THE ROAD TO THE EUROPEAN UNION

VOLUME 2

MANCHESTER
UNIVERSITY PRESS

SERIES EDITORS *Thomas Christiansen and Emil Kirchner*

already published

Committee governance in the European Union
THOMAS CHRISTIANSEN AND EMIL KIRCHNER (EDS)

Theory and reform in the European Union, 2nd edition
DIMITRIS N. CHRYSSOCHOOU, MICHAEL J. TSINISIZELIS,
KOSTAS IFANTIS AND STELIOS STAVRIDIS

German policy-making and eastern enlargement of the EU during the Kohl era
Managing the agenda?
STEPHEN D. COLLINS

The European Union and the Cyprus conflict
Modern conflict, postmodern union
THOMAS DIEZ

The time of European governance
MAGNUS EKENGREN

Greece in a changing Europe
Between European integration and Balkan disintegration?
KEVIN FEATHERSTONE AND KOSTAS IFANTIS (EDS)

An introduction to post-Communist Bulgaria
Political, economic and social transformation
EMIL GIATZIDIS

The new Germany and migration in Europe
BARBARA MARSHALL

Turkey's relations with a changing Europe
MELTEM MÜFTÜLER-BAC

Righting wrongs in Eastern Europe
ISTVAN POGANY

The road to the European Union, volume 1
The Czech and Slovak Republics
JACQUES RUPNIK AND JAN ZIELONKA (EDS)

Two tiers or two speeds?
The European security order and the enlargement of the European Union and NATO
JAMES SPERLING (ED.)

Recasting the European order
Security architectures and economic cooperation
JAMES SPERLING AND EMIL KIRCHNER

The emerging Euro-Mediterranean system
DIMITRIS K. XENAKIS AND DIMITRIS N. CHRYSSOCHOOU

Vello Pettai and Jan Zielonka
EDITORS

THE ROAD TO THE EUROPEAN UNION

VOLUME 2

ESTONIA, LATVIA AND LITHUANIA

MANCHESTER UNIVERSITY PRESS
Manchester and New York

distributed exclusively in the USA by Palgrave

Published by Manchester University Press
Oxford Road, Manchester M13 9NR, UK
and Room 400, 175 Fifth Avenue, New York, NY 10010, USA
www.manchesteruniversitypress.co.uk

Distributed exclusively in the USA by
Palgrave, 175 Fifth Avenue, New York,
NY 10010, USA

Distributed exclusively in Canada by
UBC Press, University of British Columbia, 2029 West Mall,
Vancouver, BC, Canada V6T 1Z2

British Library Cataloguing-in-Publication Data
A catalogue record for this book is available from the British Library

Library of Congress Cataloging-in-Publication Data applied for

ISBN 0 7190 6560 7 *hardback*
0 7190 6561 5 *paperback*

First published 2003

11 10 09 08 07 06 05 04 03 10 9 8 7 6 5 4 3 2 1

Typeset in Minion with Lithos
by Northern Phototypesetting Co Ltd, Bolton
Printed in Great Britain
by Biddles Ltd, Guildford and King's Lynn

Contents

List of figures and tables *page* vi
List of contributors ix
Acknowledgments x

1 Introduction: historic and historical aspects of Baltic accession to the European Union *Vello Pettai* 1

2 The political implications of the EU's enlargement to the Baltic states *Teija Tiilikainen* 14

3 Russia, the Baltic states and East–West relations in Europe *George W. Breslauer* 25

4 The effects of EU conditionality on citizenship policies and the protection of national minorities in the Baltic states *Nida M. Gelazis* 46

5 Estonia's constititutional review mechanisms: a guarantor of democratic consolidation? *Vello Pettai* 75

6 Assessing governmental capabilities to manage European affairs: the case of Lithuania *Vitalis Nakrošis* 104

7 Social protection and EU enlargement: the case of Estonia *Lauri Leppik* 140

8 Regional integration in Europe: analysing intra-Baltic economic cooperation in the context of European integration *Ramūnas Vilpišauskas* 163

9 Revealed comparative advantage in trade between the European Union and the Baltic countries *Ville Kaitila and Mika Widgrén* 205

10 Preferential trade agreements: specific aspects of EU–Baltic trade integration *Niina Pautola-Mol* 231

11 Some aspects of EU membership on Baltic monetary and exchange rate policies *Iikka Korhonen* 255

Chronologies 282
Bibliography 286
Index 291

Figures and tables

Figures

6.1 Framework for assessing governmental capabilities *page* 106
9.1 Estimates for shares of transit trade in Baltic countries' exports to EU countries in 1996 212
9.2 Estimates for Baltic countries' transit exports to EU countries, share of total exports in 1996 212
11.1 Monthly inflation in the Baltics, 6/92–12/94 258
11.2 Monthly gross wages (USD) 1/95–12/98 274

Tables

1.1 Main bilateral political and economic agreements between the Baltic states and the European Union 7
1.2 Instruments of Baltic accession to the European Union 8
5.1 Appeals heard by the Constitutional Review Chamber, 1993–99 82
7.1 Social contribution rates in the EU and Estonia 142
7.2 GDP per capita and social protection expenditure in the EU (1995) and Estonia (1997) 143
7.3 Levels of social security benefits in Estonia compared to the requirements of the European Code of Social Security 156
7.4 Classes of protected persons in Estonia compared with the requirements of the European Code of Social Security 157
8.1 Major intra-Baltic market integration agreements 176
8.2 Linkages between EU policy and intra-Baltic economic cooperation 188
9.1 Total EU exports to the Baltic countries in 1996 207
9.2 Total EU imports from the Baltic countries in 1996 208
9.3 Main EU export and import products in trade with Estonia (CN2) in 1996 208
9.4 Main EU export and import products in trade with Latvia (CN2) in 1996 209
9.5 Main EU export and import products in trade with Lithuania (CN2) in 1996 210
9.6 Estimates for transit exports from Baltic countries to the EU and EFTA in 1992 and 1994 and to EU-15 in 1996 211
9.7 Grubel–Lloyd indices of intra-industry trade between the EU and the Baltic countries, and in intra-EU trade (CN4) 213

9.8 The CN4 product groups with more than 3 million ECUs of total trade between an EU country and Estonia, and more than 80 per cent of IIT in 1996 214
9.9 The CN4 product groups with more than 3 million ECUs of total trade between an EU country and Latvia, and more than 80 per cent of IIT in 1996 214
9.10 The CN4 product groups with more than 3 million ECUs of total trade between an EU country and Lithuania, and more than 80 per cent of IIT in 1996 215
9.11 The ratio of the EU's unit export and unit import prices in trade with the Baltic countries, and in intra-EU trade (CN4) in 1996 216
9.12 Horizontal intra-industry trade in EU–Baltic trade and intra-EU trade (CN4) in 1996 217
9.13 The stocks of foreign direct investment in the Baltic countries from the EU, the United States and Russia by country of origin 218
9.14 The stock of foreign direct investment in Estonia 6/98, Latvia 9/97 and Lithuania 7/97 218
9.15 Similarity index for the Baltic countries' exports (CN4) to the EU in 1996 219
9.16 Similarity index between the Baltic countries' exports to the EU compared to intra-EU exports (CN4) in 1996 220
9.17 Estonia's exports to the EU: high Balassa indices and high trade intensity (CN4) in 1996 221
9.18 Latvia's exports to the EU: high Balassa indices and high trade intensity (CN4) in 1996 221
9.19 Lithuania's exports to the EU: high Balassa indices and high trade intensity (CN4) in 1996 222
9.20 Chi square tests for the independence of Balassa indices in Baltic–EU trade v. intra-EU trade (CN4) 223
9.21 Chi square tests of the correspondence of comparative advantage in the Baltic countries' most important EU markets with the EU countries and the other Baltic countries' comparable comparative advantages 225
9.22 Cochran's Q-test 226
9.23 EU countries' importance to the Baltic countries in their exports and imports relative to their GDP 227
10.1 Regional trade agreements of the Baltic states 237
10.2 Estonia's trading partners, per cent of total exports or imports 238
10.3 Latvia's trading partners, per cent of total exports or imports 239
10.4 Lithuania's trading partners, per cent of total exports or imports 240
10.5 Estonia's trade by groups of goods (per cent of exports or imports) 241
10.6 Latvia's trade by groups of goods (per cent of exports or imports) 241
10.7 Lithuania's trade by groups of goods (per cent of exports or imports) 242
11.1 Geographical distribution of Estonian foreign trade 263
11.2 Geographical distribution of Latvian foreign trade 263
11.3 Geographical distribution of Lithuanian foreign trade 263

11.4 Baltic foreign trade with the euro bloc under three assumptions 265
11.5 Geographical distribution of FDI stocks in the Baltics, end-1998 267
11.6 Share of foreign-currency-denominated assets and liabilities in the consolidated balance sheets of the Baltic banking systems, end-1998 269
11.7 Changes in productivity in manufacturing 274
11.8 Changes in D-Mark unit labour costs 274
11.9 Maastricht criteria for ten CEEC applicant countries in 1999 276

Contributors

George W. Breslauer is Professor of Political Science and Dean of Social Sciences at the College of Letters and Science at the University of California at Berkeley.

Nida M. Gelazis is former Research Assistant at the Robert Schuman Centre, European University Institute.

Ville Kaitila is Researcher at ETLA, The Research Institute of the Finnish Economy.

Iikka Korhonen is Research Supervisor at the Institute for Economics in Transition at the bank of Finland.

Lauri Leppik is a freelance social policy analyst.

Vitalis Nakrošis is Lecturer in Public Policy and Administration at the Institute of International Relations and Political Science, Vilnius University.

Niina Pautola-Mol is Project Officer of the Policy Advice Programme at the Delegation of the European Commission in Russia.

Vello Pettai is Lecturer and Chair of the Department of Political Science at the University of Tartu.

Teija Tiilikainen is Director of Research at the Centre for European Studies, University of Helsinki.

Ramūnas Vilpišauskas is Associate Professor of Social Sciences at the Institute of International Relations and Political Science, Vilnius University.

Mika Widgrén is Professor at the Turku School of Economics and Business Administration, CEPR.

Jan Zielonka is Professor of Social and Political Sciences at the European University Institute.

Acknowledgements

This is the second of two volumes that look at the EU's accession process in individual post-communist countries. The first volume focuses on the Czech Republic and Slovakia, while this volume focuses on Estonia, Latvia and Lithuania. The objective is to reveal the Eastern European part of the enlargement story, and to show how enlargement is being played out in the domestic politics of the candidate countries.

Both volumes result from a large-scale research project on the EU's eastward enlargement conducted by the Robert Schuman Centre for Advanced Study at the European University Institute in Florence. With the help of the Austrian Ministry for Science and Transport, the project was initiated in 1998, focusing on the Czech Republic and Slovakia. The Academy of Finland backed the second component of the project focusing on the Baltic republics. The editors are grateful to both sponsors for their initial encouragement and excellent cooperation throughout the implementation phase.

Special thanks go to Professor Paavo Okko from Turku School of Economic and Business Administration for co-chairing (with Jan Zielonka) a special Steering Committee on this project. The exceptional commitment and expertise of individual members of this Steering Committee should also be praised. They included S. Neil MacFarlane (Oxford University), Jonas Masiokas (University of Vilnius), Žaneta Ozoliņa (University of Latvia), Alari Purju (Tallin Technical University), Susan Senior Nello (University of Sienna), Pekka Sutela (Bank of Finland), Jean Trestour (European Commission), Roeland in't Veld (University of Utrecht) and Victor Zaslavsky (Libera Università Internationale degli Studi Sociali in Rome).

We are particularly grateful to Tony Mason from Manchester University Press and to the series' editor, Emil Kirchner, for their continuous support in preparing this publication. Several anonymous reviewers have helped us to improve the successive drafts of this book. Angelika Lanfranchi and Francesca Parenti provided excellent secretarial assistance.

Vello Pettai and Jan Zielonka
September 2002

VELLO PETTAI

1

Introduction

Historic and historical aspects of Baltic accession to the European Union

Within the context of the European Union's enlargement to Central and Eastern Europe, the accession of the three Baltic states of Estonia, Latvia and Lithuania arguably represents one of the most historic dimensions of this process in terms of European geopolitics and continental integration. For the first time since the days of the Hanseatic League, the EU's expansion will bring together almost the entire Baltic Sea area into one political and economic bloc. It will incorporate an area of the continent, which has long been outside the mainstream of Europe. Following centuries of Russian and later Soviet domination of the Baltic area, Estonia, Latvia and Lithuania will once again become part of European politics and development.

For the Baltic states themselves, this transformation has been no less monumental. In the space of roughly ten years the three countries have gone from being fragile and largely unknown ex-Soviet republics to having a clear and acknowledged place in the construction of Europe. To be sure, the three states' actual impact on European integration will be tempered by their small size. For example, when the Baltics join the European Parliament they will together have only 26 representatives out of a possible 732. However, for the Baltic peoples their mere inclusion in the most extensive and cohesive political formation ever created in Europe offers a much greater prospect for stable development and lasting independence than at any time in their modern history. If the full expansion of the EU proves successful, they will have an opportunity to regain their lost years and take part in the Union's future beyond that.

It is these changes as well as challenges for the future that this volume will attempt to convey by profiling a range of social, political and economic developments in the Baltic states during the 1990s and early years of the twenty-first century. Together, the ten chapters that follow tell the story of how small states struggle to establish themselves in regional and international politics, how they attempt to resolve relations with former hegemons, how they address questions of multiethnic democracy and social integration, how they build state administrations and foster democratic constitutional norms, and how they reorganise economic structures and develop foreign trade. This wide array of reforms epitomises the extent to which the Baltics' transformation since independence in 1991 has been an almost revolutionary affair. What is more, these tasks of state- and nation-building have all had to be fulfilled by countries whose combined population amounts to only 7.5 million people.

Likewise, however, this process has been equally assisted by the European Union through different channels of political and economic support. Indeed, as can be seen in many of the contributions, the European Union has itself been changed by the accession process, through not only the creation of a number of new cooperative mechanisms, but also a general shift in geopolitical focus. In this respect, the EU and the Baltic states have already forged a genuine structure of partnership and development. Naturally, as this process is carried through to full membership and is followed by further stages of European integration, the historic aspect of the Baltics' accession will fade away. For the moment, however, its place is very much on the agenda.

This introduction will begin with a brief overview of recent political development in the Baltic states – precisely to fill the gap in knowledge about who and what the Baltic states are, and to set the stage for the more detailed analyses that follow. This is because in Central and Eastern Europe attitudes and moves toward the EU have always been embedded in the parallel processes of democratic transition and consolidation. For example, one explanation behind Estonia's initial determination to remain separate from Latvia and Lithuania in the accession process lies in the fact that its domestic party system was much more tilted to the right, and pro-market liberals were more strongly in power. Thus, a key to understanding how and why the accession countries have defined their national interests and negotiating positions the way they have lies in knowing how democratic politics has itself emerged in these states and what the main issue cleavages are.

Likewise, however, it is important to place Baltic accession in the context of European integration more broadly. As Jan Zielonka notes in the companion Czech and Slovak volume to this collection, three comparative issues deserve particular attention: the role of regions and regionalisation, the challenges of state-building, and the link between politics and economics.[1] As we will see in the second half of this introduction, all three of these issues surface also in the case of the Baltic states. They offer notable lessons for the more general study of European integration.

The Baltics' long road to Europe

Through most of the twentieth century, the place of the Baltic states in Europe was by and large a marginal one. Whether this was caused by foreign domination or the three states' own halting democratic development in their one previous period of independence during the interwar years, Estonia, Latvia and Lithuania were unable to achieve an integral place in Europe until after the collapse of the Soviet Union in 1991. Nevertheless, their intuitive sense of belonging to this geopolitical region was never in doubt, and it was largely this belief which propelled the Baltics in their development during the following decade.

The original emergence of the three states as independent countries in 1918 marked an important milestone in their development as nation-states. After defeating Bolshevik, Baltic German as well as Czarist military forces, the three countries went on to consolidate their first experience at statehood by forging new political systems as well as restructuring their economic relationships away from Russia and toward Western Europe. These efforts were not easy amidst the chronic political uncertainty of interwar Europe, not to mention the impending Depression. Moreover, the configuration of European politics at the time was far less nurturing than it is today: there were few overarching political structures or organisations, which could provide even moral support for budding states such as the Baltics. As a consequence, all three countries eventually succumbed to authoritarian rule: Lithuania in 1926, Estonia and Latvia in 1934. This collapse made the states even more vulnerable when the clouds of war began to gather in the late 1930s. When Hitler and Stalin decided in their secret August 1939 protocol to divide the three territories (along with other parts of Eastern Europe) between themselves, Estonia, Latvia and Lithuania were essentially helpless. Barely a month later, Stalin moved to secure his side of the bargain by sending troops into the three states. Thereafter, the Kremlin pressured Tallinn, Riga and Vilnius into staging rigged elections (almost simultaneously), which eventually led to pro-Soviet governments that 'requested' to join the Soviet Union in August.

These events would begin the Baltic states' relegation to the Soviet bloc, not even as satellite states, but as fully subservient Soviet republics. As a consequence, the three nations would fall under the direct wrath of Stalinist terror during the late 1940s and early 1950s, including numerous deportation campaigns. They would undergo the large-scale nationalisation of private property as well as the collectivisation of agriculture. They would be directly subordinated to the Soviet command economy and would rely for the most part on the direct allocation of resources and development plans from Moscow. Lastly, they would see an unprecedented influx of Russian and other Soviet officials, workers, and simply immigrants – all of which would, especially in the case of Estonia and Latvia, transform these states' demographic compositions as well as their ethnic politics. In terms of foreign contact, the Baltic Sea became no longer a simple geographical divide with the Nordic states of Finland and Sweden; it was what constituted the iron curtain in northern Europe.

By the time Mikhail Gorbachev came to power in 1985 the Baltic peoples had much to regain. The nationalist movements, which soon emerged in all three republics, originally demanded (and indeed, hoped for) only a restructuring of the Soviet Union along more democratic, federalist lines. When these efforts were stymied by the slow pace of change across the rest of the USSR, Baltic leaders became more radical, and full independence became the central issue by the end of 1989. Still, throughout this unprecedented period of mobilisation, the independence movements in Estonia, Latvia and Lithuania never turned violent, but instead worked to quietly build up autonomous state institutions through open elections and the installation of democratic governments in 1990. These administrations launched the first efforts at economic restructuring as well as finding international support from Europe and the United States. Already then, a number of Baltic politicians would declare that eventually their states would join the European Union.

Full independence for the Baltic nations naturally came at a wholly unpredictable moment. Still, the August 1991 attempted coup in Moscow offered Tallinn, Riga and Vilnius the opportunity they had been waiting for to break their ties with the USSR in a way which would also save face for the Kremlin. From here, the three states rapidly moved to the institutionalisation of constitutional government. In Lithuania and Estonia, this took place via the adoption of brand new constitutions in 1992; in Latvia, the parliament reinstated the country's 1922 constitution, albeit with a number of improvements. By the end, Lithuania came to have a semi-presidential form of government (meaning a popularly elected president along with a prime minister answerable to parliament), while Latvia and Estonia opted for traditional parliamentary systems (although they too had presidents with mostly ceremonial functions).

In terms of party politics, the three states held fresh parliamentary elections in 1992 and 1993, which established new administrations for beginning the task of economic and social reform.[2] Here, however, the countries started to diverge, as the sometimes strident, albeit charismatic leadership of Vytautas Landsbergis and his Sajudis movement in Lithuania during 1990–92 prompted voters to revert already in 1992 to the ex-Communist, now Democratic Labour Party, led by the former Soviet chief of the republic, Algirdas Brazauskas. While this outcome was far from a return to socialist rule, it did alter the country's momentum, as the new administration of prime minister Adolfas Slezevicius eventually got caught up in a major banking scandal and delays involving privatisation. In Estonia and Latvia, meanwhile, right-of-centre coalitions were elected to power. In Tallinn, a 32-year-old historian, Mart Laar, became prime minister, and his government immediately began a determined effort to privatise the bulk of state property, open up the economy to free trade, and ally the country as much as possible to western political structures. In Riga, the government of Valdis Birkavs was led by a liberal centrist party, Latvia's Way, which also pledged rapid market reform and a pro-western orientation. However, greater instability in the Latvia party system eventually weakened the coalition's ability to maintain this course as steadfastly as in Estonia.

Still, Estonia and Latvia had one challenge, which Lithuania did not have: sizeable ethnic minorities, notably Russians. Although both Estonia and Latvia had had Russian minorities during their interwar period of statehood, the influx of new Russian immigrants during the Soviet era increased these numbers significantly. By 1989, Estonia had a Russian minority of some 30 per cent, while in Latvia it was nearly 35 per cent. In this context, Estonian and Latvian politicians had often to tread carefully, as by and large these Russian minorities were less enthusiastic about independence; they were also wary of Estonian and Latvian hopes of making their new states more Estonian- and Latvian-centred. As Nida Gelazis shows in her chapter, the question of citizenship for these Soviet-era populations was particularly controversial, not only domestically, but also internationally. Some one million people in the two states were eventually declared non-citizens based on the argument that these people had come to Estonia and Latvia during an illegal Soviet occupation. While both Estonia and Latvia eventually undertook extensive minority integration programmes in order to naturalise some of these people and rebuild social cohesion, these issues will continue to challenge the two societies well beyond their entry into the European Union.

Baltic accession and regionalisation

The argument that the Baltic states' entry into the European Union is 'historic' comes also from the ways in which the EU was itself prompted to take on board the three ex-Soviet republics despite the shadow of Russia and its geopolitical complexities. This regional aspect of Baltic accession is therefore one of the most intriguing issues for scholars of European integration, since in and of itself it will transform EU–Russian relations, and the EU will have to be ready for it as much as Riga, Vilnius or Tallinn. As Teija Tiilikainen states at the very outset of her chapter, the Baltic states will be the first EU members with outstanding border disputes with Russia. These disputes pertain to the fact that following World War II the borders of all three Baltic states were altered by Stalin, and in particular both Estonia and Latvia lost several thousand kilometres of territory to Russia. Although in many of these questions Brussels has hitherto tried to maintain a neutral stance, it is clear that after enlargement Brussels will have to defend the Baltic states more vigorously, should they come into difficulties with Russia. Naturally, Baltic–Russian relations may eventually become as amicable as they are with the other EU member state, which currently abuts Russia – Finland. However, the Baltics carry much more historical 'baggage' because of their recent past, and this baggage will inevitably be transposed into the EU.

To address some of these issues, George Breslauer therefore examines the specific evolution of Baltic-Russian relations since 1991. During the Yeltsin era, he argues, Russia was torn between three foreign policy tendencies: liberal internationalist, radical nationalist and moderate nationalist. While the liberal-internationalist trend, which was most dominant during the early 1990s, was the most open to the Baltics' re-orientation toward the West, this stance did not endure as Yeltsin's own authority waned, and rival political and economic circles emerged. Instead, the Baltics were treated to intermittent blasts of cold air from both the moderate- as well as radical-nationalist schools. In Estonia's and Latvia's case, such rhetoric usually involved treatment of the two republics' Russian minorities. For Lithuania, the problem was guaranteeing access to the heavily militarised Russian enclave of Kaliningrad. In most cases, these complaints did not go beyond hard-ball diplomacy; however, often enough they raised concerns in Western European capitals as to whether the Baltics were worth admitting into the EU, not to mention NATO. To some extent, the continued weakness of Russia allowed EU leaders to feel that their inclusion of the Baltics was safe. But it also required (and will continue to require in the future) a certain amount of simple commitment on the part of the EU that the Baltics were indeed part of Europe.

Organising accession

This commitment to making enlargement work also became manifest in the extensive array of cooperative mechanisms the EU developed during the 1990s in order to prepare all of the candidate countries for accession. While this process included much of the same legislative screening witnessed during previous enlargements, in Central and Eastern Europe accession would also require the establishment of much more extensive harmonisation programmes as well as much greater sums of financial aid. In tables 1.1 and 1.2, we see an outline of these cooperative frameworks as well as the main chronological stages of EU–Baltic relations.

As Ramūnas Vilpišauskas shows in his chapter, the EU's original approach to the Baltic states was a uniform one in relation to each country. Brussels negotiated, as well as signed, its initial cooperation agreements with the Baltic states almost in unison, mainly because it saw the three as a bloc and accession was as yet not on the horizon. After EU leaders decided, however, that eastern enlargement would definitely go ahead, the three states were increasingly treated separately. Indeed, this stance was also encouraged by Estonia, which believed that it had the best shot at rapid accession and therefore wanted to distance itself from its southern neighbours for fear of being somehow weighed down. In July 1997, the European Commission reified this dividing line by including Estonia among the first batch of countries with whom concrete accession negotiations would begin in early 1998. This caused a considerable amount of dismay in Latvia and Lithuania, which were allowed to start negotiations only a year later. Nonetheless, by 2001 these differences had been erased, as it became clear that enlargement would in fact take place in one large wave. The Baltic states were once again seen as one bloc – indeed, as part of the entire group of ten candidate countries slated to join the Union as early as 2004.

In the meantime, work continued within the EU's system of accession partnerships, national action plans, twinning schemes, infrastructural PHARE aid, and basic legislative screening and harmonisation. Through the end of 2001, the

Table 1.1 Main bilateral political and economic agreements between the Baltic states and the European Union

Dates		Main provisions
Diplomatic recognition		
Estonia	27.08.91	Delegations from the European Commission set up in each Baltic capital
Latvia	27.08.91	
Lithuania	27.08.91	
Trade and cooperation agreements		
Signed	11.05.92	Most favoured nation status, non-discrimination; extension of EU generalised system of preferences; economic cooperation in some areas
In force		
Latvia Lithuania	01.02.93	
Estonia	01.03.93	
Agreements on trade and trade-related matters		
Signed	18.07.94	Liberalisation of trade based on GATT principles; free trade in industrial goods; 4-year transition period given to Latvia, 6-year period for Lithuania; Estonia begins immediate free trade; joint committees to oversee the implementation of the agreements
In force	01.01.95	
Formal application to join the EU		
Estonia	28.11.95	
Latvia	27.10.95	
Lithuania	08.12.95	
Association (Europe) agreements		
Signed	12.06.95	The objective of Estonia, Latvia and Lithuania to become EU members acknowledged; the provisions of free trade agreement incorporated; political dialogue enacted; economic cooperation in areas such as competition policy (EU rules), movement of services, capital and labour, protection of intellectual property rights, consumer protection, approximation of laws; cooperation in other areas such as industrial policy, science and technology, energy, environment, etc.; Association Council to supervise the implementation of the agreement and Association Committee
In force	01.02.98	

Source: Adapted from R. Vilpišauskas, 'Assessing Governmental Capabilities to Manage EU Affairs', *Robert Schuman Centre Working Paper*, 58 (2000).

Table 1.2 Instruments of Baltic accession to the European Union

Instrument	*Main features*
Pre-accession strategy	
(a) Europe agreements	See Table 1.1
(b) PHARE programme	Technical assistance for transition and pre-accession measures in applicant countries
(c) White Paper preparation of the associated CEECs for integration into the internal market of the Union (1995)	Identifies key measures in each sector of the internal market and suggests a sequence in which the approximation of legislation with the EU *acquis* should be undertaken
Accession partnerships	Define country-specific needs in order to support the applicant country in its preparation for membership. Measures are based on the needs identified in the EU's 1997 Opinion documents and aim to meet accession (Copenhagen) criteria. Provide financial assistance needed for further implementation of priority measures
National programmes for the adoption of the acquis	Define actions needed to reach objectives set out in the accession partnership. Structurally are based on the Opinions and progress reports
Screening	Analytical examination of the *acquis*
Twinning	Aims at reinforcing institutional and administrative capacity. Consists of technical assistance, training programmes, exchange of experts, participation of applicant countries' officials in EU programmes
Accession negotiations	Aim at agreement between the EU and a candidate country on terms for accession

Source: Adapted from R. Vilpišauskas, 'Assessing Governmental Capabilities to Manage EU Affairs', *Robert Schuman Centre Working Paper*, 58 (2000).

Commission had issued three Regular Reports on the state of Baltic preparations for EU accession. In these assessments, all three countries were consistently deemed compliant with the general Copenhagen criteria for EU membership, both on the political (democratic governance) as well as economic (market reform) levels. More problematic were individual aspects of the *acquis* such as judicial reform, anti-corruption measures, administrative capacity and sector-specific issues. In Estonia and Latvia, minority integration remained a concern, while in Lithuania public administration reform was singled out as still needing implementation.

Baltic accession and state-building

It is not difficult to see, therefore, how this harmonisation process was equally related to the parallel process of Baltic state-building. Yet, this aspect too raises numerous questions. For instance, when and how have the institutions or policies prescribed by the EU conflicted with the budding institutions or policies of the Baltic states? Is it the case for the Baltics that because they only recently regained independence and did not have entrenched state institutions and policies before EU accession, that they are able to adopt more easily the EU's ready-made formulae? Or has the technical complexity of these policies served to overwhelm these states and their administrations, and thereby even precipitate anti-EU backlash?

In this volume, the contributions by Vitalis Nakrošis, Lauri Leppik, and Vello Pettai especially highlight these questions. To begin with, it is well known that one of the most recurring themes in the European Commission's various reports on the candidate countries has been a perceived lack of 'administrative capacity' to implement the *acquis*. Rarely, however, does one find a more precise elucidation of what these problems really are beyond a mere call for more training or staff. Vitalis Nakrošis uses the failure of Lithuania to be included within the one-time 'first circle' of EU applicant countries as an example of how weaknesses in administrative organisation and structure undermined early progress in Lithuania's European integration process. He identifies a number of the specific legacies from the communist era – such as the lack of a genuine civil service tradition, fragmented personnel management, and underdeveloped foreign relations skills – which constituted the real substance of administrative incapacity during the mid-1990s. Yet, needless to say, all three of these variables are also central to state-building and arise precisely because of the newness of state administrations. The lesson for the study of European integration is that the conditionality of such mammoth administrative agendas and action plans can easily backfire if their failures lead to public recrimination and discontent.

In Lauri Leppik's chapter, a different dimension of state-building emerges – that of building a welfare state. Although the Soviet Union might have foundered precisely on its attempt to build an all-encompassing socialism, modern societies can ill-afford to do without some kind of integrated social safety net. Yet, once again questions of administrative capacity arise to the extent that many such policies require detailed population statistics as well as record keeping. Moreover, in a free-market economy such benefits often need to be modelled mathematically so as to track changes and evaluate their effect on the labour market. In this respect, Leppik shows how Estonia's transposition of EU norms in social welfare led to an extensive restructuring of the country's social protection system. As he writes, 'The EU's co-ordination system naturally assumes that each of the [main] branches of social security . . . are present. Or, as has been said, it is not possible to co-ordinate something with nothing.'[3] Yet, since Estonia was also only beginning to develop its own social policy after decades of Soviet centralisation, the panoply of unemployment, old-age, family, disability, and other types of benefits long ago instituted in the EU took time to integrate and balance out between the needs of Estonian society and the financial means of the Estonian state. Indeed, for a state that was, for example, equally keen on gaining entrance to NATO and had therefore to reckon with a simultaneous requirement to maintain its defence expenditures at 2 per cent of GDP, an important state-building trade-off was present: whether to foster the rapid renovation of a social welfare system or prioritise national defence. In this sense, EU accession and state-building were rather paradoxically at cross-purposes.

Thirdly, Vello Pettai examines a political-institutional dimension of state-building in the form of Estonia's novel Constitutional Review Chamber. While the EU admittedly had little to prescribe or proscribe in terms of an institution like this, its effect was still felt through the European Court of Justice as well as the European Court of Human Rights (although the latter derived from the Council of Europe). It was the case law of these sister institutions, which began slowly to seep into decisions of the Estonian Constitutional Review Chamber during the 1990s. Thus, also for the Review Chamber, rapid EU accession presented a double task: first, to consolidate Estonia's democracy through a certain number of norm-building decisions, and second, to contribute to awareness-building among Estonian legal and judicial circles that soon enough Estonia would have to feel itself a part of much broader EU law. After years of sham Soviet justice, rule of law had to be built on multiple cognitive and procedural levels.

Linking politics and economics

Since the European Union represents (among other things) a major economic trading bloc, the question of how the Baltic states will fit into this open system dominates the last four chapters of our volume. The stakes in this respect were clear: already by the late 1990s up to half of the Baltics' foreign trade was with the European Union, and these figures were bound only to increase. In particular after the Russian financial crisis of 1998, a number of Baltic firms further re-oriented their activities toward the West. Although trade with Russia would eventually recover (especially as Russian–Baltic political relations stabilised), the EU's market would remain attractive, no less because of the latter's monetary union.

Yet, as all of the chapters in this book also suggest, economic relations in a context of EU accession are rarely autonomous from political processes. To begin with, political leaders generally play a crucial role in creating suitable (or simply new) economic environments for business activity. Here, the Baltic states were no exception. Ramūnas Vilpišauskas makes this point very clearly as he describes the simultaneous evolution of both EU–Baltic as well intra-Baltic economic relations. In this process, we in fact see a multi-level political game ensue, involving the EU, national Baltic politicians and localised domestic interest groups. Yet, more often than not, these relations also become a crossfire for the national politicians, who must dodge bullets from the remaining two sides. As Vilpišauskas demonstrates, on the one hand the EU served as a unique 'rules-supplier' and stimulus for greater Baltic cooperation. This was generally seen as positive by Baltic politicians. At the same time, however, domestic agricultural lobbies eventually derailed the pace of negotiations toward intra-Baltic free trade when the actual cost of such openness became apparent. In the face of Brussels and its regulatory norms, such lobby groups could not always demand exceptions or precipitate disruptions. Vis-à-vis the other Baltic states, however, such jockeying was relatively easy. To be sure, many of these tussles would have probably arisen without the EU; however, the process of EU accession had the distinct effect of transforming the situation into a multi-level political-economic game.

The issue of economic competitiveness is continued in the next chapter by Ville Kaitila and Mika Widgrén. Indeed, they raise the issue point-blank by investigating the revealed comparative advantage in trade between the EU and the Baltic states. Using a range of statistical measures, they find that most EU–Baltic trade is inter-industry trade, which assumes a degree of comparative advantage. The Baltics trade in primary goods, which they need from the EU or the EU needs from the Baltics. However, greater economic integration should lead to an increase in intra-industry trade, as Baltic firms become part of European-wide production networks. By early 2002, Estonia had neared this model the most, as many of its companies had already become integrated with Finnish and Swedish industry as a result of heavy investment by these Nordic neighbours. But Latvia and Lithuania had likewise to follow suit.

The question of intra-industry trade is also mirrored in Niina Pautola-Mol's chapter on preferential trade agreements, since such agreements can be both trade-creating (between partners) as well as trade-diverting (away from third parties). The more these agreements contribute to bringing the Baltics into an integrated economic system, the more they will stimulate phenomena such as intra-industry trade. More broadly, however, Pautola-Mol frames the issue as part of Wilfred Ethier's theory of new regionalism, which stresses that regional cooperation is characterised more and more by smaller states linking up with larger states, and that in the process these smaller states are obliged to execute extensive unilateral reforms as well as agree to deep integration. In this respect, Pautola-Mol's chapter also echoes the issue of regionalisation, although more from a purely economic perspective. Given the size of the Baltic states vis-à-vis the European Union as well as their need for post-communist economic restructuring, the Baltics' entry into the European Union matches this model to a considerable extent. At the same time, preferential trade agreements raise the question of whether or not free trade becomes jeopardised vis-à-vis third parties. As the Baltics prepare for EU accession, they (like many of the other Central and Eastern European candidate countries) will have to renegotiate trade deals they may have with outlying states (such as Ukraine). The expansion of the European Union in this respect helps the applicant countries, but may narrow the scope of free trade on a global level after these countries fall behind the common tariff and trade barrier of the EU.

Yet behind this single wall the Baltics will also benefit from a common currency, the euro. Iikka Korhonen therefore examines the implications of this union on existing Baltic monetary and exchange rate policies. Again, trade flows are an important determining factor here, since the high levels of Baltic–EU trade are an argument in favour of linking monetary and exchange rate policy to the euro. Estonia has been linked to the euro through the German mark since it introduced its currency, the kroon, in 1992. Lithuania, too, saw the writing on the wall when it switched its peg currency from the dollar to the euro in early 2002. Latvia is the only Baltic country to maintain a link with the IMF's notional currency, the SDR, although here too the SDR is heavily weighted by the euro. Thus, in terms of policy, the Baltics were generally prepared. Still, this did not mean that the euro would be introduced in the Baltics any time soon. Indeed, in September 2001 the Commission explicitly discouraged any CEECs from prematurely adopting the euro, stating in its enlargement strategy document, 'Any unilateral adoption of the single currency by means of "euroisation" would run counter to the underlying economic reasoning of EMU in the Treaty, which foresees the eventual adoption of the euro as the endpoint of a structure convergence process within a multilateral framework.'[4] However, all three Baltic states did do much to achieve monetary stability and confidence by institutionalising currency boards or other strict measures. Thus, a transition to the euro was more a question of 'when', rather than 'if'.

Conclusion

In 1991, the German sociologist Claus Offe coined the term 'triple transition' to describe the political, economic and socio-cultural challenges facing the countries of Central and Eastern Europe as they took to rebuilding their societies after communism.[5] The phrase was trenchant since it captured the unprecedented magnitude of change, which analysts and politicians (not to mention the people themselves) were beginning to realise was in store for them during the next decades. Yet, as even a cursory reading of Offe's article shows, neither he nor most other analysts at that time could imagine how these transitions would be affected – or in fact compounded – by the soon-to-be-added dimension of EU accession. In the early years of studying post-communist Europe, it was habitual to think of the transition in largely unidimensional terms. Each country certainly had a vast array of policies to reform, yet all of these seemed essentially restricted to each individual country. To be sure, there were also external factors such as international lending organisations (when the transition needed money) or international political associations (when the transition ran into trouble with democratic norms or human rights). However, these, too, were clearly exogenous parameters, and not necessarily continuous or systematic.

Yet, as this volume (as well as its companion on the Czech Republic and Slovakia) shows, such country-level isolation no longer corresponds to reality.

Certainly, each of the chapters to follow talks about the legacies and challenges of specifically post-communist transition. Even in this introduction, the three issues that have been highlighted (regionalisation, state-building, and political-economic relations) are all salient because of the nature of post-communism. However, a more profound message of this volume (and of its unique case-studies) is that *EU enlargement to Central and Eastern Europe has transformed the hitherto triangular shape of the transition into a pyramidal one, with the EU standing at the top, influencing and determining the course of all of the previously isolated parameters of change.* We can no longer speak of economic reform simply within a market system; rather, we must examine economic reform within the set chapters of the *acquis communautaire.* We can no longer speak of political reform with some general goal of 'democracy' in mind; rather, political reform means movement toward the EU's particular structure of institutions, rights and norms. Lastly, we can no longer speak of change in general socio-cultural mentalities; instead, we are dealing with a more direct convergence toward a form of EU identity and consciousness.

Naturally, none of this is harmful in and of itself. On the contrary, with hindsight it may actually seem inevitable, had transitologists really thought through what accession would mean for post-communist Central and Eastern Europe or had students of European integration turned their attention to this region earlier. Wherever the deficiency, however, it is clear from the contributions to this project that the study of Central and Eastern Europe is henceforth ineluctably tied together with the study of the EU, and that of the EU likewise with Central and Eastern Europe. The goal of this volume is to begin to show how this analytical synthesis can be achieved.

Notes

1 J. Zielonka, 'Introduction: Enlargement and the Study of European Integration', in J. Rupnik and J. Zielonka (eds), *The Road to the European Union, Vol. 1: The Czech and Slovac Republics* (Manchester, Manchester University Press, 2002), pp. 1–15.

2 For a complete overview of Baltic party politics during the 1990s see V. Pettai and M. Kreuzer, 'Party Politics in the Baltic States: Social Bases and Institutional Context', *East European Politics and Societies*, 13:1 (1999), 150–191.

3 L. Leppik, in this volume (Chapter 7).

4 European Commission, *Making a success of enlargement* (Brussels, European Commission, 2001), p. 19.

5 C. Offe, 'Capitalism by Democratic design? Democratic Theory Facing the Triple Transition in East Central Europe', *Social Research*, 58:4 (1991), 865–882.

Teija Tiilikainen

2

The political implications of the EU's enlargement to the Baltic states

The Baltic states will be the first former Soviet republics that will join the project of European unification. They will also be the first new members of the EU to have unsettled questions with Russia. All three of the Baltic states have declared that membership of the EU is only a partial solution to their present political goals – the full solution being membership in both the EU and NATO. There are a number of internal as well as external factors linked with the Baltic states, due to which the Baltic enlargement of the EU will undoubtedly bring a new political dimension to the EU agenda.

The Baltic enlargement, as part of the eastern enlargement of the EU, will pose great challenges to the EU as well as to the new member states themselves. In this chapter I will focus upon the *political challenges* of the Baltic enlargement. Most of these political challenges originate in the immediate history of the Baltic states as annexed republics of the Soviet Union. They can, however, be divided into two groups on the basis of whether the historical conditions reflect themselves in their *political thinking* and *identity* or in *social and political structures.* A third group of political challenges will consist of those changes that the Baltic enlargement will bring to the EU system concerning its borders and territory as well as its political institutions.

This discussion dealing with the political challenges of the Baltic enlargement of the EU is not in any case meant to understate the political value of the EU enlargement and has therefore to be put into its proper framework. The spread of the project of European integration into the new Central and Eastern European democracies has constituted one of the self-given dimensions of integration since the beginning of the 1990s. Any critical evaluations related to the enlargement almost without exception deal with its various details purporting to contribute to the better adaptation of the EU to the enlargement project. Hence, the purpose of this criticism is not to question the enlargement itself.

National identity in explaining national policies

In the stable system of the Cold War, subjective factors like national identities did not seem to have much importance as far as the explanation of foreign policies was concerned. It appeared as if systemic factors, factors connected with the bipolar division of powers as the backbone of the international system, could explain a major part of states' international action. In the 1990s, which has usually been characterised as a period of transition in international politics, a return to national identities has been necessary in order to cope with the vast changes that have made themselves evident since the collapse of the Cold War system.[1] Identity forms the basis for an actor's self-understanding. On the basis of identity, borders are drawn between oneself and others. The notion of identity can be connected with individuals as well as with collective actors. According to Bhikhu Parekh, every polity has a more or less coherent conception of the kind of collectivity it is, what it means to belong to it, who belongs to it or is an outsider, and how it differs from others.[2] The concept of national identity refers to *the political self-understanding of a nation* as an important basis for its policy and political choices. A national identity is not, as is usually believed, a unitary phenomenon. It is based upon a number of historical and cultural traditions, the interpretation and application of which vary from context to context. As a basis for foreign policy, national identities express themselves as worldviews, that is, as subjective interpretations concerning the international environment and one's own position in it. These worldviews furthermore express a set of values functioning as the value basis for a given policy.

The key characteristics of the Baltic identities can, consequently, be used when it comes to the understanding of their foreign policies and, at a later stage, of their policies and position as a part of an integrated Europe. A key aspect of Baltic national identities – as far as it relates to the formulation of their independent policies – is formed by their way of conceptualising their statehood. The Balts never consented to the annexation of their territories by the Soviet Union. It was seen as an illegal act, the consequence of which being that the Balts believed in the existence of their statehood throughout the occupation.[3] This belief was strengthened by the non-recognition policies of a majority of the western states as far as the valid title of the Soviet Union over the Baltic territories was concerned.

The refusal to accept an interruption in their statehood has formed the main platform for all Baltic policies after the restoration of their full sovereignty in the 1990s. The Baltic countries have applied for membership in all of the key western institutions, not on the basis of a more or less instrumental logic and reasoning, but on the basis of their political identities and historical position on the western political map.[4] An Estonian expert, Toivo Klaar, has even claimed that the restoration of Estonian independence was never seen as a goal in itself by those involved in the liberation movement. According to him it was seen as an important step on the path from being a colony of the USSR to becoming an equal partner in an integrated Europe.[5]

The cultural and historical right to western belonging, including a place in western institutions, explains not only the speed with which the Baltics' foreign policies were formulated, it also explains the firm determination with which these claims have been introduced to the western community. The two Baltic states that fell out of the originally proclaimed 'first round' of enlargement were among the most obstinate critics of the Commission's decision and referred to the political character of the decision as well as to the outdated economic statistics that had been used.[6] As membership in the EU was perceived in terms of belonging to a cultural and historical unity, it was much more difficult to consent to the differentiation of the three Baltic states in this respect than if it had been seen in purely economic terms.

Another important basis for the Baltic foreign policies is formed by the high level of insecurity that is connected with the Baltic states and their territories. The Baltic conceptualisation of threats and security policy objectives differs from the post-Cold War security policy discourse in a majority of the Western European countries. While crisis management and prevention became the main content of western security policy in the 1990s, the Balts still count on the probability of a territorial threat scenario, where their state structures are threatened by Russia.[7] The high value put on traditional national security is another element that pushes the Baltic states toward western institutions. The conception of security is also the element that explains why the Balts are still more interested in membership of NATO despite the fact that membership of the EU would undoubtedly lead to much firmer ties and interdependence with the western community.[8] As long as the Balts, however, reason in terms of traditional security, the EU will appear too weak for their purposes, since it does not include any guarantees for the territorial security of its members.

On the basis of these political identities, which to a large extent are shared equally by the three Baltic states, we can say something about the challenges they will bring to the project of European integration. Treating membership in the western community as their historical right, the Balts will certainly form a group of applicants who will be prepared to struggle hard for their membership, and who, on the other hand, will not be satisfied with any solution other than full membership. Once in the European Union, the Baltic countries will do their best in order to qualify for a place in the hard core, whether political or economic, of the EU. Moreover, until their membership in NATO is finalised, they can also be counted among those EU members who would be willing to build a collective security system of some kind within the framework of the EU.

The Baltic question seen from a Russian perspective

The Baltics' integration into western security structures appears in a slightly different light from the Russian perspective. It is just this conflict of conceptions which, when politicised, has given reason for deep mistrust between the Baltic states and Russia. Therefore, because of its importance for the situation in general, the Baltic–Russian dimension also deserves attention.

Russian political elites, for their part, generally do not admit their share of guilt regarding the fate of the Baltic states in 1940 and the war that followed. They refer to the fact that it was the Soviet Union and its communist regime, and not Russia, that stood behind this policy.[9] The goal of the Russian leadership as far as the new security system is concerned is to create a multipolar world. This would be a world where Russia, together with other great powers like the United States, Germany, France and the United Kingdom, maintain an international balance of power.

Russia treats NATO as a relic from the Cold War, which is in contradiction with the new world order. Its continued existence works, in fact, in favour of a perpetual US hegemony. Since 2000, official Russian NATO policy has become more moderate, but the basic scepticism towards NATO has not disappeared. The enlargement of NATO is, according to the most extreme Russian interpretation, seen as a project that purports to isolate Russia and surround it with antagonistic alliances. As a great power, Russia considers itself in any case entitled to certain spheres of interest, among which it counts also the Baltic states. This position is completely unacceptable for the Balts – a fact that has created a deep cleavage between Russia and the Baltic states.

The Russian conception of the European Union differs remarkably from its view of NATO. In spite of the reinforcement of its security policy dimension, the EU is not perceived as a threat to Russia, and Moscow does not therefore oppose the former's enlargement. The problem is that due to their expectations concerning security guarantees the present EU is not regarded as a sufficient solution by the Baltic states; NATO also remains a must.

History appears in social and political structures

A second political challenge that the EU will face in connection with the Baltic enlargement concerns a number of specific, unsettled problems between the Baltic states and Russia, namely, the question of borders as well as the rights and position of the Russian minorities in the Baltic states. These problems, even if settled, will include a high risk of conflict between the parties. Russia has sought to link the two problems, while the Balts have emphasised them as separate issues.

When the EU will be enlarged to the Baltic states, the new Union will include sizeable Russian minorities on its territory. While Russia has declared that the position and welfare of these minorities will constitute an immediate foreign policy interest for it, from a legal point of view the Russian minorities are not a problem for the EU. In its 1997 Opinions regarding the applicant countries' capacity to fulfil the conditions for membership, the Commission confirmed that all three Baltic countries upheld the characteristics of a democracy with stable institutions, guaranteeing the rule of law, human rights and respect for and protection of minorities.[10] As far as Estonia and Latvia were concerned, however, the Commission called on them to accelerate the rate of naturalisation of Russian-speaking non-citizens in order to enable them to become better integrated into society. In its enlargement report issued in autumn 2001, the Commission noted the positive developments, which had taken place in Estonia and Latvia concerning minorities. Both countries were said to have further progressed in the integration of non-citizens, and continued to fulfil all the recommendations of the OSCE regarding citizenship and naturalisation. It was, however, stated that due care would need to be taken in both countries to ensure that the implementation of existing language legislation took place in full respect of the principles of proportionality and justified public interest.[11]

Nevertheless, from a political point of view the large Russian minorities in Estonia and Latvia continued to form a great challenge for the EU. At the general level this meant that the issue of the Russian minorities and their position would enter into the political relations between the EU and Russia, and that this question would have the potential to affect these relations in either a positive or negative manner. Furthermore, through the reinforced position of fundamental rights in the EU, and the new capacity given to the European Court of Justice to control the application of these rights, issues related to the Russian minorities were likely to find added status on the EU agenda.[12] Lastly, those Russians who lack either Estonian or Latvian citizenship will also constitute a challenge to the EU as far as EU citizenship and its further development is concerned. For example, these people will not be entitled to Union citizenship or to the evolving political and economic rights that are vested with it. They will lack both the right to free movement in the EU area as well as basic political rights such as the right to vote or to stand as a candidate in the European Parliament or municipal elections in the member state in which one resides. The Russian minorities will give added weight to critics who say that EU citizenship reinforces the division of people living in the EU area into different categories. This is an element of EU citizenship that is directly linked to the Union's further deepening.[13]

The long and difficult process related to border agreements between the individual Baltic states and Russia is another good example of Moscow's aspirations to exert its influence on the Baltic states – aspirations that will hardly end when these states have entered the European Union. Thus far, the EU has adopted a neutral attitude towards this specific dispute – the existence of a valid border agreement with Russia has not been demanded by the EU as a condition for EU membership. It is unclear, however, what the Russian policy in this respect will be after the Baltic states will have entered the EU – whether Russia will be discouraged from continuing its manoeuvres against the Baltic states or whether it will feel it still has something to gain from foot-dragging, now with the European Union. It is, nevertheless, clear that once the Baltic states are in the Union, relations between the Baltic states and Russia will form a potential area of tension between the EU and this third state.

The Baltic states as a part of the developing EU

In addition to the political challenges that emanate directly from Baltic history, the Baltic enlargement of the EU will pose other challenges related to the general political and geopolitical characteristics of this enlargement. The first question to be asked in this connection is whether we can talk about 'a Baltic enlargement', that is, whether there is reason to assume that the Baltic states, once having entered the EU, will form a unitary subgroup within it.[14]

In spite of the active cooperation that took place between the Baltic states during the 1990s, there are some crucial differences in their political orientations that might work against their unity. Due to historical and cultural reasons, Lithuania has been more oriented towards Poland, and might see this as a useful relationship even in the EU, whereas Germany has formed the most important Central European contact for Estonia and Latvia.[15] A division of the same type has taken place as far as the Nordic orientation toward the Baltic states is concerned. For historical and cultural reasons, Estonia has been most active in its relations with Finland, Latvia with Sweden and Lithuania with Denmark. It is also a common assumption that as members of the EU the Baltic states will see more advantage in close relations with the EU's Western European members, than with its Nordic members.[16]

The Baltic enlargement of the EU will undoubtedly strengthen the position and powers of the northern members of the EU in a simple North–South constellation. In spite of their differences, the Baltic states still share with other northern EU members like Finland similar concerns related to their location on the outskirts of a united Europe, in the immediate neighbourhood of an unstable Russia, and sharing a long common border with Russia. Yet, a split has also emerged in this area – namely, Baltic attitudes toward the EU's 'Northern Dimension' programme or the Finnish initiative to integrate Russia into European and global structures through increased multilateral cooperation. Since one of the main dimensions of the programme has been to increase EU–Russian cooperation in the fields of energy, transport and commerce, the initiative has been criticised as an attempt to override the Balts' position in these fields of cooperation with Russia.[17] In this sense, the Nordic and Baltic states can be competitors vis-à-vis Russia.

The Baltic enlargement and common EU territory

Baltic participation in the EU's single market and in the unification of external borders will also bring a number of migration issues into focus, such as the question of minorities, the effectiveness of Baltic border controls, and the degree of cheap labour coming from the Baltics. Since the total population in the three Baltic states is only around 7.5 million, this pressure will not be overwhelming. However, some migration from the Baltic countries is probable due to the gap in living standards between the existing EU members and the newcomers. This migration will be divided between a number of neighbouring countries.[18]

The gate-keeping position of the Baltic states as new EU border states will be a more challenging issue. In taking on the role of an external EU border, the eastern borders of the Baltic states will be subject to particular demands concerning border control. During the late 1990s, the most serious problems in this field involved the Latvian and Lithuanian border authorities.[19] These problems usually were due to a lack of resources and were reflected, for instance, in a large number of illegal migrants using the Baltic states as passageways to Europe. In Latvia, most cases of illegal migration, smuggling and contraband tended to involve Belarus, since border controls by the Belarussian authorities were often weaker than those on the Latvian–Russian frontier.[20] Even Lithuania has most of its border problems with Belarus. In its 2001 report on the Baltic states, the Commission, however, did acknowledge the positive developments which had taken place in the border control systems of both Latvia and Lithuania.[21]

The state of Baltic border control as well as the adoption of proper legislation concerning the treatment of illegal immigrants and refugees was in the immediate interest of the EU. The EU's provisions concerning immigrants and asylum were further harmonised in the Amsterdam Treaty and it was therefore a key condition that national legislations in this area be compatible.

The Baltic enlargement and the political institutions of the EU

On an institutional level, the eastern enlargement of the EU will also constitute a challenge for the Union, and as a consequence a number of institutional amendments will need to take place on the basis of the 2000 Nice Treaty. The particular challenges resulting from the Baltic enlargement relate to the size of the Baltic states and – not unimportantly – to the different languages that the three countries will bring to the EU's political and administrative machinery.

Given their parameters, the Baltic states will be among the smallest members of the European Union. This increase in the number of small member states in an enlarged EU was one of those factors, which accelerated the institutional reforms put forth by the EU's Intergovernmental Conference of 2000. The institutional arrangement finally arrived at in the Nice Treaty will enable all the new member states to have at least one Commissioner, since the structure of the Commission will be reconsidered only when the EU has reached twenty-seven member states. This also means, however, that all of the future EU member states – including the three Baltic states – will have to assume a certain degree of EU executive power from the beginning of their EU membership. Participation in the European Council will also pose heavy demands on the Baltic states and their relatively small state administrations.

On the basis of the Council's future division of votes decided upon at Nice, the Baltic states were placed among the smallest and second-smallest powers of the club with the number of Estonian and Latvian votes (4) corresponding to that of Luxembourg and the number of Lithuanian votes (6) being identical to those of Denmark, Finland and Ireland. Still, the Nice treaty left open the question of the EU Presidency and its fate in a Union comprised of so many small states. The political and administrative capacity of the three Baltic states to carry out the immense workload of this institution – were they ever to assume the Presidency – could be questioned. This was exacerbated by the Presidency's key role in external relations and in representing the EU in international organisations.

Last, but not least, the Baltic states will bring to the EU three different languages which according to present rules will all be entitled to the position of an official language of the EU. The Baltic enlargement could thus serve as an ultimate stimulus for a reform of the EU in this respect, i.e. a switch to a limited number of working languages, if a decision upon this is not taken even earlier.

The Baltic enlargement and the CFSP

The challenges that the new Baltic members will pose to the EU's Common Foreign and Security Policy (CFSP) are most of all linked to the firm aspirations that these countries have for NATO security guarantees. Many present EU states, for example, have been concerned about the readiness of the new non-NATO EU members to contribute to the development of the CFSP if they see it as only a transitional stage on their road to NATO.[22]

The enlargement of the EU to non-NATO countries like the Baltic countries was among those factors, which created pressure also on the place of the Western European Union between the EU and NATO.[23] A new membership category 'Associate Partnership' was created within the WEU for the Central and Eastern European countries. This membership category enabled these countries to get involved in the political and operational activities of the WEU with, however, a clear difference in their rights as opposed to full members (members of EU and NATO), associate members (NATO but not EU members) and observers (EU but not NATO members). The Maastricht Treaty also included a declaration on Western European Union (Declaration 30, II) according to which 'States which are members of the European Union are invited to accede to the WEU on conditions to be agreed in accordance with Article XI of the modified Brussels Treaty, or to become observers if they so wish.' However, the abolishment of this formulation by the Amsterdam Treaty reflects a concern about the new members' willingness to use the WEU as a channel to NATO's security guarantees.

The decisions made by the European Council in Cologne and Helsinki in 1999 led to the dissolution of the WEU as an independent organisation and the construction of a military crisis management capacity directly under the political leadership of the EU. This move became known as the Common European Security and Defence Policy (ESDP). The candidate members of the EU were connected to this new policy via a promise of political dialogue and an option to contribute resources to any future EU operations. Thus the Baltic countries have shown their solidarity with the new defence dimension by committing troops to the common crisis management force. Nevertheless, the political leadership and decision-making concerning EU operations have remained firmly in the hands of the EU.

In this respect, the Baltic countries could well strengthen their role in the ESDP once they become members of NATO. As NATO members, Vilnius, Riga and Tallinn would belong to a core group of EU members as far as EU–NATO relations or the deepening of the ESDP is concerned. This development, in turn, would increase pressure on the four EU members who remain outside of NATO (Finland, Sweden, Austria and Ireland) to end their non-alignment.

In addition to this tension concerning the institutional development of the CFSP, the Baltic enlargement will be likely to increase the weight of Russia in this policy area. In the Amsterdam Treaty, the EU was given some new instruments for the conduct of its foreign relations. The category of a 'common strategy' was established to function as a general policy framework for important foreign policy areas. The first common strategy adopted by the European Council in its meeting in Cologne was the Common Strategy on Russia. Relations between the Baltic states and Russia will eventually form one of the major elements of this strategy. Secondly, in the Amsterdam Treaty the EU was given a limited treaty-making capacity in the area of foreign and security policy. This is another capacity that may very well be needed when, for instance, Kaliningrad will become a Russian enclave inside the EU.

Conclusions

The Baltic enlargement will bring totally new political challenges to the European Union. These challenges will involve the borders, ethnic minorities and political parameters of the Baltic states. At the beginning of this chapter, we posited the importance of national identities as a tool for explaining foreign policy stances. On the basis of this framework, the question becomes to what extent is it possible to anticipate the capacity of the Baltic peoples to adapt themselves to the ever deepening European Union via their national identity? To answer this question, we can use the example of two Nordic states, Finland and Sweden.

The Finnish entrance into the EU mirrored a great deal the Baltic cases, as comprehensive questions like European identity and national security dominated people's expectations. As the decision to join the EU was based upon this more fundamental context, the Finnish people have not lost their confidence in integration despite the fact that a number of the more detailed expectations have not been fulfilled. The prospect of a Finnish withdrawal from the EU does not form a political topic in Finland at all. On the contrary, by taking part, for example, in the introduction of the euro, Finland has headed towards the hard core of the European Union.

In Sweden, meanwhile, the decision to join the EU was based upon more everyday, short-term expectations which, when not fulfilled, have caused an increasing criticism of EU membership. The Swedes in general are much more sceptical when it comes to the net value of their EU membership. Their decision to stay outside the EMU reflects the fact that integration is not perceived as a comprehensive solution for the country as it is in the Finnish case.

Thus in this light there is reason to believe that in spite of all the difficulties EU membership will undoubtedly bring to the Baltic states and in spite of the Balts' own highly sceptical opinion vis-à-vis the EU, their firm aspirations of belonging to the western community will sustain the people over the long term. Indeed, even if the EU turns out to be a disappointment for the Balts, they will most likely be more inclined to change it, rather than to break away from still another Union.

Notes

1 The distinction between 'objective' and 'subjective' factors in explaining foreign policies formed one of the key debates in international relations theory in the 1990s. A good introduction to the theme can be found in M. Hollis and S. Smith, *Explaining and Understanding International Relations* (Oxford, Clarendon Press, 1991).

2 B. Parekh, 'Discourses on National Identity', *Political Studies*, 42 (1994), 492.

3 This conception even reflected itself as the starting point for Estonia's and Latvia's new nationality legislations during the beginning of the 1990s, according to which automatic citizenship was accorded only to those, who were citizens in 1940 or their descendants. See chapter 4 by Nida Gelazis in this volume; also, I. Ziemele 'The Citisenship Issue in the Republic of Latvia', in S. O'Leary and T. Tiilikainen (eds), *Citizenship and Nationality in the New Europe* (London, Sweet and Maxwell, 1998), pp. 187–204.

4 Concerning the Estonian interpretation of the situation, see P. Vares, 'Returning to Europe: A View from Estonia', in M. Jopp and S. Arnswald (eds), *The European Union and the Baltic States* (Helsinki, The Finnish Institute of International Affairs and Institut für Europäische Politik, 1998), pp. 101–112; concerning the Latvian case see Ž. Ozoliņa 'Latvia, the EU and Baltic Sea Co-operation' in the same volume, pp. 113–144.

5 T. Klaar 'Estonia's Security Policy Priorities', in G. Artéus and A. Lejiņš (eds), *Baltic Security: Looking Towards the 21st Century* (Stockholm, Latvian Institute of Foreign Affairs and Försvarshögskolan, 1998), pp. 18–32.

6 G. Avery and F. Cameron, *The Enlargement of the European Union* (Sheffield, Sheffield Academic Press, 1998), pp. 122–123.

7 S. Arnswald, *EU Enlargement and the Baltic States* (Helsinki, The Finnish Institute of International Affairs and Instittut für Europäische Politik, 2000), p. 94.

8 The larger interest in NATO membership has been confirmed by G. Vitkus, 'At the Crossroads of Alternatives: Lithuanian Security Policies in 1995–97', in Artéus and Lejiņš, *Baltic Security*, and by D. Bleiere, 'Integration of the Baltic States in the European Union: The Latvian Perspective', in A. Lejiņš and Ž. Ozoliņa, *Small States in a Turbulent Environment: The Baltic Perspective* (Riga, Latvian Institute of International Affairs, 1997).

9 A brief, but good, analysis of the Russian position can be found in E. Romare, *Rysslands syn på sin säkerhet* (Stockholm, Regeringskansliet, 1998.)

10 Avery and Cameron, *The Enlargement of the EU*, pp. 69–80.

11 European Commission, *Making a success of enlargement* (Brussels, European Commission, 2001).
12 In the Amsterdam Treaty, the European Court of Justice was for the first time given controlling powers over article F2, according to which 'The Union shall respect fundamental rights, as guaranteed by the European Convention for the Protection of Human Rights and Fundamental Freedoms, signed in Rome on 4 November 1950 and as they result from the constitutional traditions common to the member states, as general principles of Community Law.'
13 The new charter of fundamental rights covers both rights that are conferred to all EU residents and rights that are conferred to EU citizens only. Plans have existed, however, to further enlarge the rights of EU citizens. See R. Koslowski, 'EU Citizenship: Implications for Identity and Legitimacy', in T. Banchoff and M. Smith, *Legitimacy and the European Union* (London, Routledge, 1999), p. 169.
14 A good group of comparison here is formed by the Nordic states, which after the Nordic enlargement of the EU have shown a greater willingness for individual, rather than common, solutions to large political questions such as the EMU or support for Eastern enlargement.
15 A. Lejiņš, 'The Quest for Baltic Unity: Chimera or Reality?', in Lejiņš and Ozoliņa, *Small States*, pp. 147–183.
16 The Balts' intention to join NATO can be treated as a concrete fact that makes relations with leading NATO members of the EU more useful than relations with the Nordic members.
17 The main Finnish newspaper *Helsingin Sanomat* described this criticism in a September 1998 article entitled 'The Balts are Suspicious towards the Finnish Eastern Projects'. It referred to a number of Baltic newspapers that during summer 1998 had been highly critical of the Northern Dimension programme.
18 V. Kaitila and M. Widgrén, *Baltian maiden EU-jäsenyys ja Suomi* (Helsinki, ETLA, 1998), pp. 105–122.
19 See H. Mannonen, 'The Internal Security Field in the Baltics', in *The Integration of the Baltic States to the European Union* (Helsinki, Ministry of Foreign Affairs, 1997).
20 Mannonen, 'The Internal Security Field', p. 44.
21 European Commission, 'Making a Success of Enlargement' (Brussels, European Commission, 2001).
22 R. Dannreuther, *Eastward enlargement, NATO and EU*, Forsvarsstudier 1/1997 (Oslo, Institut for Forsvarsstudier, 1997), p. 65.
23 The Maastricht Treaty confirmed the role of the old European defence alliance, the WEU, as an evolving military dimension of the EU, deciding to leave all decisions of defence policy to this body.

GEORGE W. BRESLAUER

3

Russia, the Baltic states, and East–West relations in Europe

This chapter places Russian–Baltic relations during the 1990s within the context of Moscow's policies toward East–West relations in general and toward Europe in particular.[1] It analyses the thrust of Russian foreign policy under the presidency of Boris Yeltsin and the observable implications this had for the Baltic states as the latter sought to join the European Union. It then suggests a range of scenarios for the future of Russia's domestic evolution, the implications of those scenarios for its foreign relations, and the consequences of each for Moscow's relations with the Baltic states.

The chapter is cast at a fairly high level of generalisation. It does not analyse the twists and turns of Moscow's daily relations with the Baltic states during these years. Nor is it based on new research into the issue. Rather, I provide a general framework within which to locate the fairly temperate Russo-Baltic relations of the 1990s. Thus, the informational base of this 'think piece' will be familiar to specialists on Russian foreign relations. However, toward the end I will discuss the conditions under which flashpoints could arise in the relationship or a sustained heightening of hostility might take place.

Three foreign policy tendencies

One can distinguish many fine gradations among the orientations and preferences of different political actors in Moscow during the 1990s. But, basically, three coherent tendencies competed for ascendancy in Russian foreign-policy-making: liberal internationalism, radical nationalism, and moderate nationalism.[2] Each of them had historical roots, but each had also been adapted to post-Soviet conditions at home and in the world.

Liberal internationalism is a term that has its origins in western international relations theory; its initial application was to western countries. Its counterpart in Soviet days was the radical reformist, and at times 'globalist' tendency that became stronger behind the scenes throughout the post-Stalin decades and that culminated in Gorbachev's 'new thinking' about international relations.[3] In late Soviet and post-Soviet Russia, it entailed the formal rejection of proletarian internationalism and class conflict in international affairs in favour of the westernisation of Russia and its integration into European, Atlantic, and global-capitalist economic, political, and military institutions. This was a perspective that called for 'joining the West' as a co-resident of 'our common home – Europe'. Sometimes proponents of this perspective extended it to encompass the Atlantic dimension as well: 'from Vancouver to Vladivostok' (travelling from west to east, of course). The tendency viewed Europe as a more advanced civilisation – indeed, as the standard for 'civilized, normal' society – and as a reference group for emulation by Russia as it attempted to redefine itself.[4]

This tendency dominated Gorbachev's foreign policy, though it was tempered by a strained effort to maintain certain distinctive features of Soviet 'socialism' that would provide the basis for a democratic-socialist 'third way'. That strained effort was dropped after the Soviet Union collapsed. During the first year of Yeltsin's presidency, liberal internationalism prevailed in Moscow's foreign-policy-making. Essentially, this meant that Russian policy-makers were eager to cooperate with the United States and Western Europe largely on the West's terms, in hopes of securing material assistance for the transition and of rapidly integrating Russia into as many western-led multilateral organisations as possible.

Reacting in part against this concessionary, supplicant posture, and in part against the simultaneous collapse of the USSR, communism, the Warsaw Pact, and Soviet global power, a rejectionist counter-tendency emerged rapidly during 1992–93. Sometimes referred to as a 'red-brown' coalition, it united restorationist communists with reactionary and romantic nationalists. Differences within the coalition over the desirability or feasibility of restoring the USSR were less important than the common sentiment that Russia had to restore its prior glory and stand up against the dark forces in the outside world that were trying to destroy it. Let us call this tendency, following Shlapentokh,[5] *radical nationalist*, while bearing in mind that it includes many imperial restorationists as well.

This counter-tendency was based upon the search for a unique path of development for Russia and a unique role for Russia internationally. It rejected the goal of integrating the country into Europe, for it viewed Russia as surrounded by enemies on all fronts.[6] It provided the ideological foundation for a neo-fascist regime in Russia; it is what we would have to fear if 'Weimar Russia' were ever to become a prophetic metaphor for the Russia of tomorrow. In foreign policy prescriptions, the tendency can take many forms, distinguished by the scope and focus of its use of violence. It can be isolationist and focus its promotion of violence on internal enemies, both political and ethnic. Alternatively, it can be imperial-restorationist, thus exercising large-scale coercion against countries of the near abroad. Or it can also express itself in aggressive expansion beyond the boundaries of the former Soviet Union, whether coupled with, or instead of, an imperial-restorationist project. In any case, the posture toward the outside world would be decidedly confrontational. Happily, radical nationalism has been only a rhetorical tendency in Russian political and social circles thus far, though it has certainly influenced the climate of opinion in Moscow.[7]

The third tendency stood midway between the liberal internationalist and the radical nationalist. Again following Shlapentokh,[8] let us call it *moderate nationalism.*[9] This perspective rejected as excessively one-sided the concessionary terms of cooperation with the West accepted under Gorbachev and during the first year of Yeltsin's leadership. But it equally rejected the view of Russia as besieged by hostile international forces that it needed to confront in order to deter; and it resisted the temptation to embrace coercively restorationist projects. Rather, 'moderate nationalism' as a worldview seeks to combine cooperation with competition in international affairs. It views Russia as, by right, a great European power, one that wishes cooperation with Europe, even integration into European institutions, but accompanied by a special sensitivity to the maintenance of its sovereignty, autonomy, and special, great-power status. In domestic affairs, the moderate nationalists tended to be technocratic and pragmatic. In foreign relations, they were self-styled 'realists,' embracing balance-of-power, *realpolitik* theories of international organisation.

Moderate nationalism lacked idealism about international affairs and feared that liberal internationalism, as practiced earlier, was willy-nilly a prescription for being suckered by a United States that was seeking hegemony within the global system. Many of them, when forced to define their positions in ideational or identity-driven terms, embraced some variant of 'Eurasianism', which sought a distinctive identity for Russia in international affairs as a bridge between Europe and Asia due to its unique combination of both heritages. But, when discussing concrete policies, the Eurasian identity was less important than the pragmatic search for ways simultaneously to cooperate with the West, build advantageous relations with other powers throughout the world, offset US unilateralism, and define a set of foreign policy interests that were distinctive to Russia and for which it was willing to stand up. The moderate-nationalist tendency came to the fore in 1993, in a reaction against the liberal-internationalism then ascendant, expressing itself as an analytical challenge: what is Russia's 'national interest?'[10] During the late 1990s, this tendency became ever stronger, to the point that many former liberal internationalists shifted their position toward moderate nationalism. As a result, and unlike the radical-nationalist tendency, the moderate-nationalist tendency emerged ascendant within the policy-making community.

Margot Light has nicely summarised some of the points of complementarity and difference among these three tendencies.

> Both Liberal Westernizers and Pragmatic Nationalists stressed the importance of relations with the West . . . although they differed in the priority and exclusivity they accorded to these relations. Similarly, both Pragmatic and Fundamentalist Nationalists expressed Eurasianist views. The distinction between them with regard

> to Eurasia lay primarily in how they envisaged implementing their ideas. All three groups also agreed that Russia was responsible for the welfare of Russians in the diaspora. They differed, however, about what the Russian government should do to fulfil its obligations . . . All three groups insisted that Russia was, and would continue to be, a great power. They differed, however, on what the implications of great-power status were for Russian foreign policy.[11]

Yeltsin's foreign policy strategy: a synthesis

In contrast to Moscow's policies of 1988–92, Russian foreign policy after 1993 reflected an effort to *combine* the liberal-internationalist and the moderate-nationalist tendencies. The embattlement of Foreign Minister Andrei Kozyrev, and his eventual replacement in January 1996 by Yevgeny Primakov, were surface manifestations of this effort to strike a balance – or to effect what Wallender has called a 'liberal-statist synthesis'.[12] The effort to combine competitive (but not confrontational) with cooperative postures accounted for the coexistence of a persistent urge for cooperation with the West and a simultaneous urge to define and defend Russia's national pride and to assert national interests independent of western concerns. The latter expressed itself in self-assertion within the near abroad, the development of closer ties with regimes such as Iran and Iraq that affected Russia's security and material interests, efforts to balance US unilateralism through expanded ties with China and India, adoption of a limited protector role toward Serbia in the NATO–Yugoslavia confrontation, problematic arms control negotiations, and others. The tension within the liberal/moderate-nationalist coalition also explained Moscow's urge both to be integrated into Europe and to do so in ways that would not make Russia simply an instrument of Washington's foreign policy preferences.

But in both the liberal-internationalist and the moderate-nationalist worldviews, the 'idea of Europe' was both strong and positive: as a reference group in international and domestic affairs, as a partner, as an object of emulation, and as a community of which Russia wished to be a part.[13] And for the large majority of policy influentials, the idea of East–West and Russo-European cooperation was equally powerful, viewed as both desirable in its own right and as necessary for the stabilisation of both a dangerous international environment and an increasingly out-of-control domestic Russian context.[14]

What, then, were the implications of these tendencies for Russian foreign policy toward the Baltic states? Under Boris Yeltsin's rule one could see how the two tendencies combined to shape policy in this region. Moscow did prove willing to withdraw its troops from bases in the Baltic states and to dismantle advanced military installations, but it also tried to link the pace of withdrawal, rhetorically at least, to liberalisation of Estonia's and Latvia's citizenship laws. In the event, Moscow withdrew its troops and dismantled its installations, and Latvia and Estonia made limited concessions by revising their citizenship laws somewhat. Similarly, we find in Moscow's official rhetoric and discussions from this period a resigned acceptance of the Baltics as having escaped the Russian sphere of influence.[15] But we also find an insistence that the treatment of Russian minorities in the Baltic states was a legitimate ethno-national concern of Moscow's, that access to Kaliningrad was a legitimate national-security concern, and that Moscow had the right as well as the means to exercise material coercion, given Baltic dependence on Russian energy supplies, if the Baltic states rejected Moscow's right to express and act upon its concerns. Lastly, we saw a Russian willingness to endorse prospective Baltic integration into the European Union, but this was accompanied by a heightened sensitivity to Russian exclusion from EU institutions and strong opposition to the idea of Baltic membership in NATO.[16] In sum, Moscow's policies toward the Baltic states mirrored the combination of cooperation and competition in its approach to Russo-European and East–West relations more generally.

The liberal-statist synthesis was not driven solely by generalised worldviews, however. After the collapse of communism an especially powerful set of private economic interests also arose and became assertive as an actor in the formulation of Russian policies. The energy industry – LUKoil and Gazprom in particular – sought opportunities and concessions in all three Baltic states. Temporary deterioration of Moscow's relations with each state in 1998 and 1999 coincided with efforts by these conglomerates to win concessions from Baltic governments.[17] But, after those companies succeeded in their efforts, relations between Moscow and the Baltic governments returned to a state of relative equilibrium.[18]

A stable equilibrium?

Despite the tensions within the liberal/moderate-nationalist coalition, this equilibrium proved fairly stable throughout the 1990s. After 1993, variations within Moscow's policy repertoire toward the Baltic states largely stayed within the parameters outlined. Those parameters were reinforced by the European Union's and the Council of Europe's attitudes toward citizenship laws and minority rights in the Baltic states – attitudes that dovetailed with what Moscow had been advocating.

But the stability of the equilibrium was also mightily reinforced by one common characteristic of advocates of both the liberal-internationalist and moderate-nationalist tendencies in Moscow. Most of them were supremely aware of Russia's *weakness* as a state and as an international actor. This was not a matter of attitudes and preferences; it was a matter of rational calculation and perception. These might have been at variance with ideal preferences and with nostalgia for great power status. And that variance might have left individuals highly conflicted and frustrated, inclining them toward angry rhetorical outbursts at academic gatherings, at press conferences, and in some publications. But the realistic awareness of Russia's *capabilities* was a powerful source of sobriety within the process of formulating Russia's foreign policy – one that existed already in 1992 but that was greatly reinforced by the traumatic initial military defeat in Chechnya.[19] In the actual formulation of policy, pessimism prevailed about Russia's capability to assert itself as a great power and about its ability to close the gap between ideal preferences and realistic capabilities. It is noteworthy, for example, that, on many issues, Moscow's foreign policy establishment (though perhaps not its parliament) was willing to compromise and conciliate western capitals when forced to choose between a cooperative and a competitive posture.[20]

Perhaps the pithiest expression of the gap between nostalgia and sober calculation, or between affect and cognition, was stated by Aleksandr Lebed (a moderate nationalist) in his autobiography. The statement concerned the near abroad and was appropriated without attribution by Boris Yeltsin in his presidential campaign of 1996: 'Those who do not regret the collapse of the USSR lack a heart; those who believe they can restore it in its previous form lack a brain.'[21] Lebed expressed similarly moderate thoughts during a visit to NATO headquarters in autumn 1996, where he spoke about the prospect of NATO's first wave of expansion.[22]

Sources of disruption of the equilibrium

As far as strength and weakness are concerned, power is a relative, situational, and perceptual concept. Russia may have been weak in general during the 1990s, and awareness of this weakness may have shaped the general direction of its foreign policy. But in specific realms and places, Russia did enjoy sources of leverage that gave it bargaining power in interstate relations. In the Baltics, Russia had, above all, economic sources of leverage in its control of energy supplies although, admittedly, it was also dependent on transit routes through the Baltics for oil exports and many imports. Thus, in deference to the demands of LUKoil, Russia successfully imposed economic sanctions on Latvia and Lithuania in early 1998 and early 1999, respectively.[23] Russia also had military sources of leverage, especially with respect to covert operations. Russian policy-makers had political sources of leverage to encourage ethnic-Russian residents of Latvia and Estonia to politicise and dramatise their grievances. They had psychological sources of leverage in the very fact that Russia was so big, so close, so unstable, and historically so rapacious, lending magnitude as well as credibility to Russian rhetorical threats. And they had ecological sources of leverage in their capacity to ignore situations that could have drastic environmental consequences for the region. These specific forms of leverage, of course, did not ensure the *capacity* for ongoing domination, much less restoration. And the exercise of some of them could have had an adverse impact on Russia's relations with Western Europe and the United States – a cost that policy-makers of the liberal and moderate-nationalist orientation in Moscow would consider seriously before acting. Hence, they were not exercised lightly. But if our concern is the measurement of Russian weakness or strength, the point to bear in mind is that these sources of leverage would have been important in a crisis, that they were sources of strength, not weakness, even during the 1990s, and that they offset the general perception of weakness among policy-makers in Moscow.

The Putin government has thus far acted with moderation toward the Baltic states. And, following the September 11, 2001 terrorist attacks in New York and Washington, Putin has returned liberal-international viewpoints to a position of ascendancy in Moscow's foreign-policy-making. This has entailed a determined effort to ease East–West tensions, to build a long-term East–West partnership against terrorism, and to use this as a basis for firmly integrating Russia into western institutions, including NATO. The rapid turnabout holds great promise for cooperative East–West relations. But it must not be taken for granted. Flashpoints between Moscow and the Baltic governments could exacerbate relations. These could be a product of circumstances within the Baltic states or within Russia. In the Baltic countries, while great progress has been made toward economic and political revival, the unresolved questions of inter-ethnic relations and national identity could hit the surface in ugly ways, especially when economic rough patches are encountered or economic shocks take place. Moreover, the unsettled condition of Russian politics, the fragmented condition of the Russian state, the possibility that the Russian economic rebound of 1999–2002 will prove unsustainable, and the continued vitality of 'hardline' constituencies in both Moscow and Washington suggest that Moscow's cooperative urge may not remain ascendant.

It is sometimes difficult to think beyond the current rapprochement, but we can imagine a number of ways regression could take place. First, the Baltics could become a scapegoat for Russian frustration in other realms of internal or foreign policy. If Russian interests in places like the Caspian region, Iraq or Iran are damaged, either by western action or local circumstances, a ruling group could look elsewhere for a compensatory gain that is less likely to be countered effectively. Second, one could think not of a ruling group, but of a political leader who is seeking to defend his shaken authority. As Lebow has shown in the case of great power crises of the nineteenth and twentieth centuries, when leaders are on the political defensive, they often seek 'wins' by militarist means that they would not have entertained had their authority been secure.[24] Such an interpretation could be applied to Khrushchev's emplacement of Soviet missiles in Cuba. It may also explain the fact that Boris Yeltsin was willing to invade Chechnya only five years after his country had finally extricated itself from the war in Afghanistan, and less than three years after Yeltsin himself had severed Russian material assistance to the successor Afghan government. Yeltsin was decidedly on the political defensive at the time.[25] We have yet to witness Putin on the political defensive, but he will be up for re-election at a time when the Russian economy may no longer be in rebound.

A third path toward the same end is also rooted in the pathological side-effects of political competition. During political campaigns and in anticipation of political succession, candidates typically strike postures that they hope will resonate with their electoral audiences. Since there are more politicians competing for positions than there are defensible programmatic niches within a liberal-statist policy synthesis, politicians will be tempted to competitively outbid each other to attract voters who are disaffected either materially or ideologically: with promises of personal-economic relief or national-economic betterment or with promises to restore Russia's glory by one means or another. Competitive outbidding in Russian politics also means the search for scapegoats, and scapegoating of the Baltics is easy, since they are small and weak. Moreover, it is potentially less costly to treat the Baltics as the rhetorical whipping boys than to target the governments of Ukraine or Kazakhstan – assuming the competing politicians are primarily concerned with maintaining stability at home and averting destabilisation of these two large neighbours.

As long as scapegoating of the Baltics remains rhetorical, it may trigger no escalatory dynamic. But one can imagine an escalatory path of the following sort. A candidate is elected who had scapegoated the Baltics during the election campaign and feels the need politically, at a minimum, to demonstrate some progress on that score after he/she is in office. Baltic governments then react to this apparent provocation by upping the rhetorical ante, as a way of drawing the United States and Western Europe into an augmented commitment to their protection, which in turn leads to an escalation of real Russian threats. Someone would probably back down, since neither the US, Western Europe, nor Russia under a liberal or moderate-nationalist leadership, wants an East–West confrontation. But the dynamic could nonetheless exacerbate relations and, depending on the outcome, potentially undercut the credibility of both liberals and moderate nationalists within Russian politics. Note again that all three of these triggers of a possible toughening of Moscow's policies toward the Baltics could take place under a liberal/moderate-nationalist coalition and are consistent with a more general self-perception of Russia as a weak power.

There is another path to exacerbation of Russo-Baltic relations under these same conditions. The current Russian state is fragmented and corrupted throughout. That condition can be the source of provocations that are not orchestrated by either a ruling group or a president or foreign minister in Moscow. Russian military commanders in Moscow or in regions adjacent to the Baltic states may not share the moderation of the politicians in the ruling coalition. Given the poor condition of Russia's armed forces, those commanders may be more emotional about issues such as the miserable conditions in Kaliningrad or Murmansk. In view of Russia's small number of warm water ports, the same commanders may be more convinced that the Baltics are strategically vital to Russia's national security. Affectively and cognitively, such commanders may differ enough from their civilian bosses that, in a crisis, they might be willing to undertake independent actions that could escalate the crisis unnecessarily. Similarly, one can imagine provocations by uncontrolled Russian expatriate forces within the Baltic states or by local police or paramilitary organisations in regions adjacent to the Baltic states. That is, without coordination with politicians or commanders in Moscow or St Petersburg, these forces, in a crisis or in 'normal' times, could seek to elevate Moscow's commitment to their cause by initiating a crisis between themselves and Baltic governmental authorities and by then calling upon Moscow to protect them against the reaction.

With the reconsolidation of authoritarianism in Belarus, and Moscow's support for growing integration between Russia, Belarus, and others, one can imagine still another path through which provocations could upset normality in Russo-Baltic relations. An unpredictable, imperial-restorationist president in Belarus – such as Aleksandr Lukashenko – could find it convenient to distract attention from domestic conditions in that country by fabricating crises with his Baltic neighbours. And given his influence in Moscow, and his relative obliviousness to western governmental opinions, he could feel emboldened to do so with relative impunity.

All of this suggests a policy prescription. Baltic governments might be wise to increase their levels of integration, not only with Scandinavia and north-central Europe, but also with Russia's northwest region and the Leningrad *oblast'* in particular. To the extent that such integration will foster greater local Russian dependence on Baltic assets, it could create an additional constituency in Moscow for moderation and cooperation. Hopefully, this would raise Moscow's threshold for competitive or confrontational responses to crises born of provocations. From this perspective, Baltic humanitarian assistance to Kaliningrad *oblast'* in the late 1990s was salutary and wise.

NATO enlargement

The paths to crisis noted above would not necessarily require overthrow (or fundamental radicalisation) of a coalition of liberals and moderate nationalists in Moscow. But an alternative path to crisis runs through Western Europe, NATO, and the United States, and this would probably require a more fundamental shift in coalitions. This hypothetical path is triggered by the combination of NATO's first wave of expansion, that organisation's war in Yugoslavia, and the prospect of a second wave of NATO expansion that accorded membership to one or more of the Baltic states. Within the confines of this chapter I cannot discuss all the issues and contingencies associated with these past, present, and future events. But several points warrant emphasis. One lesson of the first wave of enlargement, which entailed membership for Poland, Hungary and the Czech Republic, was that the vast majority of Russian politicians of all political orientations considered NATO's expansion into Eastern Europe to be a very undesirable development.[26] Responses ranged along a spectrum from viewing it as simply unfortunate, insensitive, or unhelpful (the response of the most pro-western, liberal internationalists) to viewing it as an aggressive, hostile act of isolation and encirclement of Russia (the radical-nationalist response). Most politicians stood at points in between in their rhetoric, though with a bias toward emotional response and the imputation to NATO of hostile intent. The NATO–Russia Founding Act of 1997 marginally offset this emotion and perception, and certainly facilitated President Boris Yeltsin's and Foreign Minister Yevgeny Primakov's efforts to prevent the inevitable outcome from destroying the fabric of Russo-American and Russo-European governmental relations. But the fact that years of Russian protests did so little to prevent that outcome must certainly have affected the climate of opinion in Moscow regarding western intentions. It would be useful to know just how much of Russia's forbearance in reacting against NATO enlargement was due to restraint enforced by Boris Yeltsin and how much reflected a broader consensus within Moscow's policy-making circles about policy priorities, avoidance of adventurism, and the limits of the possible.

Although difficult to document, NATO enlargement probably had a corrosive effect on the credibility of the ruling coalition's justifications for moderation. And it forced many politicians and intellectuals to swallow a great deal of anger and disillusionment. If all other things had remained equal, the behavioural consequences might not have become apparent for quite some time, but could have manifested themselves, perhaps quite unexpectedly, at some point in the future. As Nikolai Sokov wrote in July 1998:

> Russian policy is likely to be stable for a long time, marked by explosions of strong rhetoric, but restraint in terms of action. If tension continues to build, however, policy is likely to snap at an unpredictable moment, perhaps with little apparent provocation. Russia's external relations will be guided by emotion instead of rational calculation . . . So far Russia has not truly reacted to NATO enlargement. The real response might come years from now, and is impossible to predict. To a large degree, it will be formed by the way the relationship with NATO develops in the next several years. Historical patterns warn that Russia, while appearing to drop its grievances, may at some point suddenly demand 'payment' for events everyone else will have forgotten.[27]

Obviously, the Baltic states are relevant to 'the way the relationship with NATO develops in the next several years'. The logic of piecemeal NATO enlargement entailed a felt need in the West to reassure those countries that had been left out but that were knocking vigorously at the doors. Rhetorically, western governments provided this reassurance by proclaiming that enlargement was a continuing process, that no country in Europe was excluded from the possibility of eventual membership, and that the Baltic states stood a good chance of consideration when the next wave of accessions was considered seriously in 2002. To make those assurances credible, representatives of western governments occasionally stated or hinted that the timetable for consideration might be accelerated. Such, indeed, became the most likely scenario after the September 2001 attacks in New York and Washington.

None of this public discussion, of course, completely quelled the criticism of Russian politicians and policy-makers, who argued that a second wave of enlargement that incorporated states of the former Soviet Union would entail 'consequences'. Nor is it clear that concrete reassurances to Russia, beyond those already to be found in the NATO–Russia Founding Act, could be devised that would defuse Russian concerns. After all, the Baltics, although written off by Moscow's policymakers as potential participants in the Commonwealth of Independent States, remained much more closely tied into the Russian policy-making 'psyche' than were the states of the former Warsaw Pact. Psychologically, integration of part of the FSU into a potentially hostile alliance structure evoked loss of empire, loss of great power status, a historical mindset of Russia being abused by the outside world, and a deep resentment of American unilateralism since the end of the Cold War. Politically, it evoked the ethnic Russian communities that would suddenly be living under NATO's prospective protection. Militarily, it evoked the loss of a major defence perimeter and its 'occupation' by a former enemy alliance. And emotionally, it evoked all the anger and sense of helplessness that had accumulated over the past ten years of precipitous decline in Russia. Obviously, even for those Russian elites who were most oriented toward cooperation with the West, expansion of NATO into the Baltic states would be a difficult pill to swallow.

Much of Moscow's problem with NATO's expansion into Eastern Europe was that western governments were attempting to transform an alliance against a common enemy into a security community for stabilisation of the continent, but without diminishing the military preparedness of an alliance. NATO enlargement *was* defensible, in principle at least, as an effort to use the alliance as an instrument of all-European stabilisation. Indeed, the prospect and hope for NATO membership led several governments in Eastern Europe to settle major differences between their states, and influenced the governments of Latvia and Estonia to liberalise their citizenship laws. Authorities in Moscow acknowledged that an all-European organisation for collective security, broadly defined, was a salutary prospect. They questioned, however, the choice of organisation, since NATO was the one all-European organisation in which Russia had no realistic prospect of gaining membership.

During the late 1990s, Russian commentators repeatedly stressed that Moscow must evaluate the 'threat' from NATO enlargement by asking questions about the long term. Why did the West consider NATO, and not the OSCE, the Council of Europe, the West European Union, or some hypothetical new organisation to be the most appropriate instrument for creating a pan-European security community? What was the vision in the West of the role of Russia within this security community in, say, the year 2030? Would Russia be a member of equal standing in policy-making processes within the community? If NATO was the instrument of choice, what were the prospects that Russia would also be drawn into membership? Would Baltic countries have a presumptive veto over the acceptance of new members, as the NATO rules of unanimity implied? Since Moscow never received reassuring or convincing answers to these questions, it was not surprising that it drew the conclusion that, in thirty years, NATO expansion throughout Eastern Europe and into the Baltic states (and perhaps also into Belarus and Ukraine) could erect a new political 'curtain' between Russia – even a democratic Russia – and Europe.[28]

Thus, even for those many Russian politicians who believed that NATO and NATO expansion presented no real military threat to their country, the idea of a NATO enlargement that excluded the realistic possibility of Russian membership implied heightened barriers to Russia's long-term goal of integrating itself into Europe. And, again thinking about the long term, so many twists of fate and history could intercede in that time period that an expanded NATO could easily be reconverted into an anti-Russian defence alliance, especially given the anti-Russian proclivities of almost all the new and prospective members. If those members included states of the former Soviet Union, the next Cold War, if it came to that, could leave Russia in a decidedly worse position militarily and politically than it had *circa* 1985.

For all these reasons, the dominant coalition in Moscow followed the NATO–Russia Founding Act of 1997 with an immediate effort to slow the momentum toward Baltic accession during a second wave. Prime minister Chernomyrdin, in September 1997, proposed 'confidence-building measures designed to ease tensions in the Baltic region [and] called for the Baltic states to adopt a non-bloc status similar to that of Finland and Sweden, and said that Russia was ready to offer the Baltic states (and Sweden and Finland) unilateral security guarantees'. Russia found no takers for these offers.[29]

Just as Moscow was accommodating itself to the *fait accompli* of Polish, Czech and Hungarian accession to NATO, while drawing its 'red line' against a second wave of NATO expansion, war broke out between NATO and Milosevic's Yugoslavia. The effect of this war was to greatly increase the credibility and legitimacy of anti-NATO sentiments within the Russian population, to shift the balance in elite rhetoric toward a combination of moderate- and radical-nationalist sentiments, and to throw liberal-internationalists into a state of political helplessness. The fact that the war happened to be waged against a historical Russian ally and ethno-religious associate heightened the sense of rage. But more fundamental was the fact that the war took place against Russia's will and without United Nations sanction (to avoid a Russian or Chinese veto). This suggested to policy-makers in Moscow that NATO had unilaterally declared itself to be the guardian of values in Europe, with the right to enforce its will militarily on the continent as it so chose. The net effect was both to greatly strengthen anti-western sentiments and fears within the populace and political elite and to reinforce the presumption that NATO would attempt to dictate to Moscow the terms of Russia's prospective integration into Europe.

Looking down the line, Russia's foreign policy orientations could depend on the extent to which the authorities are able to sustain the country's economic rebound of recent years. If the Russian government cannot do that much, then the situation could become all the more unpredictable. True, the combination of abject weakness and chronic instability could leave decision-makers in a sobered state of mind, totally preoccupied with domestic problems, and ever-more-eager to avoid adventurism or alienate potential sources of capital abroad. But it could equally – or more so, if the instability is chronic and socio-economic 'shock' intervene – lead to a 'snap', be it violent or electoral, that overthrows the liberal/moderate nationalist ruling coalition in favour of a radical-nationalist ascendancy. This is the scenario often referred to as Weimar Russia. It is not a likely scenario. And it is increasingly difficult to imagine in the face of these first years of apparent stabilisation and East–West détente under Putin. But it is not inconceivable and therefore warrants inclusion in a listing of possibilities.

Weimar Russia?

This scenario opens up entirely new and unwelcome possibilities. This is not the place for a full discussion of the factors pushing for and against this eventuality. The debate over the tightness-of-fit of the Weimar analogy is heating up at the moment and has spawned some very interesting insights about both the similarities and the differences.[30] Ironically, part of the justification for NATO's expansion, and for its maintaining the capacity to revert very quickly to the posture of a defensive alliance, is precisely the possibility that Russia might succumb to a neo-fascist regime that might rebuild an absolutist Russian state and take out its aggressions on its neighbours.

The country would pay a heavy economic price for such a radical-nationalist ascendancy. Hopes for debt rescheduling or relief, foreign loans, foreign direct investment, even the continuing cash flow from Western Europe for Russian sales of natural gas could be jeopardised or dashed. But, for radical nationalists, material values are less important than the advancement of national glory through domination, by whatever means. Radical nationalists display a greater willingness to act on their emotions and to exaggerate the country's potential capabilities. They typically rally constituents by scapegoating both the western world and alleged enemies within, usually linking the two by claiming that internal and external enemies are working together to destroy the country.

At present, most radical nationalists in Russia appear to share with their moderate and liberal co-politicians an awareness of Russia's weakness and a squeamishness about adventurism in foreign relations.[31] But this can change, especially if a new generation of radical nationalists follows the neo-fascist path taken by Makashov, Barkashov, the Russian National Unity movement, and others. In some regions of Russia in the late 1990s (Krasnodar, Pskov, Orel), local governments were in power that can be termed fascist and that justified themselves with fascistic themes. The open scapegoating of Jews has increased greatly since the economic crash of August 1998, replete with conspiratorial explanations for the suffering of the Russian people. We could hope that the sobering effect of nuclear weapons would dampen radical nationalists' enthusiasm for international adventurism. Thus, a pogrom mentality against ethnic minorities and liberals within Russia might substitute for the kind of overt external aggression of Hitler, Mussolini, and the Japanese government in the 1930s. But there is also that intermediate category between the 'domestic' and the 'foreign'; Russians call it the 'near abroad', which is where the Baltic states are located.

A radical-nationalist regime could more ambitiously reconcile the pogrom mentality with the fear of nuclear confrontation by cracking down simultaneously on internal enemies and on countries within the near abroad. The Baltic states would be relatively easy targets. The Yeltsin administration tried to mute domestic criticism from radical nationalists and communists by attempting to demonstrate that, even as NATO expansion proceeded apace, so too did the level of integration among members of the Commonwealth of Independent States (CIS). The political union with Belarus was pushed hard as were various forms of economic union with Ukraine, Kazakhstan, Kyrgystan, and several other Commonwealth states. While CIS integration may be a value in and of itself, it is quite possible that it became linked to the felt need for a consolidative response to NATO expansion. If this is the felt political need of a moderate regime that is trying to reconcile a strategy of integration into the West with the competitive defence of its 'national interests,' imagine how much stronger would be the response of a regime of radical nationalists that cared little for East–West cooperation except in so far as it helped to manage the nuclear danger.

I am not in the business of attaching probability estimates to alternative scenarios; whether a fascist ascendancy in Russia is a 5 per cent probability or a 25 per cent probability in the foreseeable future is unfathomable – and is probably the wrong question to ask. We can concede that it is *possible* and then suggest factors that might increase its level of probability by an indeterminate amount. That is the methodology I have employed in this chapter.

Feudalisation

To this point, I have been writing about Russia as if it were governed in the 1990s by a ruling coalition that sought to formulate policy in line with its preferences, perspectives, and perceptions, and as if that coalition had a functioning state at its disposal for the implementation of its policies. In discussing a prospective Weimar scenario in the twenty-first century, we only need to substitute a different ideological orientation and to consider how it would define and pursue ideals and interests in the world. I have altered these images only to consider the possible sources of uncontrolled provocations that could lead to crises in Moscow's relations with the Baltic states, provocations resulting from unauthorised actions by subordinates in the chain of command.

But what if we bring this last image to the forefront and treat it as symptomatic of a more general problem: the fragmentation, corruption, and criminalisation of the Russian state,[32] along with growing self-assertion by regional elites against the centre? Put differently, and even more bluntly, what if we treat Russia's state as in progressive disintegration and Moscow's leaders, be they moderates or radicals, as incapable of reversing the condition? President Putin tried to address this prospect by putting into place mechanisms for enforcing central writ in the provinces. But it remains far from clear whether central control has in fact been greatly enhanced. And should political or economic crises occur in the future, the process of fragmentation that dominated the Russian scene in the 1990s could accelerate once again. If such a condition lasted for an extended period of time – a decade, let us say – we might then be justified in projecting a scenario that we could call 'feudalisation'. Russia, in this scenario, continues a process of regional disintegration (even if this does not include formal secession by regions), with central power increasingly ephemeral or ineffectual, until the 'country' resembles a very large number of neo-feudal baronies, analogous to Europe in the early middle ages.[33]

Presumably, even under these circumstances, the Foreign Ministry would continue to negotiate on behalf of the central government, but its capacity to deliver on agreements would depend on whether that government could collect taxes and enforce or coordinate those agreements within the country. The Defence Ministry might continue to exercise formal control of the armed forces and the nuclear weapons complex, but its capacity to raise, train, and organise an army or to protect against the spontaneous disappearance of nuclear materials and weapons would always be in question. The President might hold regular summits with foreign leaders, but his capacity to negotiate anything of importance, or his ability to deliver on promises, might be hostage to his relations with regional governors and their willingness and ability to mobilise and transfer resources.

The feudalisation scenario has profound implications for international security, Russia's relations with Western Europe and the United States, and the future of the Baltic states. For a country such as Russia to be fragmented, with a collapsed state, for a long period of time could have major consequences for the construction and viability of bilateral and multilateral regimes to contain the proliferation of nuclear, biological, and chemical weapons, to prevent environmental disasters, and to combat public health threats, international organised crime, drug trafficking, terrorism, and more. In addition, the traditional state-to-state approach, whether bilateral or multilateral, would be confounded by the fact that power within Russia was dispersed among multiple regions and among formal governmental and non-governmental actors within regions. So with whom does one negotiate? The international system, in both bilateral and multilateral forums, is structured to coordinate relations among central governments that are presumably able to speak for their countries. It is much less adept at reaching solutions to problems that require negotiations between governments, on the one hand, and subnational units, on the other. All these dilemmas would perhaps be of greatest frustration to the rich democracies of Western Europe and North America, who typically take the lead in attempts to construct multilateral regimes to combat transnational threats.

For the Baltic states, feudalisation of Russia might appear to have fewer disadvantages. To be sure, it would not eliminate provocations by uncontrolled security forces; indeed, it would eliminate a possible central restraint on their activities. But that centre does not now have much restraining power in any case. To the extent that the Baltic states have more to fear from a strong central government in Moscow, feudalisation would reduce the credibility of Moscow's threats. Would those threats instead emanate from the feudal baronies of Russia's northwest region? Perhaps, if governors of those regions were inclined toward pushing around neighbouring states, individually or in combination with other regions. But most of the contiguous regions of Russia are small, poor, and very badly managed. They could hardly assert themselves as independent actors in international relations, and presumably could easily be deterred by the threat that larger states in the vicinity would support the Baltic governments. The one exception to this rule is St. Petersburg and the Leningrad *oblast'* which, if it turned fascist and assertive, could make mischief for Baltic states. However, the economic cost of doing so, both in loss of broader European support and in the disruption of trade routes through the Baltic states, would be considerable.

Presumably, the Baltic states would be vulnerable to looming environmental, public health, and organised criminal threats emanating from Russia and would have a stake in finding ways to ameliorate them. Under conditions of feudalisation, they would presumably seek to work with both European governments and the governments of whatever Russian regions have the capacity to make a difference.

Conclusion

I have indicated a number of paths through which a relatively stable equilibrium in Russian policies toward the Baltic states could be disrupted, even with a liberal/moderate-nationalist coalition in control of policy-making, causing crises in both Russo-Baltic and East–West relations: assertiveness by private economic interests that influence governmental decisions; a felt need in Moscow for a scapegoat for foreign policy setbacks; the perverse side-effects of political competition; a breakdown of administrative controls; provocations by other leaders within the CIS; a breakdown of interethnic relations within the Baltic states, leading to a felt need for Russian intervention of some sort; or the rancorous inclusion of the Baltic states in NATO.

Thus far, Russian policy toward the Baltic states has been a function of its policy in Europe, and in East–West relations, more generally. And these are functions of what kind of orientation was ascendant in Moscow's foreign policy-making circles. After 1993, the Yeltsin administration pursued a hybrid policy that combined East–West collaboration with East–West competition, based on a coalition of liberal internationalists and moderate nationalists. Such a coalition yielded a relatively stable equilibrium in Russian policies toward the Baltic states.

Some important developments took after 1999.[34] War in Chechnya resumed in the autumn of 1999 and rekindled Russian interest in selective security integration among the southern CIS states. With the exception of Georgia, the deepening of Russian security ties with the southern-tier states was voluntary, based largely on a shared perception of threat from terrorism and extremism. The rising salience of the 'threat from the south' may have reduced the profile of the Baltic states in Russian foreign and security policy, both as motivators of Russian action and as matters of domestic political disputation.

A second change was the arrival of Vladimir Putin to the prime minister's office and then to the presidency. Although it is too early to assess the impact of leadership change on Russian relations with the Baltic states, several preliminary observations seem appropriate. Putin appears to be having some success in consolidating his own authority at the centre. Coupled with the modest economic recovery stemming from higher energy export revenue and the stimulus provided by rouble depreciation, this consolidation reduced the near-term probability of both the Weimar and the feudalisation possibilities discussed above.

President Putin's initial foreign policy steps suggested continuation of the gradual eclipse of both liberal internationalism and radical nationalism. Developing policy drew upon an essentially power-political understanding of national interest, informed by a perception of the mixed (both competitive and collaborative) quality of relations with the West, and was clearly situated in the 'Eurasianist' context of Russian identity politics. How this expressed itself in the Baltics depended largely on whether the Russian policy elite perceived deepening European institutional engagement in the three states to be situated in a broader context of East–West cooperation. Of the two major forms of institutional engagement, enlargement of the European Union continues to elicit less concern in Russia than does NATO expansion.

The relatively benign view of EU enlargement results in part from the historically non-military character of that organisation. The EU's recent steps towards concretising its own security and defence identity in policy and force structure do not appear to have increased Russian concern, perhaps because those changes have created tension in the transatlantic relationship and are consistent with the Russian government's preference for multipolarity.

The major point of tension in Russian–European relations remains Kaliningrad. The region's capacity to produce problems in Russia's relations with Europe in the sphere of regional security was underlined in February 2001 by the near-hysterical NATO and EU reactions to reports that Russia had deployed tactical nuclear weapons there. Furthermore, the common external tariff wall surrounding Kaliningrad had the potential to complicate its economic recovery significantly. And the Schengen visa control regime to which Kalingrad's neighbours are obliged to adhere may create significant obstacles to the movement of Russian citizens between the enclave and the rest of the Russian Federation.

However, the EU has embarked on a series of efforts by European organisations to reduce potential friction between the three Baltic states and Russia.

Most notably, the EU imposed minority-rights conditionality on accession, deliberately excluding Latvia from the initial EU accession negotiations because of Latvia's slowness in conforming to European expectations on minority citizenship. The EU has also engaged Russia in subregional trans-border cooperative activities. Particularly prominent in the latter regard is the EU's 'Northern Dimension', adopted in 1998–99 on the initiative of Finland.[35] The objective of the Western European states in the Baltics as elsewhere is to resolve the potential tensions between Russia and themselves through constructive engagement. Whether this is feasible depends on both the evolution of the Russian polity and on broader trends in Russian–Western relations.

After September 11 2001, Russia's relations with both Western Europe and the United States warmed considerably. The shared perception of a common enemy – international terrorism – led to summit meetings between President Putin and Western leaders that stressed prospects for a long-term, multilateral rapprochement. It remains to be seen whether liberal internationalism can provide the basis for an enduring restructuring of East–West relations and the fuller integration of Russia into western multilateral institutions.

Notes

1 This is a revised version of a paper originally delivered at the conference, 'EU Challenges, Baltic Dimensions', at the European University Institute, Florence, Italy, 22–3 January, 1999. The author is grateful to participants in the conference, as well as to Matthew Bencke, Hall Gardner, Robert Legvold and Neil MacFarlane, for comments on the earlier version.

2 On 'tendency analysis', see F. Griffiths, 'A Tendency Analysis of Soviet Policy Making', in H. Gordon Skilling and Franklyn Griffiths (eds), *Interest Groups in Soviet Politics* (Princeton, Princeton University Press, 1971); for an application to Soviet foreign policy, see F. Griffiths, 'Images, Politics, and Learning in Soviet Behavior Toward the United States', Ph.D. dissertation, Columbia University (1972). For analyses of the competing intellectual frameworks in post-Soviet, Russian foreign policy, see N. Malcolm, A. Pravda, R. Allison and M. Light, *Internal Factors in Russian Foreign Policy*, (Oxford, Oxford University Press, 1996), especially chapter 2 (M. Light, 'Foreign Policy Thinking'). See also A. Arbatov, 'Russia's Foreign Policy Alternatives', *International Security*, 18:2 (1993); W. Zimmerman, 'Markets, Democracy, and Russian Foreign Policy', *Post-Soviet Affairs*, 10:2 (1994); S. N. MacFarlane, 'Russian Conceptions of Europe', *Post-Soviet Affairs*, 10:3 (1994); A. Kortunov, 'Russia, the "Near Abroad", and the West', in Gail Lapidus (ed.), *The New Russia: Troubled Transformation* (Boulder, Westview Press, 1995); V. Shlapentokh, 'How Russians Will See the Status of Their Country by the End of the Century', *Journal of Communist Studies and Transition Politics*, 13:3 (1997); C. Wallander, 'The Russian National Security Concept: A Liberal-Statist Synthesis', *Policy Memo Series*, 30 (Cambridge, Program on New Approaches to Russian Securty, David Center for Russian Studies, Harvard University, 1998).

3 W. Zimmerman, *Soviet Perspectives on International Relations, 1956–1967* (Princeton, Princeton University Press, 1969); Griffiths, *Images, Politics, and Learning*; R. Legvold 'Soviet Learning in the 1980s', in G. W. Breslauer and P. Tetlock (eds), *Learning in US and Soviet Foreign Policy* (Boulder, Westview Press, 1991); A. Brown, *The Gorbachev Factor*

(Oxford, Oxford University Press, 1996) chapter 7.

4 I. Neumann, *Russia and the Idea of Europe: A Study in Identity and International Relations,* (London, Routledge, 1996).

5 Shlapentokh, 'How Russians ill See'.

6 See V. Vujacic, 'Gennadiy Zyuganov and the "Third Road"', *Post-Soviet Affairs,* 12:2 (1996); W. Laqueur, *Black Hundred: The Rise of the Extreme Right in Russia,* (New York, Harper Collins, 1993).

7 The surprising strength of the communist party and the neo-fascist party of Vladimir Zhirinovsky in the Duma elections of December 1993 and December 1995 strengthened their ability to put the Yeltsin government on the defensive. Indeed, not unrelated, Yeltsin fired his liberal-internationalist foreign minister in January 1996. For further evidence of Yeltsin's efforts to avoid being isolated at an extreme of the political spectrum, see G. W. Breslauer and C. Dale 'Boris Yeltsin and the Invention of a Russian Nation-State', *Post-Soviet Affairs,* 13:4 (1997). During 1998–99, the most reactionary forces within the red-brown coalition have publicly condemned Jews for the problems Russia faces, sparking a heated debate in Moscow and elsewhere about the legal limits of free speech when it inflames interethnic hatreds.

8 Shlapentokh, 'How Russians Will See'.

9 Wallender, 'The Russian National Security Concept', refers to this tendency as 'statist'; Light refers to it as 'pragmatic nationalist' (Margot Light, 'Foreign Policy Thinking').

10 For an early analysis of these discussions, see S. Sestanovich, 'Russia Turns the Corner', *Foreign Affairs,* 73:1 (1994).

11 Light, 'Foreign Policy Thinking', pp. 51–52.

12 Wallender, 'The Russian National Security Concept'.

13 See Neumann, *Russia and the Idea of Europe*; MacFarlane, 'Russian Conceptions of Europe'; H. Timmerman, 'Relations Between the EU and Russia: The Agreement on Partnership and Co-operation', *Journal of Communist Studies and Transition Politics,* 12:2 (1996); D. Danilov, 'A Piece of the Partnership', *Transitions,* 4:4 (1998), 60–63.

14 The combination of cooperative and competitive postures is quite different from what it was in Soviet days. At that time, the competitive was much stronger than the cooperative. See G. W. Breslauer, 'Why Détente Failed', in Alexander George (ed.), Managing US–Soviet Rivalry, (Boulder, Westview Press, 1982). Under Yeltsin, the balance of the mix is reversed, with the cooperative strand much stronger than the competitive.

15 The Baltic states all refused to join the Commonwealth of Independent States and have gone furthest in redirecting their trade dependencies westward, while knocking most vigorously on the doors of the European Union and NATO for membership.

16 On the European Union, see Timmerman, 'Relations between the EU and Russia'; on NATO, the literature is voluminous; for an overview of the issue, see J. Haslam, 'Russia's Seat at the Table: A Place Denied or a Place Delayed?', *International Affairs,* 74:1 (1998).

17 Z. Brzezinski and F. S. Larrabee, *U.S. Policy Toward Northeastern Europe: Report of an Independent Task Force* (New York, Council on Foreign Relations Press, 1999), p. 37.

18 But for a complaint by the Latvian foreign minister that the present situation should not be treated as either normal, desirable, or stable, see V. Birkavs, 'Latvia Seeks to Reconcile the Past With a Multiethnic Future', *International Herald Tribune,* 14 (1999), p. 9.

19 On the magnitude of this trauma, see A. Lieven, *Chechnya: Tombstone of Russian Power,* (New Haven, Yale University Press, 1998).

20 It is worth noting, however, that Russia's weakness has also served as a resource by which Moscow has secured cooperative engagement from the West. Precisely because the Russian state has been too weak to control or finance initiatives required to decommission nuclear warheads, destroy chemical weapons, prevent the theft of weapons of mass destruction, clean up environmental degradation that spans national borders, and

combat other transnational threats, Russian policymakers have been able to induce or blackmail Western governments into paying the bill for such efforts. For an outstanding demonstration of this, see R. Darst, 'Bribery and Blackmail in East–West Environmental Politics', *Post-Soviet Affairs*, 13:1 (1997).

21 A. Lebed, *Za derzhavu obidno* (Moscow, Moskovskaya Pravda, 1995), pp. 409–410; for Yeltsin's paraphrase, see *The New York Times*, 30 March 1996.

22 Lebed, who was then Yeltsin's National Security Advisor, said during his visit to Brussels that 'whatever NATO decides, Russia is not going to go into hysterics'. In discussing NATO–Russia negotiations, Lebed stated: 'We propose that we should tackle all the problems oolly, on the basis of reason rather than emotion.' Leaders including Moscow Mayor Yuri Luzhkov, Liberal Democratic Party head Vladimir Zhirinovsky, and Communist Party chairman Gennady Zyuganov criticised Lebed for talking tough in Russia but pandering to NATO in Belgium. Indeed, on his first day back in Russia, Lebed seemed to validate their claim, asking attendees at a conference, 'Will NATO's expansion . . . boost Russia's security? Nobody can guarantee that it won't occur to someone . . . to do to us what was recently done to Iraq.' Lebed was referring to US missile attacks on Iraqi targets. Less than a week after his return from Brussels, Yeltsin fired Lebed. For the above quotes, see N. Buckley, 'Lebed Seeks Pact with NATO', *The Financial Times*, 8 October 1996), p. 2; 'Lebed's NATO Broadside', *The Independent* 11 October 1996), p. 15.

23 Brzezinski and Larrabee, *U.S. Policy*, p. 37.

24 R. N. Lebow, *Between War and Peace: The Nature of International Crisis*, (Baltimore, Johns Hopkins University Press, 1981).

25 See G. W. Breslauer, 'Yeltsin's Political Leadership: Why Invade Chechnya?' in G. W. Breslauer *et al.*, *Russia: Political and Economic Development* (Claremont, The Keck Center for International and Strategic Studies, 1996); E. A. Payin and A. A. Popov, 'Chechnya', in J. R. Azrael and E. A. Payin (eds), *U.S. and Russian Policymaking with Respect to the Use of Force* (Santa Monica, The Rand Corporation, 1996), pp. 25–26; V. Tishkov, *Ethnicity, Nationalism and Conflict In and After the Soviet Union*, (London, Sage Publications, 1997), p. 218.

26 As Danilov cogently puts the point, 'The broad consensus in favor of EU expansion matches the unanimity of Russia's political establishment in rejecting NATO enlargement', Danilov, 'A Piece of the Partnership', p. 61.

27 N. Sokov 'Russia's Relations with NATO: Lessons from the History of the Entente Cordiale', *Policy Memo Series*, 29 (Cambridge, Program on New Approaches to Russian Security, David Center for Russian Studies, Harvard University, 1998), p. 2.

28 For innovative proposals on how to restructure NATO to include Russia in its decision making, see H. Gardner, *Dangerous Crossroads: Europe, Russia, and the Future of NATO*, (Westport, Praeger, 1997); H. Gardner, 'NATO Enlargement: Toward a Separate Euro-Atlantic Command', Committee on Eastern Europe and Russia in NATO, internet edition, 30 January 1999; I. Straus, 'NATO's problem of decision-making – and General Marshall's Solution', internet edition, April 1999.

29 Brzezinski and Larrabee, *U.S. Policy*, p. 38.

30 See, for a sampling, A. Yanov, *Weimar Russia and What We Can Do About It*, (New York, Slovo-Word Publishing House, 1995); S. E. Hanson and J. S. Kopstein, 'The Weimar/Russia Comparison', *Post-Soviet Affairs*, 13:3 (1997); critique by S. D. Shenfield in *Post-Soviet Affairs*, 13:4 (1997) and rejoinder by Kopstei and Hanson in the same issue.

31 This was one of the findings of Shlapentokh's surveys (Shlapentokh, 'How Russians Will See').

32 See the issue of the journal *Demokratizatsiya*, 6:3 (1998), which is devoted entirely to this theme and its implications.

33 See V. Shlapentokh, 'Early Feudalism: The Best Parallel for Contemporary Russia', *Europe–Asia Studies*, 48:3 (1996).

34 My research foci have lain elsewhere since 1999. I am grateful to Neil MacFarlane (Oxford University) for adding the post-1999 reflections on Russian foreign and domestic policies.

35 For a succinct account, see H. Adomeit, *et al.*, *Russia's Futures* (Ebenhausen, Stiftung Wissenschaft und Politik, 2000), pp. 42–44.

NIDA M. GELAZIS

4

The effects of EU conditionality on citizenship policies and the protection of national minorities in the Baltic states

The protection of human rights and respect for national minorities appears at the top of the list of the European Union's accession criteria. While this reflects the EU's long-standing commitment to promoting human rights outside its borders, it is no easy task to legally determine the standard of human rights the EU will require applicant countries to meet prior to accession. EU accession demands that applicant countries exhibit the values shared by the member states. Yet, the promotion and protection of human rights does not figure among the objectives listed in Article 2 of the Treaty on European Union (TEU).[1] Although the European Court of Justice (ECJ) has been the leading institution for determining what EU rights are, it has restricted its decisions to cases in which EU laws raise human rights issues and has avoided imposing a European human rights standard on member states' actions.[2]

Despite this lack of a clear human rights agenda, however, the EU has more than any other international organisation made a clear impact on raising the standard of human rights in the Baltic states. This influence has been particularly apparent in the Baltic states' policies towards the protection of national minorities and citizenship policies. Although organisations such as the Organisation for Security and Cooperation in Europe (OSCE) and the Council of Europe have criticised the Baltic states' policies towards their Russian-speaking resident populations, they have had little effect. The first section of this chapter will address how the legal process by which the Baltic states regained their independence restricted the application of certain international human rights norms in these countries. It will be seen that due to their particular context, the Baltic states were able to bypass certain conventions of international law pertaining to citizenship.

The second part of this chapter will address the EU accession process and, in particular, the disparity between the lack of an EU human rights agenda and the relatively high human rights conditions placed on the applicant countries. Furthermore, certain EU accession requirements reflect a higher standard of human rights protection than currently practised by certain member states. It will be shown that despite this disparity, the Baltic states have made clear attempts to meet these criteria in a relatively short period of time. In conclusion, I will posit that by raising human rights accession criteria, the EU is attempting to build the foundation for increased political unity and the possibility of adopting an EU charter for human rights, which will raise the standard of human rights throughout Europe.

Baltic independence: state continuity versus secession

In their attempt to break free of the USSR, the Baltic states had open to them two distinct 'paths' to independence. On the one hand, they could have attempted to secede from the USSR based on Soviet law and formal negotiations with Moscow. On the other hand, they could insist on the internationally recognised illegality of the 1940 Soviet takeover of the Baltics and as such assert a right to immediate independence as occupied territories. In the event, the three republics' strategies witnessed a process of evolution from the first path to the second during the course of 1988 to 1990. Estonia was the first to broach the secessionist route in November 1988, when its parliament passed a declaration of republican sovereignty and thereby made it known that it was prepared to secede if its demands for greater autonomy were not met. When these attempts at dialogue with the Soviet system went unheeded,[3] emphasis in all three republics shifted to the illegality argument. Meanwhile, Mikhail Gorbachev's glasnost program and the subsequent deletion of Article 6 in many of the Soviet republics' constitutions (which granted the Communist Party monopoly power) opened the door to pluralist elections. As a result, party-like pro-independence organisations were created – the Sajudis movement in Lithuania, the Estonian Popular Front, and the People's Front in Latvia – which ran in opposition to the Communist Party in the February and March 1990 elections to the republic-level Supreme Soviets. The electoral results gave substantial majorities to each of the three opposition parties, and so the newly elected leaders interpreted the results as quasi-referendums for independence, and took steps accordingly.[4]

Immediately following these elections, the Lithuanian Supreme Soviet adopted a Declaration of Independence from the USSR on 11 March 1990. In order to formally bridge the 50-year gap between them and the internationally recognised state that had existed during the interwar period, Sajudis leaders immediately reinstated the 1938 constitution (the last of three constitutions adopted during the 22-year inter-war independence period).[5] There were two reasons for this largely symbolic act. First, after its declaration of independence, no influential Western democracy acknowledged the Republic of Lithuania. Therefore, Lithuanian leaders continued to work as they had, making sure that no legal loophole remained which Moscow might find to draw Lithuania back into its net. Secondly, because the Lithuanian Communist Party was cooperating with Sajudis in the goal for independence, it had not lost its public credibility or democratic viability. In this context, Sajudis leaders feared that if the LCP were somehow to regain power, they might insist on retaining the Soviet constitution as the basis for an independent 'Lithuanian Soviet Republic'. Thus, by reinstating the interwar constitution, Sajudis wanted to assure the West that it was determined to abandon communism and create a liberal democracy in Lithuania. Moreover, less than one hour after the reinstallation of the 1938 constitution, the Lithuanian Supreme Soviet adopted a Provisional Basic Law, which served as an interim constitution for nearly two years. In an effort to avoid calling new elections and to maintain the stability of the existing government, the Basic Law resembled the Lithuanian Soviet constitution in its provisions concerning institutions and power structures.

This move was quickly copied by the newly elected Estonian parliament, which on 30 March 1990 declared a 'Transition Period for Independence' as well as the reinstatement of the main provisos of the country's last, 1938, constitution. At the same time, the Estonians adopted a second law laying out interim governing procedures until 'fully legal authority' could be restored.[6] This was largely the same formula followed by the Latvian Supreme Soviet, which adopted a 'Declaration on the Renewal of Independence' on 4 May 1990 and reinstated its 1922 constitution.[7] In all three Baltic cases, the parliaments asserted the illegal nature of the 23 August 1939 secret deal between Germany and the USSR, which led to the loss of sovereignty of the three Baltic states. Moreover, this stance was echoed by the United States and other western democracies, who for many years had openly acknowledged that the Baltic states had in fact been illegally annexed by the USSR. It was on this basis that all three countries therefore claimed their right to re-establish their sovereignty. At the same time, however, it is interesting to note that Latvia's declaration guaranteed the protection of social, economic, cultural and political rights of 'citizens of the Republic of Latvia and those of other nations permanently residing in Latvia', including 'those citizens of the USSR who express the desire to continue living in the territory of Latvia'.[8] Yet, subsequent policies regarding citizenship rights will be seen later in this chapter to reflect a clear turnaround of this policy.

In this vein the three republics continued their fight until the August 1991 putsch in Moscow offered a window of opportunity. Taking advantage of the chaos, all three republics reasserted their declarations of independence on 20–21 August 1991. With the collapse of the USSR, western democracies began to formally recognise the Baltic states' independence, and the three states began the next phase of institution building and democratic consolidation.

Soviet-era migration

Despite the assertions of legal continuity by the Baltic states, fifty years of Soviet rule had made a lasting impact on every aspect of these societies which were impossible to ignore. The problems posed by Soviet-era migration in particular brought up ethical problems. Soviet ideology strongly supported the creation of multiethnic societies and frowned upon nationalistic sentiments. State policies were developed and implemented largely according to these aspirations.[9] The Russian language was the basic administrative language of the USSR, and while families in the non-Russian republics had a choice between sending their children to Russian or native-language schools, graduation from a Russian school generally gave individuals a privileged position in terms of securing good jobs or a university education. Moreover, the Russian language was a requisite course in all native-language schools.

More stringent measures were taken as well to manufacture multiethnic cities through forced migration within the USSR. The policies under Stalin were the most brutal, in the sense that force was used to strip the 'bourgeoisie' of their property and to send them far from their native republics. The fortunate were able to emigrate to the West, but thousands of people were murdered or forced to migrate within Soviet territory. Baltic residents were particularly targeted as anti-Soviet, with the result that tens of thousands of ethnic Estonians, Latvians and Lithuanians emigrated from their native countries during 1943–44. At the same time, incentives were given to ethnic Russians, Ukrainians, Belorussians and other groups to migrate to the Baltic states, as Soviet-era industrialisation of the Baltic states demanded a large workforce to support these initiatives. The result was that the number of ethnic Estonians, Latvians, and Lithuanians dropped tremendously between 1934 and 1959 in their respective countries: 100,000 ethnic Estonians, 169,000 ethnic Latvians and 267,000 Lithuanians vanished from census data in 25 years.[10]

Citizenship policies in the Baltic states[11]

Lithuania

Even before its declaration of independence from the USSR on 11 March 1990, Lithuania adopted its first citizenship law on 3 November 1989. This law enabled all permanent residents of the territory to gain Lithuanian citizenship, regardless of ethnicity, language, religion or employment status.[12] By the 3 November 1991 deadline for registration, 90 per cent of all residents opted to become Lithuanian citizens.[13] A second law on citizenship was passed on 5 December 1991, which entitled all citizens and permanent residents of Lithuania before 15 June 1940 and their descendants to become citizens of the newly independent state. The 1991 law also laid down the criteria for naturalisation of new citizens. One may acquire citizenship by birth or by naturalisation. The rights of children are protected to the extent that children of Lithuanian citizens (Arts 9–8), children of non-citizens permanently residing in Lithuania (Art. 10), and children born or found on the territory of Lithuania whose parents are unknown (Art. 11) are entitled to gain automatic citizenship of Lithuania.

Naturalisation of adults must follow after certain conditions are met (Art. 12). An applicant must pass a written and oral examination in the Lithuanian language and the basic provisions of the constitution, have lived in Lithuania for at least ten years, and have a permanent place of employment or a constant legal source of support. Although there is no mention in the law itself prohibiting members of the former Soviet army from gaining citizenship, the Constitutional Court has ruled that without special consent of the government, they do not qualify as permanent residents and therefore are not entitled to citizenship.[14]

It will become clear after the citizenship legislation of Latvia and Estonia have been reviewed that the Lithuanian citizenship policy is relatively liberal in comparison with the other two Baltic states. Indeed, whereas 'the Baltic states' are often invoked as having human rights and ethical shortcomings in terms of their citizenship policies, Lithuania cannot be included in such statements. Yet, the justification for the inclusion of Lithuania in this study is two-fold. First, Lithuanian leaders were more interested in building a new democratic state than relying too much on Lithuania's (problematic) interwar democratic legacy.[15] Second, in exploring the reasons behind this seemingly generous policy towards non-ethnic Lithuanians it is important to state that the 'russification' of Lithuania was executed to a far less degree than in either Estonia or Latvia. The total proportion of ethnic Lithuanians remained relatively unchanged since the interwar period, and remains at around 80 per cent. In contrast, the difference in the percentage of ethnic Latvians and Estonians in their respective countries between the 1930s and the 1990s is more profound: in 1935 the percentage of ethnic Latvians was 75.5 while in 1995 that percentage had dropped to 55.1; in 1934 Estonia, the ethnic majority made up 88 per cent of the population, while in 1989, the percentage was 61.5.[16] Therefore, the fact Lithuanians felt that they could accommodate a sizable proportion of non-Lithuanians (around 20 per cent) without sacrificing their democratic ambitions, sovereignty, or native language and culture was decisive in their decision to adopt a relatively liberal policy on citizenship.

Latvia

While Lithuania and Estonia (see below) chose to rebuild their new democracies from scratch by adopting completely new constitutions, Latvia valued the concept of state continuity to an extreme by keeping the 1922 constitution in force. To compensate for this document's short length and its lack of important elements (for example, it contained no mention of human rights), the constitution was buttressed by a series of constitutional laws, including the 4 May 1990 Declaration on the Accession to Human Rights Instruments and the Law on the Rights and Obligations of a Citizen and Person of 10 December 1991. Nevertheless, these measures were inadequate because of the absence of a law defining the status of constitutional laws vis-à-vis ordinary legislation. This meant that courts had no indicators for deciding on cases in which the rights law contradicted other laws issued by the Saeima (or parliament). Eventually, the Saeima adopted several amendments to the 1922 Constitution, which finally paved the way for judicial remedies for human rights infractions.[17] On 12 June 1996, the Saeima adopted a constitutional amendment establishing a constitutional court. The Saeima also eventually adopted an entirely new section 8 of the constitution in October 1998, which constitutionalised fundamental rights.

In the spirit of the principle of state continuity, in 1991 Latvian leaders reinstated the 1919 Citizenship Law (as amended in 1927), which granted individuals who possessed Latvian citizenship prior to 1940 automatic citizenship in the restored Latvian state. The 'Resolution on the Renewal of the Republic of Latvia, Citizens' Rights and Fundamental Principles of Naturalisation' stated that the restored state considered the 1940 USSR law on citizenship null and void, thus rendering thousands of Soviet-era immigrants to Latvia and their descendants stateless.[18] This measure was justified by the argument that since the Latvian state never legally ceased to exist, only those who were truly members of the inter-war state and their descendants had the right to participate politically in state re-creation. These 'original' citizens were thus the only residents of post-1991 Latvia entitled to participate in the first elections of the restored state. As a result of this policy, only 64 per cent of the resident population was actually eligible to participate in the 1993 elections.[19]

Finally, on 22 July 1994 a new law on citizenship was adopted by the Saeima. This law reiterated the fact that pre-1940 citizens and their descendants were entitled to citizenship and laid down the ground rules for naturalisation, but it also granted citizenship to individuals who were permanent residents of pre-1919 Latvia (the date of Latvian inter-war state creation). Unlike Lithuania, Latvia made special provisions to encourage Latvian émigrés to repatriate. The 'Transitional Provisions' of the 1994 law allow interwar citizens of the Republic of Latvia to gain citizenship without renouncing their current citizenship. Citizenship was also granted upon registration to Soviet-era immigrants of Estonian and Lithuanian ethnicity, to non-ethnic Latvians who finished Latvian language secondary schools, and to spouses (for at least ten years) of Latvian citizens (Art. 13).

Article 10 of the 1994 law indicates those who may not acquire citizenship of Latvia, even through naturalisation. This group includes:

- those who have 'turned against the Republic of Latvia's independence, its democratic parliamentary state system or the existing state authority in Latvia, if such has been established by a court decree';
- those who since 4 May 1990 have stirred ethnic hatred or racial discord through the propagation of fascist, chauvinist, national-socialist, communist, or other totalitarian ideas;
- officials of foreign states, those who have served in the armed forces or police of a foreign state (including the USSR) who were not permanent residents of Latvia prior to their conscription;
- those who have been employees, informants, or agents of the KGB or any other foreign security service;

- those who have been convicted of a crime and imprisoned for more than one year;
- and those who participated in attempts to stop the independence movement after 13 January 1991 through participation in the Latvian Communist Party, the Working Peoples' International Front of the Latvian SSR, the United Council of Labour Collectives, the Organisation of War and Labour Veterans, or the All-Latvia Salvation Committee and its regional committees.

All other residents wishing to gain Latvian citizenship are required to go through naturalisation procedures. These procedures require establishing permanent residence in Latvia for five years starting from 4 May 1990, having command of the Latvian language, history and the national anthem, and knowing the basic principles of the constitution and the constitutional law on 'Rights and Obligations of a Citizen and a Person' (Art. 12). Chapter III of the law describes the language exam, which includes testing the applicant on his or her ability to read, speak, and write in Latvian on topics from everyday life. It also states that the disabled and the elderly are exempt from taking this exam. Applicants must also show proof of a legal source of income and renounce their former citizenship (Art. 12).

To prevent what Latvian parliamentarians believed would be a run on the naturalisation office, the 1994 law also instituted a 'windows' system for naturalisation (Art. 14). This law distinguished applicants for citizenship by age and whether or not applicants were born in Latvia and separated them into eight groups accordingly. The first group (those born in Latvia who were 16–20 years of age at the time of their application) were scheduled to begin naturalisation procedures on 1 January 1996. The eighth set of applicants (those born outside of Latvia and over 30 years of age) could not begin the naturalisation procedures until 1 January 2003.

Unsurprisingly, due to the strict new citizenship law, the number of registered Latvian residents who gained citizenship between 1995 and 1997 rose by only 1.4 per cent, leaving at least 28 per cent of registered residents stateless.[20] In the face of international pressure to end the condition of statelessness within its borders, Latvia stood by its citizenship policy and asserted the latter's legality due to state continuity. Instead of amending its citizenship policies, the Latvian parliament adopted a special law on the 'Status of Former USSR Citizens who have Neither Latvian nor Other States' Citizenship' of 12 April 1995. This law applies to only those resident non-citizens who qualify for citizenship through naturalisation, thus excluding former Soviet army personnel and their families. This law affirms that stateless persons who have registered with the government enjoy the same rights as Latvian citizens according to the constitutional law on 'Rights and Obligations of a Person and a Citizen' (Art. 2). Moreover, the law also confirms that resident non-citizens have the right to travel freely; are able to admit their spouses and dependents into Latvia; maintain their native language and culture; and to receive translation services in court proceedings. The law also stipulates that resident non-citizens will not be exiled or expelled from the territory of Latvia except according to law or when a foreign state agrees to receive them.

Estonia

Like Latvia, Estonia strictly followed the principle of continuity in re-establishing its democratic state, though to a lesser extent. After the Moscow putsch and the quick adoption of a 'Resolution on the National Independence of Estonia', the Estonian parliament immediately began working on a new constitution. Moreover, as in Latvia and Lithuania at the time, the struggle for independence was linked to democratic intentions and guarantees that no attempts would be made to restrict citizenship of the independent republic on the basis of ethnic origin.[21] However, because the future citizenship policy would hit Russian-speakers the hardest, a pall was cast on these original pledges. Nevertheless, the Estonian Constitution, adopted by referendum in June 1992, included guarantees for the protection of minorities; it also guaranteed social rights to resident non-citizens. Article 28 of the Estonian Constitution stipulates 'All persons shall have the right to health care. Estonian citizens shall be entitled to state assistance in the case of old age, inability to work, loss of a provider, and need . . . this right shall exist equally for Estonian citizens, and citizens of foreign states and stateless persons who are sojourning in Estonia.' The constitution also stipulated that resident non-citizens would have the right to participate in local elections.[22] These liberal policies implied that the political consensus on the citizenship question was to create a restrictive citizenship policy and foreshadowed a protracted period of transition in which many residents would be left stateless.

In February 1992, the Estonian parliament reinstated the 1938 Law on Citizenship, as amended in 1940,[23] according to which citizenship was extended only to those residents who had Estonian citizenship prior to 16 June 1940 and their descendants.[24] An opportunity to gain citizenship automatically was also given to Soviet-era immigrants who could prove that they had supported the main political movement in favour of legal continuity, the Congress of Estonia, during 1989–91. This citizenship law was still in place for the 1992 national elections, therefore severely restricting the number of eligible voters.[25] Like Latvia, Estonia adopted a 'Aliens Act' on 8 July 1993, which was very similar to the Latvian law on resident non-citizens in terms of granting constitutional rights protection to aliens. However, unlike the Latvian law, which guaranteed that resident non-citizens would not be deported, the Estonian law included a negative incentive for non-citizens to apply for new residency permits within an established time limit or face possible expulsion from the territory of Estonia (Art. 21.7–8).

Estonia thus adopted an initial series of legislative acts on citizenship and residency. However, on 19 January 1995, the parliament adopted under pressure from nationalist deputies a new law on citizenship, which tightened some of the original naturalisation requirements. The new 'Citizenship Act' sets out nearly identical provisions for naturalisation as the Latvian citizenship law; thus, for the purposes of this study it is sufficient to have described only the Latvian law in detail. One notable difference is that there are no special provisions regarding the repatriation of Estonian émigrés, as was the case in Latvia, and no special privileges were given to Latvian or Lithuanian residents. Moreover, the Estonian law does not follow the 'windows' system, therefore naturalisation procedures were open to all permanent residents from the date the law came into force (1 April 1995). Nevertheless, naturalisation proceeded at a snail's pace: by 1997 only 1,060 applicants had managed to fulfil all the requirements to gain citizenship and in later years these figures continued to fall.[26]

International legal guidelines for citizenship

The Hague Convention on Certain Questions Relating to the Conflict of Nationality Laws of 12 April 1930 states that it is 'for each State to determine under its own law who are its nationals' (Art. 1).[27] Yet, international law and state practice do provide limits to this right. The Council of Europe has outlined several general principles which states should take into consideration when faced with the problem of citizenship. The principles relevant to the Baltic cases include prohibition on discrimination on the basis of ethnicity or language, the creation of effective links between potential citizens and the state, the avoidance of the creation of statelessness, and the right of option for residents of successor states to choose their country of citizenship. Although it should be understood that adherence to one of these principles should never be a defence against ignoring one or all of the other principles delimiting a state's nationality policy, it is useful to show the ways in which one principle may indeed limit another and that the standard of application of each principle is determined by the particular context and values of each state. Finally, the Baltic states have succeeded in defending their citizenship policies by clearly defining their status as re-established states as opposed to successor states.

Anti-discrimination principle

The prohibition of discrimination on the basis of ethnic origin, colour, religion, language, or political opinions in determining citizenship is a well-recognised limitation on a state's right to determine conditions for acquisition of citizenship. Article 1(3) of the International Convention on the Elimination of All Forms of Racial Discrimination stipulates that 'nothing in the Convention may be interpreted as affecting in any way the legal provisions of States Parties concerning nationality, citizenship or naturalisation, provided that such provisions do not discriminate against any particular nationality'. Moreover, Art. 9 of the UN Convention on the Reduction of Statelessness prohibits states from depriving 'any person or group of persons of their nationality on racial, ethnic, religious or political grounds'. Thus, the citizenship legislation of all three Baltic states becomes suspect due to their stiff language requirements and firm stances on not granting citizenship to former Soviet military personnel.

One argument offered in defence of Latvia's and Estonia's policies towards their resident Russian populations is that they serve to 'correct' fifty years of discrimination against ethnic Estonians and Latvians by Russia. Ziemele asserts that 'the measures which were undertaken by the independent governments of the Baltic states were measures of special protection in the sense of Article 26 of the ICCPR aimed at re-establishing *de facto* equality for discriminated groups in the respective societies which also involved the attribution of the status of state language to local languages.'[28]

The level of fluency required by Latvian and Estonian citizenship procedures has been criticised as unreasonable, but the international community could do little to persuade the countries to ease their demands. Indeed, most states require some working knowledge of the official language of the state prior to granting citizenship. Ultimately, the OSCE High Commissioner on National Minorities, Max van der Stoel, recommended exempting the elderly and disabled from taking language examinations as well as simplifying the exam for all applicants. In response, the exemptions were included in citizenship procedures, but both Latvia and Estonia deemed simplification of the language exams unnecessary.[29] Moreover, attempts have been made to grant non-citizens equality under the law in terms of granting resident aliens protection under the constitution, social assistance and limited voting rights.

Effective link principle

In response to the allegations that the citizenship laws of Latvia and Estonia discriminate on the basis of ethnicity and language, the effective link principle was invoked. This principle is derived from the recognition that there must be some kind of link between the state and an individual requesting citizenship. These links are very often birth, domicile and residence in the country in question.[30] Yet other criteria can be included as well, particularly in terms of the state's responsibility for defending its citizens against the actions of other states.[31] For these reasons, it is customary that successor states may choose not to grant automatic citizenship to individuals who had served in political or military capacities of the previous state.[32] This principle banished any attempts to criticise Baltic citizenship legislation on the grounds that former Soviet army, state or KGB personnel were prohibited from gaining citizenship.[33] Secondly, in the specific case of Latvia and Estonia and their additional requirement that applicants must have a knowledge of the native language, history, and constitution, the assumption was that Russians feel a stronger allegiance to Russia even if they have chosen to live in the Baltic states. Russia has certainly shown concern over the status of Russian minorities living in the Baltic states and its constitutionalised commitment to promote its interests in the 'near abroad' far surpasses any other state's claims on foreign territories. Given the history of Russian aggression in the Baltic states, Estonia and Latvia may be justified in demanding that ethnic Russians not only break their political ties to Russia, but also demonstrate a commitment to their adoptive countries.

Avoidance of statelessness principle

The principle of avoiding conditions of statelessness has become hard law since the adoption of the UN Convention on the Reduction of Statelessness. In reference to citizenship laws, Article 8 of the Convention stipulates that State Parties 'shall not deprive a person of his nationality if such deprivation would render him stateless.' The fact that 13 per cent of residents in Estonia and 28 per cent in Latvia remain stateless flies in the face of this relatively straightforward principle. Moreover, in line with the Convention on the Rights of the Child and Article 24 of the International Covenant on Civil and Political Rights, state practice has come to require that states grant citizenship to children born in their territories who would otherwise be rendered stateless.[34] On this last score, Estonia and Latvia were slow to act, adopting legislation to grant such special citizenship to stateless children only in 1998.

Right of option principle

The right of option gives residents of succession states the right to choose between taking citizenship in one of the two (or more) successor states or between the successor state and the predecessor state.[35] In cases where the option of taking the citizenship of the predecessor state is chosen, it is usually coupled with the obligation to leave the successor state.[36] It might be argued by Estonia and Latvia that the current stateless population permanently residing in the countries actually chose statelessness because they were given the option of gaining automatic citizenship by the Russian Federation. Article 13 (2) of the Russian Law on Federation Citizenship, adopted 28 November 1991, states that 'Persons born on 30 December 1922, and thereafter, who lost the citizenship of the former USSR shall be deemed in Russian Federation citizenship by birth, where they were born on the territory of the Russian Federation, or where either parent at the moment of their birth was a citizen of the USSR and was in permanent residence on the territory of the Russian Federation.' And, though restrictive, the citizenship laws of Estonia and Latvia do offer an option for residents to become citizens through naturalisation. Moreover, it is state practice that the right of option goes hand in hand with the principle of effective links, whereby nationality is granted by the country, which shares the individual's ethnic, linguistic, or religious identity.[37] In the Baltic case, this would place the primary responsibility for extending citizenship to the Russian resident populations on the Russian Federation. Yet, the resident non-citizen populations have largely chosen to remain in the Baltic states despite their stateless status.

Practice of granting nationality automatically in cases of state secession

The practice of granting citizenship to a resident population, or the principle that 'population goes with territory' is said to be an international custom, though it 'is not yet a binding rule of codified international law prescribing the automatic acquisition of the nationality of the successor state'.[38] In cases where there is a successor state and a predecessor state, the rule has been that the successor state confers its citizenship to former nationals of the predecessor state habitually residing in the successor state, in almost all cases this citizenship is conferred automatically,[39] though the right of option and effective links principles should also be considered. In instances where the predecessor state ceases to exist, as is the case of the USSR, successor states are even more strongly compelled by international practice to offer automatic citizenship to residents of their territories. Article 10 of the 1961 Convention on the Reduction of Statelessness gives effect to this obligation, providing that

> Every treaty between Contracting States providing for the transfer of territory shall include provisions to secure that no person shall become stateless as a result of the transfer . . . In the absence of such provisions a Contracting State to which territory is transferred or which otherwise acquires territory shall confer its nationality on such persons as would otherwise become stateless as a result of the transfer or acquisition.

The automatic conferment of citizenship to permanent residents of the territory of a successor state was followed only by Lithuania. Why did Estonia and Latvia diverge from this practice and how did they get away with it? To answer this question it is necessary to return to the Baltic 'path of independence' and examine more closely the principle of state continuity embraced by the Baltic states. If Estonia's original path of seceding from the USSR had been successful, the Baltic states would have had to sign a treaty with the USSR and thus be subject to the Convention on the Reduction of Statelessness, with all its implications for allocating citizenship. But, by asserting their status as continuous states, the Baltic states subverted the need to found their independence on a secession pact with the USSR. Following their re-assertion of independent statehood, interwar national laws and international treaties were again recognised.[40] And as a consequence, the two states reinstated their interwar citizenship laws, with all the ramifications these had on Soviet-era migrants. Thus, 'these states represent a special case since their claim to be identical with the three Baltic states annexed by the Soviet Union in 1940 was accepted by the international community'.[41]

As a final point regarding international guidelines on citizenship, it is worth pointing out that in 1997 the Council of Europe drew up a European Convention on Nationality in order to give hard-law backing to some of the general principles cited above. Few states have since signed the Convention, however, and none of the three Baltic states has acceded to it. Nevertheless, the Convention provides important new limitations to states' nationality policies. Interestingly, Estonian and Latvian policies towards stateless residents have created an important benchmark for citizenship policy, which was incorporated into the Convention. For example, Article 20 of the Convention requires that in cases of state succession, nationals of the predecessor state habitually resident in the territory over which sovereignty is transferred to a successor state and who have not acquired the latter's nationality shall have the right to remain in that state and those persons shall enjoy equality of treatment with nationals of the successor state in relation to social and economic rights. Moreover, resident non-citizens may not be excluded from employment in the public sphere.

Human rights conditionality in EU enlargement

While conditionality is not a new international tool for influencing state behaviour, this tool has strong potential for success in the Baltic states (relative to other developing countries) for at least two reasons. First, the Baltic states, like other post-communist countries, are in dire need of international finances to support reform, both political and economic. Second, the Baltic states have consistently asserted their 'Western credentials' and the desire to return to Europe. This desire is prompted by an even greater desire to 'leave' the East, that is, Russia's sphere of influence. Thus, even if there are significant cultural differences between the Baltic states and Western Europe, there is a strong incentive for these differences to be bridged in an effort to increase security.

Despite the Baltic states' relative willingness to go along with conditionality, the effectiveness of this tool is also dependent on donor states' and international institutions' treatment of conditionality. Peter Burnell has developed three questions for donors to ask themselves before offering aid for political changes:

> First, are they [the donors] convinced the target groups in the aid-receiving world know and understand what the donors want, and why they want it? Second, do those groups display full confidence in the donors' qualifications to suggest such advice, and if not, would they be justified in developing such a confidence? Third, are there features of the operation of political conditionality which, in the reasonable estimation of friends, could actually impede the promotion of good government and democracy, and make these pursuits more vulnerable to the indifference and hostility of their detractors and enemies?[42]

Burnell asserts that the strength and effectiveness of the conditionality tool depends on how it is used. In terms of the Baltic states, the relative strengths of international institutions to credibly employ the conditionality tool become quite clear. First, it would seem that those institutions in which the Baltic states are already members have less to offer in terms of conditionality. Indeed, the conditions placed on these countries by the United Nations, the Council of Europe and the OSCE have largely been met upon entry into the fold. Monitoring and helping to enforce treaty obligations would be their main vehicle for promoting change, although since the states under scrutiny are also equal voting partners, the rights-violating state has a greater advantage in arguing its case than affected groups within the state.[43] Nevertheless, behind-the-scenes deals seem to be struck between institutions and violator-states through funding by third parties (either other member states or other international organisations), which seem to effectively place 'helpful pressure' on problem countries.[44]

At this point, the EU holds the most leverage in terms of placing human rights conditionality on the Baltic states, in view of their applications to join. In principle, the rules are simple: apply the *acquis communautaire* and corollary association agreements, and EU admission will be granted; failure to comply will delay admission and suspend aid. Previous EU enlargements also required acceding countries to make political and economic adjustments. But the conditions placed on the post-communist countries are higher than ever for two reasons. The rapid expansion of the EU's competence since the end of the Cold War and the social and economic devastation due to the Soviet legacy in Eastern Europe have both contributed to widening the gap between Eastern and Western Europe.

The three basic requirements for membership determined at the 1993 European Council meeting in Copenhagen are:

- the applicant state must have achieved stability of institutions guaranteeing democracy, the rule of law, human rights and respect for and protection of minorities;
- the applicant state must have a functioning market economy with the capacity to cope with competitive pressures and market forces within the Community;
- the applicant state must be able to take on the obligations of membership, including adherence to the aims of economic and political union.[45]

These seemingly straightforward criteria translate to over 80,000 pages of legislation that will need to be adopted prior to accession.[46] The vast body of legislation derived from the *acquis communautaire* are presented as 'objective criteria' to be used to evaluate the ten post-communist applicant countries. The EU created these objective criteria in order to increase the transparency of the enlargement process and thus respond to allegations that it has shown favouritism to certain countries.[47] Nevertheless, each of these countries faced different challenges and were at different stages of their political and economic transitions. Thus, the complexity of the task potentially weakened the conditionality tool since the number of criteria was great, monitoring their implementation by the Commission was difficult, and the return on the investment (accession to the EU) seemed distant.

To address this weakness, the EU's Agenda 2000 initiated a new strategy, which reinforced the conditionality tool. First, those countries that had already progressed further in terms of political and economic development were grouped as 'front-runners' in the enlargement process. The Czech Republic, Estonia, Hungary, Poland, and Slovenia were thus rewarded for their strides towards democratisation and market reform. This was a sizable carrot for those included in the first wave and a notable stick for those that were left out; it also created incentives for the slackers to speed up reforms. Next, through so-called Accession Partnerships, the EU created a separate strategy for each country, complete with short- and medium-term goals. Each step taken towards reaching these goals was accompanied by promises of financial assistance through the newly created PHARE programme and other 'catch-up' facilities, directly targeting specific reform measures, such as fighting corruption, rebuilding infrastructure, and promoting foreign investment. This was a significant step in assigning different weights to the huge body of criteria and adapting an enlargement strategy compatible with each country's unique strengths and weaknesses.

So that there would be no question of its policy, the Council adopted Article 4 of Regulation 622/98 on 16 March 1998 which gave the Commission the power to suspend financial assistance if it deemed that the country in question was not progressing quickly enough, or was actually back-pedalling in its progress towards adopting the *acquis*.[48] Regulation 622/98 thus legally and institutionally enshrined the conditionality tool in the enlargement process.

Progress in keeping up with the short- and medium-term goals of the Accession Partnerships was documented in the Regular Reports by the Commission. Unlike the Agenda 2000 Opinions and the Accession Partnerships, the Reports were extremely detail-oriented summaries of the progress in meeting the accession criteria in each country, reflecting the problems met by reformers in each of the countries, as well as their achievements. As will be discussed below, the Reports allowed the EU to make adjustments in its policies to each country depending on the rate of its progress in specific areas. Although the timespan between the adoption of the Agenda 2000 Opinions and the Regular Reports was scarcely more than one year, progress in the acceding countries became clearer, as was the EU's shift in focus on certain rights. Thus, it seemed probable that the EU's standards and expectations would increase the better applicant countries performed.

Human rights in the European Union

Including requirements for human rights protection in the Association Agreements for EU accession was a practical tool for smooth integration of the post-communist democracies into the Union. Western Europe's commitment to both free market principles and open, democratic societies necessitated that newcomers share and promote not only economic ideals, but also democratic ones, of which human rights protection was an integral part.

Despite their obvious significance, however, human rights remain a contentious issue within the EU, since each member state remains committed to its own unique constitutional and ideological tradition. The inclusion of human rights in the Treaty of the European Union (TEU) after the Maastricht and Amsterdam Intergovernmental Conferences represents a small triumph for the member states in overcoming their significant political differences in this field. The absence of rights in prior treaties was not a result of their indifference to human rights, but was due to their inability to decide which rights should be incorporated as guiding principles of the Union and at what standard and how they should be applied.[49] In fact, Article 13 of the TEU actually reflects the dissonance on human rights among the member states. It states, 'Without prejudice to the other provisions of this Treaty and within the limits of the powers conferred by it upon the Community, the Council, acting unanimously on a proposal from the Commission and after consulting the European Parliament *may* take *appropriate* action to combat discrimination based on sex, racial or ethnic origin, religion or belief, disability, age or sexual orientation' (emphasis added). The EU's irresolute stance is symptomatic of its reticence to accept the responsibility of promoting human rights within its own borders.

The inability of the EU to create a human rights agenda is another consequence of this dissonance. Article 6 of the TEU states that the EU is 'founded on the principles of liberty, democracy, respect for human rights and fundamental freedoms, and the rule of law, principles which are common to the member states'. The final part of that Article states that the 'Union shall provide itself with the means necessary to attain its objectives and carry through its policies'. Nevertheless, it has not yet introduced new mechanisms for carrying out its commitment to promoting rights.[50]

The European Court of Justice has been an important forum for the EU human rights debate. Human rights conflicts have touched on other important EU principles, such as supremacy, direct effect, and subsidiarity. Regularly, cases come before the Court that raise important human rights issues, but the ECJ has not been completely consistent in its approach to these questions. Instead, its decisions reflect a 'push and pull' process in which the Court is 'at times [willing] to embrace the invitations of those actors [to review member state action under Community fundamental rights standards] and at other times [it] explicitly or implicitly has rejected them'.[51] The oscillation of the Court stems from the ongoing power balance between the EU's institutions, on the one hand, and between the EU and its member states, on the other. Thus the Court has joined that game as well, carefully balancing between protecting and increasing its sphere of competence, while equally manoeuvring around delicate relationships with the national courts of the member states. In this regard, Alston and Weiler make an important observation concerning the Court's interpretation of its competence on rights:

> In its jurisprudence, the Court has articulated three critical constitutional principles which inform this field. The first affirms that '. . . respect for human rights is a condition of the lawfulness of Community acts'. The second affirms that it is the positive duty of the institutions 'to ensure the observance of fundamental rights'. In other words, they are obligated not simply to refrain from violating them, but to ensure that they are observed within the respective constitutional roles played by each institution. Finally, the human rights jurisdiction of the Community extends only . . . in the field of Community law.[52]

The groundwork for as well as the active review of human rights in the EU and its member states have thus been laid down, even though the ECJ has taken a strong human rights stance in only a few cases.[53] For now, the role of enforcing and protecting human rights primarily falls on the shoulders of the member states, which only serves to reinforce the need to include human rights in the pre-accession criteria for EU membership.

Which rights are necessary for EU accession?

Determining what rights are essential for the creation of a common market and at which standard these rights must be protected has been a contentious issue with which the EU's institutions have been grappling. At the same time, while the conditionality tool was seen as quite strong in the EU enlargement process, human rights constitute only a subsection of the formal political criteria for EU accession. To complicate matters, the *acquis* is in the process of expanding, which means that the conditions for accession are in the process of changing as well.[54] Moreover, the basic Copenhagen conditions are largely declarative,[55] they allow flexibility of interpretation, and they do not indicate at what standards these criteria will be judged. The tools used to measure progress and the standards applied in meeting the political and human rights criteria for accession are therefore highly subjective.[56] In addition to any changes in criteria or evaluation standards that might come from the Commission, the European Parliament (EP) has taken decisions independently that may further expand the accession criteria.[57] Although the EP's role in determining accession criteria is limited, it does vote on the accession of new member states, and therefore any decision it takes can be seen as plausible additions to the already numerous accession criteria.[58] Therefore, evaluating which rights have been included in conditionality requirements for aspiring members, what standards are required, how human rights protection is measured, and how the EU will 'punish' those countries that do not comply with those conditions are all somewhat problematic.

Putting these complicating factors aside, however, the TEU does offer clues about the Commission's direction in terms of what rights are important to the EU. First, Article 6.2 of the TEU clearly states that the European Convention for the Protection of Human Rights and Fundamental Freedoms (ECHR) shall be respected by the Union and ratification of the ECHR is part of the *acquis*. The Agenda 2000 cites this article as well, which indicates its importance as a tool for evaluating the protection of human rights in acceding countries.[59] Nevertheless, the ECHR has been deemed by the ECJ as 'insufficiently precise' to clearly address European rights.[60] This has been interpreted to mean that the ECJ considers the ECHR to have set only a minimum standard for rights protection, and that the EU must provide a higher standard of protection to its citizens.[61] The ECJ has often quoted the end of Article 6.2 which stipulates that in addition to the ECHR the EU must respect rights 'as they result from the constitutional traditions common to the member states', which also implies a higher standard than that provided for in the ECHR. Thus, looking at the conventions to which applicant countries are party is a necessary but insufficient indicator of their readiness to accede to the EU.

From the Agenda 2000 Opinions, Accession Partnerships, and Regular Reports, I have determined that the EU has focused on three types of rights. My groupings do not necessarily overlap with traditional classifications of rights, and would probably be clumsy if they were used in another context. Nevertheless, I use them here in order to shed light on the EU's motivations for including certain rights over others in its human rights policy in the candidate countries. The first group includes rights which are necessary to ensure democratic rule and open societies. These democracy guarantees include access to justice, right to life, freedom against arbitrary arrest, right to privacy, freedom of association, freedom of expression, and freedom of assembly. These rights and freedoms form one of the basic processes of democracy – the right to organise politically and participate in the political process without repercussions. If these rights and freedoms are in place and function properly, then there are no impediments for a society to create and protect a shared system of values. For the EU, this category of rights is essential first of all for its symbolic significance: democracy is a European *value* and is indeed one of the unifying factors of the alliance. But the second reason for including them in the pre-accession criteria is because currently the EU can do little to influence human rights standards in the actions of member states.[62] Therefore, securing the framework necessary to help develop a national commitment to human rights is essential for any EU member state. This class of rights seems to stem from Article 177.2 of the TEU, which stipulates that 'Community policy in this area [development cooperation] shall contribute to the general objective of developing and consolidating democracy and the rule of law, and to that of respecting human rights and fundamental freedoms.' It is also consistent with the requirements for accession in previous enlargements.[63]

There is little resistance to raising the standards of this group of rights in the applicant countries. After all, it was the absence of such rights, which drove the anti-communist campaigns of the late 1980s. Nevertheless, protecting these rights is not unproblematic, first of all because of the weakness of civil society in these countries and second, because one of the legacies of the Soviet regime is the knee-jerk reaction of strengthening the state in order to regain control over unruly social elements (e.g. organised crime).

The second group of rights required by the EU involves counter-majoritarian rights. This group includes the protection and non-discrimination of ethnic minorities, non-citizens, asylum seekers, and children, and the freedom of religion. For the most part, the Accession Partnerships' Political Criteria are silent on women's rights and non-discrimination due to race, gender, disability, religion, age, or sexual orientation, which is a clear EU policy.[64] Yet, the Accession Partnerships clearly specify the demand that applicant countries sign and ratify the Framework Convention for the Protection of National Minorities (FCPNM). The FCPNM seems to be important since attitudes towards minorities and foreigners have important consequences in foreign policy and security. The Common Foreign and Security Policy sections of the Opinions concentrate on revealing the applicant countries' good relations with their neighbours, which can be destroyed easily by ill-treatment of that neighbour's diaspora populations.[65] It may also be an indication of how receptive these countries will be to the free movement of workers and capital after accession.[66]

This group of rights is somewhat more difficult to sell in post-communist societies, judging from the rise of nationalism and ethnic discrimination throughout the region. Although all three Baltic constitutions have clear provisions that promote and protect the rights of national minorities, these protections have sometimes been seen as insufficient due to the limited power of national institutions. Moreover, particularly in the Baltic states, where independence was fought for by arguing for national self-determination, and where Lithuanians, Latvians and Estonians were viewed as second-class citizens by their Soviet-era colonisers, turning the other cheek and adopting liberal policies towards the Russian minority seems unlikely. Lastly, there exist a number of Western countries, such as France and Belgium, which have not signed the Framework Convention and which therefore reflects a comparable ideological position in the general debate between valuing individual rights over group rights. To this group of ambiguous nations could be added the Netherlands, Greece and Portugal, who have all signed, but have not ratified the Convention.

The final set of rights could be grouped as quality-of-life rights. I choose this title not because I believe these rights to be less important than others, but because the Commission itself decided to put environmental protection and health care under that title instead of placing them in the human rights section.[67] I have added other rights (from the human rights section of the Opinions) to the quality-of-life rights because these rights have high price tags: the right to social security and minimum wage, education, humane imprisonment, national defence, and refugee camp conditions. Also in this group I have included the right to property and the right to strike and form trade unions because they contribute to raising the quality of life in acceding countries. These rights are primarily socio-economic rights, and form the building blocks for a modern market economy. They reflect the Union's overall objectives as derived from Article 2 of the TEU. Since most involve hefty government expenditures, it is doubtful that these countries would have developed clear policies in these fields so early in their economic transitions without EU intervention.

The effect of EU conditionality in the Baltic states

In the concluding paragraphs of each of its 1997 Opinions, the European Commission seemed to leave the impression that relatively little needed to be done in each country to fulfil Brussels's political criteria for accession. In Latvia and Estonia, only minor adjustments appeared necessary to accommodate the Russian-speaking population. The Opinion on Lithuania, meanwhile, would have had us believe that Lithuania had entirely fulfilled the political criteria.

These conclusions, however, are hardly compatible with the preceding paragraphs which raised many human rights concerns in each of the three categories or rights: democratic guarantees, counter-majoritarian rights, and quality-of-life rights.

Using the classificatory system proposed here, the Commission's Opinion as part of Agenda 2000 identified a total of 14 human rights problems in Lithuania. Five of these were problems within the category of democracy guarantees: inadequate legal recourse in the courts due to lengthy legal proceedings, a shortage of lawyers, and the absence of procedures for making police and other civil servants accountable for their actions; the second stems from the first and deals with the inadequacy of the state's attempts to prosecute alleged Nazi war criminals; third, the existence of the death penalty; fourth, inadequate protection against arbitrary arrest; and fifth, inadequate right to privacy. In the category of counter-majoritarian rights, four problems were identified: inadequate protection against anti-Semitic acts; insufficient protection of children against child pornography, child prostitution, and sexual abuse of children; the questionable abandonment of special rules originally granted to ethnic minority parties for entering parliament; and the inadequate implementation of gender discrimination laws. Finally, in terms of quality-of-life rights, the Lithuanian government was seen as having unnecessarily complicated the procedures ensuring the right to strike; it had not completed the land register necessary to assure the right to property; prison conditions were inhumane; the health care system needed serious reforms; and serious reforms were necessary in the area of environmental protection.

The Agenda 2000 Opinion on Latvia's application isolated 15 human rights breaches. Among these, two infringed upon democracy guarantees: inadequate legal recourse and the continued existence of the death penalty. Counter-majoritarian rights were the most problematic in Latvia. The eight problems identified in this category were: restriction on freedom of religion; inhumane and degrading conditions in asylum seekers' accommodation centres; inadequate protection of children; infringements of the rights of minorities to form collective groups; extremely restrictive rules for citizenship; discrimination against non-citizens; ethnic minority discrimination; and non-implementation of gender anti-discrimination laws. Within the category of quality-of-life rights, the five problems focused on by the Commission were: restriction on property rights of non-citizens; inhumane prison and army conditions; and inadequate health care system and environmental protection.

In the case of Estonia, ten human rights problems were identified in the Agenda 2000 Opinion. Breaches of democracy guarantees were identical to those identified in Latvia. Within the counter-majoritarian rights category, the four identified problems included: a lack of measures to promote the collective rights of ethnic minorities; overly-restrictive citizenship laws; discrimination against non-citizens; and insufficient implementation of gender anti-discrimination laws. Finally, the four problems identified in the quality-of-life category were: restrictions of the right to property; inhumane prison conditions; inadequate health care system; and the need to bolster environmental protection.

While the Agenda 2000 documents were successful in exploring the unique problems of each applicant country and its specific context, the subsequent Accession Partnerships seemed to indicate a return by the Commission to promoting uniform 'objective criteria'. The Commission's concentration on a small set of rights seemed to reflect their greater significance in the EU context relative to other rights problems presented in the Opinions. In the case of the Baltic states, the Accession Partnerships required all three countries to improve border management and ameliorate conditions at refugee reception facilities; improve the operation of the judicial system, implement migration policy and asylum procedures; fight against organised crime including trafficking in human beings; enforce equal opportunities between women and men; improve public health standards; strengthen environmental protection measures; and continue raising the standard of the right to property. In the Latvian and Estonian cases, measures were also mandated to promote the integration of national minorities and facilitate the naturalisation of non-citizen residents. An additional requirement was placed specifically on Estonia to reform its pension programme.

In this respect, the Accession Partnerships indicated that the most important rights problems were in the fields of counter-majoritarian and quality-of-life rights, while no mention was made of problems in democracy guarantees. Nevertheless, the Partnerships revealed an interesting development in EU financial assistance for democracy projects, which seemed to show that there was still work to be done in that field. Whereas previously the EU had channelled a mere 1 per cent of its PHARE budget to the Democracy Programme, the EU pledged subsequently to increase PHARE assistance in institution building (which involves the strengthening of democratic institutions, rule of law, etc.) to 30 per cent of the PHARE budget.[68] By contrast, the Regular Reports by the Commission not only continued to mention problems and developments in all three human rights categories, but the standard of evaluation of certain rights was actually raised. This was best demonstrated in the Lithuanian case: in the Agenda 2000 Opinion, the position of asylum seekers was deemed to be satisfactory, while in the Regular Report, a detailed critique of foreigner registration centre conditions and refugee admission procedures appeared. Another example of this was the Opinions' positive evaluation of the freedom of association in both Lithuania and Estonia on the one hand, and the Commission's comment that the NGO sectors in each country were not growing rapidly enough due to the low level of public information. However, if education of the public was to blame, it could hardly have been logical to conclude that the public was better educated in 1997 than in 1998 about associations and NGOs. Both examples showed that the EU's standards of evaluation had increased.

But the most important revelation of the Regular Reports was the dramatic progress made by the applicant countries in responding to the criticisms of the Agenda 2000 Opinions. Perhaps the most impressive performance was given by

Latvia. First, although it was not an explicit requirement by the EU, the Latvian Parliament adopted a constitutional amendment, which incorporated a bill of rights into the Satversme (Constitution). Previously, the document on the 'Rights and Duties of Citizens' existed as a regular law, with no method to check whether other legislation or state actions comply with it. Next, in spite of its controversial nature, the Parliament managed to adopt a new citizenship law, which was subsequently upheld in a national referendum. As a result, the 'window system' (which differentiated by age those who could apply for citizenship every year) was abandoned and the naturalisation process was opened to all resident non-citizens. Also, modifications to the citizenship law were made to enable children born in Latvia to stateless parents to be granted citizenship, and the procedures for naturalisation for people over the age of 65 were simplified. Moreover, the Latvian government responded to the Opinion's criticism of its discriminatory policies towards non-nationals by eliminating restrictions preventing non-citizens from working as fire-fighters, airline staff, pharmacists, and veterinary pharmacists. Likewise, unemployment benefits would now be available to non-citizens without their having to present certificates that they know the Latvian language. Progress was also demonstrated in other fields by new laws on asylum seekers and refugees, the start of prison reconstruction and modernisation projects, as well as ongoing implementation of environmental protection measures.

Lithuania also demonstrated some progress in the weak areas identified in the Agenda 2000 Opinion. In response to a call for improvements of the judicial system, several administrative changes were instituted. For example, a conservative law on preventative detention was replaced with a more liberal 'Law on Crime Prevention' which also included clear guidelines regarding search and seizure which offered greater protection of the right to privacy. In addition, another new law was introduced to increase the accountability of law enforcement and judicial officers. A law on the protection of children's rights was adopted, which was in line with the UN Convention on the Rights of the Child, and an ombudsman for the protection of children's rights was established, while another ombudsman was established to oversee implementation of the gender anti-discrimination law.

Lastly, some improvements were initiated in Estonia, although progress reports here were coupled with further criticisms and improvement requirements, indicating a heightened standard of evaluation most likely due to Estonia's greater proximity to accession than the other two Baltic states. In March 1998 the death penalty was abolished and Protocol 6 of the ECHR was ratified. Ongoing progress in the restructuring of the police and judiciary was recorded as well. In the field of counter-majoritarian rights, Estonia began a large-scale minority integration programme, including Estonian language training for non-Estonians, which was heavily supported with EU PHARE funds. The government adopted a formal policy statement calling for the development of a multicultural society in Estonia, while also respecting Estonian national rights.

At the same time, only limited amendments were made to the country's citizenship laws. For example, as in Latvia, simplified naturalisation was made possible for children of stateless parents resident in Estonia. Still, the EU remained concerned about the long-term maintenance of these efforts.

Despite the EU's many problems with creating a comprehensive human rights agenda, it was able to create and effectively promote a human rights policy in the Baltic states through conditionality in three areas: democracy guarantees, counter-majoritarian measures, and quality-of-life rights. Even in the course of one year, the three Baltic states undertook dramatic efforts to respond to the specific criticisms and concerns elaborated in the Agenda 2000 Opinions. Indeed, perhaps the 'stick' of being excluded from the first round of accession negotiations prompted Lithuania and especially Latvia to push through reforms more quickly than Estonia. Nevertheless, all three countries were issued a sizable 'carrot' to promote further development of human rights protections in the form of extensive PHARE aid devoted to human rights development programs.

The oscillation between the EU's positive evaluation of the political and human rights criteria on the one hand, and its increasing standards for rights protection in the Baltic states on the other seemed to reflect the need for diplomacy when promoting human rights outside EU borders. This need stemmed from the weakness of the EU to influence – let alone harmonise – the standards of rights protection in its member states. Thus, by stating that Lithuania, for example, has fulfilled the political criteria, the EU covered itself from accusations of imposing a double standard. Nevertheless, critiques and requirements for improvements in the field of human rights continued and the standards of evaluation actually rose with time and progress. Though highly speculative and difficult to prove, it is worth considering other effects of this policy. For instance, by demanding a high standard of protection and collectivisation of minority rights, was the EU also provoking change in the UK, Belgium and France, where individual rights had priority?[69] A better example was the demand that Latvia and Estonia simplify their procedures for granting citizenship to children born in the territory to non-citizen residents. Was it just a coincidence that Germany soon afterward adopted similar procedures as well? If there was a link, then the success of the enlargement project would be two-fold: not only did it promote rights in the applicant countries of Central and Eastern Europe, but it also influenced member state behaviour as well.

Ultimately, of course, if the EU was serious about its requirements to incorporate the stateless residents of Estonia and Latvia into these societies as citizens, there would be little to hold it back from obliging these countries to sign the European Convention on Nationality, since the 'toughest' new standards included in that agreement were in line with EU policies on granting long-time residents rights almost equal to those of citizens. Yet, this might in time compel countries with large resident-alien communities such as Germany to do the same. Moreover, if, for instance, resident-alien communities residing in EU member states acquired limited political rights, such as the non-citizens' right to vote in local elections in Estonia, this could in turn lead to rethinking the concept of EU citizens and expanding EU citizenship to long-time residents – that is, third country nationals – or at least granting them equal free-movement rights as enjoyed by EU citizens.[70]

Conclusions

This chapter has explored the difficulty with which the international community has attempted to influence change in the Baltic states' policies on citizenship and the protection of national minorities during the 1990s. The inability of organisations such as the OSCE and the Council of Europe to reverse discriminatory policies in the Baltic states was due to the lack of progress in international law since the end of World War II regarding nationality policy. Only after the failure of international law to offer a remedy for statelessness in the Baltic countries was an effort made to bring law up to speed with contemporary values, which strive to raise the principle of non-discrimination above nationalist sentiments.

The great success of the EU enlargement process in promoting change in the Baltic states' policies, not only towards the Russian minority but also in terms of other human rights, stemmed from an effective use of conditionality. With the promise of accession, the Baltic states sought to remedy the condition of statelessness in their territories and abandoned certain discriminatory policies. Ultimately, this fact that applicant countries were complying with relatively high human rights criteria prior to accession would surely raise the standard of human rights protection in the EU and create a foundation for the EU to step up political integration and the adoption of a comprehensive human rights agenda.

Notes

1 See M. Nowak, 'Human Rights "Conditionality" in Relation to Entry to, and Full Participation in the EU', in P. Alston, M. R. Bustelo and J. Heenan (eds), *The EU and Human Rights* (Oxford, Oxford University Press, 1999).

2 See D. S. Binder, 'The European Court of Justice and the Protection of Fundamental Rights in the European Community: New Developments and Future Possibilities in Expanding Fundamental Rights Review to Member State Action', *Harvard Jean Monnet Working Paper*, 4/95, p. 71.

3 This was in part because the Kremlin itself started to throw cold water on Article 72 of the USSR constitution, which provided for possible secession. Indeed, ultimately Gorbachev had the entire article repealed and replaced by a complicated law, which actually made secession all but impossible. This therefore also spurred the Balts' shift to legal continuity arguments. See R. Karklins, *Ethnopolitics and Transition to Democracy: The Collapse of the USSR and Latvia* (Baltimore, The Johns Hopkins University Press, 1994), p. 28.

4 It is important to mention that the electorate in 1990 included all residents of the territory of each republic – giving all people, regardless of their ethnic origins or date of

arrival in the republic the right to cast a vote. The clear electoral defeat of the Communist Party indicated that votes were not cast along ethnic cleavages; it is clear that many ethnic Russians chose to support the independence organisations over the Communist Party. Latvia offers the clearest example that non-Latvians also supported independence: the People's Front gained two-thirds of all seats in the Supreme Soviet, even though the ethnic breakdown in 1990 Latvia was 52 per cent Latvian; 34 per cent Russian; 4.5 per cent Belarusian; 3.5 per cent Ukrainian; 2.3 per cent Polish, and 1.3 per cent Lithuanian. In Latvia and Estonia, the fact that ethnic minority groups supported the initial independence movements was later dismissed, and these same groups were largely excluded from future elections due to restrictions on citizenship rights.

5 See 'Constitution Watch: Lithuania', *East European Constitutional Review*, 1:1 (1992),. 5.

6 See V. Pettai, 'Estonia: Positive and Negative Institutional Engineering', in A. Pravda and J. Zielonka (eds), *Democratic Consolidation in Eastern Europe: Institutional Engineering* (Oxford, Oxford University Press, 2001), p. 96.

7 Section 3 of the 'Declaration of the Renewal of Independence', 4 May 1990.

8 Section 8 of the 'Declaration of the Renewal of Independence', 4 May 1990.

9 See G. Smith, 'Nationalities Policy from Lenin to Gorbachev', in G. Smith (ed.), *The Nationalities Question in the Soviet Union*, (New York, Longman Publishing Group, 1990), pp. 1–20.

10 See Appendix 2, Table I in M. Lauristin and P. Vihalemm (eds), *Return to the Western World: Cultural and Political Perspectives on the Estonian Post-Communist Transition* (Tartu, Tartu University Press, 1997), pp. 305–306. This table also indicates an even greater loss suffered by the Jewish populations in the region: between 1934 and 1959, 56,000 and an astounding 204,000 Jews 'disappeared' from Latvia and Lithuania respectively.

11 In the following sections dealing with the genesis of citizenship legislation in the three Baltic states I have tried to restrict myself to the major laws that have been passed and the end result of this process. Needless to say, this process has been messy and many political and legislative twists and turns have been excluded if they did not result in lasting policies.

12 See Z. Petrauskas, 'Issues of Citizenship in the New Constitutions', Report presented at the Council of Europe's UniDem Seminar on Citizenship and State Succession, Vilnius, 16–17 May 1997 (Strasbourg, Council of Europe, 1998), p. 27.

13 Council of Europe: Doc. 6787, 'Report on the Application of the Republic of Lithuania for Membership of the Council of Europe', 2 March 1993, p. 11.

14 See I. Ziemele, 'The Role of State Continuity and Human Rights in Matters of Nationality of the Baltic States', in T. Jundzis (ed.), *The Baltic States at Historical Crossroads* (Riga, Academy of Sciences, 1998), p. 260

15 This partial dismissal of the principle of continuity is also apparent in the reticence of Lithuanian politicians to invite World War II émigrés into the political sphere of the restored state. For instance, the electoral law requires ten-year residence for repatriated émigrés before they can run as candidates in elections. Also, dual citizenship is strictly limited, therefore forcing repatriated émigrés to cut their ties to the countries where they settled. These measures have become less stringent, to the point that Valdas Adamkus, formerly a US citizen, was elected president in 1997. See N. Gelazis, 'Institutional Engineering in Lithuania: Stability through Compromise', in A. Pravda and J. Zielonka (eds), *Democratic Consolidation in Eastern Europe: Institutional Engineering* (Oxford, Oxford University Press, 2001).

16 Data on ethnic composition of the Baltic states is found in I. Ziemele, 'The Role of State', p. 260.

17 See I. Ziemele, 'Incorporation and Implementation of Human Rights in Latvia' in M. Scheinin (ed.), *International Human Rights Norms in the Nordic and Baltic Countries*, (Dordrecht, Martinus Nijhoff Publishers, 1996), p. 78.

18 See I. Ziemele, 'The Role of State', p. 260.
19 See 'Constitution Watch: Latvia' *East European Constitutional Review*, 2:3 (1993), 11.
20 These percentages were calculated from the 1997 official Population Register of the Latvian Citizenship and Immigration Board, as reported in the *Latvia: Human Development Report 1997* (Riga, UNDP, 1997), p. 49. Since these numbers only include residents who have actually registered with the government, this number reflects the minimum possible number of stateless persons residing in Latvia.
21 See Aleksei Semjonov 'Citizenship Legislation, Minority Rights and Integration in Estonia', paper presented for the ECMI Baltic Seminar 'Minorities and Majorities in Estonia: Problems of Integration at the Threshold of the EU' (Flensburg: European Center for Minority Issues, 1998), p. 5.
22 Although many constitution-drafters at the time assumed that this would also give resident non-citizens the right to run for elected office in local councils, the 19 May 1993 electoral law denied non-citizens this right. David Laitin explains that 'Most delegates of the Riigikogu knew that they were breaking the spirit, if not the letter, of the Constitution, but the political goal of undermining the power of the current city councils in the northeastern cities proved of greater importance to them.' See D. Laitin, 'The Russian-Speaking Nationality in Estonia: Two Quasi-Constitutional Elections', *East European Constitutional Review* 2–3:4–1 (1993–94), 25.
23 The 1940 amendments to this law dramatically changed what had been originally (in 1938) a relatively liberal law that simplified naturalisation procedures for those who had permanently resided in the territory of Estonia for at least ten years, did not envisage any formal exam for knowledge of the Estonian language, and gave automatic citisenship to children born in Estonia to stateless parents. See Semjonov, 'Citizenship Legislation', p. 7.
24 See Ziemele, 'The Role of State', p. 257.
25 The 1992 figures during the constitutional referendum show that only around 60 per cent of the 1990 electorate was able to participate. See Semjonov, 'Citizenship Legislation', p. 6.
26 See Semjonov, 'Citizenship Legislation', p. 7.
27 LNTS. Vol. 179, p. 89, as cited in Council of Europe: 'On the Consequences of State Succession for Nationality', Report adopted by the European Commission for Democracy through Law at its 28th Plenary Meeting, Venice, 13–14 September 1996, Science and Technique of Democracy Collection, No. 23 (Strasbourg: Council of Europe Publishing, 1998), p. 21.
28 Ziemele, 'The Role of State' p. 264.
29 See appendix of the 'Statement by Romans Baumanis, Head of the Delegation of Latvia', agenda item 16: Rights of Persons Belonging to National or Ethnic, Religious, and Linguistic Minorities, 54th Session of the Commission on Human Rights, Geneva, 31 March 1998.
30 Council of Europe, 'On the Consequences', p. 22.
31 Nottebohm Case (Second Phase), Judgment of 6 April 1955, ICJ Reports 1955, p. 23, as cited in Council of Europe, 'On the Consequences'.
32 Council of Europe, 'On the Consequences', p. 14.
33 Although international law and practice allows states to deny citizenship to military and government personnel of foreign states, this has become an excuse for Estonia to deny residence permits and even deport (former Soviet) Russian soldiers who are married to Estonian citizens. Certainly, the international community should demand that the right of families to stay together be protected at a higher standard than the right of states to deny citizenship on the basis of the effective links principle. See 'Estonia to Expel Eight Russian Reserve Officers', *RFE/RL Newsline*, 11 June 1997. Subsequently, the Estonian Supreme Court upheld the appeal of one such ex-officer to stay in Estonia with his family.

34 See Ziemele, 'The Role of State', p. 262.
35 See P. Weis, *Nationality and Statelessness in International Law* (Alphen aan den Rijn, Sijthoff & Noordhoff, 1979), p. 43.
36 Council of Europe, 'On the Consequences', p. 45.
37 *Ibid.*, p. 46.
38 *Ibid.*, 'On the Consequences', p. 39.
39 *Ibid.*, 'On the Consequences', p. 14.
40 Ziemele cites different acts on the part of the international community, which support the claim of the Baltic states' re-establishment of independent statehood. For instance, the fact that some countries withheld formal recognition of the Baltic states independence due to the pre-existing recognition granted to the interwar states and the act of British and French banks returning gold reserves deposited by the interwar republics based on *restitutio ad integrum* were both indicators that the international community accepted the Baltic states' actions. See Ziemele, 'The Role of State', pp. 255–256.
41 Council of Europe, 'On the Consequences', p. 38.
42 See P. Burnell, 'Good Government and Democratization: A Sideways Look at Aid and Political Conditionality', *Democratization*, 1:3 (1994), p. 503. Although Burnell deals with democratic conditionality, I assume that human rights conditionality falls within the general goal for good government and democratisation.
43 Take, for example, the carefully worded diplomacy of the UNDP regarding the state language policies in Latvia and Estonia: 'Another challenge in some countries of the region is to ensure that "the restored state" and "restored citizenship" based on ethnicity do not lead to ethnonationalism. Although there has been an understandable reaction to the previous era, which was characterised by an "over-integrationist" tendency, there are dangers associated with "ethnic democracy" that have emerged in countries such as Estonia and Latvia. The fear, which may not be justified, is that the character of democracy is inclined to ethnic favoritism.' UNDP Regional Bureau for Europe and the CIS, *The New Yalta* (New York, 1998), p. 27. I believe that any reasonable observer of the stringent citizenship requirements (based on knowledge of the national language) and the restrictive language laws (which demand that workers pass language exams before they receive jobs or licences) shows beyond a doubt that these regimes practise 'ethnic favoritism'. The question might be posed instead regarding whether or not these practices amount to blatant discrimination.
44 In the specific case of the OSCE's High Commissioner on National Minorities, Stefan Vassilev recounts, 'the mandate of the HCNM does not provide any real 'sticks'. This is true, as far as direct means of pressure or imposition are concerned. In practice, however, the HCNM has 'indirect' or 'hidden' means. Indeed, there are many efforts in Central and Eastern Europe to obtain international financial and economic aid, as well as membership in the European Union, the North Atlantic Treaty Organisation and the Western European Union . . . In addition, the HCNM has the political support of the OSCE and its Chairman-in-office, as well as general and specific support of the OSCE key member states.' See Stefan Vassilev 'The OSCE High Commissioner on National Minorities: A Non-Traditional Approach to Conflict Prevention', in UNDP Regional Bureau for Europe and the CIS, *The New Yalta* (New York, 1998), p. 144.
45 The fourth condition addresses the EU, not the candidate countries: '4) the EU must be able to absorb new members and maintain the momentum of integration.' European Council in Copenhagen, 21–22 June 1993, Conclusions of the Presidency, SN 180/93, p. 13.
46 See H. G. Krenzler 'Preparing for the Acquis Communautaire', in Michelle Everson, rapporteur, *Robert Schuman Centre Policy Paper*, 6 (1998), p. 6.
47 *Ibid.*, p. 9.
48 'Article 4: Where an element that is essential for continuing to grant pre-accession assistance is lacking, in particular when the commitments contained in the Europe Agreement

are not respected and/or progress towards fulfillment of the Copenhagen criteria is insufficient, the Council, acting by a qualified majority on a proposal from the Commission, may take appropriate steps with regard to any pre-accession assistance granted to an applicant State.' Council Regulation (EC) No. 622/98 of 16 March 1998 on assistance to the applicant States in the framework of the pre-accession strategy, and in particular on the establishment of Accession Partnerships, *Official Journal* No. L 085, 20/03/1998 P. 0001–0002.

49 See M. Colvin and P. Noorlander, 'Human Rights and Accountability after the Treaty of Amsterdam' *EHRLR* (1998), 191–203.

50 P. Alston and J. H. H. Weiler, 'The European Union and Human Rights: Final Project Report on an Agenda for the Year 2000', in *Leading by Example: A Human Rights Agenda for the European Union for the Year 2000: Agenda of the Comité des Sages and Final Project Report*, (Florence, Academy of European Law, EUI, 1998), p. 26.

51 Binder, 'The European Court', p. 9.

52 Alston and Weiler, *Leading by Example*, p. 47.

53 Binder, 'The European Court'.

54 Krenzler, 'Preparing for the Acquis', p. 7.

55 *Ibid.*, p. 9.

56 See H. G. Krenzler 'The EU and Central-East Europe: The Implications of Enlargement in Stages', *Robert Schuman Centre Policy Paper*, 2 (1997).

57 One example is the EP's 'Résolution sur les droits des homosexuels et des lesbiennes dans l'Union européene', B4–0824 et 0852/98, which includes: '2) demand à tous les pays candidats d'abroger leurs dispositions législatives violant les droits de l'homme des homosexuels et des lesbiennes, en particulier celles qui prévoient des différences d'âge pour les rapports homosexueles; 3) invite la Commission à tenir compte du respect des droits de l'homme des homosexuels et des lesbiennes lors des négociations relatives à l'adhésion des pays candidats.'

58 It is difficult to measure the importance of the EP's additional 'conditions' in the negotiations between candidate countries and the Commission. Nevertheless, at least in Lithuania, the EP's resolution on the rights of homosexuals has been co-opted by NGOs and the media, and has thus entered the public debates on the criteria for EU enlargement. See 'Lietuvos gejai: bilietas i Europos Sajunga' (Lithuania's gays: the ticket to the EU) in *Veidas*, 41 (8–14 October 1998), p. 22.

59 See, for example, 'Agenda 2000: Commission Opinion on Estonia's Application for Membership of the European Union', in *European Commission Bulletin of the European Union Supplement* 11 (1997), p. 15.

60 See Case 44/79, *Liselotte Hauer* v. *Land Rheinland Pfalz*, 1979 ECR 3727 (1980) 3 CMLR 42 (1979).

61 Binder, 'The European Court', pp. 6–7.

62 *Ibid.*, pp. 6–7.

63 The 'Declaration for Democracy: stipulated that 'respect for and maintenance of representative democracy and human rights in each member state are essential elements of membership in the European Communities', Copenhagen European Council, 7–8 April 1978, *EC Bulletin*, 3, 1978.

64 This reflects the dissonance surrounding Article 13 of the TEU discussed above. Moreover, although excluded from the human rights section, gender discrimination and equal opportunity is briefly mentioned in the Opinions under section 3.5, Economic and Social Cohesion: Employment and Social Affairs.

65 The link between human rights and security is documented under point 5 of the Human Rights Agenda adopted by the Comité des Sages. Alston and Weiler, 'Leading by Example', p. 4.

66 This argument is seemingly weakened by the fact that, whatever its difficulties in

protecting individual rights, the ECJ has consistently been able to protect the rights of EU citizens living and working outside their home countries. Nevertheless, it is still in the EU's interests that new member states be friendly to non-nationals, at the very least because it will make the EU's and ECJ's work easier.

67 Although the EU may not see these as human rights issues, many East European countries have included the right to a clean environment and right to adequate health care in their constitutions. For example in the Lithuanian constitution, Articles 53 and 54 enshrine the right to healthcare and a clean environment. Furthermore, the fact that these rights have been constitutionalised does not necessarily mean that they would be implemented even without EU pressure. Such rights are seen by many East European leaders as 'aspirational' and governments often postpone addressing such rights in favour of concentrating on economic reform.

68 S. S. Nello and K. E. Smith, 'The Consequences of Eastern Enlargement of the European Union in Stages' *Robert Schuman Centre Working Paper*, 51 (1997), p. 12.

69 *Ibid.*, p. 20.

70 For a review of the rights of third-country nationals under EU law, see A. C. Oliveira, 'The Position of Resident Third-Country Nationals: Is It Too Early to Grant Them Union Citizenship?', in M. La Torre (ed.), *European Citizenship: An Institutional Challenge* (The Hague: Kluwer Law International, 1998), pp. 185–199.

VELLO PETTAI

5

Estonia's constitutional review mechanisms

A guarantor of democratic consolidation?

In the European Commission's Agenda 2000 report on Estonia, it was concluded that 'Estonia presents the characteristics of a democracy, with stable institutions, guaranteeing the rule of law, human rights and respect for and protection of minorities.'[1] In particular, the report noted that 'In Estonia's institutions the Supreme Court plays an important role in upholding democracy and the rule of law.' Yet, in the remainder of the over 100–page report there was little additional elaboration of this statement, except to say that 'Petitions addressed to the Supreme Court are rising in number, even though most of them are groundless.'[2]

As other chapters in this volume note, the EU's 1993 Copenhagen criteria for admission into the European Union are relatively general; likewise, the EU's *acquis communitaire* has little to say about the specifics of democratic government or rule of law. Thus, it is perhaps not surprising that the EU's own reports sail over some of these points. Yet, the goal of democracy forms the backbone of what the EU represents as a political community. Moreover, although many conventional studies of democratic transition in post-communist Europe have addressed the institutionalisation of democracy within the legislative as well as executive branches of government, few have investigated how such norms have been fostered and supported by the judicial branch. Thus the EU's pithy assessment of Estonian courts actually raises a number of questions, which this chapter will seek to address. Namely: what has been the real contribution of the Estonian Supreme Court to the upholding of Estonia's democracy and the rule of law? How has, in particular, the Court's Constitutional Review Chamber (the CRC, or the 5-justice sub-section of the Supreme Court, which is responsible for exercising constitutional review in Estonia) influenced the evolution of Estonia's democratic government as well as the provision of justice in the legal system? How does and will Estonia's constitutional review mechanism compare with other such institutions in the European Union once Estonia becomes an EU member? What are the broader European trends that this mechanism will be likely to encounter in the future? This chapter will attempt to bring this critical, yet understudied, dimension of Estonia's institutional framework closer into focus with particular reference to the issue of democratic consolidation and political stability in Estonia over the long term. It will approach the issue from a predominantly political science perspective, analysing the Court's cases with this standpoint in mind. While other studies have been done of the Court's legal performance,[3] the approach taken here will be more interpretive and analytical.

This chapter will address these issues by breaking them down into sections and beginning with a conceptual discussion of the link between constitutional courts and democratic consolidation. Although so much has been written on democratic transition and consolidation, it is surprising to notice how little these studies have included the development of constitutional review mechanisms in post-authoritarian countries. Secondly, I will review the history and structure of constitutional review mechanisms in Estonia. While Estonia had certain elements of a review mechanism in place before its annexation by the Soviet Union in 1940, its real experience with this kind of institutional process has developed only since 1993. Thirdly, I will analyse the case history of the current CRC during the 1990s (39 rulings through the end of 1999) based on five general categories: separation of powers, breach of powers, public policy-making, fundamental rights and freedoms, and international treaties. While these categories are somewhat arbitrary (and many cases of the CRC have straddled the different categories), they all address certain key principles of democracy, which must be safeguarded.[4] To the extent that Estonia's Constitutional Review Chamber has been called upon to adjudicate these questions, I will argue that Estonia's emerging democracy has been strengthened.

Constitutional review, constitutionalism and democracy

The issue of constitutional review goes far beyond the fine points of judicial procedure or legal technicality. At heart, it concerns the stability and functionality of the democratic process itself. For at the national level a country's constitutional review mechanisms serve as the essential third pillar in the separation of state powers. In most democracies (and especially in parliamentary ones) the legislative and executive branches of government naturally balance each other. While parliament can approve and dismiss the prime minister, the prime minister generally has power over the actual machinery of government (including both material as well as coercive resources) and can sometimes force his/her own policies on parliaments through the threat of confidence votes and/or deal-making.

Still, in order for democracy to work it is the judiciary which must play the additional role of overseeing both of these institutions from the standpoint of what keeps the whole political system together – the constitution. The question of constitutional review thus reverts to what is an even more important prerequisite for democracy: constitutionalism. Respect for and adherence to the one document that constitutes the basic rules of the political game (and thus personifies the entire essence of *democratic* management of power) can never be taken lightly or assumed, not only in consolidating democracies, but also in consolidated ones. On the contrary, such respect must be buttressed through effective monitoring and arbitration procedures, which must additionally have the legitimacy to make binding decisions. As Allan R. Brewer-Carías writes, 'if written constitutional systems pretend to have a supreme, obligatory and enforceable law, they must establish means for the defence and guarantee of the constitution'.[5]

Constitutional review mechanisms have thus become a ubiquitous and inherent part of democratic governance, particularly from 1945 onwards. Yet, we must also not forget that constitutional review mechanisms serve a second important function alongside resolving institutional disputes – namely, the protection of fundamental rights and freedoms in society. In contemporary constitutional practice, such rights and freedoms are also enshrined in basic law. However, their protection and realisation is again never automatic, but must instead be continually monitored and safeguarded through judicial means. For it is by no means a rare occurrence that both the executive and the legislature will, for example, agree on some coercive measure to promote order or efficiency in society, but at the expense of one or more of the fundamental rights and freedoms declared sacrosanct by the constitution. If such actions are allowed to stand, they can eventually lead to popular discontent or, at the very least, popular alienation. In these cases, the judiciary and its constitutional review mechanisms must be able to maintain a necessary balance. They must defend not only institutional stability, but also societal stability.

Lastly, it is worth noting how little attention constitutional review mechanisms have received within the vast scholarly literature on democratic transitions and consolidation.[6] While many scholars speak of the need for 'democratic political culture', and others even stress the importance of constitutionalism for democratic viability, there has been scant interest paid to the actual institutional mechanisms that are supposed to bring about these results. In particular, during the early years of a democratic regime, newly created institutions (both legislative and executive) are likely to be highly sensitive about their mutual balance of powers and the practical operation of those prerogatives. Executives, who often face the need to implement decisive political, economic or social reform, may seek dominance in the new political system, while legislatures, acting as the newly installed 'body of the people', may desire instead to limit governmental power. These are confrontations, which in consolidating democracies have quite frequently led to major institutional tensions or tugs-of-war, and which in some cases have led to democratic breakdown. Witness the struggles in Russia during 1993, Peru in the early 1990s or Venezuela in 1999. Indeed, the Baltic states themselves had a legacy of institutional weakness from the pre-war period. Although admittedly these particular problems were not caused directly by an absence of constitutional review mechanisms, they might perhaps have been better managed had such procedures been in place.[7] Thus, the issue is a topical one both from a theoretical as well as an empirical standpoint.

Constitutional review in Estonia

Having experienced just twenty years of independence between the two world wars and fifty years of Soviet domination thereafter, Estonia's constitutional as well as judicial practice has been fairly limited. In 1920, the country adopted its first constitution after convening a special Constituent Assembly in 1919. The regime that was chosen was a strongly parliamentary one, in which the executive branch had relatively few autonomous powers and was beholden to the legislature for constant support. Although members of the Constituent Assembly did consider one proposal for instituting a system of constitutional review through the Supreme Court, this idea was eventually dropped.[8] Instead, the concept was subsumed under Estonia's basic administrative court procedure whereby the courts were given the right to rule on the legality of at least administrative acts with regard to the rights and complaints of plaintiffs. Yet, parliamentary acts were off limits, which epitomised again the parliamentary bias of the regime.

Eventually, this general institutional weakness (along with growing political discord and economic hardship) led to the rise in the early 1930s of proto-authoritarian groups calling for decisive constitutional reform. A new constitution, sponsored by these groups and calling for a strong presidency, was put to a referendum in 1933. Although the measure passed by a significant margin, its implementation was pre-empted in March 1934 by the caretaker prime minister at the time, Konstantin Päts, who staged a coup d'état to prevent the new forces from taking power. Päts banned all political parties and installed an authoritarian regime for the next three years. In 1937, however, he allowed a constituent assembly to draft a new constitution, which installed a much more presidential system.

Under the new regime, begun in 1938, there was again no specific institution charged with binding constitutional review. However, the system did create the office of a legal chancellor (to be appointed and dismissed by the president), who was to be sent drafts of all major laws, regulations, decrees, and edicts drawn up by the executive branch of government with a view to exercising limited constitutional review over them. In this respect, the legal chancellor's job was preventive as opposed to judicial, however, his decisions were restricted to the executive.[9] Additionally, Article 121 of the 1938 constitution stated that, 'Initiation and procedures of the judicial control over the constitutionality of the exercise of the state power shall be determined by law.' However, during the subsequent two years that the constitution functioned until the Soviet takeover in 1940, agreement was not reached as to what this paragraph should mean in practice and whether full-scale constitutional review (including over parliament) could or should be created by a separate law.

The issue of protecting the constitution, monitoring institutional prerogatives, and strengthening democratic stability were all tasks, which Estonia's first era of independence ultimately did not succeed in accomplishing. While low levels of democratic culture as well as the prevailing authoritarian mood in Europe as a whole contributed greatly to this outcome, these factors could not outweigh the intrinsic advantages to be gained from an effective mechanism of constitutional review. In the fifty years of Soviet domination to follow, popular hopes often seemed lost as to whether another opportunity would ever arise for constructing an independent democratic state. In 1991, however, that chance did arise, and this time Estonia would work toward a more comprehensive political system.

Estonia's leap to freedom in the midst of the attempted putsch in Moscow in August 1991 was accompanied by a bold decision to immediately convene a new constitutional assembly for the drafting of a fresh constitution. This assembly met for eight months through to the spring of 1992, by which time an initial draft was completed.[10] The new basic law mandated a parliamentary system with a prime-ministerial government and cabinet. At the same time, a ceremonial president would be elected by the legislature (or in case of deadlock, an electoral college). Thus, the regime sought to avoid the 1920s dominance of parliament, while equally preventing an over-bearing executive. On 28 June 1992, the constitution was adopted by a popular referendum.

While the constitutional assembly's deliberations were often protracted over such things as the mode of election for president, the need for some kind of constitutional review was never disputed. Instead, according to the protocols of the assembly, the only concerns raised were in regard to the mechanics.[11] In the end, Estonia's new constitutional review mechanism came to stand on three channels of judicial appeal – the president, the legal chancellor, and the lower courts – all leading to the five-member Constitutional Review Chamber (CRC) of the Supreme Court, which would have final decision-making authority.[12] The CRC is elected from among the full 17–member Supreme Court, but its chair must be the Chief Justice. The system is thus a concentrated one (as opposed to a diffuse one), along the lines of those adopted in Germany, France or Italy.[13] However, being a judicial body the CRC cannot take up cases on its own, but instead must rely on appeals from other designated institutions. Moreover, as we will see below, the court is restricted in its rulings only to those points of law brought before it.

Institutions of constitutional appeal

The legal chancellor

The creation of a post of legal chancellor for the new constitutional system was an idea derived from the 1938 constitution. However, the profile of the office was significantly modified in that henceforth it was to be an independent institution, elected by the parliament for a seven-year term. More importantly, the legal chancellor's responsibilities would now include the monitoring of all legal acts in the country (from the parliament to the government all the way down to local municipalities) from the express point of view of their constitutionality. The job was specifically defined in Article 139 of the constitution as 'an independent official who shall review the legislation of the legislative and executive powers and of local governments for conformity with the Constitution and the laws'.[14] Although the constitution uses merely the verb 'review', the legal chancellor's actual oversight activities take place on several levels. At a pre-emptive level, the legal chancellor has the right by law to attend all sessions of both the government as well as parliament. In this capacity he is also sent copies of all draft laws and decrees from both institutions, which he then has an opportunity to screen before their adoption.[15] At a second level, the legal chancellor may be called upon to interpret an existing law not only by members of parliament or government officials, but also by average individuals.[16] Finally, the Legal Chancellor's Act requires that a copy of any legal act passed by an executive or legislative body at either the national or local level be sent to the legal chancellor's office within ten days of its passage.[17] Although this means that literally thousands of acts are forwarded to the legal chancellor each year and it is physically impossible for him to review each and every one, it does provide a formal mechanism for him to keep abreast of legal regulations in the country.[18]

Procedurally, if the legal chancellor believes some legal act is in violation of the constitution,

> he or she shall propose to the body which passed the legislation to bring the legislation into conformity with the Constitution or the law within twenty days. If the legislation is not brought into conformity with the Constitution or the law within twenty days, the Legal Chancellor shall propose to the Supreme Court to declare the legislation invalid.[19]

Thus, at this most peremptory level the legal chancellor performs an *ex post* review function, whereby the legislative or executive body under question is initially given a chance to amend its act, but it may thereafter be taken to the CRC if the legal chancellor is not satisfied with its response.

During his seven-year term in office, Estonia's first legal chancellor, Eerik-Juhan Truuväli, protested a total of over 240 legislative acts passed by the government, the Riigikogu or individual local authorities.[20] Of these, two-thirds concerned local governments, although a large number involved acts of the government (30) or individual ministers (26). Only 16 arose in connection with laws passed by the Riigikogu. Moreover, in only 12 instances was Truuväli unable to resolve his protests through consultations; these cases he eventually appealed to the CRC, where he lost only once.

The courts

The role of the lower courts in initiating constitutional review procedures is quite standard and straight forward. If in the process of hearing a case the court comes to the conclusion that a particular legislative act is unconstitutional, it must dismiss the law from consideration in the case and rule without it. Thereafter, an appeal is filed immediately with the CRC, which must review the case within two months. Thus, the appeal is made on behalf of the lower court and does not involve in any way the original parties to the case. It is the court, which argues (usually simply in writing) its case against the respective executive or legislative authority that originally adopted the legal act. If the court is found to be right, then the act is rescinded. However, if the court is wrong, then current procedure does not allow the previous court case to be reopened. This is a flaw that had still to be remedied.

The president

Within Estonia's constitutional review procedure, the president is the only institution which has the right to appeal laws passed by the Riigikogu to the CRC before they take effect. Thus, he or she is the only one, who can exercise formal preventative or *ex ante* constitutional review.[21] Under Article 107 of the constitution, the president has the responsibility for promulgating laws adopted by parliament. However, if the president is opposed to a law, he or she may refuse to promulgate it and return it to parliament for reconsideration. If the parliament passes the law again in its identical form, then the president must sign the legislation, or he or she may appeal to the CRC for a ruling on the law's constitutionality. Thus the president can exercise a suspensive veto over parliamentary legislation, but he or she cannot completely override the parliament. Moreover, the fact that any dispute between the parliament and president can ultimately lead to the CRC means that any objections to a law that the president has are obliged from the very beginning to centre on mostly legal (instead of political) arguments, since the president knows that if he or she is to be assured of victory, the case will have to stand up to the potential scrutiny of the CRC, where only constitutional arguments prevail. Thus, the rules have an objectifying effect on disputes.

The CRC in practice

In addition to the specific provisions of the constitution, a separate law, the Constitutional Review Court Procedure Act also regulates the work of the CRC.[22] This act specifies the deadlines, requirements and rules for reviewing appeals to the CRC. In addition, in terms of precise actions, the CRC may issue essentially two kinds of rulings. The first is to rule against the appeal based on insufficient arguments, and the second is to declare the appeal valid either fully or partially. In the latter case, the legislative act in question is struck down based on the degree to which the CRC finds in favour of the applicant as well as the degree to which the applicant him- or herself has sought the act to be declared unconstitutional. This is because paragraph 4.3 of the Constitutional Review

Court Procedure Act limits the CRC to exercising judicial review only in relation to those points of law specifically brought before it. Thus, the CRC cannot take up separate points, which it believes are unconstitutional. However, it can and often has raised arguments in relation to the given points, which were not brought out by the parties involved.[23]

Since its inception in May 1993 through to November 1999, the CRC heard a total of 39 cases.[24] As indicated in table 5.1, the most active year for the CRC was 1994, when 11 cases were considered. Although initially the president as well as the legal chancellor took the lead in submitting cases, the lower courts began in 1995 to be more active in using their constitutional review prerogatives, and by 1997 they had moved ahead of the other two institutions. The Riigikogu was challenged the most by these actions, as a total of 21 laws were contested. The executive (both government and individual ministers) was challenged 12 times and local governments 6. In a few cases, appeals to the CRC involved more than one government decree or point of law. As a result, the CRC was obliged to make more than one ruling, sometimes upholding one aspect of an appeal, but dismissing another.

Table 5.1 Appeals heard by the Constitutional Review Chamber, 1993–99

	Year							
	1993	*1994*	*1995*	*1996*	*1997*	*1998*	*1999*	*Total*
Appeals made by:								
President	2	3	–	1	–	2	–	8
Legal Chancellor	2	6	–	1	–	3	–	12
Lower courts	–	2	4	2	3	5	3	19
Total rulings	4	11	4	4	3	10	3	39
Type of legal act contested								
Law	2	7	3	2	–	6	2	22
Government decree	–	2	–	2	2	2	1	9
Ministerial decree	–	1	1	–	–	1	–	3
Local government legislation	2	2	–	–	1	1	–	6
Ruling of the Constitutional Review Chamber								
Act declared unconstitutional	3	9	2	3	2	8	2	29
Act already repealed by the time of the CRC's ruling	–	2	–	1	–	2	1	6
Act declared constitutional	1	1	2	1	1	–	1	7

In terms of the five categories to be discussed below (separation of powers, breach of powers, rights and freedoms, public policy-making), cases involving breach of powers predominated. This was understandable, since four possible institutional actors (the parliament, the government, individual ministers, and local governments) and their legal acts could all come under this category. International treaties, meanwhile, were raised more rarely, although here the number was likely to grow as Estonia came closer to joining the European Union and its legal acts were subject to greater scrutiny vis-à-vis EU norms.

Separation of powers

Estonia's adoption of a new constitution in 1992 was a decisive step toward building a new and comprehensive democratic order. It was in contrast to a number of other ex-communist countries (such as Poland and Hungary), which had initially simply amended their old constitutions as a way of institutionalising democracy. Still, the Estonian decision also created an entirely unknown and untested institutional configuration. Not only were the parliament, government and courts all expected to become serious institutions (in contrast to the old Soviet ones), but in addition the 1992 constitution had created several new offices, including a presidency, a legal chancellor, and an auditor general. Although the constitution did set forth a fairly comprehensive system of separation of powers among these different institutions, it was clear that many details would still have to be settled, both through additional legislation as well as simple precedent. Where agreement could not be reached as to these details, the CRC was frequently called upon to arbitrate.

The president v. parliament

In any political system an essential axis of power is that which exists between the president and parliament. During the work of the Constitutional Assembly of 1991–92, there were considerable debates as to whether Estonia needed a president at all, and if so what prerogatives he or she should have. In the event, the new constitution created a largely ceremonial presidency, but which included a limited power of veto in the area of legislation. In September 1992, a special presidential election was held, at the end of which Lennart Meri, a writer, film-maker and former foreign minister, was elected to office. Meri was an excellent choice for his stately demeanour and strong commitment to democracy; however, he was also well-known for his independent-mindedness and political self-assurance. As a result, he was likely to have a keen awareness of institutional prerogative as well as of institutional precedent, sitting as the first president. Indeed, Meri was the first of Estonia's three constitutional oversight institutions to appeal a case to the CRC, just two months after the chamber was formed.

Through 1999 the CRC heard four major cases concerning the president's institutional powers. In each case, the issue involved laws, which the Riigikogu (Parliament) had attempted to pass in order to flesh out practical procedures and relations involving the president. Meri, however, sought to block what was to his mind over-regulation of these matters, and in general he was victorious. The only exception was the very first law, which Meri appealed and which was simultaneously the CRC's very first case.[25] In this instance, Meri had vetoed a law, which mandated that the official state seal (to be used for confirming the credentials of ambassadors as well as letters regarding the ratification or denunciation of international treaties) would be kept in the office of the state secretary, and not in the president's office. Meri claimed that since it was his job to appoint and recall ambassadors as well as to sign necessary treaty letters (based on Articles 78.2 and 78.6 of the constitution), the entrusting of the state seal with an official of the executive branch would *de facto* mean his subordination to the executive branch. In turn, Meri asserted that this was a violation of the principle of separation of powers, as enshrined in Article 4 of the constitution.

In some sense, the question seemed a pedantic one; but in the context of evolving institutions, it was the first test of strength between the parliament and the president. In its ruling, the CRC sided with the parliament, arguing that although the president was responsible for appointing and recalling ambassadors as well as signing treaty notices, the government was equally responsible (under Articles 87.1 and 87.7 of the constitution) for the execution of foreign policy. As a result, the CRC claimed the state seal was essentially a technical matter and that its location in the state secretary's office could not prevent the president from fulfilling his constitutional duties. Meri's appeal was denied.

In February 1994, however, the president challenged the parliament on a new issue, this time involving his right to bestow state medals and awards. In the constitution, only a general reference is made to this right: the president shall 'confer state awards, and military and diplomatic ranks' (Article 78.15). The Riigikogu therefore had to pass supplementary legislation, spelling out this procedure in more detail. In its law adopted in December 1993 the Riigikogu called for the establishment of a special commission, which would review and present to the president a list of candidates for the range of state awards conferred each year on Estonia's independence day (February 24). President Meri objected to this provision, arguing that the committee (whose membership was also mandated by the law) would be able to pre-select candidates and therefore restrict his formal institutional prerogative. In this case, the CRC ruled that the president had to have full autonomy in both drawing up as well as selecting his award recipients. Any commission forced upon him by the parliament was interference in the president's constitutional duties and therefore unconstitutional.[26]

This was an important message to the parliament in that where the constitution had left such discretionary powers to the president, the head-of-state was to have wide-ranging autonomy in establishing the exact modalities of its execution. In April 1998, the CRC reiterated this point, when President Meri appealed a similar case involving his right to grant clemency or reduce criminal sentences (Art. 78.19). Finally, in June 1994 a fourth and most consequential defence of the presidential institution came, when Meri vetoed the Riigikogu's attempt to regulate the presidency in general through a Presidential Procedure Act. In this instance, the law sought to lay down the procedure (mentioned in Article 109 of the constitution) whereby the president would be authorised to issue decrees with the force of law in special situations where the parliament was prevented from coming together. The law stated that first the speaker of parliament would have to certify that the parliament was unable to come together, and that second the prime minister would have to confirm that there was a 'matter of urgent state need' at hand, which required legislation by presidential decree. President Meri argued that these two specific modalities (not mentioned in the constitution) infringed on his constitutional rights and duties as head-of-state in such situations, and were thereby unconstitutional. Again the CRC agreed with the president and struck down the law. Subsequently, the Riigikogu was so deterred from touching the issue again, that a presidential procedure act was never re-drafted until 2001.

The parliament v. the government

A second type of separation of powers concerns the relations between parliament and government. This issue was first raised in November 1994 based on a case brought by the legal chancellor. The legal chancellor protested the Riigikogu Procedural Act (or basic rules of order in parliament), which allowed MPs to serve concurrently on the executive boards of major state-owned firms. The boards were intended to supervise general management at the few key enterprises still left in state hands both during and after large-scale privatisation. Having MPs in particular serve on the boards was seen as a way of securing political consensus for the management of state assets. Yet, the legal chancellor saw the issue as a conflict of interest between the legislative and executive branches. He argued that because the MPs were receiving remuneration for their work and were viewed on a par with board members drawn directly from the executive, they were in fact working simultaneously as members of both the legislative and executive branches, and were therefore in violation of the constitution's Article 4. In its ruling, the CRC agreed with the legal chancellor's case, saying that,

> Any situation of conflict of interest, in which a state employee simultaneously fulfils essentially contradictory tasks as well as seeks contradictory objectives, can precipitate deficiencies in the execution of his official responsibilities as well as create the pre-conditions for corruption. Conflicts of interest must be avoided in all state institutions.[27]

Still, the issue was a delicate one, since it contained important practical implications. According to Article 64.2 of the constitution, if a member of parliament assumes a position in any other branch of government, he or she automatically forfeits their seat in parliament. Thus, if this provision were strictly adhered to and the CRC decided to rule against the parliament, the result would have been to automatically throw out a large number of MPs from the parliament and bring chaos to the legislature's work. Instead, the CRC set an important precedent by granting the MPs one month, in which to make their choice between the parliament and the executive boards. Although the Constitutional Review Chamber Procedure Act does not expressly allow for such timedelays, it was clearly warranted in this case.

Breach of powers

In Estonia's constitution there are a number of important principles about how questions of policy are to be legislated and by whom. Firstly, Article 104 lists a total of 17 specific laws or domains in relation to which the Riigikogu can pass laws only with an absolute majority of its members. These include the state budget, various electoral laws, laws relating to the structure of the Estonian government as well as other state institutions. Any law pertaining to these areas, which is passed without such a majority, is unconstitutional. Secondly, if a particular aspect of any one of these domains is by chance legislated within the context of some other law (which needs only a simple majority to pass), such an act can also be found unconstitutional. Thirdly, the constitution contains several paragraphs on fundamental rights and freedoms as well as other institutions' rights, which stipulate that restrictions on these rights can only be legislated by a law, not by any other legal act such as a decree. Any attempt to regulate these areas through other such means is equally unconstitutional. Fourthly, Article 87.6 states explicitly that the government of the republic shall 'issue regulations and orders on the basis of and for the implementation of law'. This means that the government can issue decrees only on the basis of specific paragraphs in law authorising it to do so. Moreover, these paragraphs must be explicitly cited in the text of the decree. As will be seen below, this was a particular area of focus for the CRC during the 1990s, as many government decrees during the early years of Estonia's new constitution were sloppily drafted and thus unconstitutional. Lastly, local authorities are also bound by national law when adopting their own regulatory ordinances, despite the fact that the constitution's Chapter 14 on local government equally makes reference to their autonomy in deciding their own affairs. Where municipalities overstepped these boundaries or adopted regulations not sanctioned by law, the CRC struck them down. In this section, therefore, I will review four types of breach of power, involving the parliament, the government, individual ministers, and local governments.

The parliament

An important principle that the CRC repeatedly sought to enforce during its first six years concerned the Riigikogu's constitutional responsibility to fulfil its legislative duties. This referred to the parliament's obligation to adopt laws and decide matters delegated to it by the constitution, instead of passing them off to the executive to decide. In one of the CRC's earliest decisions, it made this argument very clear. In November 1993, President Meri challenged the Riigikogu's adoption of the Tax Regulation Act.[28] In the original law, the Riigikogu had authorised the Minister of Finance to scrutinise and define the nature of taxes levied by local governments on their territory. While the CRC struck down the law on the principle of local government autonomy, it also noted that the law was an attempt by the parliament to delegate to the executive a job (defining local taxes), which the constitution had specifically assigned to the legislature

(Arts 113 and 157.2). Thus, the CRC did not shy away from admonishing the parliament based on the latter's obligation to fulfil its legislative functions. Moreover, in 1994 the CRC reiterated this stance in connection with an appeal by the legal chancellor concerning a law regulating surveillance activities by the police.[29] Again, the Riigikogu had attempted to pass on the modalities of authorising such surveillance to the Defence Police, although it included within these rules a requirement that the consent of a justice of Supreme Court must also be obtained. Nevertheless, the CRC ruled that such circumstances had to be spelled out specifically in law, otherwise they would violate basic rights and freedoms. *Inter alia*, the CRC stated, 'That, which the legislature has been authorized or obligated to do by the Constitution, can not be delegated to the executive branch, even temporarily or under the possibility of control by the judiciary.'[30]

The government

A second institution, which was caught more than all others breaching its constitutional powers, was the government and its individual ministers. Of the CRC's 39 cases through 1999, executive-branch breach of power was at issue in 12 of them. Most notably, the matter was raised in December 1996 when a 1994 government decree regulating the import of vodka was challenged by a lower court in a criminal case.[31] At issue was the fact that although the decree referred to Estonia's Consumer Protection Act of 1993 as its basis in law, the text itself did not actually cite a specific paragraph from the law. Thus, the decree was formally unconstitutional. Although in the months that followed the decree's adoption, the Riigikogu amended the Act to authorise the government to take action in the specific sphere of vodka importing, the CRC ruled that such initial violations of constitutional law could not be legalised *post hoc* and were in any case a dangerous sign of legal arbitrariness. The justices argued that on the one hand,

> The objective of the right given to the Government of the Republic to issue decrees is to reduce the burden on the legislature and to hand the technical specification of norms over to the government, so as to guarantee flexible administrative activity as well as to avoid the overburdening of laws with useless individual regulations. At the same time, the circumscription of executive power by law is necessary for maintaining control over the democratic nature of exercising state power, and for preserving general legal order as well as protecting constitutional rights and freedoms.[32]

Thus, while the two aspects were significant, the latter was constitutionally more important.

Likewise, in March 1999 the CRC clipped the government's wings after the latter had attempted to restrict the right to free enterprise by banning the sale of brand-new consumer appliances at municipal markets.[33] The regulations had been part of a general government endeavour to channel the sale of consumer appliances into licensed retail stores. However, ruling on two separate cases brought by lower courts (in which the defendants had been fined by local authorities for violating the government decree), the CRC found that following Article

31 of the constitution on free enterprise[34] such restrictions could only be legislated by law. The relevant point in the decree was therefore declared unconstitutional.

Government ministers

The issue of government ministers overstepping their legal prerogatives arose in the CRC only three times during its first six years. In all of these cases, the respective decrees were declared unconstitutional, although in one case the decree was rescinded before the CRC handed down its ruling. For example, in January 1995 the CRC heard a lower court appeal involving a 1994 decree issued by the Interior Minister concerning residency permits for non-citizens.[35] Although the lower court had ruled that the decree was unconstitutional because a section of it violated the principle of rule of law (Art. 10), the CRC ruled instead that the decree was actually unconstitutional because Estonia's respective law on aliens did not explicitly authorise the Interior Minister to issue such decrees; only the full government had actually been authorised. Thus the ruling was an important case, where the CRC sought to correct an error, which had slipped by not only the lower court, but also the legal chancellor.

Local government

Lastly, the CRC was called upon to adjudicate alleged breaches of power by local authorities. Indeed, in mid-1993 the CRC was instrumental in resolving one of Estonia's most serious ethnopolitical conflicts after the mostly Russian towns of Narva and Sillamäe in Estonia's northeast held local referendums on whether to demand territorial autonomy from Tallinn. The conflict was ignited by minority Russian opposition to a new and controversial Aliens Act, which threatened to revoke many Russians' right to residency in the republic.[36] In their opposition to the new legislation, the local authorities in Narva and Sillamäe decided to play one of their last remaining cards, which was to call a referendum on territorial autonomy. The move was a challenge to Tallinn's central authority, but it also raised the spectre of secessionism in the northeast, since many feared that territorial autonomy would become the basis for a future move to join the Russian Federation. After some intense political mediation by moderate Russian leaders from Tallinn as well as officials from the OSCE, a compromise was struck in which the Estonian government agreed not to interfere with the balloting, while the local Narva and Sillamäe authorities agreed to accept a future ruling from the Constitutional Review Chamber as to the referendums' constitutionality. The deal eventually held, since the referendums took place in mid-July without major incident, while immediately thereafter the Legal Chancellor submitted an appeal to the CRC to declare the referendums unconstitutional.

For the CRC, the autonomy issue was clearly one with important ethnopolitical consequences, which it could not easily overlook. Although the referendums themselves had already been somewhat discredited by news reports indicating widespread procedural errors during the poll, the Estonian government was still keenly interested in having the actions themselves struck down by the CRC. This was made easier by the fact that both the Narva and Sillamäe authorities had themselves formulated their decisions in a contradictory legal matter, leaving the way open for the CRC to dismiss the referendums on essentially technical grounds.[37] More specifically, the Narva and Sillamäe local councils had inappropriately used in their original resolutions the formal term of 'referendum', which according to the constitution's Article 105.1 can be initiated only by the Riigikogu. Although the Sillamäe City Council had also included the term 'resident poll' in its phraseology, the CRC maintained that the essential misuse of terms meant that the two referendums were legally speaking unconstitutional. Additionally, the CRC noted that although both the constitution (Art. 154) as well as Estonia's Local Government Organisation Act give municipalities the right to decide matters of local importance, the question of territorial autonomy was fundamentally a national one, which local governments could not raise unilaterally. Thus, based on these two arguments, the CRC threw out the Narva and Sillamäe referendums, and in turn the rulings were accepted by the two local governments.

In terms of the full range of cases concerning local government breaches of power it is interesting to note that all of these appeals have been raised so far by the Legal Chancellor, and not for instance by the local courts.[38] During his 1993–2000 term in office, Eerik-Juhan Truuväli had to deal in particular with Tallinn city authorities, appealing first a case in 1994 regarding the capital's decision to begin clamping illegally parked cars, and again in late 1998 after the city began charging a fee for cars entering the municipality's old town.[39] In both cases, Truuväli argued that Tallinn had overstepped its legal bounds, since neither the clamping of cars nor the charging of what he alleged was a tax on vehicles entering the old town had been authorised by national legislation. (In the first case, the reason was that the clamping of cars did not exist among the range of punishments allowed by Estonia's Administrative Code, while in the second the charging of entrance fees for vehicles was not included within the list of taxes local governments were permitted to levy according to Estonia's tax code.) These two Tallinn decisions therefore constituted a breach of power. Although both practices were viewed by many people as important measures for controlling traffic in and around the city centre, the legal issues predominated for the CRC, which ruled in the Legal Chancellor's favour and struck down the Tallinn decisions on both occasions. Indeed, in the latter instance, the effect was immediate in that as soon as the ruling was announced, newspaper reporters in cars tried to force their way into the old town for free, and city authorities were left pondering as to what measures they could still take to nevertheless curb the new traffic.

Rights and freedoms

In a number of instances, the legislative acts, which the CRC struck down on legal-technical grounds, also concerned various rights and freedoms. As a result, the CRC's action was in favour of not only legal propriety, but also the defence of constitutional rights. For example, the CRC's ruling in January 1994 striking down the Riigikogu's attempt to authorise the Defence Police to engage in surveillance activities was based on the grounds that such activities must be spelled out in law and not delegated *carte blanche* to the executive. This was in part a technical argument; however, as one Estonian scholar of the CRC has written, the decision also established important principles in regard to rights protection, since:

> [1] the term 'law' used in the restriction clauses of the Fundamental Rights and Freedoms Chapter of the Constitution has to be interpreted as an act of the Riigikogu, and
>
> [2] the restrictions to the fundamental rights and freedoms are unconstitutional if they are not provided for in a way detailed enough to enable the subjects of law to determine their conduct on the basis of informed choice.[40]

Likewise, the CRC applied this principle in its March 1999 ruling concerning the right of individuals to sell brand-new goods at local markets, for in that decision the CRC said that the constitution allowed for such restrictions to be imposed, but that these had to be legislated by law, not government decree.[41]

A more serious case of fundamental rights, however, arose with the passage of a Police Service Act by the Riigikogu in May 1998. This law allowed police commanders to transfer a rank-and-file officer to another department or precinct without the officer's consent even if that entailed an additional change in residence for the officer. President Meri promulgated the law in early June. However, in mid-September the legal chancellor launched an appeal to the CRC charging that the provision regarding officer transfers violated Article 34 of the constitution, which guarantees the right of legal residents to 'choice of residence'.[42] According to the legal chancellor, this principle was completely inviolable, since the constitution does not state (as it does regarding, for example, the right to free enterprise) that this right can be circumscribed by the law. Thus, even though the Riigikogu had attempted to legislate the flexible transfer of police officers via a fully fledged law, the CRC agreed with the legal chancellor that this was not enough and that such a restriction of rights was unconstitutional in whatever form.[43]

In May 1996, President Meri also raised the issue of fundamental rights when he challenged the Riigikogu's passage of the Non-Profit Organisations Act. The law as originally passed by parliament excluded the right of minors to register non-profit organisations. This decision, however, was according to the president in violation of the constitution's Article 48, which states that 'Everyone has the right to form non-profit undertakings and unions.' More specifically, since the constitution does not expressly restrict this right to adults or allow it to be circumscribed in any way by law, the Riigikogu's action had no legal basis. On this score again, the argument was about basic rights, and the CRC concurred with the president.[44]

Public policy-making

As was argued above, two of the most important domains of constitutional review involve institutional prerogatives and the protection of fundamental rights and freedoms. In contemporary debates over constitutional theory, however, a third area of judicial influence has emerged in relation to public policy-making. With the evolution of judicial activism in many countries, supreme and constitutional courts have often become involved in adjudicating (and essentially deciding) important public policy issues hitherto determined solely by the executive and legislative. This trend has raised concerns, however, that the courts are 'distorting' policy by removing it from the domain of direct public control (within the executive and legislature) and transferring it to the judicial arena, where the public has less access. The issue is a significant one for post-communist countries, since as a rule these states have been faced with important, and oftentimes controversial socio-economic reforms. In the event of adroit manipulation by political actors or simple activism by the courts, such policies can easily become 'distorted'.

With regard to this danger, Estonia's system of constitutional review offered few worries in the sense that cases could be brought to the CRC by only three particular institutions. The consequence of such a system was to limit the type and range of cases brought to the CRC, in addition to focusing them more on legal, rather than political arguments. In other constitutional systems (such as in Estonia's Baltic neighbour Lithuania), access to the constitutional court was broader, including the right to appeal by parliamentary deputies or in some cases by individual plaintiffs. The result here was that such parties could use this access for political purposes by challenging public policy, for instance, on certain constitutional grounds. In particular, this could be the case for an opposition minority in parliament angered by some government decision. Constitutional appeals could also be used as a delaying tactic or as a publicity stunt in order to put pressure on a government to back down.

Thus, while the hypothetical danger of policy distortion existed, in Estonia it was generally ruled out because of the narrow structure of the constitutional review mechanism. Indeed, in the CRC's first six years of existence there were only four instances, in which government-initiated and parliament-approved public policies were overturned by the CRC.[45] Moreover, in three of these four cases the CRC interpreted the issue as one of 'rightful expectations', since the state had attempted to reverse policies and procedures, which individuals had come to expect would continue and they were therefore placed at a disadvantage when the state suddenly changed its rules. Only in one celebrated case involving housing privatisation (to be discussed below) did the CRC alter an entire dimension of the Riigikogu's basic policy scheme, eventually resulting in the re-drafting of these provisions.

The Constitutional Review Chamber first addressed the issue of public policy in 1994, when a lower court challenged a 1993 amendment to Estonia's farming legislation, in which tax breaks for new farmers established in 1989 and set to last for five years were prematurely abolished. The issue emerged from a lower court case in which a farmer in the northern county of Harjumaa had sued the local tax authorities for property taxes levied upon him under the new tax amendments. The lower court sided with the farmer and in the process declared the new taxes unconstitutional.

The CRC's ruling turned out to be important, since in it the CRC made one of its first attempts to flesh out the meaning of the constitution's Article 10 concerning the sanctity of rule of law. Specifically, Article 10 states that,

> The rights, freedoms and duties set out in this Chapter shall not preclude other rights, freedoms and duties which arise from the spirit of the Constitution or are in accordance therewith, and conform to the principles of human dignity and of a state based on social justice, democracy, and the rule of law.[46]

For the CRC, this paragraph symbolised the constitution's commitment to general European legal norms and standards, which included the principle that legal acts can not have retroactive effects. As the CRC's ruling declared,

> The Constitution along with laws and other legal acts adopted in compliance with it are intended to establish regularity and stability in society. It is through this that a solid foundation for the legal enjoyment of fundamental rights and freedoms is established and that legal security as a social value develops.[47]

By ruling in favour of the lower court (and indirectly the Harjumaa farmer), the CRC affirmed that individuals had a right to expect the continuation of a government policy as long as the particulars of that policy were in still operation. In the case of the Harjumaa farmer, he had a right to expect his tax break would last for five years, if that was how the state had originally promised. The state had no right to reverse its promise no matter how expensive it might have become for the state or regardless of government or policy shifts.

In later court practice, this interpretation of Article 10 would become a mainstay of judicial principle. For in 1998 the issue arose again, this time in relation to property restitution. In all post-communist countries, a major element of economic restructuring has been property reform. Moreover, in most countries of Central and Eastern Europe this issue has broken down into two parts: privatisation and property restitution. The latter concerns the return or compensation of property to owners, from whom it had been confiscated or nationalised following the original communist seizure of power. Depending on the timing and modalities of that seizure, a number of post-communist parliaments approved elaborate schemes for owners to reclaim their property and/or receive compensation from the state for property since destroyed or lost. In Estonia, a comprehensive Property Reform Foundations Act was adopted in June 1991 under pressure from right-wing forces calling for a full-scale restitution policy. As a result, the new law established wide-ranging procedures, whereby former owners as well as their individual relatives or inheritors could apply either for the return of their former property (e.g. farms, houses, land, industrial buildings) or for appropriate compensation from the state if this property had been lost or declared a state asset (e.g., stocks and bonds).

Although the policy as a whole was not widely contested, many of the specific rules were criticised by more moderate politicians for their liberality, especially in relation to the number of relatives and inheritors or former owners, who were declared eligible to reclaim property, as well as the amount of compensation possible for each claimant. As a consequence, in 1996 the centrist government of prime minister Tiit Vähi began drafting a new law to amend these two provisions as well as reform other aspects of the entire policy. The Property-Reform-Related Legislation Amendment Act of January 1997 decided to remove one category of relatives (the wives of children of former owners) from being eligible to reclaim property, while also abolishing the right to compensation for those claimants whose property had been physically destroyed since nationalisation.

These amendments had been agreed in political terms by the government and parliament and indeed were promulgated into law by President Meri. Yet, fundamentally they were in violation of the principle of rightful expectations, as the rules of the restitution policy had now been altered before the full term of claims processing had been completed. Specifically, in the case of both modifications, the Amendment Act specified that anyone belonging to these two categories and whose restitution application had been processed by their respective local government *before* the Act took effect (in February 1997) could maintain their rights as claimants. Anyone, whose claim, however, had not been processed by then, would lose their rights and either have their claim denied (as in the case of wives of the children of former owners) or see their compensation denied (as in the case of those with destroyed property). The amendments thus had quite an arbitrary effect, since in some counties local commissions had been able to process their restitution applications more quickly, while in others they had not. An individual may have submitted his or her claim in full compliance with the law before the original deadline (in December 1991), but now would potentially see it denied for reasons beyond his or her control.

This contradiction was not raised by either the President (in promulgating the law) or the Legal Chancellor (in ostensibly reviewing all legal acts in Estonia); however, within two months the issue reached the courts and a decision would soon follow from the CRC in September 1998.[48] In April 1997, the government of the small parish of Pühalepa on the Estonian island of Hiiumaa, had approved a pair of property compensation claims after the Amendment Act had taken effect. The local county governor protested these settlements in the local court, claiming that the Pühalepa authorities had to follow the new law and deny any future compensation requests. Yet, the local court overruled the governor and declared instead the compensation clause of the Amendment Act to be in violation of the Constitution's Article 10. In its appeal to the CRC, the Hiiu County Court specifically cited the CRC's 1994 ruling on farming policy and claimed that this was an analogous violation of the principle of rightful expectations. In its ruling on the issue, the CRC agreed with the applicability of Article 10 in this case, and in addition noted the relevance of Article 12 on the equality of individuals before the law. The CRC said that even if the government and parliament had wanted to avoid further social injustices by abolishing the right to compensation, the reversal of policy to the detriment of those still within the policy implementation process was itself a larger social injustice.[49]

This decision, therefore, set a precedent with regard to the second major policy change engendered by the Amendment act – namely, the claimant rights of wives of children of legal owners. In January 1999, the Tallinn Administrative Court received a case involving one such plaintiff, and in due fashion proceeded to throw out the provision of the Amendment Act relating to her restriction. Although later in the CRC, representatives from both the Estonian government as well as the Riigikogu again attempted to claim that the law was in accordance with the constitution, the CRC repeated its arguments from the previous two policy instances and struck down the second policy amendment.[50] In both cases, therefore, all individuals with claims for property were returned to their original equal status in order to allow all of their requests to be processed equally. Although officials in charge of restitution policy were disappointed by their defeat as well as fearful that the CRC's decisions would re-open claims processed in the meantime on the basis of the new amendments, there was nothing they could do but to follow the rulings and deal with the new situation.

Essentially, the issue in these cases was one of consistency in policy, and not the policy itself. A more serious challenge to policy-making by the government and parliament came, however, in 1995 when a lower-court case involving housing privatisation reached the CRC.[51] At issue here was a provision in the Housing Privatisation Act of 1993, which mandated that all Soviet-built apartments were to be subject to privatisation by their occupants regardless of whether the apartment had been built by the state, a municipality, a state enterprise or certain semi-state cooperatives, which also frequently provided housing for their workers. The law was in contradiction to a previous one from 1992, which had sought to prepare the ground for privatisation by formally 're-nationalising' the property of the aforementioned semi-state cooperatives in order to bring all property under state control, for this original law had renationalised only that property which had originally been given to the cooperatives free of charge by the state. Anything that the cooperatives had built with their own resources (including apartment buildings) could continue to belong to the cooperatives, which were now viewed as essentially private enterprises. Still, in the course of developing its full-scale housing privatisation policy in 1992–93 the Estonian government and parliament had become increasingly concerned that because the number of such cooperative-built apartments was fairly large, their continued possession by the cooperatives and exclusion from the general state policy of housing privatisation would deprive the tenants living in these apartments from the privileges of voucher-based privatisation and instead subject them to market prices that the cooperatives would be able to charge for their ostensibly private ownership of the apartments.

The idea to extend the scope of state control over these apartments thus arose from a fear of socio-political tensions if this cooperative property were not renationalised. Yet, within a few months of this decision a former-Soviet retail agricultural cooperative, the ETKVL, refused to privatise some choice apartments it had built in downtown Tallinn, claiming that such state-imposed privatisation terms constituted a violation of its property rights according to Article 32 of the constitution.[52] In a case lodged against the cooperative's ownership rights and brought by some tenants living in the ETKVL apartments, the Tallinn City Court ruled that the ETKVL was indeed not obliged to privatise its apartments on general terms, but rather that if the state placed such demands upon it, it could demand just compensation for such expropriation of property.

After hearing the case in April 1995, the CRC sided with the lower court (and the ETKVL) and struck down the disputed provisions of the Housing Privatisation Act. In its decision, the Chamber noted that, 'To force one subject of private law to hand over its property to another subject of private law can not be considered [a legitimate] pursuit of public interest.'[53]

The ruling thus vindicated the ETKVL's position, while the state's scheme for housing privatisation was dealt an important setback. For the ETKVL, it had successfully used the courts to reverse a political decision by the government and parliament, even though these institutions had sought to defend the broader interest of thousands of apartment tenants. In resolving the dispute, the CRC took a legal stance, denying the state's prerogative to freehandedly reorganise property relations despite the fact that just a few years earlier all property had essentially belonged to the state. Moreover, the CRC was unmoved by arguments in favour of allowing property reform to be quick and decisive so that the country would have a faster transition to a market economy. On the contrary, it refused to allow the property rights of these cooperatives to be fudged, since such enterprises (and in particular the apartments they had built with their own resources) were now essentially private and therefore protected by the 1992 constitution.

In response to its setback, the Riigikogu returned to the drawing board and in December 1995 adopted a new law mandating the same privatisation of apartments, but this time offering cooperatives such as the ETKVL the chance to take the state privatisation vouchers they were set to receive and use them to privatise in turn other land belonging to them. In this way, some sort of meaningful compensation would be offered to the enterprises involved, while also allowing for the privatisation process to encompass the initially left-out tenants. The issue reflected a deep commitment on the part of several members of the Riigikogu to find a just solution to the privatisation problem and to not be deterred by the CRC's earlier ruling. Yet, for the Legal Chancellor, who was now following the matter closely, the new law did not appear to solve the problem, and as result in June 1996 he launched his own appeal to the CRC, seeking the annulment of the new privatisation amendments.

In his arguments, the legal chancellor repeated the points cited by the CRC in its previous ruling, as well as stressing the fact that the new compensation scheme still fell far short of the market value of these apartments and therefore was unjust.[54] In addition, the legal chancellor cited the European Convention on Human Rights and its provisions concerning the sanctity of private property. Although Estonia in ratifying the ECHR had adopted certain reservations with regard to these particular property provisions (citing the need to enact certain necessary socio-economic reforms as part of the transition to a market economy), the legal chancellor argued that the Property Reform Foundations Act (and by implication all laws relating to property reform) had been left out of the specific laws Estonia had cited in connection with its treaty reservation and that therefore Estonia was also bound by the ECHR in this case.

In resolving this second round of debate concerning housing privatisation, the CRC was obliged to approach the issue from a different angle, since in this case the appeal came from the legal chancellor and was therefore an instance of abstract judicial review. This fact altered, in particular, the CRC's standpoint toward the legal chancellor's claim that the compensation being offered by the new privatisation scheme was unjust. On the contrary, ruled the CRC, only the cooperatives themselves could contest through the regular courts the amount of compensation being offered. Abstract judicial review could not be used in this case. Moreover, the CRC noted the fact that since the Riigikogu had now tried twice to resolve this privatisation question, there seemed to be a legitimate public interest at stake, which the Chamber was not in a position to dispute, especially under conditions of abstract review. As a result, the CRC backed away from challenging the Riigikogu again, and instead it denied the legal chancellor's appeal.

International treaties

Article 123 of Estonia's constitution states that in cases where national legislation conflicts with international treaties duly ratified by parliament, the provisions of the international treaty shall apply. As a young state with few international commitments (and even less public awareness of such obligations), this provision was rarely raised in the CRC during its first several years. Still, in the few cases in which it did arise, controversy arose as to how its practical effect should be interpreted. In a major case from 1998, the Constitutional Review Chamber appeared in fact to overlook the relevance of certain international covenants binding on Estonia and instead privileged narrow domestic political imperatives.

One of the first CRC's references to Estonia's international treaty obligations was made in connection with President Meri's appeal of the Non-Profit Organisations Act in 1996.[55] In that decision, the CRC concurred with another of President Meri's arguments which stated that the restriction on the right to establish non-profit organisations to adults was also in violation of Article 15.1 of the UN Convention on the Rights of the Child, which Estonia had ratified in 1992. In its ruling, the CRC made explicit reference to Article 123 of the constitution as a further basis for its finding in favour of the president.

Similarly, the CRC was swayed by international arguments in a May 1998 decision concerning a government decree regulating the validity of seamen's passports for citizens and non-citizens. The government's decree differentiated between the two status categories by allowing citizen seamen full rights to enter and exit Estonia regardless of the national registry of the ship on which they were working, while non-citizen seamen would have this travel right only if they were working on an Estonian-registered vessel. The CRC, hearing the case on appeal from a lower court (which had in turn ruled on a specific case brought by a non-citizen seaman), ruled that the government's decree was in violation of Article 5 of the International Labor Organisation's Convention No. 108, which governs the issuing of seamen's passports.[56] The Chamber again made specific reference to Article 123, while Chief Justice Rait Maruste submitted a concurrent opinion recalling Estonia's political decision to join the EU and the responsibility that this would increasingly place on the country to respect *inter alia* the free movement of persons.

Yet, arguably the CRC faltered with regard to international law in February 1998 when it implicitly sanctioned the imposition of Estonian language requirements for candidates running in parliamentary and local government elections in contradiction to Article 25 of the International Covenant on Civil and Political Rights.[57] The measures were originally passed by parliament in November 1997 through amendments made to the Language Act. The amendments included two dimensions, the first concerning language requirements for electoral candidates, and the second mandating a tightening of Estonian language proficiency requirements for non-Estonian employees in both the public and private sectors. In vetoing the bill the first time around, President Meri cited two considerations. First, he argued that the language requirements for state- and private-sector employees had been worded too vaguely, that they therefore violated the constitution's Article 11, which states that 'Rights and freedoms may be restricted only in accordance with the Constitution. Such restrictions must be necessary in a democratic society and shall not distort the nature of the rights and freedoms restricted.' In this respect, the President maintained that the ambiguously worded language requirements would distort the right of individuals to non-discrimination in employment. Secondly, the president claimed that because the task of controlling an electoral candidate's knowledge of Estonian would according to the law be assigned to the executive branch (specifically the Minister of Education), this provision would constitute a serious violation of the separation of powers (Art. 4 of the constitution) since the executive would potentially be able to harass these candidates later on if they were elected members of parliament.

Admittedly, the president, too, did not cite the ICCPR in arguing against the electoral language requirements nor did he invoke the supremacy of international treaties. Politically, it was easier for him to stress the legal technicalities, instead of appearing to defend minority Russian interests. However, the Constitutional Review Chamber viewed the situation differently, since it had by this time set a precedent of frequently adjudicating cases based on arguments not expressly raised by the applicants themselves. In this instance, therefore, the CRC could have argued persuasively that language requirements for electoral candidates ran counter to the ICCPR's Article 25.[58] The argument behind this logic would have been that the democratic electoral process must be completely free and that voters must be allowed to choose whomever they wish to represent them without the pre-selection or restriction of candidates based on discriminatory rules (such as gender, education, property ownership, and also language). To be sure, an elected body can mandate just one language as its operating language. However, in this case the 'electoral market' – and not the state – must be the one to force candidates to know enough of the state language in order to be a credible candidate and do an effective job once in office.

In adopting its original law, the Riigikogu had clearly been motivated by nationalist desires to make sure that no non-Estonian-speaking person was elected to parliament or a local council, where he or she would not be able to perform their duties because of insufficient language skills. This was particularly the fear regarding municipalities in heavily Russian northeast Estonia, since in local elections non-citizens had the right to vote (Art. 156 of the constitution) and in these municipalities ethnic Russian candidates were more likely to be elected. Admittedly, the constitution's Article 6, which enshrines Estonian as the state language, also requires by implication that the local councils be run in Estonian (whatever their ethnic composition). However, if several of the council members were to turn out to be non-Estonian-speaking, then the councils would effectively become Russian-speaking and illegal. As a result, the sponsors of the bill in parliament (mostly from the nationalist Pro Patria party) were looking for a way to nip the non-Estonian-speaking candidate problem in the bud.

In its ruling, the CRC was ultimately swayed by these nationalist arguments, for although the CRC struck down the amendments to the Language Act, it did so precisely on the basis of the legal-technical arguments, and indeed rejected most of the rights-based considerations.[59] In addition to recognising the President's argument that allowing the executive branch to enforce the level of language knowledge of elected MPs would be a violation of the separation of powers, the CRC also raised a second technical argument, which was that the restrictions had been incorrectly legislated. Namely, because the new requirements were a matter of electoral procedure, the CRC noted that such changes had to be legislated through the respective laws governing Riigikogu and local elections and not through the Language Act as such. What was more, these two electoral laws were among those acts required by Article 104 of the constitution to be passed by an absolute majority of the parliament, which was not the case with amending the Language Act. Thus, the CRC stuck wholly to technical arguments.

Indeed, in responding to the rights-based issues, the CRC dismissed these, citing both the constitution's Article 6 as well as, more interestingly, the constitution's Preamble as justifying language requirements. In particular, the Preamble's fifth paragraph declares that the Estonian state shall be one, which guarantees 'the preservation of the Estonian nation and culture through the ages'. For the justices of the CRC, this was an important principle, based on which the state had the right to take measures, which protected the Estonian language, to the extent that language was viewed as an essential element of Estonian nationhood. Moreover, the CRC attempted to link the issue to effective democracy by arguing that,

> Article 1 of the Constitution declares that Estonia is a democratic republic. Democracy fulfils its objective only when it functions. One pre-condition for the functioning of democracy is that those individuals who exercise power understand wholly what is happening in Estonia and use in their dealings one [single] communicative system. Thus, in a representative democracy as well as in the business of the state the establishment in Estonia of a requirement to use Estonian language is in harmony with the public interest, as well as justified from the perspective of historical-derived circumstances.[60]

While this argument would seem entirely valid for requiring the use of Estonian in local council or business, it did not address in any way the issue of restricting candidate rights during elections themselves. In its ruling, the CRC left out any mention of the ICCPR and thus gave general sanction to official language enforcement measures beyond what international covenants allow.

Moreover, the CRC reiterated its stance in November 1998 after the issue came up again via a lower court and in relation to the specific case of a local government deputy.[61] This time the CRC struck down provisions of the original Language Act (not the 1997 amendments), which had established (in general terms) language requirements for local deputies as well as delegated the enforcement of those requirements to the government.[62] The CRC again said that any language requirements had to be legislated via the local government electoral law and that such restrictions had to be specific. Admittedly, in this new ruling the CRC acknowledged the argument that any restrictions of rights have to comply with the constitution's Article 11 on democratic norms. However, it also implied that the goal of protecting the Estonian nation and culture (as stated in the constitution's preamble) was an overriding concern and that language requirements had merely to avoid being too excessive.[63]

Conclusion

In its first six years of operation, Estonia's constitutional review mechanism served to lay down several important principles of constitutional procedure as well as political balance. Through appeals launched by the president, the legal chancellor as well as the lower courts, the Constitutional Review Chamber had to deal with a wide range of issues relating to the separation of powers, the breach of powers, fundamental rights and freedoms, public policy-making, and international treaties. In its rulings on these five issue areas, the CRC took in particular a hard line in relation to (1) the requirement that rights and freedoms could only be restricted by law, and (2) that state institutions could not overstep their authority when adopting legal acts. Indeed, the numerous cases, which emerged in these domains, seemed to attest to some of the growing pains of Estonian democracy as the parliament, government, individual ministers, and local governments all learned to play their roles and fulfil their constitutional responsibilities. In this respect, the CRC helped prove the value of such oversight mechanisms not only for constitutionalism, but also for democratic consolidation. For in such budding democracies, the powers and prerogatives of state institutions had to be monitored, both to settle political disputes between institutions as well as to prevent the abuse of power. On many occasions such controversies were over legal-technical matters. Moreover, one cannot point to any single case as being necessarily monumental for securing constitutionalism. They all contributed their own stone to building up Estonia's new constitutional edifice and its proper defence. Their key effect was in safeguarding the system as a whole – for Estonia and for future membership in the European Union.

Notes

1 European Commission, 'Conclusion', in *Agenda 2000: Commission Opinion on Estonia's Application for Membership of the European Union* (Brussels, 1997).
2 European Commission, 'Functioning of the Judiciary' in *Agenda 2000.*
3 P. Roosma, 'Methods of Constitutional Interpretation in the System of Checks and Balances: Development and Practice of Constitutional Review in Estonia' (A Thesis on Comparative Constitutional Law, Legal Studies Department, Central European University, Budapest, 1997); R. Maruste and H. Schneider, 'Constitutional Review in Estonia: Its Principal Scheme, Practice and Evaluation', in R. Müllerson *et al.* (eds), *Constitutional Reform and International Law in Central and Eastern Europe* (The Hague, Kluwer Law International, 1998); P. Roosma, 'Constitutional Review under 1992 Constitution', *Juridica International*, 3 (1998), 35–42; H. Schneider, 'Relations Between State Bodies in Implementing Constitution', *Juridica International*, 3 (1998), 10–24.
4 For similar categorisations, see Schneider 'Relations', and Roosma, 'Protection of Fundamental Rights and Freedoms in Estonian Constitutional Jurisprudence', *Juridica International*, 4 (1999), 35–44.
5 A. R. Brewer-Carías, *Judicial Review in Comparative Law* (Cambridge, Cambridge University Press, 1989), p. 124.
6 See, for example, S. Mainwaring *et al.*, *Issues in Democratic Consolidation* (Notre Dame, University of Notre Dame Press, 1992); G. Di Palma, *To Craft Democracies* (Berkeley, University of California Press, 1990); J. Linz and A. Stepan, *Problems of Democratic Transition and Consolidation: Southern Europe, South America, and Post-Communist Europe* (London, The Johns Hopkins University Press, 1996); but also even J. Elster and R. Slagstad, *Constitutionalism and Democracy* (Cambridge, Cambridge University Press, 1988).
7 For background, see G. von Rauch, *The Baltic States: The Years of Independence, Estonia, Latvia, Lithuania, 1917–1940* (New York, St Martin's Press, 1974).
8 The proposal was to have the Supreme Court be the institution, which would promulgate all laws, and thereby serve as an instance of constitutional review over all legislation.

However, this was dropped because of the obvious complexity such a system would entail; Roosma, *Methods*, pp. 7–8.

9 Maruste and Schneider, 'Constitutional Review'.

10 V. Pettai, 'Estonia: Positive and Negative Engineering', in A. Pravda and J. Zielonka (eds), *Institutional Engineering in Eastern Europe* (Oxford, Oxford University Press, 2001), pp. 111–138; also, R. Taagepera, 'Estonia's Constitutional Assembly, 1991–1992', *Journal of Baltic Studies* 25:3 (1994), 211–232.

11 Roosma, *Methods*, pp. 15–27; V. Peep, *Põhiseaduse ja põhiseaduse assamblee* (Tallinn, Juura, Õigusteabe Aktsiaselts, 1997).

12 The full Supreme Court can also hear constitutional review cases, if one member of the CRC requests it.

13 For more on the difference between diffuse and concentrated systems, see A. R. Brewer-Carías, *Judicial Review in Comparative Law*; E. McWhinney, *Supreme Courts and Judicial Law-Making: Constitutional Tribunals and Constitutional Review* (Dordrecht: Martinus Nijhoff Publishers, 1986); H. Schwartz, 'The New East European Constitutional Courts', in A. E. D. Howard (ed.), *Constitution Making in Eastern Europe* (Washington, D, The Woodrow Wilson Center Press, 1993).

14 All English-language quotations of the Estonian constitution are taken from the translation issued by the Estonian Translation and Legislative Support Centre, which has been officially sanctioned for informational purposes. 'Constitution of the Republic of Estonia', *Estonian Legislation in Translation, Legal Acts of Estonia* 1 (1996).

15 'Õiguskantsleri seadus' [Legal Chancellor Act] (1999) section 2. Indeed, according to Eerik-Juhan Truuväli, Estonia's Legal Chancellor from 1993 to 2000, this level of review has been one of the most important, since most questionable issues have been resolved precisely at this stage. Interview, 3 September 1999, Tallinn.

16 Over the years, many politicians have indeed used this provision in order to get an immediate opinion on particular political disputes.

17 'Õiguskantsleri seadus' [Legal Chancellor Act] (1999), section 16.

18 In addition, Estonia's 15 county governors are also responsible for reviewing the legality of local government acts.

19 'Constitution', Art. 142.

20 Data collected by the office of the legal chancellor.

21 As noted above, the legal chancellor can also influence the drafts of legal acts to be adopted by the government, since he is sent all materials, which are considered by the cabinet. However, this is only an informal review occasion.

22 'Põhiseaduslikkuse järelevalve kohtumenetluse seadus' [The Constitutional Review Court Procedure Act], *Riigi Teataja* 1, 25 (1993), Art. 435.

23 For instance, in a November 1994 ruling nullifying a Tallinn City Council decision to begin clamping illegally parked cars in the city, the CRC cited its own arguments concerning procedural violations by the council, which were in addition to the legal chancellor's arguments concerning property rights. See 'Riigikohtu põhiseaduslikkuse järelevalve kolleegiumi otsus', *Riigi Teataja*, 1, 80, 1377 (1994).

24 One 1998 appeal by the legal chancellor concerning a local municipality was submitted, but later withdrawn.

25 'Riigikohtu põhiseaduslikkuse järelevalve kolleegiumi otsus', *Riigi Teataja*, 1, 43, 636 (1993).

26 'Riigikohtu põhiseaduslikkuse järelevalve kolleegiumi otsus', *Riigi Teataja*, 1 , 12, 229 (1994).

27 'Riigikohtu põhiseaduslikkuse järelevalve kolleeiumi otsus', *Riigi Teataja*, 1, 80, 1379 (1994), 2275.

28 'Riigikohtu põhiseaduslikkuse järelevalve kolleegiumi otsus', *Riigi Teataja*, 1, 72/73, 1052 (1993).

29 'Riigikohtu põhiseaduslikkuse järelevalve kolleegiumi otsus', *Riigi Teataja*, 1, 8, 129 (1994).
30 'Riigikohtu põhiseaduslikkuse järelevalve kolleegiumi otsus', *Riigi Teataja*, 1, 8, 129 (1994), 228.
31 'Riigikohtu põhiseaduslikkuse järelevalve kolleegiumi otsus', *Riigi Teataja*, 1 1997, 4, 28 (1996) and 'Riigikohtu põhiseaduslikkuse järelevalve kolleegiumi otsus', *Riigi Teataja* I 1997, 4, 29 (1996).
32 'Riigikohtu põhiseaduslikkuse järelevalve kolleegiumi otsus', *Riigi Teataja*, 1 1997, 4, 28 (1996), 147.
33 'Riigikohtu põhiseaduslikkuse järelevalve kolleegiumi otsus', *Riigi Teataja*, 3, 9, 89 (1999).
34 Article 31: 'Estonian citizens have the right to engage in enterprise and to form commercial undertakings and unions. Conditions and procedure for the exercise of this right may be provided by law.'
35 'Riigikohtu põhiseaduslikkuse järelevalve kolleegiumi otsus', *Riigi Teataja*, 1, 9, 112 (1995).
36 This was on top of Estonia's exclusionary 1992 citizenship law, which denied automatic citizenship to most Russians in the country because they were Soviet-era occupation immigrants and thus considered non-citizens.
37 'Riigikohtu põhiseaduslikkuse järelevalve kolleegiumi otsus', *Riigi Teataja*, 1, 59, 841 (1993) and 'Riigikohtu põhiseaduslikkuse järelevalve kolleegiumi otsus', *Riigi Teataja*, 1, 61, 890 (1993).
38 The president, obviously, cannot touch local government decisions, as his powers pertain only to parliamentary acts.
39 'Riigikohtu põhiseaduslikkuse järelevalve kolleegiumi otsus', *Riigi Teataja*, 1, 80, 1377 (1994) and 'Riigikohtu põhiseaduslikkuse järelevalve kolleegiumi otsus', *Riigi Teataja*, 1, 80, 1378 (1994). Also, 'Riigikohtu põhiseaduslikkuse järelevalve kolleegiumi otsus', *Riigi Teataja*, 1, 113/114, 1887 (1998).
40 Roosma, *Methods*, p. 60.
41 'Riigikohtu põhiseaduslikkuse järelevalve kolleegiumi otsus', *Riigi Teataja*, 3, 9, 89 (1999).
42 Section 34: Everyone who is legally in Estonia has the right to freedom of movement and to choice of residence.
43 'Riigikohtu põhiseaduslikkuse järelevalve kolleegiumi otsus', *Riigi Teataja*, 1, 104, 1742 (1998).
44 'Riigikohtu põhiseaduslikkuse järelevalve kolleegiumi otsus', *Riigi Teataja*, 1, 35, 737 (1996).
45 'Riigikohtu põhiseaduslikkuse järelevalve kolleegiumi otsus', *Riigi Teataja*, 1, 66, 1159 (1994); 'Riigikohtu põhiseaduslikkuse järelevalve kolleegiumi otsus', *Riigi Teataja*, 1, 42, 655 (1995); 'Riigikohtu põhiseaduslikkuse järelevalve kolleegiumi otsus', *Riigi Teataja*, 1, 86/87, 1434 (1998); 'Riigikohtu põhiseaduslikkuse järelevalve kolleegiumi otsus', *Riigi Teataja*, 3, 9, 90 (1999).
46 'Constitution', Art. 10.
47 'Riigikohtu põhiseaduslikkuse järelevalve kolleegiumi otsus', *Riigi Teataja*, 1, 66, 1159 (1994), 1868.
48 'Riigikohtu põhiseaduslikkuse järelevalve kolleegiumi otsus', *Riigi Teataja*, 1, 86/87, 1434 (1998).
49 *Ibid.*
50 'Riigikohtu põhiseaduslikkuse järelevalve kolleegiumi otsus', *Riigi Teataja*, 3, 9, 90 (1999).
51 'Riigikohtu põhiseaduslikkuse järelevalve kolleegiumi otsus', *Riigi Teataja*, 1, 42, 655 (1995).

52 Section 32.1: The property of every person is inviolable and equally protected. Property may be expropriated without the consent of the owner only in the public interest, in the cases and pursuant to the procedure provided by law, and for fair and immediate compensation. Everyone whose property is expropriated without his or her consent has the right of recourse to the courts and to contest the expropriation, the compensation, or the amount thereof.

53 'Riigikohtu põhiseaduslikkuse järelevalve kolleegiumi otsus', *Riigi Teataja,* 1, 42, 655 (1995), 1405.

54 'Riigikohtu põhiseaduslikkuse järelevalve kolleegiumi otsus', *Riigi Teataja,* 1, 87, 1558 (1996).

55 'Riigikohtu põhiseaduslikkuse järelevalve kolleegiumi otsus', *Riigi Teataja,* 1, 35, 737 (1996).

56 'Riigikohtu põhiseaduslikkuse järelevalve kolleegiumi otsus', *Riigi Teataja,* 1, 49, 752 (1998).

57 Estonia ratified the ICCPR on 21 January 1991.

58 To wit, 'Every citizen shall have the right and the opportunity, without any of the distinctions mentioned in article 2 and without unreasonable restrictions: 1 To take part in the conduct of public affairs, directly or through freely chosen representatives; 2 To vote and to be elected at genuine periodic elections which shall be by universal and equal suffrage and shall be held by secret ballot, guaranteeing the free expression of the will of the electors; 3 To have access, on general terms of equality, to public service in his country.'

59 'Riigikohtu põhiseaduslikkuse järelevalve kolleegiumi otsus', *Riigi Teataja,* 1, 14, 230 (1998).

60 *Ibid.*, p. 409.

61 'Riigikohtu põhiseaduslikkuse järelevalve kolleegiumi otsus', *Riigi Teataja,* 1, 98/99, 1618 (1998).

62 The reason for this additional case stemmed from the fact that in the previous appeal brought by the president only *amendments* to the Language Act were considered. In the Language Act itself, however, there were general provisions that the CRC also found unconstitutional, but could not consider because the original appeal by the president did not raise them. Indeed, since the Language Act was a law that had already been passed, objections to it could not even be appealed by the president, but only by the legal chancellor or via the lower courts. In this case, the Electoral Commission of Estonia had attempted to remove a Russian deputy from the town of Maardu for not knowing enough Estonian, but the district court ruled that the case's basis in the Language Act was unconstitutional.

63 Ultimately, the *Riigikogu* did pass amendments to both electoral laws establishing language requirements for electoral candidates, and President Meri promulgated the amendments despite protests from both Russian community leaders as well as organisations such as the OSCE and the Council of Europe. The legal chancellor, too, was also opposed to challenging the laws. Thus, the issue remained a thorn in Estonia's human rights record until November 2001, when the Riigikogu finally repealed the amendments under direct pressure from the OSCE and the European Union. The irony was that many of the same deputies who had voted for the language requirements in 1997–98 were now obliged to reverse their vote in the face of international pressure.

Vitalis Nakrošis

6

Assessing governmental capabilities to manage European affairs

The case of Lithuania

When in 1997 Lithuania failed to be invited to the first round of European Union (EU) accession negotiations, the news triggered a frenzy of defensive posturing and finger pointing throughout the Lithuanian political class. The EU policy of the government of Gediminas Vagnorius endured a particularly difficult period, since it was the target of the greatest criticism, not only from the European Commission,[1] but also from the national legislature.[2] In response, the Lithuanian government blamed the EU's pressure to decommission Lithuania's Soviet-era nuclear power plant at Ignalina for the country's failure to secure a place amongst the 'ins'.[3] This analysis attempts to bring a cool head to the debate by arguing that weak governmental capabilities to manage EU matters were the primary factors delaying the progress of Lithuania's accession to the EU.[4]

This research question is important for several reasons. From the theoretical perspective, an analysis of Lithuanian governmental capabilities may shed some light on the evolution of governmental capabilities to manage EU matters in small and post-communist countries. The question resonates with Olsen's argument that the focus of scholarly attention has to be moved from examining formal changes to the EU's organisation and functions to looking at institutional capabilities for action.[5] In addition, since this research question examines the EU's impact on the development of governmental capabilities in Lithuania, it is similar to Grabbe's assertion that it is important to consider the extent to which the EU affects domestic EU policies in the Central and Eastern European countries (CEECs).[6] Lithuania's governmental capabilities for administering EU matters will affect not only Lithuania's ability to benefit from EU membership, but also the EU's governance capacity, in particular the uniform application and enforcement of the *acquis communautaire.*

The importance of government capability extends well beyond Lithuania's EU policy, however. In all transitional countries, state capacity building – needed for the protection of law and order as well as for the enhancement of economic prosperity – is essential in the process of transition. As Norgaard has concluded, 'Lithuania has to improve the technical capacity and administrative efficiency of the state administration' in order to successfully manage the process of economic transition, which involves among other things the regulation of economic activities.[7] Thus, this analysis can help illuminate the extent to which Lithuanian governmental capabilities allow for the effective management of transition and delivery of public goods. Finally, this research question can also shed some light on the current (and future) value and legitimacy of the Lithuanian state, measured in terms of its effectiveness and efficiency in delivering its goals.[8]

It is important to define the relationship between the process of national adaptation to European integration and the evolution of governmental capabilities to administer European affairs.[9] While the analysis of national adaptation is often limited to detailing the substitution of old institutions and policies with new ones in response to explicit or implicit European requirements, the analysis of governmental capabilities has the potential to delve deeper by looking at the extent to which the adaptation process leads to the emergence of adequate governmental capabilities. In addition, the fact that the EU's PHARE programme explicitly refers to reinforcing administrative and institutional capacity in the CEECs as one of its most important objectives allows one to examine the impact of not only domestic reform, but also European efforts to develop governmental capabilities in Lithuania.

Conceptualising governmental capabilities

The development of governmental capabilities will be analysed primarily by looking at Lithuania's ability:

- to transpose EU law (which currently dominates Lithuanian EU policy);
- to anticipate the impact of EU law at the national level;
- to form coherent negotiating positions for representing its interests at the EU level; and
- to implement and enforce the *acquis.*

This analysis is primarily concerned with the adequacy of Lithuanian governmental capabilities or, in other words, the extent to which Lithuanian governmental capabilities allow for the effective administration of various EU matters. Effectiveness is defined here as the degree to which Lithuanian authorities are able to achieve objectives, laid out either separately by the Lithuanian government or jointly by the Lithuanian government and European institutions. Lithuania's governmental capabilities will be analysed by looking at the evolution of institutional constraints upon the effective administration of EU matters. The assumption is that as constraints become less binding, Lithuanian governmental capabilities will become more adequate. It is expected that institutional constraints, defined by internal and external factors, affect

Figure 6.1 Framework for assessing governmental capabilities

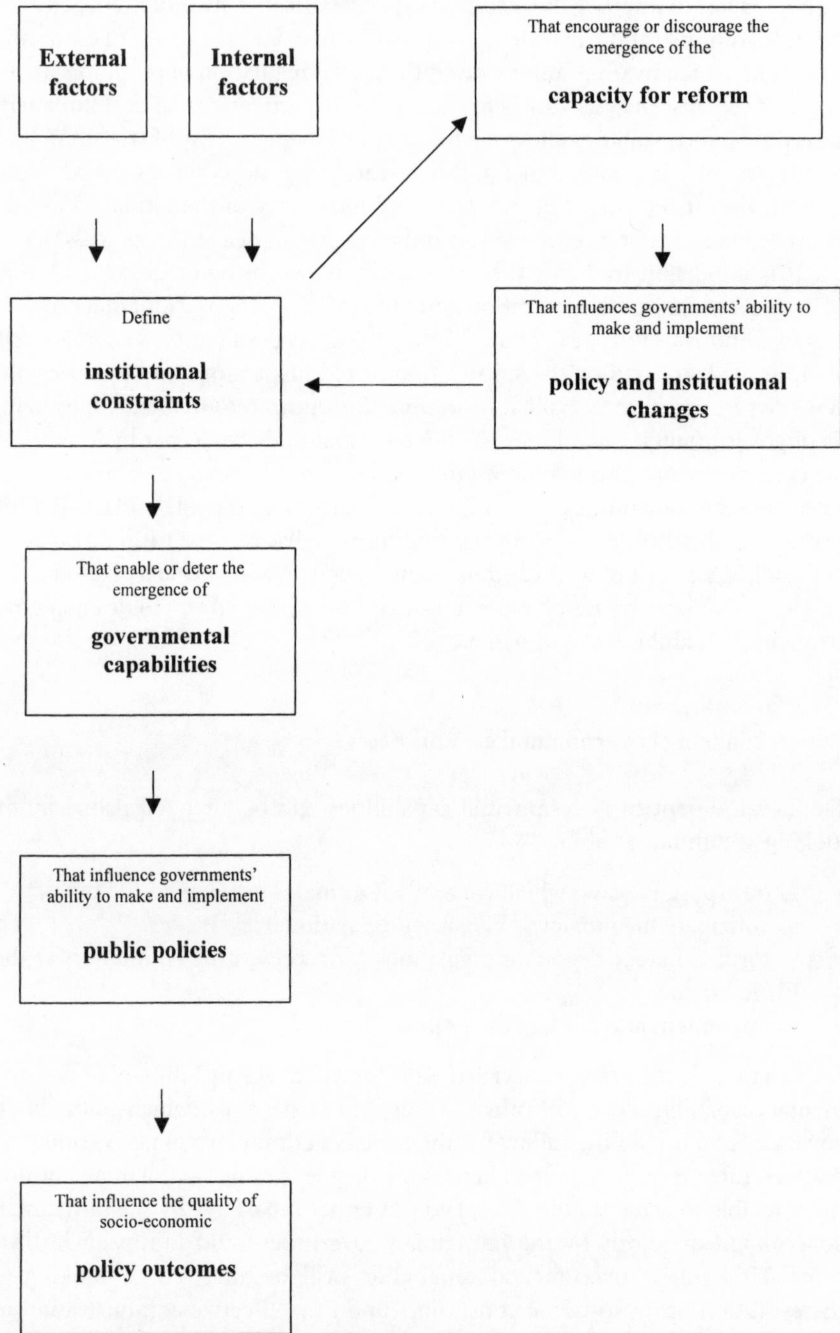

Source: Adapted from R. K. Weaver and B. A. Rockman (eds), *Do Institutions Matter? Government Capabilities in the United States and Abroad*, Washington, DC, The Brookings Institution, p. 9.

governmental capabilities in the way specified in figure 6.1. As the analysis will suggest, the level of constraints on Lithuania's administrative capacities were still quite high in the late 1990s. To illustrate this the analysis will also examine in greater detail Lithuania's management of its National Programme for the Adoption of the *Acquis* (NPAA).

In this analysis, the term 'governmental capabilities' refers to the ability of the Lithuanian government to exercise EU matters through both individual institutions and institutional relationships. This can be contrasted with the primary emphasis of many previous studies on individual institutions. The Commission in its 1997 *avis* and subsequent regular reports on the CEECs utilised the single institution as a main unit of analysis for evaluating administrative and institutional capacity.[10] Similarly, another study stressed the importance of human resources within individual institutions in the adoption of the *acquis*.[11] Yet, the focus on individual institutions is too narrow as it omits institutional relationships, which have a significant impact on governmental capabilities. Institutional relationships are important because the administration of EU affairs includes extensive coordination of inter-ministerial matters at the domestic level, at the EU level and at the domestic–EU interface.[12] From the theoretical perspective, the most appropriate unit for analysis within public administration must not be the single organisation, but, rather, organisational networks.[13]

Since the institutional constraints that affect governmental capabilities are usually defined by a highly complex set of factors, one needs to define the scope of this analysis. It is not aimed to provide an all-encompassing conceptualisation of governmental capabilities. Even if that were possible, the number of factors involved would make the analysis unwieldy. This analysis is primarily concerned with the impact of independent variables found within the administrative and governmental level on the evolution of governmental capabilities. This focus can be in part justified by the fact that Lithuania, along with the other CEECs, inherited an administrative structure, which is highly dependent on political institutions. Its power to administer EU matters is strengthened by the very nature of the EU, which delegates the primary responsibility for EU matters to the administrative level.

One must recognise that a number of institutional constraints matter to governmental capabilities. The most significant of these that are examined in this analysis are the following:

1 Institutional constraints that affect capabilities of individual institutions

- ministerial organisation;
- number of officials and their distribution;
- staff management, including recruitment, training, career development, pay conditions, turnover;
- ministerial decision-making, including intra-departmental relationships;

2 Institutional constraints that affect institutional relationships

- government organisation, including the establishment of coordinating institutions or committees;
- distribution of officials and their mobility within the civil service;
- formal and informal governmental decision-making processes, including coordination and implementation processes and culture;
- institutional networks, including the integration of interest organisations into the policy process and the emergence of 'policy communities'.

Political factors are also addressed in this analysis, although it is difficult to hypothesise the way in which they affect governmental capabilities. While political factors have the potential to influence considerably governmental capabilities – through individual personalities, party politics in the legislature and executive, and coalition politics in the cabinet – their impact is highly contingent on the uncertain transition environment, which depends, among other things, on the ideological composition of governing coalitions. Finally, it should be noted that both the evolution of judicial capabilities and the impact of institutional constraints at the sub-national level fall outside the scope of this study.

The new institutionalist approach

This analysis adopts the new institutionalist approach as the most relevant framework for the assessment of governmental capabilities to manage European matters in transition countries. As is well known, the basic claim of this approach is that institutions matter. First, it adopts a wide interpretation of what constitutes an institution. According to one definition, institutions include formal institutions, informal institutions and conventions, the norms and symbols embedded in them as well as policy instruments and procedures.[14] A key advantage of this definition is that it allows for an examination of the informal aspects of politics and policy-making, which are crucial for the understanding of post-communist politics and policy-making.

More specifically, the chapter uses two conceptions of new institutional theory – both normative and historical institutionalism – to analyse the evolution of governmental capabilities in Lithuania.[15] The first school of normative institutionalism is associated with the work of March and Olsen.[16] Its most fundamental proposition is that institutional behaviour is shaped by the logic of appropriateness defined by the values internal to the institution. By shaping institutional behaviour, institutions can constrain or facilitate policy change. It is the logic of appropriateness that guides institutional behaviour by setting 'parameters of acceptable behaviour'.[17]

The analysis tests the proposition that institutional and policy changes are dependent on the extent to which the old logic of appropriateness is institutionalised.[18] In other words, it is expected that the more institutions are embedded in existing institutional settings, the less latitude there will be for policy and institutional reform. Institutionalisation (or embeddedness) is defined here as 'the emergence of enduring practices and rules, structures of meaning, and resources'.[19] In order to explain different levels of embeddedness, which vary across institutions and more significantly across nations, one must make cross-institutional and cross-national comparisons. Thus, a comparative dimension is introduced into this analysis. Emphasis is put on possible sources of divergence between Lithuania and other countries, where different sets of constraints impact upon the development of governmental capabilities.

The propositions of another school of new institutionalism, historical institutionalism, will be tested in this analysis as well. Its fundamental proposition lies in 'path-dependency', according to which reform outcomes are dependent on initial conditions. In the context of transition, it is useful to interpret this argument in two ways by employing two different timespans. First, path-dependency can be equated with the impact that inherited institutions exert upon administrative reform, thus linking the evolution of governmental capabilities to, for example, a country's post-communist heritage. Alternatively, path-dependency can be equated with the impact of initial decisions on administrative reform, thus linking the evolution of governmental capabilities to policy and institutional choices made during the transition. Therefore, it is predicted that both institutions inherited from the past affect the evolution of governmental capabilities through constraints upon decision-making[20] and initial reform choices affect the evolution of governmental capacities by foreclosing other options later on.

Historical institutionalism assesses both the evolutionary and transformative models of change.[21] From the evolutionary perspective, institutional change is viewed as incremental and not challenging deeply embedded institutions. Thus, in our context, one can predict that the evolution of governmental capabilities is subject to a series of incremental rather than radical changes. This analysis also expects different institutions to be subject to different change patterns depending on their embeddedness. Alternatively, from the transformative point of view, institutional development can be seen as interrupted by a window of opportunity that brings the possibility for significant change, but does not guarantee it. If such opportunities are exploited, policy or institutional changes may be introduced, which entail clear departures from previously established patterns. It is important to note that both internal and external forces can 'open' a window of opportunity. Thus, the evolution of governmental capabilities is marked by a window of opportunity, which may lead to significant policy or institutional changes.

In sum, the first section of this analysis outlines the main externally derived institutional constraints on Lithuanian capabilities to manage EU matters, namely those required by the EU itself. I will argue that during the late 1990s there was a noticeable discrepancy between the nature of Lithuanian administration and the EU's requirements. The second section attempts to determine the extent to which Lithuanian governmental capabilities for administering EU matters were hampered by domestic institutional constraints on the Lithuanian EU policy, in particular the administration of the National Programme for the Adoption of the *Acquis*. These institutional constraints are divided into the constraint of inadequate human resources and that of ineffective policy coordination. The third section focuses on the EU's impact on the evolution of governmental capabilities in Lithuania through its financial assistance and agenda-setting instruments.

The impact of external factors on Lithuania's administration

This section provides a detailed examination of the external factors affecting governmental capabilities to manage European affairs. The analysis assumes that they affect governmental capabilities by defining institutional constraints, as specified in figure 6.1. In addition, the binding character of institutional constraints depends primarily on the extent to which the nature of the Lithuanian administration (internal factors) matches the EU-level requirements (external factors).[22] To determine the specific manifestations of a 'mismatch', it is necessary to undertake a detailed examination of EU requirements and the characteristics of Lithuania's state administration.

One of the main characteristics of the EU is the very large volume of EU legislation. In the mid-1990s it was estimated that the *acquis* consisted of over 20,000 regulations and 2,000 directives, with approximately 80 per cent of member states' socio-economic legislation originating in the EU.[23] For a country like Lithuania, however, its ability to adjust to this volume of EU legislation within a relatively short period of time was limited by the relatively small size of its administrative structure – just 11,000 officials. To be sure, administrative adjustment pressures varied considerably across sectors. But this also put limits on the even evolution of governmental capabilities across different policy fields. Therefore, well-developed policy areas in the EU, such as agriculture or environment, posed more problems for Lithuanian authorities than underdeveloped policy areas, such as transport.

Lithuania's accession to the Common Agricultural Policy (CAP) was particularly problematic, since it contained numerous provisions, ranging from the enforcement of veterinary standards, to the imposition of various production quotas, to the monitoring of 'set-aside' rules. The following example was particularly illustrative. In 1995, a newly-built Lithuanian pig farm, with an annual capacity of 54,000 animals and in full compliance with EU veterinary standards, applied for an export licence to the EU market. The Commission, however, refused to issue an export licence on the grounds that there was no guarantee that every pig within a 300–kilometre radius of the farm had been vaccinated against swine fever – this despite the fact that the required 300-kilometre radius actually extended beyond Lithuania's jurisdiction into neighbouring countries.[24] In this respect, complying with EU institutional rules turned out to be simply impossible. In addition, administrative adjustment was made difficult by the 'moving target' problem. This involved the fact that certain *acquis* areas, such as finance, agriculture and structural funds, were subject to radical overhaul, which in turn rendered the adjustment process in the CEECs even more precarious.

Another feature of the EU was its emphasis on the regulation of economic activities. Adjusting Lithuania's administration to the European pattern of regulation required huge reform efforts, including the establishment of new regulatory institutions and the development of new regulatory skills. Lithuania inherited regulatory frameworks incompatible with those of the EU member states, particularly in the area of environment, which was significantly underdeveloped. Regulation in Lithuania still followed the rule inherited from the communist tradition according to which 'everything that is not explicitly allowed is forbidden'. Moreover, a number of European regulatory requirements (e.g. air quality standards) entailed significant policy innovations for the member states themselves,[25] let alone new members like Lithuania. The principle of mutual recognition of regulatory standards (e.g. professional standards) required knowledge of regulatory legislation that was enacted not only by the EU, but also by its member states. It was hardly surprising then that the extent of reforms demanded by the EU meant that an entire decade could well pass before regulation was made more effective, even in the most advanced CEECs.[26]

In addition to regulatory requirements, CEE administrations needed to adjust to European financial control requirements. In order for the CEECs to accede to the CAP and other structural funds, their financial control mechanisms had to be brought in line with those of the EU. The development of financial control, much like the development of regulatory institutions, was again limited by the post-communist legacy. The CEECs inherited no independent financial control or audit institutions and they had 'no experience of modern "project administration" including public procurement with contracts awarded through tendering procedures'.[27] During the late 1990s, financial control in Lithuania was executed through rudimentary laws on budgeting, state control and local self-government. In this respect, the Lithuanian government still needed to strengthen its internal financial control functions and establish an external performance control function.

Lastly, the implementation and enforcement of European legislation frequently required significant human and budgetary resources, often more than applicant countries could afford. The CEE 'skeleton public administrations and skeleton budgets' put limits on their abilities to apply the *acquis* effectively.[28] This constraint appears to have been most acute in the case of environmental legislation. The adoption and enforcement of about 300 pieces of EU environmental legislation would be impossible without significantly strengthening existing environmental institutions. For example, in 1998 it was estimated that approximately 15 new officials would need to be recruited to the Lithuanian Environment Ministry and another 20 to its regional departments by 2002 in order to undertake the heavy workload.[29] To ensure effective implementation and enforcement of environmental provisions, new institutions would need to be established, including a national agency for environmental protection or a chemical substances control agency. In terms of budgetary resources, it was estimated in 1998 that the implementation of only 15 of the most costly pieces of EU environmental legislation would require approximately 3.1 billion ECU. Excluding the most expensive directive (70/220/EEC on car pollution), which would be paid for primarily by the private sector, in 2010 the implementation of the remaining 14 most costly pieces of environmental legislation would cost Lithuania a projected 381.9 million ECU, which amounted to 6 per cent of Lithuania's 1996 gross domestic product.[30]

With regard to the limited availability of human resources it is important to note that this constraint was more restrictive for some CEECs than others due to significant variations in the size of CEE administrations. The similar scope of EU matters and, in turn, similar workloads with which all applicant countries were confronted rendered the size constraint more binding in Lithuania, where approximately 11,000 officials were employed in the central government. By contrast, some 100,000 officials were employed in the Polish central government.[31] Thus, if Poland appeared to be facing a scarcity of human resources in the transposition of the *acquis*,[32] the problem would be even more severe in Lithuania.

Yet, this constraint did not preclude Estonia and Slovenia, both with relatively small civil services, from gaining entry into the first wave of EU accession negotiations. This can be explained by two major factors. First, the size constraint had not yet fully materialised by 1997. The readiness of the CEECs to accede to the EU was judged by a number of criteria, and progress in implementing and enforcing the *acquis* was not the most important. It has been pointed out that 'the capacity to transpose and implement the *acquis* [. . .] was of little importance for the selection of formal negotiation partners. Although Slovenia's score on this point fell [sic] of all associated countries except Bulgaria and Romania, it was admitted to the top group due to its good political and economic record'.[33] Yet, with time there was a gradual shift of focus from the transposition of the *acquis* to the application of EU laws and regulations, which meant that the human resources constraint would become more acute, posing greater difficulties for Lithuania, not to mention the other small states of CEE. Second, the factor of population size must be viewed in the context of other constraints, particularly the human resource constraint. The Hungarian experience showed that governmental capabilities were unlikely to be enhanced by merely increasing the number of officials: while the number of Hungarian officials grew from 65,000 in 1989 to some 100,000 in 1995, the effectiveness of public administration, including coordination, did not improve.[34]

As a result, it is quite likely that the constraint of an inadequate civil service will become even more binding after EU membership, since it will bring the loss of a significant number of the most experienced and senior staff, as they leave to serve in EU institutions. This was the case in many countries, including Spain, where civil servants from the Spanish accession management team took up positions in the EU institutions or the Spanish Permanent Representation.[35] As a consequence, the Spanish government lost a considerable amount of its capacity to coordinate its domestic decision-making on EU matters.[36] For Lithuania, EU membership will heighten the need to improve its ability to formulate coherent negotiating positions to ensure that its interests are well represented at the EU level.[37]

Domestic constraints on capacity building

The foundation of Lithuania's EU policy from an internal point of view was essentially laid by an important governmental decree from 1995. This decree established the general institutional structure, which would consist of a high-level coordination committee (the Governmental Commission for European Integration), its secretariat, a coordinating institution (the European Integration Department within the Ministry of Foreign Affairs (MFA)) and, finally, special European affairs units within every ministry through which the involvement of policy ministries was ensured. The MFA assumed the lead responsibility for EU matters, stemming from its responsibility for coordinating external economic issues and the management of foreign affairs.

During the second half of the 1990s, this framework became the institutional baseline for policy implementation; however, this did not mean that subsequent institutional evolution was not marked by significant changes. After the establishment of the initial machinery in mid-1995, a first window of opportunity to introduce significant institutional changes opened in late 1996. Immediately after the autumn 1996 parliamentary election, which brought to power a coalition government dominated by the conservative Homeland Union, the institutional machinery was overhauled. A Ministry of European Affairs and a Negotiations Delegation were established, thus representing a clear departure from the existing institutional framework.

A new window of opportunity emerged in mid-1998 after a seemingly unrelated event spurred a series of developments that directly impacted institutional reform. When the Minister for European Affairs Laima Andrikiene was involved in a car accident, leading to one casualty, her political legitimacy both in the public and the cabinet was compromised. This in turn triggered a government re-organisation in which the number of sectoral ministries was reduced from 17 to 14. In terms of Lithuania's coordinating machinery, the Government Commission for European Integration was strengthened, and a European Committee replaced the Ministry of European Affairs. As a consequence, the Ministry of Foreign Affairs was also weakened by this reshuffle, as it now lost the lead policy-coordinating role to the European Committee. The MFA was left with only the coordination of the implementation of the Europe Agreement, providing necessary technical assistance and support to Lithuania's negotiation team, and controlling cooperation within the framework of the EU's Common Foreign and Security Policy.

Thus we see that significant changes in Lithuania's EU institutional structure were precipitated by internal political forces in the form of government turnovers (late 1996) or shifts among political personalities (mid-1998). Moreover, local reformers used the Commission's criticism with regard to Lithuania's relatively slow progress towards EU membership as a justification for making politically difficult changes. This reveals the contribution of external forces on the evolution of Lithuania's institutional machinery, primarily in the form of the Commission's criticisms. Nevertheless, national forces remained the primary force behind turning windows of opportunity into significant institutional changes.

The mere assessment of institutional adjustments does not allow one to examine the effectiveness of Lithuanian EU policy. Thus, our analysis proceeds with a more specific analysis of Lithuanian EU policy by looking at the role of the civil service and policy coordination. It attempts to determine how the mismatch between the nature of Lithuanian administration and the EU's requirements affected Lithuanian EU policy, and, more importantly, to what extent Lithuania's potential capacity for administering EU matters was adequate.

Capabilities of individual institutions: the constraint of an inadequate civil service

With the increasing scope of EU matters, the burden on Lithuania's civil service in terms of administration increased substantially. After 1995 every ministry established a special division or department for European affairs. The size and effectiveness of these offices varied considerably. Often, these departments simply oversaw ministerial liaison with other ministries or the legislature, while other ministerial divisions dealt with substantive matters falling under ministerial jurisdiction. In addition, there was a shift of responsibilities from coordinating institutions to sectoral institutions that bore the majority of responsibility for sectoral alignment of national law with the *acquis*. If until 1995 the Ministry of Foreign Affairs was responsible for virtually all Brussels business, by 1999 every ministry was involved in the administration of EU matters. Nevertheless, this section will argue that during the late 1990s Lithuania's civil service was still plagued by a lack of information and expertise on European affairs, which could best be explained by the persistence of institutions inherited from the communist past along with forces attributable to the transition process.

One of the first reasons for these difficulties was paradoxically an excess of administrative autonomy. Throughout the decade of the 1990s, Lithuania was slow to build up a uniform civil service. In large measure, this was attributable to the post-communist heritage, since under the Soviet system there had been no concept of a civil service. Rather, most departments of government maintained direct responsibility for all aspects of personnel management, including recruitment, training and promotion. Under this principle of ministerial autonomy, which persisted after independence, it was assumed that each institution best understood its own reform needs and was best placed to reform itself.

Yet without any effective central steering, the ability of individual central government institutions to increase their administrative capacity was also limited and irregular. They functioned in a highly regulated environment that limited their ability to change the existing logic of appropriateness. Naturally, those institutions whose leaders were able to recognise the gap between old practices and new demands were more responsive. Nevertheless, the ability of individual institutions to see this discrepancy was not sufficient to ensure successful adaptation across the board.

Secondly, the ability of Lithuania's civil service to manage European affairs effectively was constrained by a low degree of internal coherence. Due to the absence of a civil service under communism, Lithuania inherited a specialist-biased and fragmented administration, which continued to limit effective coordination after independence. This trend was further exacerbated during the transition process by a failure to establish a uniform civil service and by the deliberate decision to keep individual central government institutions weak in order to prevent the possible dominance of a single authoritarian politician over the entire central government. Nevertheless, a few positive trends should be noted, such as the emergence of a network of European 'cadres', or individuals sharing similar values acquired during education, training or from working together. This network, which linked the European Committee, the European Integration Department in the MFA and individual European integration units in sectoral ministries, appeared to have contributed to greater coherence in Lithuanian EU policy by fostering coordination among sectoral policy institutions.

Thirdly, the communist era left behind a major separation between expertise in technical sectoral matters and expertise in foreign affairs, including foreign languages and diplomatic skills. Although in some cases this gap was not so consequential since the exercise of EU responsibilities required both types of expertise, it was still manifested in the institutional organisation of Lithuanian administration. Special units, with experts in foreign (including European) affairs, were responsible for the administration of foreign and European affairs, while other units were responsible for technical sectoral matters. Given this distinction, the exercise of EU responsibilities required extensive internal coordination between two types of administrative units, which was frequently ineffective.

Fourthly, Lithuania's public sector was often not capable of recruiting and retaining qualified personnel. Instead, the fast-growing private sector attracted not only the best university graduates, but also the best officials from the civil service by offering higher salaries and better incentive structures. Moreover, during the years of transition Lithuania's civil service was subject to a high degree of politicisation, stemming in part from the existence of two competing political parties (the Lithuanian Democratic Labour Party and the Lithuanian Conservatives). In the absence of effective civil service regulation regarding job security, the political polarisation led to numerous politically motivated appointments and dismissals. Consequently, job security was lacking, and chances for promotion were largely based on political loyalty rather than performance. The problem as a whole was reflected in the relatively high employment volatility within Lithuania's civil service: in 1997, the average career length in Lithuania's civil service was less than 3.8 years.[38]

The adoption and implementation of civil service legislation was not a priority in Lithuania during the early years of the transition. Although the Lithuanian government finally adopted a Law on Officials in 1994, it failed to develop an autonomous and professional career civil service. The Law on Officials did not unify the diverse remuneration and grading systems within the public administration. Nor did it introduce effective mechanisms for the implementation and enforcement of its provisions. It contained no administrative appeal system to challenge politically motivated appointments or dismissals, thus leaving the careers of officials subject to the whim of political appointees. As a result, the Lithuanian government decided to draft new civil service legislation rather than to enforce the old one. The new Law on Civil Service would be geared towards creating a career system.

Lastly, the training of officials was still governed by general labour law rather than by any civil service legislation. As a result, each state institution was bound by law to set aside a minimum of 3 per cent of its total remuneration budget for training purposes. In reality, however, much less was allocated for this purpose. For example only 0.54 per cent of the state budget was spent during the first three quarters of 1998.[39] Moreover, training possibilities were frequently incidental and driven more by external assistance programmes than by a comprehensive national programme. Perhaps the only exception here was training geared toward the European 'cadres'. Nevertheless, the effectiveness of many training programmes was constrained by a weak ability among officials, in particular mid-career civil servants, both to absorb new skills and to apply them in daily work. A survey of training programmes revealed that only 49 per cent of all participants were capable of applying the knowledge acquired during the training programmes.[40]

In the absence of a comprehensive training strategy and a school for coordinating training programmes, the activities of more than 20 training institutions were left uncoordinated and ineffective. This situation stood in sharp contrast to Poland, where the Polish National School of Public Administration was launched already in 1990 and a comprehensive training programme was implemented. To address Lithuania's training deficiencies, a Strategy for Training of the Lithuanian Civil Service for Accession to the European Union was drafted and a Lithuanian Institute of Public Administration was established in 1999. However, it would take some time for these new institutions to become fully operational and thereafter produce necessary results.

Institutional relationships: the constraint of ineffective policy coordination

Apart from the civil service, it is important to consider how institutional relationships that fall under the category of 'policy coordination' also inhibited Lithuania's ability to manage EU affairs effectively. For example, effective policy coordination was often constrained by a lack of expertise and information on EU matters. Likewise, given the highly technical and specialised nature of these EU affairs, mobility among officials within the civil service was severely limited. Instead, other coordination mechanisms were needed. Nevertheless, it is important to note that the problem of weak coordination was not confined to Lithuania. Among the first-wave CEE countries, Poland was singled out in 1998 for insufficient ministerial coordination of its accession talks.[41] Even the administrations of many member states – including Germany, Greece, Portugal and Spain – suffered from ineffective policy coordination.[42]

Formal coordination structures

During the early accession period, Lithuania's coordination mechanisms were meant to steer EU policy among a range of different institutions including the formal cabinet, inter-ministerial legal working groups and other state bodies such as the European Committee and decreasingly the Ministry of Foreign Affairs. Coordination also encompassed not only the synchronisation of policy positions, but also the drafting of new legal acts.

Ostensibly at the highest level of policy coordination was the Governmental Commission for European Integration (GCEI). The GCEI was a cabinet-level committee created in 1995 and headed by the prime minister. Yet, during its first years of activity, the GCEI failed to become a 'real decision-making body' due to an infrequent schedule of meetings, an absence of formal decision-making powers (its decisions had to be referred to the full cabinet for approval) and a *de facto* control over the GCEI's agenda by the Ministry of Foreign Affairs.[43] In mid-1998, the GCEI was reorganised, after which its position was strengthened by instituting more frequent meetings and increasing its size. In addition, the GCEI was empowered to make legally binding decisions through the Government Chancellery. These reforms nevertheless failed to produce changes in the old pattern of agenda-setting. GCEI's agenda continued to be set almost entirely by the European Committee and dominated by the National Programme for the Adoption of the *Acquis*. Sectoral institutions were not inclined to place their issues on the GCEI's agenda due to its limited capacity for arbitration and the principle of ministerial autonomy.

A second distinctive feature of Lithuania's EU machinery was an underdevelopment of coordination capacities also at lower levels of administration. For example, during the 1990s Lithuania never established a formal coordination committee to bring together permanent officials, such as the heads of European affairs units in the ministries. In turn, this incapacity often led to policy overload at upper levels of government. Yet, where these senior positions were also plagued by political appointments and instability, coordinating capacity was virtually non-existent. Lastly, although Lithuania also had 12 legal coordinating committees, or low-level working groups responsible for the alignment of Lithuanian legislation with the EU's *acquis*, their efforts were largely ineffective due to a lack of clearly defined objectives and accountability to the sectoral policy ministries or to the European Committee.[44]

Thirdly, the evolution of coordinating capabilities in Lithuania was constrained for a certain period of time by the existence of two concurrent secretariats, one based in the Ministry of Foreign Affairs and the other in the now-defunct Ministry of European Affairs. This situation resulted in a considerable degree of confusion over the two institutions' respective roles in the area of European affairs and therefore required additional coordination activity between the two. Fortunately, the replacement of the Ministry of European Affairs in 1998 with the European Committee helped to bring significant clarity to the distribution of functions between the two secretariats. Despite these improvements, however, neither of the secretariats was capable of forecasting the potential *impact* of new EU legislation – a standard task of member state institutions such as the French SGCI (the General Secretariat of the Inter-Ministerial Committee on European Economic Co-operation), the Spanish SECE (the Secretariat of the State for the EU) or the British European Secretariat. This also stood in contrast to Hungary, where a Strategic Task Force for European Integration within the Prime Minister's Office, had long been working to determine the costs and benefits of Hungary's accession to the EU.[45]

As a result, Lithuania's early accession mechanisms represented a balance between a fairly heavy central coordination (the European Committee had a staff of approximately 70) and extensive ministerial involvement through the individual legal working groups. By contrast, the United Kingdom had a relatively light coordinating machinery (the European Secretariat had a staff of 20)[46] while Poland's coordinating machinery was extremely heavy (the Committee for European Integration had in 1998 the largest staff of any CEEC, 160[47]). Thus, judging by the considerable responsibilities of the European Committee, Lithuania's coordinating machinery was definitely lightweight. Comparable coordinating institutions in the EU member states (e.g. with staffs over 50) had much more extensive functions than Lithuania's European Committee. At the same time, in Lithuania total staff size was not always indicative of real responsibilities, in part because such relationships were rarely checked systematically. Instead, departmental competition over staff remuneration budgets often came into play as much as sound administrative logic.

Processes, procedures and culture

Beyond the formal network of EU-related institutions in Lithuania there was also the question of interaction among these bodies. In this domain, Lithuania suffered from a weak system arbitration of inter-ministerial conflicts. During the early years of Lithuania's accession, when disputes inside the bureaucracy could not be solved at lower levels, the GCEI was mandated to intervene. However, the GCEI's steering and arbitration capacity was limited by the collegiate nature of governmental decision-making and high ministerial autonomy. Although these principles are common to every modern bureaucracy, their effect in Lithuania was exacerbated by the lack of cohesion within the civil service (in contrast to Great Britain, Ireland or Denmark) and the lack of a consensual decision-making style (as in the Netherlands or Belgium). In addition, because the prime minister chaired the GCEI, the GCEI's capacity for arbitration depended greatly on the prime minister's willingness to intervene, which was generally very limited.

This constraint invariably fed into the difficulties that the European Committee faced in exercising its functions, since it derived its authority from the GCEI. The European Committee was not willing to become involved in arbitration (even though there was a constant need for it) unless it was called up to do so by the GCEI. By contrast, when conflicts of interest arise among Dutch sectoral institutions, the Dutch Ministry of Foreign Affairs attempts to settle them by acting as 'an honest broker', while unsettled issues are referred by the Dutch prime minister to a cabinet sub-committee (the Council for European Affairs) where conflicts are arbitrated before they reach the cabinet.[48]

As a consequence, Lithuania's policy coordination culture remained inadequate to meet the growing needs of the country's accession to the EU. Policy coordination was narrowly equated with central control. Such elements as 'the definition of an institutional mission and role', 'the institutional embodiment of purpose', 'the defence of institutional integrity' and 'the ordering of internal conflict',[49] which are crucial for effective policy coordination, were often missing. The embedded principle of ministerial autonomy hindered the evolution of extensive information-sharing networks that would have facilitated policy coordination. Though the European Committee did supply guidelines for the administration of EU matters, which sectoral institutions had to follow, they were not extensive and often originated in the Commission or the EU Delegation in Vilnius. The practice of exchanging information through circulation lists was still underdeveloped, though copying letters to interested parties was becoming increasingly widespread. At the level of working groups and committees, the flow of information between legal working groups and responsible institutions was inadequate.

The coordination of policy implementation was particularly weak in Lithuania. This stemmed largely from the lack of an appropriate implementation culture. Under the communist administrative system, characterised by an excessively hierarchical and legalistic nature, officials were primarily concerned with carrying out formal orders rather than implementing their substantive provisions.[50] In Lithuania after the first years of independence, the implementation of government assignments continued to be monitored on a similar basis. This was, for example, in contrast to the UK, where the deeply embedded norm that the effective implementation of EU law must be ensured is viewed by the

British European Secretariat as 'one of the key oversight tasks'.[51] In addition, the example of Austria illustrates that EU membership is likely to demand more flexibility from Lithuania's administration. After Austria's accession to the EU, its deeply embedded principle that 'all state behaviour has to be based on written law' tended to limit the flexibility necessary to conduct negotiations at the EU level.[52]

Policy networks

The effective management of European affairs also depends considerably on the relationship between the civil service and specialised interest organisations. The administrations of EU member states usually draw their expertise and information from various non-governmental organisations. In addition, they rely on professional organisations for the implementation and enforcement of regulatory requirements, e.g. safety at work standards. In most member states professional organisations of actuaries, accountants or veterinarians exercise self-regulation.[53] Under the principle of partnership, professional organisations and other groups are entitled to be involved in the administration of EU structural funds. In an attempt to increase their performance, several member states have consolidated their links with different interest organisations.[54]

Conversely, the involvement of Lithuanian interest organisations (and subnational authorities) in domestic decision-making on EU matters remained minimal during the 1990s. As a result, Lithuanian authorities were not capable of drawing from their groups' expertise and information on EU matters. The internal organisation of Lithuanian interest groups was generally weak, and there were no strong links between interest organisations and the Lithuanian EU policy-making process. Lithuanian business and professional organisations were too weak to exercise self-regulation or delegated regulation. This meant that the Lithuanian government, along with other CEE governments, had to assume a greater degree of responsibility for regulatory activities than their West European counterparts, even though the government was not always best placed to do so in terms of knowledge and experience.[55] Furthermore, the development of policy networks, akin to those in EU member states, was limited by a concomitant struggle to replace old policy networks, which collapsed as a result of the elimination of central control through communist party links and the privatisation of state-owned enterprises. For example, severe tensions between revamped 'old' trade unions and new unions obstructed the integration of the labour sector as a whole into policy networks and thus their impact on EU matters.

In contrast to most EU member states, where domestic policy communities are actively involved in the national EU decision-making process, Lithuania was also missing an intellectual discourse on European issues. Domestic policy communities had the potential to accumulate institutional memory on European matters and promote adjustments to domestic EU policy. In Lithuania, however, the evolution of policy communities seemed trapped in a vicious circle: on the one hand, the problem of instability in Lithuania's civil service could have been greatly alleviated by the evolution of such external policy communities, yet the fact that the civil service was itself so unstable likewise hindered the emergence of any policy communities. In Hungary, for example, the strategic task force served as a kind of policy community. By acting as an advisory body to the integration cabinet and the secretariat, the task force linked various research institutes, universities, chambers of commerce and private companies in 19 working groups, thereby generating expertise and information.[56]

Furthermore, Lithuania missed out on an opportunity to take advantage of regional cooperation networks. The ability of Lithuanian authorities to learn from more advanced CEECs was limited by several factors. Besides the Lithuanian government's limited capacity to foster regional cooperation on EU matters, neighbouring countries also seemed to lack the will to work together with Lithuania on EU matters. For instance, Estonia clearly emphasised its desire to work on furthering its EU agenda independently of the other Baltic states, while Poland worked closely with Hungary on EU matters. After 1997, Lithuania attempted to increase its cooperation with Latvia, as illustrated by a greater frequency of bilateral meetings between Lithuanian and Latvian authorities. Nonetheless, it was not surprising that cooperation among the first-wave applicants became more intense at the expense of the second-wave applicants, when in 1997 the Luxembourg European Council first decided to open accession negotiations with only five CEECs.

The weakness of policy coordination in Lithuania threatened to become even more severe after the country's accession to the EU. EU membership would further increase the administrative workload of Lithuanian authorities, as they would become involved in all stages of the European policy-making process, ranging from agenda-setting to policy enforcement. In terms of different coordination levels, EU membership would bring the need for extensive policy coordination at the domestic level, at the EU level and at the domestic–EU interface.[57] Moreover, weak coordination would only serve to limit Lithuania's ability to maximise its advantage from EU membership, for example, through its inability to define a coherent position in its negotiations, which was of particular importance for small states in order to ensure the representation of their interests at the European level.

A case study: the implementation of the National Programme for the Adoption of the *Acquis* in Lithuania

In order to illustrate a number of the conceptual problems detailed above, it is worth profiling a specific case of Lithuanian governmental capacities: the National Programme for the Adoption of the *Acquis* (NPAA). Within the EU's enhanced pre-accession strategy of the late 1990s, the NPAA was the primary instrument for the implementation of the Accession Partnership launched with each applicant country. The Accession Partnership, adopted by the EU's Council or heads-of-state, listed broad priority objectives for each applicant country and linked all forms of assistance (and in particular the PHARE programme) to their achievement. The direct relationship between the NPAA and the Accession Partnership reflected in turn the way in which measures were enacted by member state administrations to implement EU legislation. Thus, an analysis of Lithuania's NPAA will illuminate well the country's abilities and inabilities to enact EU policy measures at the domestic level during the late 1990s.

It is necessary to note at the outset that the NPAA represents one of three integration programmes that were launched in Lithuania in response to changing circumstances. When the Commission adopted its White Paper in 1995,[58] the Lithuanian government adopted a National Programme for Legal Harmonisation in order to transpose the *acquis* outlined in the White Paper. Second, the NPAA was created in 1998, following the adoption of the Accession Partnership. Finally, when the Commission began publishing its regular reports on the progress of accession, Lithuanian authorities began reciprocating with a series of Action Programmes, which would address the deficiencies outlined by the Commission in its most recent report until the next one was drafted. Thus, each integration programme emerged as a response to new circumstances, although often these were as a result of changes in the EU's own pre-accession strategy, rather than in strategic integration objectives.

Since all of these integration programmes basically shared the same objective – namely, to increase Lithuania's ability to comply with the *acquis* – they ultimately exhibited a high degree of overlap, thereby adding to administrative costs and contributing to confusion. An abundance of 'programmes' and 'action plans' could replace the need for a comprehensive integration strategy. Indeed, the preparation of an integration strategy was circumscribed by insufficient strategic planning and predictability not only in Lithuania, but also in the EU itself. Frequent changes in the EU's approach to enlargement imposed severe limits on Lithuania's ability to design a comprehensive integration strategy.

In the absence of such a strategy, however, Lithuanian authorities were more exposed to a variety of external and internal demands, often with conflicting priorities. The Commission's proposals needed to be balanced against Lithuania's organisational goals. This, in turn, promoted a reactive approach to the administration of EU matters in Lithuania, which further fuelled institutional uncertainty and aggravated human resource constraints. This entire situation was manifested in the absence of a rational approach to legal harmonisation with the *acquis* based on a prior assessment of possible domestic impacts of particular *acquis* provisions. The fact that the Lithuanian government delayed the implementation of several NPAA measures through the enactment of government decrees reflected the fact that the NPAA was organised without sufficient knowledge about the NPAA's funding and without an assessment of what was necessary for the achievement of Accession Partnership priorities.

To these problems of policy consistency was added Lithuania's own problem of ministerial autonomy. Because the NPAA was primarily drafted by sectoral institutions, it was more akin to a collection of sectoral measures than to a consistent policy programme. As a result, such sectors as regional policy and economic policy were under-represented in the NPAA,[59] and this did not go unnoticed by the Commission, which stated in 1998 that 'an operational institutional structure for the implementation of regional policy has not been established in Lithuania' and 'Lithuania has not yet established a medium term economic strategy'.[60]

Apart from these issues, of utmost importance was the absence of an institution to check for discrepancies between national sectoral measures and the Accession Partnership priorities. In an environment characterised by a high degree of ministerial autonomy and weak control by the political executive, sectoral institutions were not willing to present detailed measures, which would have to be formally executed in a tightly controlled process. Thus, it was not surprising that such sectors as audio-visual policies were initially left out by Lithuanian authorities in the first draft of the NPAA, even though they were listed in the Accession Partnership. Additionally, most of the NPAA's measures were related to sectoral reform rather than to the implementation of EU law.[61]

The European Committee, which was formally responsible for the NPAA's administration, did not check (and actually had no capacity to check) the extent to which the implementation of sectoral measures was consistent with the Accession Partnership priorities. Thus, it was possible that the NPAA's implementation would not lead to the full transposition of the *acquis* into national law. The European Committee acted primarily as a 'post office': it collected sectoral inputs into the NPAA and then exercised only formal and hierarchical control over their execution. In this respect Lithuanian officials themselves conceded that the performance of the European Committee did not differ much from that of its predecessor, the Ministry of European Affairs.[62] As a solution, some officials suggested more effective monitoring of the NPAA, possibly including regular reports on the NPAA's implementation. Here, the example of Spain was insightful, since in this case the implementation of EU directives of an inter-ministerial or problematic nature are subject to more extensive oversight.[63]

It is interesting to note that during the late 1990s, only the EU commented on the mismatch between NPAA measures and Accession Partnership priorities. This reveals that the steering of the NPAA was exercised more by the Commission than by the Lithuanian government.[64] It was the Commission which came to the conclusion that not all Accession Partnership measures had been reflected in the NPAA; that the NPAA did not cover the entire *acquis*; that the inclusion of some NPAA measures lacked sufficient justification; that information on the financial and staff resources necessary for the achievement of the NPAA's measures were insufficient; that responsible institutions were not clearly spelled out; and that detailed implementation schedules for NPAA's measures were missing.[65] These were all critical points, which Lithuanian officials themselves appeared to overlook.

Next, the administration of the NPAA also suffered from a high degree of formalism and rigidity. The NPAA itself along with all changes to it had to be approved by the government. Delaying the implementation schedule was possible, but not looked upon favourably. Although sectoral institutions were entitled to amend the list of measures for which they are responsible, they were allowed to do so within a restricted time period. Apart from this, the formal control exercised by the European Committee over the work of NPAA also hindered flexibility. Since the cost of correcting errors was high, the adjustment of sectoral measures to new circumstances was infrequent. Sectoral institutions had limited incentives to seek efficiency gains, since funding was allocated for separate measures, and only a limited possibility existed for redistributing resources among them.

Ineffective policy implementation was also evident in the work of the NPAA. By late 1998, approximately 40 per cent of the NPAA's measures planned for 1998 had not been carried out on time, although this implementation record differed widely across sectors. For example, the so-called 'reinforcement of institutional and administrative capacity,' was one of the most overdue for implementation. By late-1998, Lithuanian authorities had managed to carry out only five administrative reform measures out of 28.[66] The late implementation of major legislative acts in this field was strangely attributed by the government to the fact that 'many legal acts are being harmonised with European Union requirements and are co-ordinated with the other national legislation',[67] although there was no EU legislation in this field.

Behind this slow governmental and legislative decision-making process was, of course, the fact that most public institutions were burdened with an enormous workload. This was hardly surprising, since most pieces of EU legislation need to be incorporated into national law through parliamentary laws and governmental decrees. By contrast, in long-standing member states such as Denmark 85 per cent of EU legislative acts were administratively transposed through 'a law of authorisation'.[68] As a result, in an effort to shorten the lengthy procedures by which European legislation was incorporated into the Lithuanian legal system, it was decided in early 1999 to prioritise the transposition of EU law. A special 'fast-track' deliberation system for European matters was launched. Its essence was that draft legal acts that were related to the transposition of EU legislation, would be marked with an 'E' (for Europe) and attributed a preferential status in the governmental decision-making system. However, its effectiveness was limited and, despite this improvement, it was clear that without a fundamental overhaul of the governmental decision-making system or of the transposition process, the mere introduction of a 'fast-track' system was unlikely to solve the problem. For with the advantage of streamlining the deliberation of EU matters came the concomitant disadvantage of delaying the deliberation of other public matters, which may be conducive to the transition process. Additionally, the opportunities offered by the 'fast-track' system were soon exhausted given the increasing amount of EU matters.

Lastly, slow implementation of the NPAA could also be attributed to limited financial resources. The general uncertainty about the funding of the NPAA's measures frequently triggered intense competition for budgetary appropriations among sectoral institutions. The total size of the budget appropriations requested for achieving the NPAA's measures in 1999 amounted to almost 2.5 billion lits ($625 million). This represented an astounding 17–fold increase from 1998.[69] For example, some sectoral institutions, assuming that the NPAA's implementation would be separately funded, increased the number of proposed sectoral measures and requested commensurate financing for their implementation. A case in point was the Ministry of Agriculture, which was uncertain about the funding of agricultural measures listed both in the NPAA and the government's policy programme and therefore attempted to secure additional funding for the achievement of the same measures by listing them in two different programmes.

This example demonstrated the need for a clear position as to the funding of the NPAA's implementation before its preparation could be started. Nevertheless, the position of Lithuanian authorities remained ambiguous, and through 1999 the NPAA's funding was not linked up to the annual budgetary process. Thus, due to the combination of at least three different factors – namely, the existence of overlapping programmes, the absence of an effective monitoring system to determine the appropriateness of measures, and the absence of a comprehensive integration strategy – it was very difficult to match public resources with real funding needs. For example, in 1999 it was estimated that national funding for the NPAA would cover only 50 per cent of actual needs.[70] The achievement of many other measures would instead be partially or wholly funded by foreign assistance programmes, including PHARE. Meanwhile, the danger persisted that various action measures would be used to legitimise sectoral demands for increased appropriations rather than for the advancement of Lithuania's accession to the EU. Thus, it was highly likely that some measures, including those of utmost importance, remained short of funding.

The EU's impact on the evolution of Lithuanian governmental capabilities

The problem of inadequate governmental capabilities concerned not only Lithuania's authorities, but also those of the EU since the accession of ten CEE countries to the EU was likely to exacerbate administrative deficiencies already existing in the EU. Therefore the EU needed to close the gap between the inability (or even unwillingness) of CEE governments to implement comprehensive administrative reform programmes and the basic requirement that new members must have effective civil services as well as effective coordination and monitoring instruments. The EU faced considerable constraints, however, in effecting administrative reform both in the existing member states and the candidate countries. Since administrative reform falls within the exclusive domain of national sovereignty, the EU was not capable of directly imposing its own administrative solutions upon any candidate countries.[71] These difficulties in turn shaped the way in which the European institutions were able to influence the management of EU matters in the CEECs. The following analysis conceptualises EU pressure by making a distinction between its financial aid and agenda-setting power.

It was to be expected that the EU's influence, particularly through the PHARE programme, would produce 'policy learning' effects in the CEECs, defined in terms of improved knowledge and skills regarding EU matters. As a result of 'changing perceptions of how the policy problem in question is to be defined, and what appropriate solutions are', policy learning may be translated into important institutional or policy changes.[72] The importance of learning in the transition countries is manifested in the argument that the long-term nature of institutional development in these countries can be explained by the substantial need for 'the gradual accumulation of experience and the acquisition of skills'.[73]

The analysis here is limited because, 'empirically, it is extraordinarily difficult to show that the EU context actually induced processes of policy learning'.[74] Thus, the EU's impact on policy learning in Lithuania will be analysed by looking at the extent to which the evolution of the PHARE programme specifically facilitated policy learning in the Lithuanian civil service. This approach can be partially justified by the uniformity of the EU's pre-accession strategy with regard to all the CEECs, even after the Luxembourg summit differentiated between them.

The analysis also makes an assessment of the EU's impact on the domestic policy-making process, since one can expect that the form EU influence takes, and the extent to which it is translated, is mediated by domestic institutional settings. The EU's impact is mediated by national institutions, which have a monopoly of power in translating EU pressure into institutional and policy changes. Thus, the analysis assesses the extent to which the EU's influence actually generated policy learning in the Lithuanian civil service and the extent to which new knowledge and skills have produced institutional and policy change. The case of fisheries administration examined below provides an example of the interplay of these factors.

The EU's financial assistance and policy learning

The EU's key instrument to enhance the effectiveness of managing European affairs in the CEECs has been its financial assistance through various aid instruments, and in particular through the PHARE programme. PHARE aims at strengthening the public administration sector so that it can assume the obligations of EU accession and membership. In Lithuania, PHARE funded civil servant training, the preparation of a draft Law on Civil Service, the modernisation of civil servant training centres and support for the establishment of the Lithuanian Institute of Public Administration.

The evolution of PHARE reveals the increasing ability to generate policy-learning effects. The 'demand-driven' PHARE suffered from several sets of problems during first years of operation in Lithuania. First, the EU was criticised for seeming more concerned with channelling money to its highly paid consultants rather than actually assisting the CEECs.[75] For instance, the European Investment Bank and the OECD estimated that 75 per cent of PHARE allocations to the CEECs were channelled through European consultants operating in the region. The effectiveness, efficiency and relevance of PHARE suffered from its rigid tendering and contracting procedures, leading to long gaps between the presentation of assistance proposals and their implementation.[76] Even one of the commissioners responsible for PHARE was forced to admit that bureaucratic procedures and the lack, or low quality, of specialist knowledge hampered the effectiveness of European assistance to the CEECs.[77] Additionally, the generation of policy-learning effects was circumscribed by the limited dissemination of knowledge and skills, although the limited PHARE budget pointed to the importance of spreading new knowledge as widely as possible.[78]

Second, the limited success of technical assistance was also attributed to the limited capacity of the CEECs to absorb technical assistance due to their weak and ill-adapted administrations as well as a lack of experience in managing foreign assistance programmes. The effectiveness, efficiency and sustainability of PHARE projects were considerably undermined by the low degree of stability within the post-communist administrations. According to one analysis, 'the officials and ministers dealing with PHARE change quite regularly, often causing lack of institutional memory which affects the running of programmes'.[79] The Project Management Units (PMUs), which were set up within relevant sectoral ministries to support the administration of PHARE, suffered from significant staffing problems,[80] high staff turnover and inappropriate role definition.[81] Additionally, the low planning capacity of the beneficiary countries hindered their ability to identify and prepare high quality PHARE projects.[82]

It is interesting to note that PHARE assistance considerably differed in its effectiveness, efficiency and sustainability across countries. The evaluation of two PHARE programmes found Lithuania's record to be the worst of the four countries evaluated (Bulgaria, Hungary, Lithuania and Poland).[83] To a large extent this stemmed from low planning capacity and instability within Lithuania's civil service, illustrated by the fact that Consulta, a state-funded agency for enterprise restructuring, was losing its PHARE-trained staff due to an insufficient commitment from the Lithuanian government to the agency's future; ultimately, the agency was liquidated.[84]

In terms of different skills, the fact that European assistance took the form of a hierarchical imposition of the *acquis* also had unequal effects on the development of governmental capabilities.[85] In essence, the skill of facilitating 'policy management', important for the transposition of the *acquis*, was preferred over the development of 'policy entrepreneurship' skills, key not only for the successful implementation and enforcement of the *acquis* but also for the future participation of the CEECs in the European policy process. This circumstance, in turn, accounts for the fact that the process of transposing the *acquis* in the CEECs was more often driven by the rule 'the faster, the better' than based on a prior assessment of the possible domestic impact of particular EU provisions.

The final set of PHARE deficiencies can be explained by its 'demand-driven' nature. In the absence of specific funding priorities, PHARE was primarily executed on the basis of the beneficiaries' needs and to the extent that these were possible to determine. Due to this recipient orientation, PHARE was sometimes forced to support ineffective policies, such as in Bulgaria, which lacked sound restructuring policies, or Lithuania, where there was little stability in the privatisation policy.[86] Most importantly, PHARE aid was not based on a principle of conditionality,[87] which would have linked PHARE assistance to a set of *ex ante* conditions (to be fulfilled prior to starting a PHARE project) or *ex post* conditions (by making future PHARE projects contingent on the success of existing ones).

A major breakthrough came in 1997, when the EU explicitly acknowledged institutional and administrative capacity in the candidate countries as the prime issue area for EU membership preparation, and it re-orientated the PHARE programme from a 'demand-driven' to an 'accession-driven' programme. Thereafter, 30 per cent of total PHARE assistance was allocated to the reinforcement of administrative and judicial capacity in the CEECs.[88] More importantly, new forms of technical assistance were spelled out, including such important instruments as curricula development, bilateral cooperation and secondments. As a result, the fact that these changes would presuppose greater involvement by both the European institutions and the member state administrations in PHARE management was likely to produce even greater policy-learning effects.

Furthermore, the 1997 reforms attempted to improve the effectiveness, efficiency and sustainability of PHARE assistance through the principle of conditionality. Article 4 of a new regulation empowered the Council to 'take appropriate steps,' which would include cutting or suspending financial assistance if any of the CEECs failed to satisfy its commitments under the Europe Agreement or progress towards fulfilling the Copenhagen criteria or the Accession Partnership priority objectives (*ex ante* conditionality).[89] Moreover, progress of the individual CEECs would be reviewed every one or two years, rendering the partnership in the next year dependent upon progress achieved in the past (*ex post* conditionality).

However, despite their advantages the new PHARE rules were criticised by CEE officials.[90] They pointed out that while demanding higher administrative responsibility for managing EU affairs, the reforms sacrificed autonomy. Additionally, the new PHARE rules were seen as less relevant for more advanced CEECs which had greater planning capacity and more effective management. Nevertheless, the Commission quickly utilised its new powers by cutting Poland's allocation of PHARE funding for 1998 by 34 million ECU (or 16 per cent) on the basis of inadequately prepared applications for various PHARE projects.[91]

In an attempt to address the constraint of the low quality of PHARE expertise in the CEECs, the Commission launched the 'twinning' framework as part of PHARE. Its basic objective was to transfer 'the vast body of administrative and technical expertise' from the member state administrations to the CEECs by seconding national experts to the candidate counties.[92] The main advantage of twinning was to result from the direct transfer of expertise and information rather than through the involvement of private consultants, who sometimes lacked technical knowledge in different policy fields. Thus, twinning was supposed to significantly improve the transfer of knowledge to the applicant countries and corresponding policy learning.

However, the positive effect of twinning was circumscribed by several factors. Even though the Commission decided to pay a supplement to the seconded national officials and their respective departments through the PHARE programme,[93] this often had little effect on reducing the limited ability (or even unwillingness) of the member state administrations to send their officials to the CEECs for sufficiently long time periods (in principle for 12 months) due to the limited number of qualified officials. As a result, only a few member states presented any twinning offers to Lithuanian authorities during the late 1990s. Moreover, during the presentation of these proposals, the representatives of one member state admitted that they would be willing to form a 'twinning team' with other member states because they had limited capacity to achieve all twinning goals by themselves.[94] More importantly, the effectiveness of twinning was undermined by long selection procedures, even longer than those for the selection of private consultants. In an attempt to close the gap between the immediate need for PHARE expertise in the structural funds area and long selection procedures for twinning, Lithuanian authorities even asked the Commission to replace half of the twinning assistance with private consultants. However, confident in the effectiveness of twinning, the Commission rejected this option.[95]

In early 1999 a second major shift occurred, when responsibility for PHARE was extensively devolved to the EU's delegations in the CEECs themselves. The main principles underlying these new adjustments included the decentralisation of PHARE management and the establishment of independent financial institutions and greater transparency. Under the new rules the delegations would not only approve the terms of reference, but also the entire tender dossier with evaluation documents on behalf of the Commission. Meanwhile, the CEECs were likely to benefit from greater decentralisation through more direct contacts with Community officials and broader responsibilities. These new relationships would likewise lead to greater learning effects.

Finally, it is necessary to cite the EU's decision to use PHARE money for funding the participation of the CEECs in various Community programmes, which in particular contributed to policy learning among interest organisations. After 1998 Lithuania became a beneficiary of three European cultural programmes, namely Ariane, Kaleidoscope and Raphael. In addition, it was fully associated with the Fifth Framework Programme for Research and Technological

Development. In 1999, it joined the Medium-term Community Action Programme on Equal Opportunities for Men and Women.[96] Discussion also began regarding Lithuania's participation in the SAVE II programme for the promotion of energy efficiency, the EU's programme on the prevention of AIDS and other communicable diseases as well as its programme on drug dependence.[97]

To overcome the limited ability of the CEECs to pay their financial contributions for participation in these and other Community programmes, PHARE co-funded the CEECs' annual fees. Under the terms and conditions adopted by the Association Council, Lithuania paid only 10, 30 and 50 per cent of the cost of its participation in Kaleidoscope and Raphael from its national budget in 1998, 1999 and 2000 respectively.[98] The remaining percentage was financed from Lithuania's annual PHARE allocations.

The evolution of the PHARE programme reveals a great deal about both the EU's policy preferences and its understanding of the CEECs administrative reform needs. The 1994 PHARE reforms were illustrative of the EU's initially limited commitment to increasing the ability of the CEECs to meet the obligations of EU membership. Behind this stood the fact that according to one Community official 'the level of seriousness about enlargement [in the EU] is not minimal, it simply does not exist'.[99] Conversely, the 1997 PHARE reforms revealed not only increasing European commitment, but also increasing understanding of the internal institutional factors that prevented external efforts from making the management of EU matters more effective. The 1999 reforms were the most significant in terms of policy learning. By aiming to prepare the CEECs for the administration of future structural funds through the decentralised management of PHARE the EU rendered internal constraints less binding, and thus advanced the emergence of adequate governmental capabilities to manage EU matters.

The EU's power of agenda-setting

The EU also influenced the capacity of the CEECs to manage EU affairs by setting both the formal and informal agenda of the CEE governments.[100] The Commission set the informal agenda by identifying specific problems for the CEECs to tackle along with recommended policy solutions. The importance of EU membership for the CEECs as well as their limited domestic expertise on EU matters facilitated the EU's ability to exercise its agenda-setting power. It is relevant to note that although the Commission certainly did not have a monopoly over the actions of the CEE governments, it was better placed to do so than other European institutions or even the individual member states. For Brussels enjoyed a formal executive authority delegated to it by the Council for eastward enlargement; in addition, it possessed both necessary expertise and financial resources. Because of the wide scope of the Accession Partnerships, the Commission's influence over policy-making in the CEECs went 'beyond the EU's role in the domestic policy processes of its member states'.[101]

Still, the EU's agenda-setting instruments also varied in their effectiveness. Initially, bilateral meetings between CEE and European officials within the framework of the Europe Agreements served as an informal agenda-setting instrument. Their effectiveness was limited, however, by the fact that the Association Council met once a year, while the Association Committees met once or twice a year. Nevertheless, they still acted as an important agenda-setting instrument by serving as constructive forums for discussing broad, but essential, policy issues.[102] Their effectiveness only began to wane as the number of the associated countries increased from three (Hungary, Poland and Czech Republic) to ten and EU officials were simply unable to keep up the pace.[103] In response to this, the 1994 Essen summit adopted a multilateral approach termed 'structured relationship' or 'structured dialogue', in which heads-of-state as well as sectoral ministers from both sides would debate European affairs in larger gatherings.

However, the influence of this structured relationship on agenda-setting soon became limited for several reasons. First, similar to the meetings held within the framework of the Europe Agreements, the structured relationship meetings were normally held only once a year – except in the case of the Council of Justice and Home Affairs and the General Affairs Council, both of which met twice a year. Secondly, these meetings were not preceded by any prior exchange of information or preparatory expert meetings. Consequently, they are weakened by broad agendas, extremely limited time and divergent views among the CEECs.[104] Although several changes (including the deficiencies cited above) were agreed upon in order to enhance the structured dialogue,[105] few substantial improvements resulted.[106] Finally, the effectiveness of the structured relationship was frequently impeded by a lack of knowledge on EU matters or institutional memory in the CEECs due to the unstable nature of CEE administrations discussed above.

A far more effective device for agenda-setting came from the Commission's 1997 opinions on the readiness of the CEECs to accede to the EU as well as its subsequent regular reports on the candidate countries' progress. In its original opinions, the Commission identified specific obstacles to meeting the obligations of EU membership and offered policy proposals for their resolution.[107] However, the Commission's opinions proved to be insufficient for overcoming internal institutional constraints. For instance, although the Commission spurred the development of Lithuanian regional policy by pointing out that its absence would hinder Lithuania's accession to the EU, progress in this area remained limited due to weak inter-ministerial coordination and a lack of expertise and information on EU regional policies. The possibility of delayed EU membership did not serve as a sufficient threat to the Lithuanian government to prompt reform in its regional policy institutions and rules.

Rather, it would appear that the EU had greater effect in prompting Lithuania to strengthen its internal administrative reform. In this domain, a number of policy solutions identified by the Commission were negotiated into short-term or medium-term reform objectives and embodied in the Accession Partnership agreement between the EU and Lithuania.[108] This agreement included, among other things, the introduction of a comprehensive training programme for state officials on EU matters. More importantly, progress on implementing these reform objectives was clearly linked to EU's continued financial assistance. This reflected the EU's increasing understanding that its ability to influence the performance of CEE administrations depended largely on establishing a link between its two main influence mechanisms: financial assistance and agenda-setting.

As a result, the 1998 PHARE programme for Lithuania, which amounted to 29.1 million ECU, was designed on the basis of priority objectives specified in the Accession Partnership. The programme covered five broad objectives: justice and home affairs, environment, energy, transport, and reinforcing institutional and administrative capacity. The last objective was the most significant in terms of financial resources: a total of 11.8 billion ECU was allocated for this objective. Most importantly, the implementation of the 1998 PHARE programme was linked to conditionality through the Financing Memorandum, signed between the European Community and the Government of Lithuania in late 1998.[109] In this memorandum, EU funding was made contingent on the existence of a sufficient level of commensurate staff people on the Lithuanian side, to be financed from the national budget and who would work in the policy fields of agriculture, regional policy and cohesion, environment and transport. This reflected the Commission's concern about the need for human resources in Lithuania in order to effectively manage individual assistance projects foreseen by the 1998 PHARE programme. The principle of conditionality was also established in relation to the adoption of new legal acts in the policy fields of social security, environment and energy. Finally, the EU required Lithuania to establish proper coordination mechanisms to avoid fragmentation of justice and home affairs actions and to supply national budgetary funds to co-fund transport projects.

Lastly, the EU helped set Lithuania's agenda through a number of informal means. These included conveying the Commission's preoccupations either indirectly through the EU Delegation or PHARE office in Vilnius or directly from Brussels through DG 1A or sectoral DGs. For instance, it was through these institutions that the Commission repeatedly expressed its concern about Lithuania's capabilities to administer a special project for structural funds in the PHARE programme. The Commission even requested a clear definition of administrative resources needed for the effective exercise of the project along with a detailed staffing plan. The repeating reference to national administrative resources showed that the Commission was ready to use all agenda-setting instruments to achieve its objectives. Nevertheless, the informal agenda-setting instruments of the EU were less powerful by definition. By being less institutionalised they did not necessary or immediately resonate within the entire Lithuanian administration.

Conclusion

This chapter has presented a framework for the study of governmental capabilities, based on new institutionalist theory and applied to the administration of EU matters in Lithuania during the country's early accession period. The inadequacies of Lithuanian EU policy were evidenced by the ineffective management of the National Programme for the Adoption of the *acquis* during the late 1990s. In part, these difficulties could be explained by the binding nature of institutional constraints. These included both internal factors (Lithuania's post-communist legacy and transition process) and external factors (the EU's policy-making nature). Together these generated a mismatch between the basic characteristics of Lithuania's public administration and the EU's accession requirements.

In terms of responding to EU pressure, the ability and willingness of Lithuanian authorities to close the capability-requirements gap depended substantially on the pressure exerted by EU institutions (particularly the European Commission) through the latter's agenda-setting instruments. Additional policy and institutional change was facilitated by the EU's PHARE programme, which generated significant policy learning effects in Lithuania's administration. Lastly, the EU's decision to link its financial assistance to agenda-setting through the principle of conditionality considerably strengthened Lithuania's internal reform efforts.

Within the Lithuanian central government, meanwhile, domestic decision-making practices helped to explain the uneven pattern of concrete institutional and policy change. This pattern was marked, on the one hand, by radical changes undertaken to the country's central government structure as well as its institutional structure for coordinating EU matters, and on the other hand, incremental changes meant to improve ministerial and governmental decision-making processes and staff management practices. This contrast was explained by different 'path-dependency' levels, which in turn were influenced by the extent to which different institutions were embedded into national institutional settings. Lithuania's formal institutional structure, which was determined by initial reform choices during the transition period, was less institutionalised than decision-making processes and staff management practices, which were inherited from the communist past.

The different levels of embededdness can also be explained by the higher sensitivity of formal institutional structures to political pressures that often sprung from the dissatisfaction of political institutions with government performance. This was illustrated by the example that major changes to the Lithuanian institutional structure for coordinating EU matters were precipitated by political factors. For Lithuanian policy-makers this contrast implied that the real challenges to Lithuanian EU policy lie not in the formal government structure, but in the wider institutional framework within which it operated.

Thirdly, we saw that the institutional constraints that hindered the development of governmental capabilities during the late 1990s were generally more conditioned by internal rather than external factors. Since the Lithuanian EU policy was still dominated by the transposition of EU legislation into national law, institutional constraints that resulted from the mismatch between the nature of Lithuanian administration and the EU requirements had not yet fully materialised. For Lithuanian decision-makers this meant that the most needed reform efforts were those which would address the binding character of *internal* factors.

Lastly, it is important to place the development of adequate governmental capabilities into the context of EU enlargement, for the absence of adequate governmental capabilities in Lithuania demonstrated not only the country's limited capacity to fulfil obligations of EU membership, but also its limited ability to negotiate favourable terms of accession to the EU. Naturally, this problem was endemic to all of the CEE countries and even to many current EU member states, particularly in the area of implementing and enforcing the *acquis*. Still, the candidate countries would have to comply with a wider *acquis* than the existing member states, since they would have no 'opt-out' possibilities and a very narrow scope to negotiate long transitional periods. These factors would place specific burdens on the state capabilities of the CEECs, and as a result the question of managing EU matters was far from a short-term concern.

Notes

I gratefully acknowledge helpful comments provided by H. Grabbe, M. Haverland, J. P. Olsen, J. Trestour, T. Verheijen, R. Vilpišauskas and J. Zielonka.

1 See Commission of the European Communities, *Agenda 2000: The Commission Opinion on Lithuania's Application for Membership of the European Union* (1997) and Commission of the European Communities, *Regular Report from the Commission on Lithuania's Progress Towards Accession* (1998).
2 See Lietuvos Respublikos Seimas, *Lietuvos Respublikos Seimo Europos Reikalu Komiteto Isvada-Pranesimas apie Nacionalines Acquis Priemimo Programos Vykdyma ir Siulymai, Kaip Gerinti Sios Programos Administratima* (Valstybes Zinios, 1999).
3 See *Lietuvos Rytas*, 18 March 1999, 'Komisijos atstovas vel pagrasino Lietuvai', p. 2 or *Agence Europe*, 22 July 1998, 'Closure of Ignalina Nuclear Power Plant has to be part of Lithuanian Energy Strategy, says van der Broek'.
4 This analysis defines EU matters (or Lithuanian EU policy) by making an arbitrary distinction between the administration of EU matters and the administration of non-EU matters for analytical purposes. I am aware that isolating European affairs from other public affairs is increasingly difficult with the expansion of EU business during the pre-accession process.
5 J. P. Olsen, *European Challenges to the Nation State*, Arena Working Paper, 14/95 (University of Oslo, 1995), p. 3.
6 H. Grabbe, 'A Partnership for Accession? The Nature, Scope and Implications of Emerging EU Conditionality for CEE Applicants', *Robert Schuman Centre Working Paper*, 12 (1999).
7 O. Norgaard, *The Baltic States after Independence* (Aldershot, Edward Elgar, 1996), p. 225.
8 J. P. Olsen, *Europeanization and Nation-State Dynamics*, Arena Working Paper, 9/95 (University of Oslo, 1995), p. 16.

9 See S. S. Andersen and K. A. Eliassen (eds), *Making Policy in Europe: The Europeification of National Policy-Making* (London, Sage, 1993); J. P. Olsen *Europeanization and Nation-State Dynamics*; J. P. Olsen, *European Challenges to the Nation State*; S. J. Bulmer and M. Burch, 'Organizing for Europe: Whitehall, the British State and European Union', *Public Administration*, 76:1 (1998), 601–628; K. Hanf and B. Soetendorp (eds), *Adapting to Europen Integration: Small States and the European Union* (London, Longman, 1998); C. Knill, 'European Policies: The Impact of National Administrative Traditions', *Journal of Public Policy*, 18:1 (1998), 1–28; C. Spanou, 'European Integration in Administrative Terms: A Framework for Analysis and the Greek Case', *Journal of European Public Policy*, 5:3 (1998), 467–484; M. Haverland, *National Autonomy, European Integration and the Politics of Packaging Waste* (Amsterdam, Netherlands School for Social and Economic Policy Research, 1998).

10 See Commission of the European Communities, *Agenda 2000* and Commission of the European Communities, *Regular Report*.

11 H. G. Krenzler and M. Everson, 'Preparing for the Acquis Communautaire', *Robert Schuman Centre Policy Paper*, 6 (1998), 6.

12 V. Wright, 'The National Coordination of European Policymaking: Negotiating the Quagmire', in J. Richardson (ed.), *European Union: Power and Policymaking* (London, Routledge, 1996), p. 149.

13 B. G. Peters, 'Managing Horizontal Government: The Politics of Coordination', *Public Administration*, 76:3 (1998), 297.

14 S. J. Bulmer, New Institutionalism and the Governance of the Single Market', *Journal of European Public Policy* 5:3 (1998), 370.

15 B. G. Peters applied a similar research strategy to the analysis of managerial reform in the United States. See B. G. Peters, 'The New Institutionalism and Administrative Reform: Explaining Alternative Models', *Estudio/Working Paper Centro de Estudios Avanzados en Ciencias Sociales*, 113 (1998).

16 J. G. March and J. P. Olsen, 'The New Institutionalism: Organizational Factors in Political Life', *American Political Science Review*, 78 (1984), 738–749.

17 Peters, 'The New Institutionalism', p. 8.

18 A similar hypothesis was tested by Knill. C. Knill, 'European Policies: The Impact of National Administrative Traditions', *Journal of Public Policy*, 18:1 (1998), 1–28.

19 Olsen, *European Challenges*, p. 5.

20 This proposition was borrowed from J. Pontusson, 'From Comparative Public Policy to Political Economy: Putting Political Institutions in Their Place and Taking Interests Seriously', *Comparative Political Studies*, 28:1 (1995), 118–119.

21 S. Bulmer and M. Burch, 'Organising for Europe: Whitehall, the British state and European Union', *Public Administration*, 76:1 (1998), 605.

22 The EU-level requirements can be divided into explicit and implicit. If the former refer to different *acquis* or Accession Partnership provisions, the latter refer to 'coordination and planning mechanisms, rebalancing of politics–administration relations, continuity, respect for formal rules and obligations, [. . .] effective monitoring and control mechanisms, and increased transparency'. See C. Spanou, 'European Integration in Administrative Terms: A Framework for Analysis and the Greek Case', *Journal of European Public Policy*, 5:3 (1998), 474.

23 G. Majone, 'A European Regulatory State', in J. Richardson (ed.), *European Union: Power and Policymaking* (London, Routledge, 1996), p. 266.

24 House of Lords, Select Committee on the European Communities, *Enlargement and Common Agricultural Policy Reform*, HL Paper 92 (London, HMSO, 1996), p. 30.

25 Majone, 'A European Regulatory State', p. 265.

26 R. Baldwin, *Toward an Integrated Europe* (Washington, Centre for Economic Policy Research, 1994), p. 193.

27 A. Pratley, 'Financial Control and Audit in the European Union', in OECD, *Effects of European Union Accession, Part 1: Budgeting and Financial Control*, Sigma Papers, 19 (Paris, OECD, 1997), p. 152.
28 *Financial Times*, 12 March 1997, 'Uncertain Map of the Future', p. 17.
29 Lithuanian Ministry of Environment, *Mid-Term Reform Strategy for Environment* (Internal Documents, 1998), p. 9.
30 Lithuanian Ministry of Environment, *Mid-Term Reform Strategy*, pp. 10–11.
31 J. J. Hesse, 'Rebuilding the State: Public Sector Reform in Central and Eastern Europe', in J.-E. Lane (ed.), *Public Sector Reform: Rationale, Trends and Problems* (London, Sage, 1997), p. 138.
32 A. Mayhew, *Recreating Europe: The European Union's Policy towards Central and Eastern Europe* (Cambridge, Cambridge University Press, 1998), p. 230.
33 F. Schimmelfennig, 'The Eastern Enlargement of the European Union: A Case for Sociological Institutionalism' (University of Konstanz, unpublished paper, 1998), pp. 28–29.
34 OECD, *Country Profiles of Civil Service Training Systems*, Sigma Papers, 12 (Paris, OECD, 1997), p. 83.
35 L. Metcalfe, *Trends in European Public Administration*, Working Paper (Maastricht, European Institute of Public Administration, 1993), p. 4.
36 Metcalfe, *Trends in European Public Administration*, p. 4.
37 For example, in an attempt to cope with its under-representation at the European level, Great Britain introduced at one point a fast-track recruitment system for European posts. H. Wallace, 'Relations between the European Union and the British Administration', in Y. Meny, P. Muller and J. L. Quermonne (eds), *Adjusting to Europe: The Impact of the European Union on National Institutions and Policies* (London, Routledge, 1996), p. 66.
38 European Committee under the Government of Lithuania, *Lithuania's Progress in Preparation for Membership of the European Union, July 1997 – July 1998* (Vilnius, 1998), p. 111.
39 *Respublika*, 17 November 1998, 'Orientuoti viesojo valdymo reformos zingsniai: Valdymo reformu ir savivaldybiu reikalu ministro p. K. Skrebio pranesimas LR Seime 1998 m. lapkricio 12 d', p. 9.
40 *Kauno diena*, 5 December 1998, 'Ar verta valdininkui mokytis?', p. 8.
41 *The Wall Street Journal Europe*, 30 April 1998, p. 1; *Financial Times*, 28 July 1998, 'PM to Spearhead EU Bid'.
42 L. Metcalfe, 'International Policy Coordination and Public Management Reform', *International Review of Administrative Sciences*, 60:2 (1994), 289.
43 K. Maniokas and G. Vitkus, 'Lithuanian Euro-institutions and Democracy', NATO Research Fellowship Programme, Final Report (Unpublished Paper, 1998), p. 28.
44 Lietuvos Respublikos Seimas, *Lietuvos Respublikos Seimo Europos Reikalu Komiteto Isvada-Pranesimas*, p. 21.
45 'Hungarian Task Force Supports Country's Integration Goals', *Public Management Forum*, 2:4 (1996), 3.
46 Bulmer and Burch, 'Organizing for Europe', p. 614.
47 T. Verheijen, 'The Management of EU Affairs in Candidate Member States: Inventory of the Current State of Affairs', in OECD, *Preparing Public Administrations for the European Administrative Space*, Sigma Papers, 23 (Paris, OECD, 1998), p. 20.
48 B. Soetendorp and K. Hanf, 'The Netherlands: Growing Doubts of a Loyal Member', in K. Hanf and B. Soetendorp (eds), *Adapting to European Integration: Small tates and the European Union* (London, Longman, 1998), pp. 41–42.
49 Wright, 'The National Coordination', pp. 148–149.
50 N. Barr, 'The Forces Driving Change', in N. Barr (ed.), *Labor Markets and Social Policy in Central and Eastern Europe: The Transition and Beyond* (Oxford, Oxford University Press, 1994), p. 105.

51 Barr, 'The Forces Driving Change', p. 621.
52 P. Luif, 'Austria: Adaptation through Anticipation', in K. Hanf and B. Soetendorp (eds), *Adapting to European Integration: Small States and the European Union* (London, Longman, 1998), p. 126.
53 Mayhew, *Recreating Europe*, p. 222.
54 France, for instance, set up a number of 'mobilisation groups' in an attempt to facilitate the exchange of information between its bureaucracy and interest organisations. See S. Mazey and J. Richardson, 'Promiscuous Policymaking: The European Policy Style?', in C. Rhodes and S. Mazey (eds), *The State of The European Union: Building a European Polity?*, 3 (London, Longman, 1995), p. 353.
55 Mayhew, *Recreating Europe*, pp. 222–223.
56 See M. A. Rupp, 'The Pre-accession Strategy and the Governmental Structures of the Visegrad Countries', in K. Henderson (ed.) *Back to Europe: Central and Eastern Europe and the European Union* (Philadelphia, UCL Press, 1999), p. 98.
57 Wright, 'The National Coordination', p. 149.
58 Commission of the European Communities (1995), *Preparation of the Associated Countries of Central and Eastern Europe for Integration into the Internal Market of the Union*, COM (95) 163 Final, 3 May.
59 Lietuvos Respublikos Seimas, *Lietuvos Respublikos Seimo Europos Reikalu Komiteto Isvada-Pranesimas*, p. 15.
60 Commission of the European Communities, *Regular Report*.
61 Lietuvos Respublikos Seimas, *Lietuvos Respublikos Seimo Europos Reikalu Komiteto Isvada-Pranesimas*, p. 15.
62 Interviews with senior Lithuanian officials, December 1998 – January 1999.
63 F. Morata, 'Spain: Modernization through Integration', in K. Hanf and B. Soetendorp (eds), *Adapting to European integration: Small States and the European Union* (London, Longman, 1998), p. 105.
64 The Commission's steering ability is facilitated by its perception as being at the top of administrative hierarchy, in the same way as Moscow was perceived under Soviet rule.
65 Commission of the European Communities, *Regular Report*.
66 Lietuvos Respublikos Seimas, *Lietuvos Respublikos Seimo Europos Reikalu Komiteto Isvada-Pranesimas*, p. 26.
67 Government of the Republic of Lithuania, *Action Programme of the Government of the Republic of Lithuania for 1997–2000: At a Half-way Point the Major Part of the Measures Stipulated for Four Years Have Already Been Implemented* (Vilnius, 1999).
68 S. Z. von Dosenrode, 'Denmark: The Testing of a Hesitant Membership', in K. Hanf and B. Soetendorp (eds), *Adapting to European Integration: Small States and the European Union* (London, Longman, 1998), p. 55.
69 *Lietuvos Rytas*, 26 November 1998, 'Biurokratu armija is valstybes kaulija milijardus litu', p. 3.
70 Lietuvos Respublikos Seimas, *Lietuvos Respublikos Seimo Europos Reikalu Komiteto Isvada-Pranesimas*, p. 18.
71 J. Fournier, 'Governance and European Integration: Reliable Public Administration', in OECD, *Preparing Public Administration for the European Administrative Space*, Sigma Papers, 23 (Paris, OECD, 1998), pp. 124–125.
72 T. Conzelmann, '"Europeanization" of Regional Development Policies? Linking the Multi-level Governance Approach with Theories of Policy Learning and Policy Change', *European Integration Online Papers*, 2:4 (1998), 8.
73 EBRD, *Transition Report 1998: Financial Sector in Transition* (London, EBRD, 1998), p. 5.
74 C. J. Bennet and M. Howlett, 'The Lessons of Learning: Reconciling Theories of Policy Learning and Policy Change', *Policy Sciences*, 25:2 (1992), 292–294, quoted in Conzemann, '"Europeanization" of Regional Development Policies', p. 8.

75 J. Zielonka, *Policies Without Strategy: The EU's Record in Eastern Europe*, Working Paper, 97/72 (EUI, Robert Schuman Centre, 1997), p. 4.
76 *An Evaluation of Phare Customs Programmes*, Final Report (1998).
77 *Financial Times*, 10 June 1993, 'Brittan Admits Flaws in Aid', p. 3.
78 *An Evaluation of Phare Restructuring and Privatisation Programmes*, Final Report (1998).
79 Mayhew, *Recreating Europe*, p. 145.
80 Pratley, 'Financial Control', p. 152.
81 *An Evaluation of Phare Customs Programmes.*
82 *An Evaluation of Phare Cross-Border Co-operation Programme*, Final Report (1998).
83 *An Evaluation of Phare Banking Sector Programmes*, Final Report (1998).
84 *An Evaluation of Phare Restructuring and Privatisation Programmes.*
85 J. Caddy, 'Harmonisation and Asymmetry: Environmental Policy Coordination between the European Union and Central Europe', *Journal of European Public Policy*, 4:3 (1997), 325.
86 *An Evaluation of Phare Restructuring and Privatisation Programmes.*
87 *Ibid.*
88 In late-1997, the Luxembourg European Council decided that the remaining 70 per cent of the overall amount, previously allocated to investment projects, would be spent on investments related to the adoption and implementation of the *acquis*. Commission of the European Communities (1997), *European Council: Conclusions of the Presidency* (Bulletin of the European Union).
89 'Council Regulation No. 622/98 of 16 March 1998 on Assistance to the Applicant States in the Framework of the Pre-Accession Strategy, and in Particular on the Establishment of Accession Partnerships', *Official Journal of the European Communities*, L 85, 20 March 1998 (Office for Official Publications of the European Communities), p. 2.
90 See *Financial Times*, 22 December 1997, 'EU Conditions for Aid Under Attack', p. 2.
91 *The Economist*, 6 June 1998, 'Humble Pie for Poland', p. 51.
92 Commission of the European Communities, *Regular Report.*
93 *Agence Europe*, 23 October 1998, 'Commission to Launch "Twinning" in January 1999, with Dispatch of First National Officials to the Ministries of Countries Candidates for Accession'.
94 Interview with senior Lithuanian officials, January 1999.
95 Interview with senior Lithuanian officials, December 1998–January 1999.
96 *Agence Europe*, 30 December 1998, 'European Commission Interim Report on the Action Programme on Equal Opportunities for Men and Women Takes Stock of Progress Achieved and Describes Actions to Be Developed'.
97 *Agence Europe*, 11 May 1998, 'Commission proposes that Council authorise participation of several CEECs in a number of Community programmes'.
98 See 'Decision No. 4/98 of the Association Council Adopting the Terms and Conditions for the Participation of Lithuania in the Community Programmes in the Field of Culture', *Official Journal of the European Communities*, L 35, 9 February 1999 (Office for Official Publications of the European Communities), pp. 42–44.
99 *Financial Times*, 16 November 1995, 'Brussels Keeps Shut the Gates to the East', p. 25.
100 Formal agenda-setting is defined as the ability to set the procedural agenda, while informal agenda-setting as the ability to set the informal or substantive agenda. See M. A. Pollack, 'Delegation, Agency, and Agenda-setting in the European Community', *International Organization*, 51:1 (1997) 121.
101 See Grabbe, *A Partnership for Accession?*, p. 11.
102 For instance, in early 1999 the EU–Lithuanian Association Council meeting discussed the national energy strategy, public administration reform, border control and control of illegal migration. See *Lietuvos Rytas*, 23 February 1999, 'Liuksemburge – apie Lietuvos ateiti', p. 2.

103 Mayhew, *Recreating Europe*, p. 163.
104 V. Birkavs, 'Planning EU Integration after Cannes', *Public Management Forum*, 1:3 (1995) 1.
105 *Agence Europe*, 27 February 1998, '15 Member States and 9 Associate Countries Make Improvements to "Structured Dialogue"'.
106 Rupp, 'The Pre-accession Strategy', p. 94.
107 J. Fournier, 'Administrative Reform in the Commission Opinions Concerning the Accession of the Central and Eastern European Countries to the European Union', in OECD, *Preparing Public Administrations for the European Administrative Space*, Sigma Papers, 23 (OECD, 1998), p. 113.
108 'Council Decisions 98/259/EC – 98/268/EC', *Official Journal of the European Communities*, L 121, 23 April 1998 (Office for Official Publications of the European Communities).
109 See Special Provisions (Annex C), 'Financing Memorandum between the European Community and the Government of Lithuania', 10 December 1998. Under the Financing Memorandum, Lithuania was obliged to meet a number of priority objectives specified in the Accession Partnership agreement, while the Commission was obliged to fund their implementation.

Lauri Leppik

7

Social protection and EU enlargement

The case of Estonia

It is no secret that the impact of EU accession on the ten applicant countries from Central and Eastern Europe (CEE) has been and will continue to be wide-ranging and deep. These implications include political, legal, fiscal and commercial issues as well as countless others. The main objective of this chapter will be to examine the most important implications for social policy in the case of one CEE country, Estonia.

Although a number of factors likely to influence applicant-country social protection systems could be identified, this chapter will concentrate on legal and policy factors. In particular, the implications of taking over the *acquis communautaire* in the field of social protection will be in the centre of the analysis. Based on the principle of subsidiarity, the area of social policy in the EU is primarily within the competence of the member states. On that basis it could be argued that the applicant countries should not have serious problems in meeting the requirements of the *acquis* and that the implications of accession should be minor. On the other hand, some authors have argued that a premature imposition of EU social regulations on many of the CEE applicant countries might prove unsustainable given current levels of economic development in these societies.[1] This chapter will therefore take a closer look at these issues and try to establish to what extent these assumptions are valid.

In the first section a brief overview of the development and current structure of the Estonian social protection system is provided. The aim is not to give a detailed description of the national system, but to provide necessary background information for evaluating the impact of accession-related factors. In the following sections, more specific issues related to the *acquis* as well as other political conditions in the field of social protection are analysed. The chapter will argue that by the late 1990s Estonia had already fulfilled or exceeded most EU requirements; however, application of the *acquis* upon accession will have important indirect implications.

Overview of the social protection system of Estonia

All of the current schemes of social protection in Estonia were either created or radically reformed after the restoration of independence. For example, under the Soviet regime there was no minimum income guarantee; family benefits were limited to low-income families; there were no unemployment benefits; health care was free of charge. After 1991, all of these aspects (along with many others) changed. The previous health care system with state-managed hospitals was radically reformed and a system of health insurance based on sickness funds was established. The same year also saw the introduction of unemployment benefits. The Soviet pension law was suspended in 1992 and a new, contribution-based (or social-tax-financed) state pension system was created. Universal family benefits and funeral grants were introduced in 1993. A system of minimum guaranteed income benefits as well as a basic social services structure were both established in 1995.

As a result, the current social security system of Estonia consists of five schemes:

1. pension insurance (including national, old age, invalidity and survivors' pensions);
2. health insurance (including medical treatment, sickness and maternity benefits);
3. family benefits (including birth grants, child benefits, child care allowances etc.);
4. unemployment benefits (including unemployment allowances, labour market grants, retraining stipends);
5. funeral grants.

All of these schemes are administered by the national government. In terms of financing, however, the pension as well as health insurance schemes are financed from social tax revenues, while the family benefit, unemployment benefit and funeral grant schemes are financed from the general state budget. In this respect, the first two schemes are considered 'contributory' social security schemes or insurance-type schemes, while the latter three are non-contributory. For the pension and health insurance schemes, the current rate of social tax is 33 per cent.[2] However, all of this is paid by the employer, based on a firm's gross payroll. This makes Estonia somewhat exceptional compared to the EU countries, where employees generally contribute as well (see table 7.1.).

In addition, Estonia has a separate system of social welfare, which includes national- and local-level social assistance benefits and social services. These are administered by local governments, although the cash benefits are funded from the national budget. Lastly, some additional benefits and most social services[3] are financed by local taxes.

In terms of eligibility, social security and social assistance rights in Estonia are primarily residence-based. This means that along with citizens Estonia's

Table 7.1 Social contribution rates in the EU and Estonia

	Total	*Employee*	*Employer*
Austria	40.40	17.20	23.20
Belgium	39.68	13.07	26.61
Germany	40.20	20.10	20.10
Greece	35.06	11.65	23.41
Finland	30.70	7.70	23.00
France	48.75	15.87	32.88
Ireland	16.25	7.75	8.50
Italy	55.54	10.19	45.35
Luxembourg	26.70	12.50	14.20
Netherlands	53.80	42.85	10.95
Portugal	34.75	11.50	23.25
Spain	37.2	6.40	30.80
Sweden	35.89	3.95	31.94
UK	20.20	10.00	10.20
Estonia	33.00	0.00	33.00

Source: MISSOC 1996.

sizable non-citizen population is also covered. Residence is the only criterion for receipt of national pension, family benefits, funeral grants and social assistance benefits, when a contingency occurs. For old-age, invalidity and survivors' pensions, and unemployment benefits, fulfilment of an additional employment-related qualification period is required.

Regarding health insurance, individuals are insured, firstly, on the basis of having paid social taxes, but since a number of other population categories (e.g. pensioners, children, registered unemployed, military personnel, parents on parental leave, etc.) are equalised with the insured, the coverage is nearly universal.[4]

As for cash benefits, flat-rate benefits prevail. National pensions, family benefits, unemployment benefits and funeral grants are all flat-rate benefits. Old-age, invalidity and survivors' pensions consist of a flat-rate amount supplemented with an employment-related amount (until 1998 depending on how many years an individual was gainfully employed, from 1999 depending on the amount of social tax paid on the wage). Sickness cash benefits are currently the only case of an earnings-related benefit, while the social assistance or minimum guaranteed income benefit is the only means-tested benefit.

In the late 1990s, social protection expenditures in Estonia accounted for 16–17 per cent of GDP. In comparative terms, this placed Estonia fairly far behind the average levels of GDP spending on social protection elsewhere in the EU (see table 7.2). However, it should be kept in mind that at least in the OECD countries the share of social protection expenditure in GDP correlates with the GDP per capita, meaning that more affluent countries spend relatively more on social protection than lower-income countries.[5]

Table 7.2 GDP per capita and social protection expenditure in the EU (1995) and Estonia (1997)

	GDP per capita ECU	*GDP per capita PPP*	*Social protection expenditure in GDP (%)*
Luxembourg	32,249	29,027	25.3
Denmark	24,747	19,555	34.3
Germany	22,610	19,075	29.4
Austria	22,006	19,171	29.7
Belgium	20,613	19,629	29.7
Sweden	20,116	17,513	35.6
United Kingdom	20,116	16,613	27.3
France	20,109	18,433	30.6
Netherlands	19,673	19,567	31.6
Finland	18,857	16,668	32.8
Italy	14,249	17,768	24.6
Ireland	13,780	16,070	19.9
Spain	10,989	13,316	21.8
Greece	8,395	11,367	21.0
Portugal	8,068	12,059	20.7
Estonia	2,800	7,000	17.3

Sources: Eurostat (1998); Social protection in Europe (1997).

While the overall tax burden in the late 1990s was around 34–35 per cent of GDP, social protection expenditures amounted to nearly 50 per cent of consolidated general government tax spending. Social protection expenditures were financed predominantly from social security contributions of employers (social tax), which in 1996 accounted for 71.5 per cent of the total expenditure. General state taxes made up 25.5 per cent and resources of local government comprised the remaining 3 per cent of the total expenditure.

Estonia as a hybrid European system

With this background information in place, the next question becomes, how does Estonia's social protection system compare to that of the EU? In order to answer this question, it is worth assessing, first, the overall philosophical orientation of Estonia's social protection system.

Within the EU, the practices of the existing member states vary as a result of different historical, cultural and political factors. The systems have often been divided into four groups or so-called geo-social models of social protection.[6]

The first group is comprised of the Scandinavian countries: Denmark, Finland and Sweden. Here social protection is seen as a civil right, coverage is fully universal. Everybody is entitled to a flat-rate basic amount when a risk arises, while those gainfully employed receive additional earnings-related benefits through mandatory occupational schemes. General taxation plays a predominant role in financing. As a rule, state authorities are responsible for the administration, and there is a unitary system which integrates different branches of social protection. The only exception to this public core is unemployment insurance, which is voluntary and managed by the trade unions.

The second group consists of the UK and Ireland. Similar to the Scandinavian case, social coverage is universal or nearly universal; however, the basic amounts of benefits are more modest, and there is a wider use of means-testing. Health care is financed from general taxation, but contributions play an important role in the financing of cash benefits. As in Scandinavia, public authorities are responsible for administration, and the delivery system is integrated. The role of social partners in policy development and management, however, is marginal.

The third group includes Germany, France, the Benelux counties and Austria. Here the coverage relies largely on the so-called 'Bismarckian' tradition, where cash benefits are mostly earnings-related and predominantly contribution-financed. Professional funds play a prominent administrative role, although the involvement of social partners is also high. Administration of social protection is often segregated and different rules apply to different occupational groups.

The fourth group encompasses the southern states: Italy, Spain, Portugal and Greece. The institutional design here is similarly a mixed pattern. In the area of cash benefits, there are fragmented 'Bismarckian' systems, which offer rather generous pensions. However the system has substantial gaps in coverage, while the safety net is weak. At the same time, the health services are national with universal coverage. Occupational funds and social partners play a prominent role in cash benefit schemes, but not in health care.

The Estonian case does not completely match any of those geo-social models. Geographically, the Scandinavian model should be closest, but from the social aspect this is not fully the case. Rather, Estonia's universal (or nearly universal) coverage, substantial role of flat-rate benefits with relatively low replacement rates and publicly administrated schemes with a minor role for the social partners make the 'Anglo-Irish' model the closest match. But here we also see substantial differences, including Estonia's greater preference for contribution-based financing (in particular, the contribution-financed health insurance system) as well as its limitation of means-testing to the minimum income guarantee (and not to other social security schemes). As a result, this comparison serves primarily the purpose of identifying potential partners for Estonia in future EU social policy debates. In order to understand more specifically the impact of EU accession on Estonia's social protection system, it is necessary to turn to the actual requirements of the *acquis* and other binding norms.

The general role of social policy among accession criteria

Although during the general process of EU enlargement there was broad agreement that economic and political criteria would play a primary role in weighting different applicant countries, views about the relevance of social policy differed quite substantially from one actor to another. For example, the European Commission's 1995 White Paper on preparing the countries of Central and Eastern Europe for 'Integration into the Internal Market of Union' stated the member states' position very clearly, 'The European Councils have emphasised that approximation in the social area must not be neglected by the association countries and forms an essential part of their preparations for accession to the Union.'[7]

Nevertheless, the Commission's own views in the White Paper were more neutral: 'The inclusion of legislation in the fields of competition, social and environmental policy, parts of which are essential to the functioning of the internal market, will ensure a balanced approach.'[8] In part, this discrepancy echoes a broader argument according to which the Commission has been a central actor in attempts to construct a larger 'social dimension' of the Union, while the Council (or the member states) has been wary of such a move and/or prevented it.[9] Still, as the title of the White Paper on market integration suggests, the internal market played a dominant role during debates of this early period. Moreover, the White Paper referred only to the assumption of EU 'hard law' (or regulations and directives), which in the social policy field was rather limited. 'Soft law' in the social field (meaning recommendations, resolutions and other documents) was left out entirely.

The legal measures described in the White Paper were broken down into two levels of priority: stage I measures reflected issues of highest priority, while stage II measures were considered secondary. Remarkably, both the main topics of social protection, which were raised in the White Paper, i.e. equal treatment of women and men in social security schemes and coordination of social security for migrant workers, were classified in the second stage.[10]

Furthermore, the social dimension also received relatively little attention in the Commission's *avis* or Agenda 2000. On the one hand, the questionnaire, which was sent to the applicant countries and on the basis of which the avis was later compiled, did make reference to some pieces of social policy 'soft law'.[11] In addition, the so-called TAIEX harmonograms and 'screening lists'[12] also contain bits of 'soft law'. Yet in the Agenda 2000 itself, as well as in subsequent progress reports and even during the actual screening process, attention was concentrated only on formal EU directives and regulations.

Considering the importance of the welfare state in forming a 'European identity', it would seem surprising that social policy – and social protection in particular – was given such limited consideration among the political criteria for accession. This is all the more puzzling given the political importance attributed to some other criteria – e.g. the integration of ethnic minorities – in relation to which even some of the current member states reveal weaknesses. The question becomes, why did the Union not impose conditions in an area, where it was strong, while at the same time putting forward conditions in areas where it had a mixed record itself?

It could be argued that the EU's vagueness about social policy accession criteria was a reflection of divided visions within the Union about the proper role of social policy. The EU's benign neglect of social policy during the early accession process therefore reflected a more serious underlying split on European social policy. To be sure, issues such as minority rights were also controversial for the EU member states, but at least at the level of general values the prevailing position was much more unanimous.

However, it could also be argued that the EU's limited stipulation of political conditions in the field of social policy was a logical consideration due to the level of economic development of the CEE applicant countries. In their analysis of which EU policies should come first and what should come last when taking over the *acquis*, Smith *et al.* argued that as the harmonisation of social (and environmental) policy[13] was not necessary to the functioning of the single market, this sector should be left among the last areas where policy alignment would be implemented.[14] They warned that premature harmonisation could damage the competitiveness of the CEE countries. Further they maintained that with the exemption of some elements of these policies, 'process regulation' could be left for a transition period *after* formal accession, and should not form a part of pre-accession strategy. Similarly, Rollo found that a full application of the EU's social (and environmental) policy requirements by the CEE countries was not sustainable at current levels of economic productivity.[15] Admittedly, in most cases these authors did not back up their claims with any detailed analysis or cite particular policies. Often they also referred to the general 'social dimension'[16] of the EU, and not simply to social protection, as studied here. However, even in the latter domain the potential for new burdens on the CEE countries was there.

Europe Agreement

In principle, the core legal instrument, which provided for the approximation of legislation and cooperation between the EU and Estonia during the pre-accession period, was the Europe Agreement, or the 1995 treaty, which established an association between the two sides. While the basic objective of the document was 'to provide an appropriate framework for the gradual integration of Estonia into the European Union', it also contained certain provisions on social security. In general, these were presented by the Commission as a preparatory stage towards implementation of more complex EU social security coordination regulations.[17] As a result, the respective provisions of Estonia's Europe Agreement (Art. 37–39) were limited to just three questions:

1 the export of pensions linked to old age, death, work accident or occupational disease (with the exception of non-contributory benefits);
2 the equal treatment of persons with respect to family allowances;
3 the aggregation of insurance periods completed in the various member states for the purpose of pensions and annuities with respect to old age, invalidity and death and for the purpose of medical care for workers and their family members.

These 'partial coordination' provisions reflected the EU's general social security coordination policy towards third states, which had association or cooperation agreements with the Community.[18] However, the provisions were not fully reciprocal.[19] The first two (export of pensions and granting of family allowances) were symmetrical, while the third was applied only to Estonian nationals. As the Europe Agreement did not establish free movement of workers, there was also no aggregation of insurance periods across the EU border for establishing rights to social security benefits. Only insurance periods completed by Estonians in different member states could be added up. Furthermore, the application of these provisions was limited to citizens only.

The primary impact of the Europe Agreements' social security provisions on Estonia would arise from the obligation to export pensions. Estonian law limits the payment of pensions to persons resident on the territory of Estonia. Only in cases, where Estonia had concluded a separate bilateral social security agreement, could pensions be exported to other countries. (As of 2001, these countries included Finland, Latvia, Lithuania and Ukraine.) Still, this experience of social security coordination is rather limited, as all of these agreements came into force only in 1997. As a result, Estonian (and other CEE) employees legally resident and working in the member states were considered to be third-country nationals, and confronted the typical problems associated with such status. Even when covered by social security in a given member state, there was no guarantee that these rights could be retained if the person moved to another EU country[20] or returned to Estonia.

In sum, the role of the Europe Agreement in preparing for implementation of EU social security coordination regulations in Estonia is rather small. (Furthermore, even by 2001 these provisions had not yet entered into force because of the absence of implementing provisions.) Instead, Estonia would gain much more experience in social security coordination via specific, bilateral agreements as well as through participation in the EU PHARE Consensus Programme, which also sought to provide advice on social protection.

Conditions set in the Agenda 2000 and Accession Partnership

Although the EU generally paid little attention to social protection within the scope of its pre-accession requirements, some notable references relating to this domain did arise as a result of the Commission's Agenda 2000 opinion and within the subsequent Accession Partnership. For example, in its 1997 *avis* on Estonia the Commission included four general statements on social protection. First, under economic criteria and also in the final conclusions, the opinion expressed concern that 'reform of the pension system has not yet started'. Second, under the human rights section it noted that Estonia 'has not signed the European Social Charter'. Third, it acknowledged that Estonia was 'in the process of preparing a number of social reforms replacing earlier laws'. However, ultimately it maintained that 'Continued efforts are required to ensure that measures of social protection are developed.'

In relation to more specific areas such as social security for migrant workers, the Commission found that 'accession does not, in principle, pose major problems', adding that '[m]ore important is the administrative capacity to apply the detailed coordination rules in cooperation with other countries. Estonia appears to have many administrative structures required to carry out these tasks, but further preparation and training will be necessary before accession'.

With respect to pension reform, the descriptive and analytic part of the *avis* made no further reference to this subject. For example, it did not state what problems were observed regarding the present system or what was to be the expected outcome of reform. Indeed, since the regulation of pension systems in the EU is within the competence of the member states, the grounds for putting forward such a condition was unclear. Nevertheless, in Estonia's subsequent Accession Partnership with the EU, Tallinn committed itself in the short term to adopting key legislation related to pension reform, while in the medium term it pledged a 'further development of social protection'.

In this respect, the only substantive requirement to come out of the Agenda 2000 document was for Estonia to sign the European Social Charter. On 4 May 1998, Estonia signed the revised, 1996, version of the European Social Charter, followed by ratification in May 2000. As a result, the *avis* was clearly a factor accelerating this process. Likewise, it could be said that the Accession Partnership had an accelerating effect on pension reform, for even though Estonia's pension reform package had essentially been elaborated before the *avis* was announced, the commitments taken in the Accession Partnership helped to sustain the reform timetable during a period of minority government in Estonia as well as general political squabbles over the issue.

The *acquis* in the field of social protection

As is generally known, the first principle of EU enlargement is that applicant countries must accept the *acquis communautaire* in full. No permanent opt-outs are possible.[21] Let us therefore make a short inventory of what in legal terms is exactly required in the field of social policy. The binding *acquis communautaire* of the European Union in the field of social policy has been limited to the four major issues:

1 coordination of social security schemes for migrant workers;
2 equal treatment of men and women;
3 health and safety at work;
4 some questions of labour law.

Out of these four areas, only the first two are concerned with social protection; the other two fall under the broader domain of 'social regulation'. Yet, as the Commission points out, all four of these areas have an internal market reasoning among its justifications, and therefore contribute to a certain 'level playing field' within the EU.[22]

Coordination of social security schemes in the EU

The EU social security coordination rules serve the objective of facilitating the freedom of movement of workers. In the words of the 1995 White Paper:

> Without such protection, the existing disparities between the social security systems of the different member states would adversely affect people moving across frontiers. They would risk losing all or part of their rights acquired or in the process of being acquired under national legislation, when leaving their country to work, to look for a job or to stay elsewhere in the Community.[23]

With respect to areas subject to coordination, all of the classical branches of social security are covered, including:

- sickness and maternity benefits;
- invalidity benefits;
- old-age benefits;
- survivors' benefits;
- work accident and occupational disease benefits;
- death grants;
- unemployment benefits;
- family benefits.

With respect to procedures, the EU's coordination rules are based on four key principles:[24]

1 *Equal treatment of one's own nationals and nationals of the other member states.*[25] Intra-Community migrant workers are subject to the same obligations (e.g. with respect to the payment of social contributions) and are entitled to the same benefits as the nationals of that state based on national legislation.
2 *Applicability of only one state's legislation for each individual.* This principle protects against both positive and negative conflicts of law, ensuring that persons can't be entitled to the same benefits from two countries simultaneously, while guaranteeing that they are always insured somewhere, but do not have to pay social security contributions in more than one state. The

main rule here is the principle of *lex loci laboris*, i.e. legislation of the state of employment is applicable.

3 *Retention of acquired rights.* Persons who have acquired rights for social security benefits in one member state maintain these rights irrespective of any movement of residence to another member state. This implies intra-Community export of benefits (primarily pensions) for the persons concerned.

4 *Aggregation of periods of insurance or residence.* In case the right to benefit is subject to a qualification period or the amount of benefit depends on the period of insurance or residence, periods completed in other member states are also taken into account. When paying out pensions, a *pro rata* principle is used. Each member state involved has to pay that share of the total amount, which corresponds to the insurance period completed in that state.

With respect to the implementation of these coordination regulations, the White Paper clarified that, 'The extension of these Regulations . . . should not be thought of in terms of gradual development [stage I, stage II . . .], but rather as a single step to be taken after accession.' The Commission also stressed not only in its White Paper, but also in the Agenda 2000 and the Accession Partnership that the most important factor here was a candidate country's administrative capacity to apply the detailed coordination rules in cooperation with other states. In addition, in many cases technical adaptations would be needed to the regulations themselves, in particular, to their annexes. These would also necessitate specific negotiations and take time.

The impact of EU social security coordination on Estonia

As the 'migrant worker regulations' deal only with social security coordination and not with harmonisation, no formal changes to national legislation were necessarily incumbent on Estonia. Nevertheless, this did not mean that the principle of coordination would leave Estonia's social protection system unaffected. In fact, there were a number of ways in which these rules would influence national systems.

The EU's coordination system naturally assumes that each of the eight branches of social security listed above is present. Or, as has been said, it is not possible to coordinate something with nothing. Of course, this does not mean that all benefits present in one state should have analogues in every other state. Nevertheless, there is an assumption that some sort of protection has to be offered against the eight social risks. This basic assumption was satisfied in the case of Estonia (as well as for all other CEE countries).

Second, the application of coordination rules has financial implications. It adds a financial burden to existing social security schemes, since the regulations give persons moving within the Union new rights. However, the resulting financial implications are not of the same degree across countries; they vary depending on the number of migrants[26] and the provisions of national legislation.

In the case of Estonia, the two largest social protection schemes, i.e. health insurance and pension insurance, will be the most influenced. In line with the balanced budget doctrine of Estonia, these schemes have applied a prudent 'closed envelope' financing approach, meaning the levels of expenditure (in the case of pension insurance: the level of pensions) are determined on the basis of incoming revenues.[27] In this situation, an additional burden does not necessarily imply increase of expenditures, but it will affect the redistribution pattern of the schemes. The burden arises most notably from the following aspects:

1 According to Estonian social security legislation, the payment of pensions and other benefits is limited to those residing in Estonia. Export of benefits is not provided, except under a bilateral social security agreement. With accession, the right to a pension will be extended to the whole territory of the Union.[28]
2 With accession, those covered by health insurance in Estonia will obtain a right to emergency medical care in any other member state. This includes those travelling as tourists in the member states who will no longer be obliged to buy private travel insurance, but will be insured by the public purse.
3 In the case of migrant workers from the other member states whose dependent family members do not transfer their residence, Estonia would have to refund the medical care (not only emergency, but also regular) delivered in another member state to those family members.

The burden on health insurance is expected to be more significant as compared to that of pension insurance. In the latter case, exported pensions (or parts thereof) are still paid according to Estonian rates. In the former case, treatment costs will have to be refunded by the Estonian health insurance system on the basis of the actual amounts incurred in EU member states. Given the existing differences in the cost of medical services between Estonia and the current EU member states, the effect is estimated to amount to 3 per cent of the current health insurance budget.[29]

For Estonian tourists to EU countries, the risk or potential need for emergency medical care is currently an individual responsibility. Under EU rules this will become a collective responsibility. As higher-income persons tend to travel more often, the obligation to reimburse treatment costs thus means that higher-income people will absorb in relative terms more resources from the health insurance funds.

At the inter-state level, differences in medical care (given also the fact that they are likely to be maintained, as health care is a closed and highly regulated sector) mean that the effects of reimbursement are disproportional to lower-income countries.

Although, in theory, the social security coordination rules should not discriminate against specific types of schemes, the reality is somewhat different. Some types of schemes are more suited to coordination than others. From the state's perspective (and not necessarily from the perspective of concerned individuals), the most problematic are residence-based schemes, which offer universal flat-rate benefits with no qualification period.[30] As access to these benefits is relatively easy, coordination can increase costs significantly. Finland and Sweden, where universal benefits are widespread, modified some characteristics of their universal schemes before entering the Union. As universal flat-rate benefits have also been the predominant type of cash benefit in Estonia, accession will force a tightening of the eligibility criteria and the introduction of *pro rata* principles into benefit calculation methods.

The regulations implicitly favour schemes designed to protect an economically active population by offering earnings-related benefits, or benefits which relate to either previous earnings, previous insurance contributions, previous periods of insurance coverage or any combination of these factors. In other words, the regulations are built around a typical Bismarckian model of social security. Another favourable option for the states would be targeted means-tested benefits, which escape coordination as they are considered social assistance, not social security. Also, in-kind benefits (as opposed to in-cash benefits) are largely non-problematic as they are not exportable.

Solutions to these problems have been suggested, but so far rejected.[31] It is important to recall here that the system of social security coordination was developed as a measure of 'market-building', and has been locked into this. Changing the current principles of coordination to accommodate better residence-based schemes is regarded by some actors as a 'spillover' into a 'non-market' area, and has therefore drawn both praise and criticism.

Social security coordination rules also have a substantial indirect impact upon future policy-making in the area of social security. They limit the policy options otherwise available.[32] For example, a state may not limit social security benefits only to its nationals. Or, in case there is such a limit, the coordination rules would extend these benefits automatically to all nationals of the member states (and also stateless persons and refugees). Likewise, a state may not limit the payment of social security benefits to its own territory. Or, again, if this were done, the coordination rules would extend the payment of such benefits to the whole territory of the Union.[33] Nonetheless, it remains the case that such limitations can still be imposed with respect to nationals and territories of third countries.

The fact that the EU social security coordination rules do not yet apply to third-country nationals may also have important implications in relation to the Russian-speaking minority in Estonia. In particular, those Russian-speakers, who have opted for Russian Federation citizenship and who number around 100,000 people or 7 per cent of the population, will not have the additional rights arising from coordination regulations once Estonia has joined.[34] This may create a new separation line among Russian-speakers, but may also prompt some of these Russian-speakers to give up Russian citizenship and apply for Estonian nationality.

It should also be mentioned here that some of the current member states have shown a reluctance to open up their labour market to nationals from Central and Eastern Europe once these states join, and they have suggested the use of transition periods on the free movement of labour for the first seven years after enlargement. If these transition periods are implemented, they will also have important implications for social security coordination. If workers are not allowed to move freely from the moment of accession, this will decrease demand for social security coordination with a subsequently lower burden for the national schemes of CEE countries. From this perspective, the controversial issue of transition periods on free movement could be regarded as a measure softening the expected burden on social security.

Equal treatment in social security

Equal treatment of men and women in social security schemes is the second most important issue of EU competence in the field of social protection. In fact, it is the only area in the field of social protection where the EU has imposed formal standards upon the member states. The principles of equal treatment are prescribed in the directives 79/7 and 86/378. The first of these directives deals with statutory social security schemes and the second with occupational social security schemes. The main principle of the directives is that there should be no discrimination (direct or indirect) on the grounds of gender with respect to access to benefits (eligibility criteria), calculation of contributions and benefits. However, the directive on statutory social security schemes allows the member states to make some temporary derogations from this main principle and exclude from its scope pension age eligibility and advantages with respect to raising children. In relation to occupational social security schemes, no exceptions are permitted, but as occupational social security is not developed in Estonia, this directive will have only limited practical implications.

Gender equality provisions have required extensive reforms in the current member states often with remarkable financial implications. This has been mainly as a result of social security schemes being based on a male breadwinner family model in the traditional Bismarckian social security system. In contrast to the situation in the member states when these directives were adopted, Estonia has a relatively good starting position.

In general, social security rights in Estonia are individual, not rights derived from the employment status of the spouse. Therefore, equal treatment in social security, at least in legal terms, is to a great extent already in place. There has been some positive discrimination, as certain provisions have been more favourable for women. The number of such provisions has been reduced, but a few cases still remain.[35] In 1998, the Estonian parliament decided to gradually equalise the pension age of men and women at the level of 63 years by the year 2016. Indeed, the EU equal treatment principle was used to back up this plan.[36] Other positive discrimination provisions related to advantages with respect to raising children or to special protection for motherhood, thus falling under exceptions where differential treatment was allowed by EU law.

European social protection minimum standards

The Treaty of Amsterdam introduced several changes into the 'social dimension' of the Union. As one particular point, the new Article 136 refers to the 1961 European Social Charter, thereby linking this key convention of the Council of Europe to the Union *acquis*. While this change was undoubtedly a step forward for the European social dimension, it is likely that this reference was introduced also with the EU's eastern enlargement in mind. For, considering the fact that all of the current member states are Contracting Parties of the Charter, this reference did not impose any new commitments on them. Rather, it is possible that the inclusion was regarded as a preventive measure against possible social dumping in the light of future enlargements. The move is all the more curious given that hitherto the member states had not agreed to adopt social protection standards within the European Union itself, but had instead recognised social standards within the framework of the Council of Europe. This paradox can be seen as an attempt by the current EU member states to keep their 'economic self' and 'social self' in separation.

Regardless of these motives, however, the shift in EU social policy standards as a result of the Amsterdam treaty remained for Estonia something it would need to take into account. Article 12, paragraph 2, of the European Social Charter requires the Contracting Parties, 'to maintain the social security system at a satisfactory level at least equal to that required for ratification of International Labour Convention (No. 102) Concerning Minimum Standards of Social Security'. To see what this provision means for Estonia, it is useful to compare Estonia's system of social security not so much to the 1952 ILO Convention, but rather to the requirements of the European Code of Social Security,[38] which is almost identical to it.[38] Furthermore, Article 12 of the European (revised) Social Charter,[39] which will supersede the original Charter, refers to the European Code of Social Security. As Estonia has ratified the European (revised) Social Charter, the standards of the Code have more practical relevance for Estonia.

Although both the Social Charter and the Code describe the so-called 'European social protection minimum standards', both instruments are characterised as enacting an *à la carte* standard, meaning within certain limits states may choose their own standards. The Code covers the following nine branches of social security: medical care, sickness benefits, unemployment benefits, old-age benefits, employment injury benefits, family benefits, maternity benefits, invalidity benefits and survivors' benefits. Respecting the degree of diversity of social security systems all over Europe, the Code (and the earlier ILO convention) was constructed in such a way as to accommodate different solutions with respect to classes of protected persons, forms of cash benefits, financing and administration. The Contracting Parties are free to choose:

- whether to protect classes of employees, the economically active population, or all residents;
- whether to pay cash benefits either as flat-rate, earnings-related or means-tested;
- whether to finance social security through general taxes or social contributions of employers/employees;
- whether to administrate the schemes of social security through government departments, autonomous public-legal institutions or through the private sector.

The minimum social security standards of the Code tackle three groups of questions:[40]

- standards relating to the number of protected persons;
- legal qualification criteria (e.g. maximum waiting period, eligibility conditions, duration of benefit, etc.);
- standards relating to the level of benefits.

Lastly, for ratification of the Code a state has to comply either:

- with at least six substantive parts relating to the different branches of social security, provided that the part on medical care counts as two parts, and the part on old-age pensions counts as three parts; or
- with at least three parts, including at least one of the following: unemployment, old age, employment injury, invalidity or survivors' benefits; and it must furnish proof that for the remaining branches some of the standards of the Code are exceeded.

An analysis of Estonia's social security legislation and practice against the requirements of the Code shows that by the late 1990s the Estonian social security system already exceeded the requirements of the Code in the branches of medical care, sickness cash benefits, family benefits, maternity benefits and survivors' benefits (see tables 7.3 and 7.4). Concerning old age pensions, the level of benefit in Estonia matched the level set by the Code. In the branches of invalidity, unemployment and employment injury, the benefit levels were below the standards of the Code. In the branches of unemployment benefits and employment injury benefits, some additional legal qualification criteria (i.e. the waiting period and in-kind benefits to be provided) had not been satisfied.

In sum, it can be said that Estonia exceeded the standards of the Code as far as the numbers of protected persons were concerned, but with respect to three branches of social security (unemployment, invalidity and employment injury) it was below the standards on the level of benefits. As the analysis shows,

Table 7.3 Levels of social security benefits in Estonia compared to the requirements of the European Code of Social Security

Contingency	*Rate of benefit (%) for standard beneficiary by the Code*[a]	*Respective % in Estonia prescribed*
Sickness	45	60/80[b]
Unemployment	45	12.1[c]
Old age	40	40.0[c]
Employment injury		
Incapacity to work	50	100.0
Total loss of earning capacity	50	38.4
Survivors	40	79.8
Family benefits	1.5[d]	9.6
Maternity	45	100.0
Invalidity	40	38.4
Survivors	40	79.8

Notes: [a] Contracting Parties are free to choose whether this rate relates to the previous earnings of the beneficiary (possibly subject to a ceiling) or to the wage of an adult male labourer (OAML) or the rate is determined according to a prescribed scale subject to a means-test. [b] Of the previous earnings of the beneficiary: 60% in case of in-patient treatment; 80% in case of out-patient treatment. [c] Of the wage of an OAML. [d] Total value of all benefits shall represent 1.5 per cent of the wage of an OAML multiplied by the total number of children of all residents.

Estonia would be able to ratify the Code, complying with at least five parts of it. Compared to Italy, which has ratified only four parts of the Code, or Ireland, United Kingdom and Switzerland, which have ratified five, the Estonian score is not bad. Ratification of the other parts would require a restructuring of the schemes, which indeed Estonia was beginning to undertake during 2000 (e.g. the unemployment insurance scheme to be introduced from 2002).

Of course, given the fact that the standards of the Code were developed by the states themselves,[41] their adoption in fact reflects nothing more than the objective situation and understandings regarding social protection, which existed in Europe during the 1960s. Indeed, considering also that the Code was (as was mentioned earlier) merely a modification of the ILO's Convention no. 102, it could be said that European standards were already then short of the broader European trend. Lastly, considering the level of social protection that actually exists in the current EU member states, the standards of the Code are in general relatively low.

Although the Code allows for substantial flexibility, from today's perspective it looks biased in many respects. First, it assumes that social security schemes are

Table 7.4 Classes of protected persons in Estonia compared with the requirements of the European Code of Social Security

Contingency	*Category of the population*	*% of the population category which must be covered*	*% covered in Estonia*
Medical care	Residents	50	97.5
Sickness	Economically active residents as a part of total population	20	43.0
Old age	Economically active residents as a part of total population	20	43.0
Family benefits	Economically active residents as a part of total population	20	100.0
Invalidity	Economically active residents as a part of total population	20	100.0
Survivors	Economically active residents as a part of total population	20	100.0
Unemployment	Employees	50	100.0
Employment injury	Employees	50	100.0
Maternity	Employees	50	100.0

built around a male breadwinner family model. Second, it favours schemes with narrow coverage and high levels of benefits over schemes with universal coverage and lower levels of benefits. Third, within the domain of family benefits and maternity benefits it does not foresee an option for residence-based schemes.

As already noted, most social security schemes in Estonia are residence-based with universal coverage (or nearly universal in the case of medical care). So far, only the schemes for old age pensions and unemployment benefits are designed to protect primarily (but not exclusively) the economically active population. Concerning the borderline case of old-age pensions, problematic for Estonia is the fact that the Code considers a standard beneficiary to have 30 years of contribution or employment record. In Estonia, the average length of service of all pensioners is 42 years. While the Estonian 'standard beneficiary' has a substantially longer employment record than the 'standard beneficiary' described in the Code, persons with 30 years of pensionable length of service end up with relatively modest pensions.

In an attempt to modernise the Code and potentially raise the level of some of its social security norms, the European (revised) Code of Social Security[42] was drafted in the 1980s. Yet, following the change in Europe's economic climate during the late 1980s, none of the member states of the Council of Europe has ratified this new version. Estonia exceeds the requirements of the revised Code concerning the branches of medical care, family benefits and maternity benefits, but is below the standards in relation to the other branches. However, as compliance with at least three parts are required for ratification of the new Code, and no special weights are given to any of the branches, Estonia would also be able to ratify the revised Code, though only the minimum.

In sum, the analysis of the Estonian social protection system against the standards of the European Code of Social Security revealed a number of structural aspects where Estonia's systems still differ from the common practice in Western Europe. These aspects included the lack of supplementary pension schemes, contributory unemployment insurance and a separate scheme for work accidents and occupational diseases.[43] Although the Code does not require the setting up of those schemes, this has been the practice in a majority of EU member states, and the standards have been elaborated on the basis of this practice.

The indirect implications of accession: the fears of social dumping

Accession is certainly not a finishing line. After accession Estonia will continue to find itself amidst a number of new and different influencing factors. At the same time, it is important to note that while the influences before accession were mainly unilateral, the influences after accession will be, at least in theory, reciprocal.

One major concern in connection with the social implications of eastern enlargement is the issue of 'social dumping'. As defined by Goodhart, social dumping may be viewed as a process whereby capital will flow to areas where labour costs are lower and labour least protected, dragging down the labour standards elsewhere.[44] Discussions about social dumping in Europe date back before even the creation of a common market. Still, the impending accession of ten CEE applicant countries to the EU – together with their considerably lower levels of income – has given a new impetus to this debate. The fear of social dumping is clearly present in the White Paper.

> Competition could be distorted if undertakings in one part of the Community had to bear much heavier costs than in another and there would be a risk of economic activity migrating to locations where costs were lower. Such costs include . . . social protection. The implementation of high common standards of protection is among the Union's objectives and at the same time helps to ensure this 'level playing field'.[45]

However, the question remains to what extent this danger (at least in relation to social protection) is a true concern, and to what extent the concern was expressed by the Commission merely to please some of the member states.

In my opinion, the 'social dumping' argument seems to be exaggerated. First, labour costs are not the only factor attracting direct foreign investments;

rather, they are one factor among several others, including the proximity of markets, labour quality and availability, transportation, financial incentives, etc. Second, indirect labour costs – which include such factors as social tax – are often in relative wage terms comparable to those of the current member states. If labour costs still play a certain role in attracting foreign direct investment to Estonia, it is because of low direct labour costs in absolute terms (and in relation to labour productivity), not because of indirect labour costs. Lastly, as has already been noted, a substantial part of EU social legislation is there to encourage labour mobility, the underlying idea being that labour seeks places where it is best rewarded by capital. At the same time, the fear of social dumping comes with an implicit idea that the opposite is not acceptable, i.e. that capital should not be allowed to seek places where labour is cheapest.

Another fear sometimes presented is that of 'social tourism'. In some member states there is a concern that large differences in social entitlements may cause migratory pressures from the CEE states. However, this fear is also largely unfounded. Substantial obstacles to such an option are already established in the *acquis*. A sufficient means of living and adequate medical insurance are already preconditions for exercising the freedom of movement of persons (i.e. non-workers) as set by relevant EU law.[46] Furthermore, 'medical tourism' or patients seeking higher quality medical care in other member states, is restricted by Regulation 1408/71, which requires an individual to obtain a special certificate or prior authorisation from the competent institution of his/her home country before being entitled to medical care in another member state.

Conclusions

Estonia's accession to the EU will have implications for its entire political, economic and social structure. In this analysis of pressures Estonia faced during the pre-accession period within the domain of social protection, the picture was somewhat mixed. As far as legal requirements were concerned, the social protection 'gap' of Estonia was rather small. This was because the degree of 'hard law' in this field was limited and therefore there was not much to harmonise.

At the same time, some structural characteristics of Estonia's social protection systems were identified, which deviate from the 'norm', and can thus legitimately be seen as a 'gap'. These included the absence of supplementary pension systems, low unemployment benefits, a weak system of work accident and occupational disease benefits.

The direct effect of accession upon social protection systems and policies was likely to be small, but there will be important indirect implications. Social security coordination extends the rights of Estonian citizens moving across Europe, while also adding a certain degree of financial constraint to its existing schemes of pension and health insurance. Lastly, while Estonia's absolute level of social protection expenditure was lower than among the existing EU states, this gap could be linked more to the general differences in wealth, and not so much to any specific lack of social protection.

Notes

1 A. Smith, P. Holmes, U. Sedelmeier, E. Smith, H. Wallace and A. Young, 'The European Union and Central and Eastern Europe: Pre-accession Strategies', *Sussex European Institute Working Paper*, 15 (1996).
2 Of the 33 per cent that is collected, 20 per cent is allocated for pension insurance, and 13 per cent for health insurance.
3 Except technical aids for the disabled and special institutional care for the mentally handicapped, which are financed by the state.
4 In 2000, 93.5 per cent of the total population were covered with health insurance, the remaining are guaranteed minimum emergency care on the basis of means-testing.
5 See F. Scharpf, 'Balancing Positive and Negative Integration: The Regulatory Options for Europe' *Robert Schuman Centre Policy Paper*, 97/4 (1997).
6 Commission of the European Communities, *Preparation of the Associated Countries of Central and Eastern Europe for Integration into the Internal Market of the Union* (Brussels, Commission of the European Communities, 1995).
7 Commission of the European Communities, *Preparation of the Associated Countries.*
8 *Ibid.*
9 M. Gold, 'Overview of the Social Dimenion', in M. Gold (ed.), *The Social Dimension: Employment Policy in the European Community* (Basingstoke, Macmillan, 1993), p. 15.
10 Indeed, the Commission stated that implementation of coordination regulations should not even be thought of in terms of stages.
11 Namely, the Council Recommendation of 24 June 1992 on common criteria concerning sufficient resources and social assistance in social protection systems (92/441/EEC) and Council Recommendation of 27 July 1992 on the convergence of social protection objectives and policies (92/442/EEC)
12 Instruments developed by the Commission to monitor the developments in the pre-accession period.
13 Or what they call 'process regulation' as opposed to 'product regulation'.
14 Smith *et al.*, 'The European Union and Central and Eastern Europe: Pre-accession Strategies'.
15 J. Rollo, 'Economic Aspects of EU Enlargement to the East', in M. Maresceau (ed.), *Enlarging the European Union: Relations Between the EU and Central and Eastern Europe*, (London, Longman, 1997).
16 It should be clarified here that the concepts of 'social dimension' and 'social policy' are broader than that of 'social protection'. Though in general social protection expenditures constitute a major share of total public social expenditures, this does not take into account, for example, health and safety regulations, which do not constitute a burden for public expenses, but for private companies, which may have difficulties shouldering them.
17 Namely, Council Regulations (EEC) No. 1408/71 and 574/72.
18 For example, the social security clauses in the CEE association agreements and in the earlier Mediterranean Cooperation Agreements were identical. M. Cremona, 'Movement of persons, establishment and services' in M. Maresceau (ed.), *Enlarging the European Union: Relations Between the EU and Central and Eastern Europe* (London, Longman, 1997), p. 198. Also, S. Pisarro, 'The Agreements on Social Security between the Community and Third States: Legal Basis and Analysis', in 'Social Security in Europe:

Equality between Nationals and Non-nationals', Report from the European conference on social security, November 1994, Oporto, 1995.

19 Cremona, claiming the opposite, makes a mistake here. Cremona 'Movement of Persons, Establishment and Services', p. 199.

20 Except when a bilateral social security agreement existed between those states covering all residents, not only nationals.

21 C. Preston, *Enlargement and Integration in the European Union* (London, Routledge, 1997), p. 228.

22 Commission of the European Communities, *Preparation of the Associated Countries.*

23 *Commission of the European Communities,* Preparation of he Associated Countries.

24 For a more detailed analysis, see F. Pennings (ed.), *Introduction to European Social Security Law* (Boston, Kluwer Law International, 1994).

25 The regulations apply also to stateless persons and refugees, but not to third-country nationals.

26 The word 'migrant' is not used here in a strict sense. The regulations apply also to temporary visitors, like tourists.

27 That is, from the 13 per cent and 20 per cent part of the social tax respectively.

28 As noted above, the exportability may arrive earlier, in case implementation rules are adopted for the relevant provisions of the Europe Agreement. However, as of December 2001, these implementation rules were not yet adopted.

29 Calculations of the author on the basis of current and predictable flows of tourists.

30 See also M. Sakslin, 'Can Principles of the Nordic Conventions on Social Protection Contribute to the Modernisation and Simplification of Regulation (EEC) No. 1408/71?', in *25 Years of Regulation (EEC) No. 1408/71 on Social Security for Migrant Workers: Past Experiences, Present Problems and Future Perspectives* (Stockholm, Report from the European conference on social security June 1996, Stockholm, 1997).

31 D. Pieters, 'Towards a radical simplification of social security coordination', in *25 years of Regulation (EEC) No. 1408/71 on social security for migrant workers: past experiences, present problems and future perspectives,* (Stockholm, Report from the European conference on social security June 1996 Stockholm, 1997).

32 S. Liebfried and P. Pierson, 'Social Policy', in H. Wallace and W. Wallace (eds), *Policy-making in the European Union,* (Oxford, Oxford University Press, 1996).

33 There are still some exceptions to this principle, as noted also above.

34 The size of this group (incl. those with Ukrainian or other CIS country citizenship) is about 110,000 persons or 8 per cent of the total population.

35 For a more detailed analysis of Estonian social security legislation in the light of EU law on equal treatment of men and women, see F. Pennings and L. Leppik, 'The Consistency of Estonian Social Security Law with EU Legislation on Equal Treatment of Men and Women', *Final Report for the EC PHARE Consensus Programme* (Tallinn, 1998).

36 Although, as noted, the relevant directive allows member states to exclude from its scope the pension age in statutory pension schemes.

37 European Treaty Series No. 48 (signed at Strasbourg on 16 April 1964).

38 The only differences are that the ILO Convention No. 102 allows for certain temporary derogations, and the minimum number of parts to be ratified is enacted slightly differently. For the rest, the two instruments are identical. In fact, the level necessary for the ratification of the Code is generally considered to be slightly higher than that of the ILO Convention.

39 European Treaty Series No. 163 (signed at Strasbourg on 3 May 1996).

40 Holloway has given the label of 'partial alignment' to this mode of legal harmonisation. J. Holloway, *Social Policy Harmonisation in the European Community* (Farnborough, Gower, 1981)

41 That is, member states of the Council of Europe in 1964.

42 European Treaty Series No. 139 (signed at Rome on 6 November 1990).
43 The government has since addressed these problems. Legislation on supplementary pensions entered into force from August 1998, unemployment insurance scheme was introduced from January 2002 and work accident-occupational disease insurance is envisaged.
44 D. Goodhart 'Social Dumping within the EU', in D. Hine and H. Kassim (eds), *Beyond the Market: The EU and National Social Policy*, (London, Routledge, 1998).
45 Commission of the European Communities, *Preparation of the Associated Countries.*
46 Directive 90/364/EEC of 28 June 1990 on the right of residence says very explicitly, 'member states shall grant the right of residence to nationals of member states who do not enjoy this right under other provisions of Community law . . . provided that they themselves and the members of their families are covered by sickness insurance with respect to all risks in the host member state and have sufficient resources to avoid becoming a burden on the social assistance system of the host member state during their period of residence'.

Ramūnas Vilpišauskas

8

Regional integration in Europe

Analysing intra-Baltic economic cooperation in the context of European integration

At the beginning of the 1990s, Estonia, Latvia and Lithuania re-emerged as independent actors in the international system. The new Baltic policy-makers were faced with a range of options in choosing their cooperation partners and the type of cooperative arrangements that best suited their particular needs and interests. These decisions had to be taken in the midst of a changing international security and economic order, and coordinated with domestic economic and political reforms and newly established laws and institutions. Thus, the prioritisation of foreign policy goals was to a large extent determined by the aims of political and economic reform (transition to the market economy and democratic governance) and perceived external threats and opportunities.

If during the period prior to independence Baltic cooperation had been one of the most significant foreign policy priorities for Estonia, Latvia and Lithuania, then following 1991 it would be membership in the European Union that would become the more overarching goal to which all three states would tailor their international policies. In this new context, intra-Baltic relations took on a different meaning. Henceforth, such cooperation would be interlinked with different EU-related processes such as the signing of bilateral agreements with the EU, implementation of pre-accession arrangements and the opening of accession negotiations.

Yet, factors accounting for the *choice* in favour of a cooperative policy orientation do not necessarily explain the *dynamics* of cooperation and the particular forms such cooperation will assume. This chapter will therefore address policy developments that in general terms can be defined as the impact of a large regional arrangement on small neighbouring countries and their cooperative dynamics, and the interaction of regional integration and sub-regional cooperation processes. In more concrete terms, to what extent can EU policy account for the development of intra-Baltic economic cooperation during the 1990s? Does the role of the EU explain the timing and the type of Baltic economic agreements, the successful conclusion of some cooperation schemes – for example, free trade and the removal of non-tariff barriers – and the failure of others – namely, a customs union? Or does a satisfactory explanation of the cooperative dynamics between the Baltic states and instances of protectionism or non-cooperation need to include other factors – for example, sub-national interest groups or transnational actors? How do the characteristics of transition in the three countries influence the dynamics of regional cooperation? Finally, how is further integration into the EU likely to affect cooperation among the Baltic countries?

Baltic cooperation provides an interesting case study for testing arguments from several theoretical domains: regional integration and cooperation, the political economy of transition and the role of institutions. First, an overview of the literature on Baltic cooperation will be presented to expose the gaps that this study aims to fill. Next, I will present the framework of analysis to be used in this study, followed by an empirical part, which will test the propositions by analysing the dynamics of intra-Baltic economic cooperation since the beginning of the 1990s. The chapter will conclude with an outline of possible future cooperation dynamics between the Baltic states.

Explaining intra-Baltic cooperation

Since the mid-1990s intra-Baltic cooperation has attracted the attention of both Baltic and foreign analysts, resulting in a number of works dedicated to the issue. Most of the literature on intra-Baltic cooperation has focused on military and security issues or the geopolitics of the Baltic region.[1] Analysts have identified a number of factors affecting the level of intra-Baltic cooperation, including: the level of external threat and the balance of power in the European or transatlantic security architecture; the geographical position of the three countries; historical experiences and links; the size of the Baltic states; or internal resources. Usually a combination of factors is used, and most studies employ methodological features from the realist tradition.[2]

At the same time, a number of studies have analysed institutional aspects of Baltic cooperation, thereby diverging from the realist perspective.[3] The level of institutionalisation of Baltic relations is perceived to be a function of institutional capacity and functional scope, or the convergence of national interests. The role of sub-regional Baltic institutions is usually compared to that of national decision-making institutions. Furthermore, by implicitly considering regional institutions as factors influencing and fostering cooperation, these studies supplement those centred around the unitary state actors and the concept of balance of power in an interstate system.

Finally, a few analysts have discussed the dynamics of intra-Baltic economic relations.[4] This type of analysis draws from theories of regional economic integration or concepts of international trade and factor movements in general. The assumption unifying these analyses is the causal relationship between regional economic arrangements and the economic welfare of individual state actors. Moreover, this interest in intra-Baltic trade agreements has been associated with a critical importance given to international economic relations for economic reform and the growth of the small and open Baltic economies. However, specific calculations (for example, concerning trade creation or diversion caused by Baltic cooperation) have not been produced for a number of reasons, including the transitional character of the Baltic economies and the quality of statistical data.

Several observations can be made regarding the existing literature on intra-Baltic relations. First, analysts attribute cooperation between the Baltic countries – and even their efforts to accede to the EU – primarily to security factors. While the importance of security in explaining the Baltic countries' foreign policies is not disputed here and security considerations often account for the initial decision of states to cooperate, it cannot explain the development of cooperation or the particular form it may take. Certainly, there are opportunities for external forces to change the perception of the security situation and to alter the cooperative dynamics. Nevertheless, radical changes in the external security environment cannot explain the starts and stops of intra-Baltic economic cooperation. Moreover, systemic explanations focused on security factors usually downplay the importance of domestic factors. Therefore, while I do not question the importance of security motives, I will deal with this factor as a given during the period analysed.

Second, the emphasis in the existing literature on historical legacies or norms and identities has similar limitations. While history, culture and identity might explain certain tendencies, commonalties or differences in behaviour, they do not seem to be able to account for incremental policy developments. Historical legacies and culture can be treated as constraints within which actors take decisions. For example, the argument of a 'European identity' might explain the 'return-to-Europe' policies of Baltic policy-makers. Likewise, the argument alleging the 'lack of a common Baltic identity' could be used to account for divergent perceptions and foreign policies among the three states. However, such factors cannot plausibly explain why a free trade area, rather than a customs union, has been established by the Baltic states.

Third, theories of economic cooperation and integration can explain and predict the possible impact of economic agreements on the welfare of the countries involved or third parties. Thus, they can provide an understanding of the policy-makers' motivations for using economic agreements to achieve their political goals. They can also explain the possible impact of market integration on both foreign and domestic actors. However, they are unable to provide 'explanations of the political choices that produce integrated areas'.[5] Their insights need to be incorporated into a wider framework that analyses the development of cooperation/integration processes, and the role of the actors and institutions involved. Such a framework is discussed in the following section.

Conceptualising cooperation

The question of why nations cooperate and integrate has been discussed extensively by international relations scholars. This chapter offers a different perspective from the works discussed above and analyses intra-Baltic economic cooperation by employing concepts drawn from liberal explanations of international cooperation and the political economy of regional integration. This section proceeds by first defining the dependent variable of economic cooperation among the Baltic states. Subsequently, the independent variables are discussed. The focus is placed on the effects of EU policies, which, it is argued, have been a major factor behind intra-Baltic economic cooperation. However, to explain the dynamics of intra-Baltic economic cooperation, in recent years in particular, domestic factors have to be taken into account. The formation of new interest groups as well as institutional channels for these groups to voice their preferences have allowed for an increasing articulation of demands both for and against the integration of national economies. The assumption is that domestic politics matters even when actors respond to external effects, and that both international and domestic levels of analysis can be combined into a coherent analysis.[6] Finally, the definition of actors and processes is followed by the next section, which applies the framework to explain the dynamics of Baltic cooperation.

This chapter adopts the definition of international cooperation suggested by Keohane, who maintains that cooperation 'takes place when the policies actually followed by one government are regarded by its partners as facilitating realisation of their own objectives, as the result of a process of policy coordination'.[7] As Milner observes, this definition assumes 'that an actor's behaviour is directed toward some goal(s)'.[8] Therefore, analysis of cooperation requires understanding how particular objectives are formed and prioritised. Regional cooperation may facilitate achieving goals, both in the external environment and in the domestic arena. Second, Keohane's framework implies 'that actors receive gains or rewards from cooperation'.[9] Thus, the issue is how the distribution of gains is perceived by participating actors, and how cooperative measures influence the chances of achieving other objectives of governmental actors as well as the distribution of gains among domestic economic groups.

Intergovernmental cooperation may vary by issue, scope and form. However, economic cooperation in one particular area, for example trade, is likely to have political effects and facilitate the achievement of other political objectives. As Feldstein has stated, 'economic cooperation is part of the more important process of international cooperation'.[10] This is certainly true in the Baltic case. Economic cooperation acquires political meaning, and may also contribute to achieving certain political objectives. Sub-regional economic cooperation is seen and supported by the EU as an important supplement to the stability and security of the region. Therefore, although this chapter focuses on intra-Baltic economic cooperation, the political significance of that cooperation derives from the importance attached to it by the leaders of the Baltic states as a means to advance another objective: integration into the EU. This argument is especially convincing given that 'most of the economic arguments favouring regional integration are not met by integration among the Baltic countries'.[11] Thus, the level of economic interdependence does not in itself provide a strong case for policy coordination and market integration.

Furthermore, analysis is focused on cooperation in the area of economic exchange. The choice is based on several grounds: (1) economic exchange has probably been the most advanced area of intra-Baltic cooperation, in some aspects surpassing multilaterally accepted requirements for regional agreements; (2) it is characterised by both successes and failures allowing different outcomes of cooperation dynamics to be compared; and (3) it illustrates how domestic politics matters even when cooperation objectives are strongly motivated by the external environment. The dependent variable of this study is, therefore, the scope of intra-Baltic cooperation in the field of economic exchange, or market integration. It addresses both successful and unsuccessful attempts to cooperate, including unilateral, competitive or conflicting behaviour reducing benefits to other actors, as well as inactivity.[12]

Cooperation can be pursued in different forms and in different settings. It may vary from *ad hoc* measures to agreements having long-term effects, to the creation of common institutions that further facilitate cooperation by reducing transaction costs and uncertainty, limiting asymmetries of information, or even acquiring an independent role in the policy-making process. In the Baltic case, several institutionalised settings – the Baltic Council of Ministers, the Baltic Assembly, and the Baltic Council – provide opportunities for regular policy coordination and the negotiation of trilateral agreements. The fact that these regional institutions do not possess independent authority differentiates Baltic cooperation from the three states' integration into the EU, with the latter implying not only the linking of economic domains and participation in common policies, but also eventually delegating authority to supranational institutions.

The impact of a regional union on neighbouring countries

The observation that the EU has had an important effect on intra-Baltic cooperation is not new.[13] However, a systematic analysis of this causal effect and possible future developments has yet to be conducted. While regional integration – and in particular that of the EC/EU – has been analysed extensively by scholars, the external effect of integration is 'a topic that both political scientists and economists have mostly overlooked'.[14] As a rule, analysis has been limited to a fixed number of participants and their integration choices without extending the scope to include its impact on external actors or their reactions. This applies to both neo-functionalist and intergovernmentalist perspectives on integration.[15] 'New' political economy approaches to regional integration – liberal intergovernmentalism, multi-level governance or reformulated versions of neo-functionalism – have mainly focused on explaining the advances of integration within the EC.[16] Although successive enlargements of the EC/EU have received considerable attention, the main issue has been, to use Gower's expression, 'the old academic chestnut' on the interrelationship between widening and deepening.[17] Thus, the emphasis has been on the impact of the enlargement on the status and prospects for further integration inside the EC/EU.

In contrast to political analyses, economic perspectives on integration have addressed external impact, mainly by employing the concepts of trade creation and trade diversion.[18] In addition to traditional welfare-oriented explanations, other forms of 'non-traditional' gains from regional trade agreements (for example, bargaining power) which link regional integration to the external environment have also been discussed.[19] These explanations represent a broader interest in regional integration and regionalism that has increased after the acceleration of EC integration in the 1980s and the subsequent wave of new regional agreements in the 1990s.

Lastly, one example of an inclusive approach explicitly addressing the external effects of integration is a general explanation of regional integration suggested by Mattli.[20] This chapter adopts some of his observations, although with significant modifications. Therefore the argument is briefly presented first, followed by suggested modifications that seem to be appropriate in the Baltic case. Mattli argues that for an integration scheme to succeed, two sets of conditions need to be satisfied: demand side and supply side. The demand for regional rules, regulations and policies by market players seeking to internalise externalities that arise from economic and political uncertainty is the driving force of regional integration. Furthermore, the potential gains from market exchange within a region must be significant. The second condition for integration to succeed is the willingness and ability of political leaders to accommodate demands for deeper integration. Willingness depends on the economic situation and growth prospects of the home market. Ability in turn depends on solving collective action problems, which is facilitated by an existence of 'commitment institutions' and a regional leader – a dominant member state acting as the focal point of coordination and as the 'paymaster', easing distributional tensions. The presence of these conditions is likely to make integration efforts successful. In turn, successful regional integration is likely to have an impact on outside countries by creating externalities such as the loss of market access and investment diversion. Outsiders, especially during economic slowdowns, will seek to join the union, demonstrating the so-called 'first integrative response'. However, if the union has no incentive to accept new members, outsiders might respond by creating their own regional group, employing the so-called 'second integrative response'. Again, for this project to succeed demand and supply conditions need to be met.

This chapter builds on the basic premises of the approach suggested by Mattli. It considers both governments' willingness and ability to cooperate as well as specific market demands. Particular importance is given to the role of leadership and the 'commitment institution' in solving coordination problems by providing common rules and side-payments. Nevertheless, Mattli's arguments are modified and supplemented to better fit the Baltic case in several respects. I will argue that the role of the regional leader may be played by an external regional union, which the neighbouring countries aspire to join when a clear leader is lacking among the sub-regional states. The external group – in this case, the EU – provides rules for intra-Baltic cooperation, thereby facilitating the choice between multiple equilibriums, over which sub-regional members might have diverging interests. The leadership role of the EU is backed by financial assistance. Yet, in both respects the role of the external leader is limited. The provision and adoption of the rules for sub-regional cooperation depend on the prospects for integration of individual countries into the regional union. Thus, willingness to cooperate depends not so much on economic gains but on the facilitation of integration into the regional union. While financial assistance can facilitate the administrative aspect of sub-regional cooperation, it is usually not sufficient for making side-payments to domestic groups dissatisfied by redistribution. Furthermore, the scope of this analysis is extended to include opposition to integration and transition related issues such as uncertainty, lack of resources and changes in political and economic institutions which impact on both the ability of governments to cooperate and the channelling of market demands. Finally, 'the second integrative response' is seen as a complimentary rather than an alternative policy of sub-regional cooperation, and therefore it could more appropriately be called 'a modified first integrative response'. The dynamics of sub-regional cooperation are directly conditioned by the prospects and prerequisites for integration into the regional union. Thus, the starting point of this analysis is 'a modified first integrative response'.

To present a simplified picture, neighbouring countries express their willingness to join a regional integration scheme. For a number of reasons, the regional union finds it too costly to accept new members, but does not dismiss the possibility of enlargement some time in the future. Meanwhile it encourages outsiders to cooperate amongst themselves and supplies the schemes of market integration as well as financial support and leadership. The regional union thereby acts as a catalyst for outsiders to cooperate. Cooperation is further facilitated by conditions such as the security situation, recent cooperative experiences, common objectives, and the demands of actors' benefiting from integration. At the same time, other factors such as divergent preferences in achieving policy objectives or protectionist demands of actors standing to lose from market integration threaten cooperation. In sum, this chapter addresses the impact of (1) the regional union that outsiders aspire to join and (2) domestic actors' preferences on sub-regional cooperation. Other factors are taken as given.

The impact of a regional union on the scope of sub-regional cooperation among neighbouring countries can be assessed by examining the union's policy towards the individual countries and how particular decisions addressed to them as a group or individually affect sub-regional cooperation. The analysis would be incomplete, however, without examining the reactions of the sub-regional group and how they contribute to or threaten the level of sub-regional cooperation.

This analysis establishes a clear link between sub-regional cooperation and the policies of the regional union. As was indicated above, sub-regional cooperation is perceived by participating actors not as an alternative but as a stepping-stone to individual integration into the regional union. For the purposes of this analysis, integration refers to the process of an independent state joining a regional union by way of removing barriers to free exchange and movement of factors of production (negative integration), adoption of certain common rules and policies (positive integration), delegation of authority to supranational institutions, and participation in common decision-making procedures. Thus, unilateral adaptation rather than joint decision-making is emphasised. The focus of this analysis is on sub-regional actors, and their strategies vis-à-vis the neighbouring regional union. Integration refers to the gradual process evolving in stages that can be identified for analytical purposes. The integration process includes: (1) the establishment and intensification of diplomatic and economic relations; (2) a pre-accession stage when the regional union explicitly acknowledges the possibility of eventual membership and supplies schemes designed to prepare applicants for integration into the common market and accession; (3) the accession negotiations, during which individual applicants agree with the union on the (negotiable) conditions of membership, and further proceed with adopting rules governing the common market and common policies; and (4) the accession itself, after which the new members acquire the right to participate in the decision-making process, though transition periods may be agreed in a limited number of areas. The main proposition is that there is a link between the dynamics of sub-regional cooperation and the integration of individual members of a sub-region into the regional union. Participation in the different stages of integration implying divergent prospects for union membership is likely to act as a barrier to cooperation and encourage non-cooperative policies, while being in the same stage increases incentives to cooperate. While the date and the strategy of EU accession was not clear, each of the Baltic states faced a strategic dilemma: trilateral cooperation would have been useful for all of them, however, each had an incentive to pursue unilateral policies hoping to be among the first to accede to the regional union.

Cooperation policies and institutional transition

One of the basic assumptions of this analysis is that governments act as utility maximisers, and are willing to cooperate when (regional) cooperation is likely to promote the chances of achieving their objectives.[21] For cooperation to occur, governments must be both willing and able to cooperate.[22] While willingness depends on how cooperation measures are perceived to influence the achievement of other objectives (other policy goals more specifically, or re-election chances more generally), the ability of states to cooperate depends on the resources available and a leader that could serve as a focal point for coordination of rules and policies. However, governments as well as other actors act in concrete institutional and organisational settings and power configurations, both domestic and international, which structure their behaviour. They can be constrained by available resources, including finances and expertise, both of which have been particularly scarce during the transition process. The role of governments has been quite complicated during the transition period, given the high degree of uncertainty, information asymmetries, lack of expertise and other resources, or in more general terms, the instability resulting from a radical change of political and economic institutions.[23]

Faced with uncertainty and meagre resources, the Baltic governments have been more likely to follow external advice and adopt existing regimes governing economic relations. The 'anticipatory adaptation' (to use Nicolaidis's term) of regimes governing economic relations of industrialised democracies was at the heart of the transition to a market economy and democratic governance.[24] It formed a part of the learning and imitation process of the policy-makers in transitional countries and expressed itself in policy-makers advocating the direct import of other cooperation models or protection patterns.[25] This process of adaptation to a large extent has been taking place irrespective of external demands.[26] Nevertheless, an external coordinator – the EU – has proved to be necessary for overcoming problems of coordination, and for finding agreement on specific forms of sub-regional cooperation.

By virtue of the importance attached to it by Baltic leaders, the EU has assumed the role of external coordinator in this process by providing rules for regional cooperation and domestic policy-making, often in close coordination with other suppliers of aid, trade and financial regimes. The role of the EU as an external coordinator helped to solve coordination problems in intra-Baltic cooperation when the three were all 'vaguely and diffusely in favour [of cooperation], but their preference for forms and terms [made] agreement on the specific cooperative enterprises difficult'.[27] Coordination problems particularly hampered intra-Baltic economic cooperation during the early 1990s. The prospect of EU membership, integration based on rules supplied by the EU and the realisation that sub-regional cooperation is likely to advance integration into the EU, have all played a role in designing and implementing schemes for intra-Baltic economic cooperation.

Motivations

The motivations behind the Baltic states' desire to join the EU represent a mixture of ideological, historical, security and economic factors. Officials from all three states have repeatedly stated the importance of promoting economic growth and development; security aspects; social welfare; and participation in common European matters. Although the importance of security, identity, history and international status is not disputed (indeed, they have been driving forces in the orientation of the Baltic states' foreign policies towards the EU), the emphasis in this chapter is on economic factors. The EU has been perceived as a centre of economic prosperity and as a source of economic modernisation for the Baltic economies. Its importance as a source of economic opportunities and resources (finance, market access, expertise, and rules) has provided a strong impetus for raising EU membership to the top of the Baltic states' foreign policy goals. At the same time, given its more limited opportunities, intra-Baltic economic cooperation has come to be seen as instrumental for advancing the individual countries' integration into the EU.[28] Naturally, there are a number of additional reasons (including history, identity, security) why intra-Baltic cooperation has been on the agendas of the Baltic states since their re-entry into the international system. Advances in the field of sub-regional economic cooperation, however, have been directly linked to EU policy towards Central and Eastern Europe, and the Baltic sub-region in particular, and to the utility attached to the sub-regional cooperation by the Baltic governments as maximising their chances of EU membership.[29]

The EU's policy towards the Baltic states has also been based on a mixture of motives and factors. As is the case in EU policy towards Central and Eastern Europe in general, EU policy towards the Baltic states has resulted from the complex interaction of EU institutions, member states, interest groups and external actors, each motivated by its own security, economic and other interests and considerations. This process has received considerable attention, and it is beyond the scope of this chapter to address the issue directly.[30] The content and form of EU policies toward the Baltic states and the impact of these policies on intra-Baltic cooperation is of greater relevance here.[31] This chapter therefore emphasises the importance of the EU as a regional actor represented by its institutions, particularly the Commission, which 'played the pivotal role as the guardian of the process of rapprochement of Western and Eastern Europe' and in forming EU policy towards the Baltic states.[32]

The picture risks being incomplete without taking into account the policies of certain EU member states that have shown a particular interest in the Baltic countries, such as the Nordic countries and Germany. Most of these countries are geographically close to the Baltic states and have particularly strong security and economic interests in intensified intra-Baltic cooperation. Yet, their interests have been translated into policies towards the Baltic states mainly through the internal bargaining processes of the EU. Therefore, they will not be addressed in this chapter since, as mentioned above, this study will leave out the question of how EU policy towards the Baltic states is developed, and what actors and interests have shaped it.

Market demands

The EU factor alone, it is argued, does not account for the starts and stops of intra-Baltic economic cooperation. Recent developments have shown that economic interest groups have an increasing influence on intra-Baltic cooperative policies, and their influence is likely to increase further in the future. Market integration measures have a direct impact on economic actors' activities, with some standing to gain from the removal of barriers to exchange and the reduction of transaction costs, while others stand to lose due to redistribution effects. This creates incentives for economic interest groups to lobby for or against further integration. The role of economic interest groups in advancing integration in the EC/EU has been widely acknowledged.[33] Importantly, as was noted several decades ago, 'the list of . . . actors should include not only groups which perceive themselves [as having] benefited [from] integration but also groups opposed to it'.[34] It is often assumed that economic groups characterised by a higher degree of internationalisation – meaning export-oriented economic policy, extensive participation in intra-industry trade, wide-ranging multinational enterprises – are more likely to support market integration measures and resist protectionism.[35] Enterprises using local resources and selling their products in the domestic market are more likely to call for protectionist measures under the actual or anticipated pressure of adjustment. Thus, various domestic groups are likely to 'demand different policies, and a government's economic policy choices often will reflect the underlying preferences of the strongest and best-organised interests within society'.[36]

The relative absence of the activities of economic interest groups in the context of intra-Baltic cooperation, in particular those favouring integration, can largely be explained by the transition process itself and the initial absence of functioning markets and institutional channels for voicing demands. At the outset of political and economic reform, changing rules and institutional structures had (to varying degrees in different states) deprived economic groups of their former influence. As some have noted about the transition process in Central and Eastern Europe, 'the new economic and political environment confronted all interest groups with a loss of power'.[37] Moreover, in the Baltic states popular perception largely associated support for transition goals with the support for the re-establishment of statehood, which reinforced opportunities for 'extraordinary politics', and provided policy-makers with more room for policies disadvantaging special interests.[38]

These opportunities, resulting from a combination of the above-mentioned factors, were exploited to varying degrees in the three Baltics, depending on the structure of their national economies, their institutional structures of policy-making, their ideological commitments and reform strategies. For example, relatively large agricultural sectors in Lithuania and Latvia have allowed agricultural interests to exert greater influence on policy-makers than in Estonia. The prevalence of large-scale, outdated industries in these two countries also seemed to generate stronger protectionist interests, which have been identified as an important constraint to the adoption and implementation of economic policies.[39] At the same time, in Lithuania the government's power to introduce legal changes to the trade regime by decree has made it easier for interest groups there to influence government policy. Moreover, governments headed by economic technocrats have in general been less vulnerable to economic interest groups, while governments formed as the result of a 'protest vote' have been more reserved towards market integration and more inclined to support large disadvantaged groups (votes) and better organised lobbies (funds).

The latter phenomena could be observed in particular after a certain level of stability in the newly established political institutions had been achieved. New institutions 'gradually produce their own social and economic basis'.[40] Policy-makers learn how to take advantage of potential votes or funds. Disadvantaged or nascent groups learn how to play according to the new rules of the game in order to advance their interests by using newly established interest intermediation structures, old-time connections from the former regime or by voicing open protest. Although these protests often arise due to the general economic situation (for example from a decline in production or income levels), they frequently target the liberalisation of international economic transactions and specific policies of intra-Baltic market integration. The patterns of lobbying have been dependent largely on the speed and openness of privatisation, which created opportunities or barriers for influencing policy-making and implementation and receiving special privileges.

The other explanation for the relative absence of observed market demand for intra-Baltic market integration lies in the small size of the sub-regional market. Combined, the three states form a market of around 7.5 million consumers. At the start of the transition, intra-Baltic trade constituted only a small fraction of the total foreign trade share in each of the three countries. Although the volume of intra-Baltic trade has been increasing, its share has remained comparatively small despite trilateral free trade agreements. Therefore, the relatively small potential for economic gain from market exchange might have reduced incentives for lobbying in support of further integration[41] Since such labour-, skill- and resource-intensive industries as clothing, footwear and textiles favour small and flexible units of production, possibilities for economies of scale in the region seem be limited.[42] To be sure, certain developments in foreign direct investment in the Baltic states and intra-Baltic investments during the late 1990s signalled the beginning of a tendency toward informal integration. An increasing involvement by foreign investors who treated the Baltic states as one market, the internationalisation of Baltic companies, and individual signs of market concentration (for example in the financial services sector) all exerted a certain degree of indirect pressure on governments to proceed with removing non-tariff barriers and harmonising market regulations, using EU rules as a guide. Still, except for the occasional statement, these groups did not conduct any visible lobbying efforts to further market integration.

By contrast, demands for protection were much more visible, and eventually led to an exchange of protectionist measures among the Baltic states following the pattern of tit-for-tat policy.[43] These (non-tariff) protectionist measures were taken in response to lobbying by local economic interest groups who experienced adjustment problems as a result of the economic crisis in Russia. Crisis 'may bring new players into the game,' or provide an opportunity for previously ignored groups to advance their own interests.[44] Because of their size, the Baltic states rely heavily on international economic exchanges and, in respect to Russia and the EU, all three states are characterised by a very small influence capability and a high degree of sensitivity.[45] The economic crisis, which began in Russia in the summer of 1998, caused a decrease in sales for Baltic exporters, which in turn triggered demands for protectionism. To paraphrase Winters, adjustment pressure caused by the fall of demand in one market can translate into a greater pressure for protection from another.[46] The issue became linked to intra-Baltic economic cooperation and was manipulated via non-tariff barriers – namely, product standards and administrative rules – to satisfy the demands of local producers, mainly agricultural groups. These developments cast a new light on the political economy development of intra-Baltic economic cooperation and showed the limits of the EU acting as an indirect coordinator and leader.

The dynamics of intra-Baltic economic cooperation

The period under analysis begins in the early 1990s, when the Baltic states re-established statehood and began to conduct independent policies. During the independence struggle itself, the three states had already gained a considerable degree of experience in coordinating their political efforts. Following August 1991, intra-Baltic cooperation remained among the main priorities of their foreign policies. Already on 8 November 1991, the first institutionalised setting for intra-Baltic cooperation – the Baltic Assembly – was created. The Assembly, which was modelled on the cooperative institutions of the Nordic countries, was made up of representatives from the three legislative bodies of the Baltic states. Six committees within the Assembly were further created to promote discussion and offer recommendations to the Baltic governments on matters of common interest, including legal, social and economic affairs, environment and energy, communications, education and culture, and security and foreign affairs.

In September 1993, an agreement on creating a Council of Ministers was reached among the three Baltic prime ministers, and on 13 June 1994, the Baltic Council of Ministers was established. Its tasks include taking decisions with regard to the recommendations of the Baltic Assembly, carrying out assignments in accordance with intra-Baltic agreements, and addressing matters of common interest. The Baltic Council of Ministers is chaired by the three prime ministers and conducts work at three levels: the ministers of foreign affairs, the Baltic Cooperation Committee (which coordinates the activities of the Council between the meetings of the ministers), and the Committees of Senior Officials (which cover about twenty issue areas and are permanent working bodies of the Council on a branch-ministerial level). Decisions of the Baltic Council of Ministers are made on the basis of consensus and are binding for the Baltic states, except when they contradict the internal laws of each state and in such cases require approval by the state's legislature.[47] The Baltic Council, established in April 1996, is a joint session of the Baltic Assembly and the Baltic Council of Ministers. The Baltic Council adopts declarations and meets annually. Finally, presidential summits have also become common practice ever since these institutions were created and elections carried out.

In a relatively short period, a dense network of coordination has been established between the Baltic states. Their work and impact have been highly dependent on the issue area and the potential for gain by each of the governments. Although intra-Baltic cooperative measures have been agreed upon and implemented in a number of areas comprising about twenty-five trilateral agreements, the discussion below is limited to policy measures related to subregional market integration and trade policy measures in particular. The main intra-Baltic trade and integration agreements are summarised in table 8.1.[48]

Table 8.1 Major intra-Baltic market integration agreements

Dates	*Main provisions*	*References to the EU*
Free trade agreement		
Signed: 13.09.93 *In force* 01.04.94	*Objectives*: to establish a free trade area in industrial goods (HS 25–97); to promote mutual trade, productivity and economic growth; guarantee fair competition; to promote development of trade in the Baltic sea area; to encourage cooperation in other economic areas *Measures:* the elimination of all export and import duties with several exceptions relating to export restrictions; a standstill clause on qualitative export or import restrictions; elimination of quantitative restrictions with some exceptions; non-discrimination and national status principles; special provisions relating to restructuring. *Rules of origin and safeguards:* Baltic origin cumulation; general GATT based safeguards *Dispute settlement mechanism:* joint committee to oversee the implementation of the agreement, settle disputes, to provide a setting for exchange of information and consultations	The parties see the agreement as a means to reinforce participation in European economic integration (Preamble)

Dates		*Main provisions*	*References to the EU*
Agreement on free trade in agricultural goods			
Signed	16.06.96	*Objectives:* to establish a free trade area in agricultural, food and fisheries products (HS 01–24); to promote development of mutual trade and fair competition *Measures:* the elimination of export and import duties and quantitative restrictions; a standstill clause; non-discrimination and national status principles *Rules of origin and safeguards:* Baltic origin cumulation; general GATT based safeguards *Dispute settlement mechanism:* joint committee created under the previous agreement	The parties declare their intention to participate in European integration processes, and the agreement is to promote this objective (Preamble)
In force	01.01.97		
Agreement on abolishing non-tariff barriers			
Signed	20.11.97	Objectives: to abolish non-tariff barriers to trade; develop a free trade area. *Measures:* the mutual recognition of sanitary, phytosanitary and technical standards applied to products and production processes (HS 01–97); harmonisation in line with EU and other relevant international institutions' rules; a standstill clause; non-discrimination and national tatus principles; establishment of Information centre *Rules of origin:* Baltic origin cumulation *Dispute settlement mechanism:* joint committee to oversee the implementation of the agreement, settle disputes, to provide a setting for exchange of information and consultations	The final objective of EU membership acknowledged; the intra-Balltic cooperation and integration into the EU should proceed in parallel (preamble) EU rules on product and process standards form a basis for mutual recognition and work of local certification agencies
In force	01.07.98		

Source: Respective trilateral trade agreements.

The idea of an intra-Baltic free trade area was first raised during the beginning of the 1990s. Like a number of other suggestions for intra-Baltic economic cooperation, this concept (together with references to the Benelux countries or other models) was brought up repeatedly by policy-makers and analysts of the three states, but with little progress toward forging an agreement on its substance, form and implementation. Economic cooperation measures were absent during the first years of the 1990s. The idea of a free trade area finally received strong political support during a meeting of the Baltic heads-of-state in Jurmala, Latvia, in August 1993, when the three leaders approved the draft of a free trade agreement. The meeting of the three Baltic prime ministers in Tallinn in September

1993 also approved the draft. This led to the signing, on 13 September 1993, of 'the biggest agreement ever signed among the Baltic countries' – the intra-Baltic free trade agreement.[49]

Yet, the accord had one major deficiency: it excluded agricultural goods. Indeed, an agreement to abolish barriers to trade in this area would require additional efforts. After several rounds of intense negotiations, an agreement on agriculture was finally reached in June 1996 and came into force in January 1997. In November of that same year, an agreement on abolishing non-tariff barriers to trade was reached, and came into force in July 1998.

Nevertheless, and as stated above, a comprehensive analysis of cooperation dynamics between the Baltic states must include not only trilateral agreements that were successful, but also those that failed. This aspect of Baltic cooperation includes the customs union agreement that has not been implemented despite numerous pledges to do so and the lack of a concrete schedule. Another category includes unilateral protectionist measures that favour one country's domestic interests over another's, and violate mutual commitments. These are briefly discussed next.

The idea of creating an intra-Baltic customs union was discussed at the governmental level in Tallinn in April 1991. During a meeting of the three governments in September 1991, a statement 'On the Establishment of a Customs Union on the Territory of Estonia, Latvia and Lithuania' was issued. This question was repeatedly discussed at the level of the three countries' policy-makers and senior officials during the following years.[50] However, no cooperative measures were implemented in this field. The efforts were revived with a resolution on the establishment of a customs union signed by the prime ministers of the three countries in February 1995. A deadline of 1998 was set up for establishing the intra-Baltic customs union. Another impetus was given by signing an agreement to lift tariff measures on trade in agricultural goods. More specific steps were elaborated in another resolution signed by the prime ministers in February 1997. The commitment to create a customs union in 1998 was reiterated again during the signing of the agreement on abolishing non-tariff barriers in November 1997. However, an intra-Baltic customs union (as well as less developed initiatives of the Baltic common market) was not created, and it is not likely to be in the future.

EU and intra-Baltic economic cooperation

The period of uncertainty

The initial years of EU-Baltic relations were marked by a group approach taken by the EU towards the three Baltic states. Although the EU conducted negotiations with each country bilaterally, general policy ranging from the establishment of diplomatic relations to the initiation of individual trade agreements had a strong group or 'Baltic sub-region' emphasis. The group approach towards the

Baltic states was reinforced by support of intra-Baltic cooperation measures, which EU representatives had encouraged on various occasions directly and indirectly by urging the strengthening of economic cooperation among transition countries in general. The economic cooperation of the Visegrad countries, and the EU statements that economic integration of transition countries should proceed in parallel with their integration into the EU, have provided Baltic policy-makers with a model to follow. Once the prospect of integration into the EU became more certain, and Baltic leaders realised that intra-Baltic economic cooperation was likely to maximise their chances for EU integration, they were willing and able to proceed with sub-regional cooperation. These developments are discussed below.

The EC recognised the independence of the three Baltic states on 27 August 1991, and in April 1992 EU ambassadors to each Baltic state began their work.[51] In a meeting with the foreign ministers of the Baltic states held at the beginning of September, EC representatives suggested including the three states in the PHARE program, thereby differentiating them from the other former Soviet republics. In addition, the EU decided to model its future trade and cooperation agreements with the Baltics along those lines adopted for other Central and Eastern European countries (CEECs), not the Soviet successor states. In September 1991, negotiations on a 'first generation' of trade and cooperation agreements were initiated. The agreements were signed in May 1992 and came into force at the beginning of 1993. The agreements were supplied by the EU and their enforcement upgraded the trading status of the Baltic states in the general 'pyramid of preferences' of the EU by extending most-favoured-nation trading status and the generalised system of preferences. In addition, the agreements abolished specific import restrictions previously applied to the Baltic economies.

Already during these negotiations on trade and cooperation, representatives of the Baltic states raised the issue of association with the EU. Their aim was to conclude association agreements similar to those signed by the EU with the Visegrad countries, and thereby gain inclusion into the group of countries recognised as prospective EU members. This hope was expressed by the foreign ministers of the Baltic states when the trade and cooperation agreements were signed in May 1992. The Estonian foreign minister, Jaan Manitski, called the accords 'our first step back to Europe', which he hoped would lead to full EC membership within a few years.[52] The recognition that these agreements could lead to EU membership was also included in their preambles. The Baltic states again expressed their wish to join the EU in the conference of 64 countries on aid to the former Soviet Union in Lisbon at the end of May 1992.[53] From here the conclusion of Europe agreements and eventual EU membership moved to the top of the Baltic governments' agendas. The attitude of EU policy-makers, however, remained rather reserved. While EU leaders emphasised during the Lisbon meeting the importance of regional cooperation between the 'newly independent states', the specific question of developing EU relations with the Baltic states was not addressed.[54]

Yet, despite this uncertainty, the EU assumed a leading role in supporting economic and political reforms in these countries. For example, the EU Commission acted in close coordination with international financial institutions, when it made aid conditional upon the adoption of International Monetary Fund economic recovery programs. A part of PHARE funds and technical assistance measures was also directed towards facilitating economic liberalisation and supporting economic cooperation by improving the administration of trade and supporting the development of exports. Trade liberalisation and sub-regional cooperation between the transition economies was encouraged as part of the EU's general support for economic transformation and democratic consolidation.[55] Already in July 1992, G-7 leaders urged 'all CEECs to develop economic relations with each other'.[56] This was directed in particular towards the Visegrad countries, but it also provided a model for the Baltic states to follow.

Furthermore, the EU conducted its policy towards the Baltic states using other regional institutions, in particular the Council of Baltic Sea States (CBSS). The CBSS was created in 1992 during a meeting in Copenhagen, where ten countries and the Commission of the EU were represented. It has since become an important institution for the development of ties between the Baltic states and the EU, and for the EU's support of sub-regional cooperation. Its importance was underlined by the fact that it included Germany and Denmark as well as the then non-EU Nordic countries, which have become the main supporters of the Baltic states' integration into the EU.[57] 'The Baltic Sea dimension' of EU policy was strengthened further after Sweden and Finland became members of the EU in 1995.

Budding EU influence

The situation in the Baltic states during the first years of transition was characterised by radical political and economic institutional changes, which imposed constraints on intra-Baltic economic cooperation. As one Baltic policy-maker acknowledged at that time, 'the tense domestic situation' rendered advancing sub-regional cooperation impossible.[58] Uncertainty and a lack of resources limited the ability of governments to implement sub-regional cooperation schemes. The work of the one already established intra-Baltic institution – the Baltic Assembly – was hampered by meagre financial resources, while the level of expertise for designing sub-regional market integration schemes was low as well. This was a period of learning, based on a mixture of institutional imitation and innovation. Absence of a regional coordinator and supplier of cooperation rules made commonly acceptable agreement on the form and substance of economic cooperation more complicated, although various proposals (often based on references to the Benelux or other models) were discussed.

The Baltic states established various foreign trade regimes in 1992 and 1993, ranging from a very liberal one applied by Estonia to more protectionist ones (particularly in the trade of agricultural goods) applied by Latvia and Lithuania. The introduction of market institutions and national currencies created the necessary basis for sub-regional economic cooperation, although different levels of progress in each of the three states posed temporary limits. In 1993, Estonian officials referred to Lithuania's slow progress in introducing a national currency and instituting a visa regime for CIS nationals, as an obstacle to trilateral trade agreement.[59] Likewise, Estonia's willingness to proceed with trilateral economic cooperation was also decreased temporarily by the formation of a left-wing government in Lithuania in 1992. Referring to 'the anti-business policies' of the new Lithuanian government, right-wing Estonian government officials considered concluding a bilateral free trade agreement with Latvia instead.[60] These differences, however, proved to have only a temporary effect on intra-Baltic relations.

The prospects for intra-Baltic economic cooperation began to change in 1993, and a major push in this regard was given by EU policies. The first indication of change in EU policy towards the Baltic states – brought about by a major effort by the Danish government – was an invitation to participate in an intergovernmental EU integration conference organised in Copenhagen on 13–14 April 1993. The conference brought together representatives from the EU, EFTA and CEECs, and its final declaration acknowledged the aim of several participating countries (meaning the Baltic states) to become EU members.[61] The following months were characterised by initiatives and responses from the Baltic states, which led to the intra-Baltic free trade agreement. Several days after the conference, the EU troika and Commissioner Hans Van den Broek held a meeting with the foreign ministers of the Baltic states during which issues of EU relations and economic liberalisation and cooperation within the Baltic region were discussed.[62] The Baltic states' representatives raised the issue of establishing a free trade area with the EU. However, the response from the EU, namely Belgian Foreign Minister Willy Claes, was that the three 'should first improve cooperation among themselves'.[63] He also indicated that the Baltic states could learn from the Benelux example.

Prior to the meeting with EU representatives, the Baltic prime ministers met in Vilnius to discuss their relations and common position towards the EU.[64] The leaders met again in the beginning of June, just before the EU summit in Copenhagen, and issued a joint document urging the EU to begin talks on association with the Baltic states.[65] Although the 21–22 June EU Summit did not recommend beginning association negotiations, the decision to ask the Commission to develop proposals on free trade agreements with the Baltic states marked a step towards integration of the three into the EU. The conclusions of the Copenhagen Summit also stated that the accelerated opening of EU markets to transition countries is expected 'to go hand in hand with further development of trade between those countries themselves'.[66]

These decisions strengthened the perception that the Baltic governments' major objective – EU integration – was likely to be facilitated by sub-regional cooperation. This was very explicitly stated by the leaders of the three countries during a meeting in Jurmala, in August 1993, when the three presidents jointly declared their intention to integrate into the EU, and that the aim to achieve Baltic integration was a step towards integrating the sub-region with the EU.[67] Indeed, the intra-Baltic free trade agreement was signed on 13 September. It was modelled on the bilateral free trade agreements that the Baltic states concluded the year before with the EFTA countries.

The conclusion of this agreement was declared to be a major step towards the integration of the three into the EU. The intra-Baltic free trade agreement was clearly perceived by the Baltic states' leaders as maximising their chances to integrate into the EU. As Estonian President Lennart Meri remarked, 'we can't re-enter Europe through three doors and then get together there'.[68] The instrumental value of the agreements was reaffirmed during the meeting of the foreign affairs ministers of the three states in December, following the decision of the Commission to begin discussions on Baltic free trade agreements. Subsequently, the ministers appealed jointly for prompt ratification of the intra-Baltic free trade agreement, and declared that this 'would pave the way for more lucrative treaties with the EU in the immediate future'.[69]

The intra-Baltic free trade agreement was positively evaluated by the EU Commission, which was at the time preparing bilateral free trade agreements with the Baltic states. A memorandum on the free trade agreement between the EU and Latvia prepared in September stated that the intra-Baltic free trade agreement would assist in their future integration into the EU.[70] The preparation for talks on the Baltic states' free trade agreements with the EU took place in the second half of 1993. At the beginning of December, the Commission presented the Council with its recommendation to negotiate free trade agreements, 'taking into account specific features' of the three Baltic countries. The latter qualification probably referred to the still unclear policy concerning their possible accession. The Commission also noted that the conclusion of the free trade agreements would ensure that existing agreements between the Baltic states and the Nordic countries would be compatible with the *acquis communautaire* after the accession of Sweden and Finland.

On 7 February 1994, the EU Council confirmed the Commission's mandate to negotiate free trade agreements with the Baltic countries. The Council and the Commission issued a declaration acknowledging the importance of strengthening integration between the Baltic states and the EU and stating that the free trade agreements would constitute an important step to this end. The declaration also stated that 'the Council will take all necessary steps with the aim of negotiating and concluding Europe agreements as soon as possible in recognition of the fact that Estonia, Latvia and Lithuania are to become members of the EU through the Europe Agreements'.[71] Thus, the EU explicitly acknowledged the aim of the Baltic states to become EU members. Although the Europe Agreements were to become the main instruments of integration, the strategy for integration was still uncertain.

In subsequent months, bilateral negotiations on free trade agreements between the EU and the Baltic states took place. The three agreements, which were supplied by the EU and modelled on interim agreements concluded earlier with other CEECs, were signed on 18 July 1994, and came into force in January 1995. Although the three agreements resulted in different provisions concerning the speed and scope of liberalisation,[72] they did explicitly recognise the need for continuing intra-Baltic cooperation by asserting that closer integration between the EU and the Baltic states and the Baltic states themselves should proceed in parallel.[73] In addition, they also reflected (to a certain extent) differences in the economic policies of each of the Baltic states, which were conditioned in turn by domestic political-economic processes.

Pre-accession and the development of the group approach

Between 1994 and 1996, the EU continued its group approach in bilateral relations with the Baltic states, although it gradually shifted its emphasis to the individual progress of each applicant in terms of future EU accession. The EU decided to begin negotiating Europe Agreements with the three even before the free trade agreements came into force. In August 1994, negotiations were opened simultaneously with all three countries. Although they were conducted bilaterally, the agreements were all signed on 12 June 1995. The Europe Agreements incorporated the free trade agreements and added new dimensions to the Baltic states' relations with the EU, including political dialogue and economic cooperation in a number of areas, and the approximation of laws in line with the *acquis*.

The Europe Agreements marked a new stage in Baltic integration into the EU and upgraded their status to that of other associated countries.[74] The agreements came into force only in February 1998, after ratification by the Baltic states' parliaments, the EU member states' parliaments, and the European Parliament. Nevertheless, even before this official date, Brussels decided that the three countries could still be included in the EU's pre-accession strategy.[75] In parallel, the EU took every opportunity to stress the need for advancing sub-regional cooperation. For instance, during a visit to the Baltic states to discuss the Europe Agreements, Commission representatives indicated that 'it could only be in the Balts' interest to cooperate closely with each other'.[76] The preambles of the Europe Agreements include the recognition of 'the need for continuing regional cooperation among the Baltic states'.[77] Representatives of other EU institutions made similar statements. In January 1995, a delegation from the European Parliament called for greater intra-Baltic cooperation, stressing the importance of free trade between the Baltic states.[78] In May 1996, the president of the European Parliament suggested during a speech before the Estonian parliament that the Baltic countries should 'cooperate more closely in order to better their chances of EU membership'.[79]

These statements represent a shift from *ad hoc* encouragement to a more coherent EU policy towards sub-regional economic cooperation in the CEECs. This policy was most explicitly laid out in the 1994 Essen summit conclusions, which stated that 'being aware of the role of regional cooperation within the Union, the Heads of State or Government emphasise the importance of similar cooperation between the associated countries for the promotion of economic development'.[80] This statement was included in a section of the pre-accession strategy, allowing some analysts to conclude that intra-regional cooperation had become a requirement for EU membership.[81] Furthermore, on 24 October 1994 the Council adopted a 'Communication on Orientation for a Union Approach towards the Baltic Sea Region', presented by the Commission. This document acknowledged that 'the forthcoming enlargement of the EU and the move towards closer relations with the countries of the Baltic create a need for an overall Union policy for that region'.[82] The EU's approach was based on the regional dimension of cooperation and, among other things, supported greater cohesion between existing regional initiatives and cooperation in trade and economic matters. It also foresaw the financing of regional projects, such as infrastructure, under the PHARE framework.

On 29 May 1995, the Council adopted a set of conclusions on EU policy towards the Baltic Sea region, and reaffirmed its policy of promoting 'initiatives to expand trade between the Baltic Sea States which are not members of the Union by providing suitable assistance, e.g., in the customs field'.[83] The Council also asked the Commission to prepare a report on the current state of and prospects for cooperation in the Baltic Sea region. At the end of November 1995, the Commission presented this report, in which financial contributions from the EU and other institutions and countries provided during the first half of the 1990s to the Baltic Sea region were assessed and future projections presented.[84] According to the Commission, between 1990 and 1994, a total of 206 million ECU were provided to the Baltic states in the context of national PHARE programs, most of which were concentrated on economic stabilisation and restructuring. Multi-annual Indicative Programs for the period between 1995 and 1999, covering an estimated total of 430 million ECU, were prepared for the three countries.[85] These measures were expected to focus on pre-accession, medium-term restructuring, infrastructural investment and regional cooperation. The Commission concluded that 'the scope for the development of such a specifically regional Union approach to the countries of the Baltic Sea region exists, based upon a deepening of the Union's own bilateral relationships and supported by the active encouragement and support of inter-regional and sub-regional cooperation'.[86]

In December 1995, EU leaders asked the Commission to propose 'a suitable regional cooperation initiative' to be presented during the conference of the Council of Baltic Sea States scheduled for May 1996.[87] Following this decision, the Commission adopted a Communication on a regional cooperation initiative in the Baltic Sea region on 10 April 1996. It proposed 'strengthening democracy, political stability and economic development in this region . . . by taking full advantage of existing cooperation instruments', and fostering regional cooperation.[88] This implied not only support for cooperation in the whole region but also for sub-regional arrangements, such as the intra-Baltic economic cooperation schemes. The position of the EU was then presented at the Visby meeting of the Council of the Baltic Sea States on 3–4 May 1996, which was attended by the President of the Council and the President of the Commission. The declaration adopted in Visby called for increased cooperation in several areas, including economic development and integration, and stressed its support for the 'early realisation of a free trade area between Estonia, Latvia and Lithuania'.[89]

Thus, the EU gradually developed a policy towards sub-regional cooperation, consisting of: (1) general support for intra-regional economic cooperation measures as an element of economic transition; (2) an emphasis on sub-regional cooperation as an element of preparation for accession; (3) the supply of rules for sub-regional cooperation based on the EU's integration record; and (4) financial support for sub-regional initiatives. It should be noted that financial support was targeted towards improving administrative capabilities, fostering exports and, increasingly, pre-accession measures. It did not, however, provide for redistribution purposes and side-payments to groups facing adjustment pressure due to liberalisation and market integration, as has been the case within the EU. Leaving aside the issues of sufficiency, efficiency and necessity of concrete support measures, EU policy in support of intra-Baltic cooperation schemes, backed by the supply of rules and some resources, seems to have played a major role in advancing intra-Baltic economic cooperation insofar as it was perceived by the leaders of the Baltic states as maximising their chances for EU integration.

Differentiation and accession negotiations

A change in EU policy towards the Baltic states (as well as towards the other Central and Eastern European applicant countries in general) became apparent after the July 1997 announcement of the Commission's Opinions on the applicant countries. The group approach towards integration of the applicant countries was abandoned in favour of an individual one. Although the proposal to begin accession negotiations with some countries, and not others created new groups of 'ins' and 'pre-ins,' the result in the case of the Baltic states was their clear differentiation. This change was echoed in intra-Baltic relations. Although the EU continued emphasising the importance of sub-regional cooperation, the potential benefits of intra-Baltic economic cooperation as a means for maximising the chances of EU membership decreased (particularly in the case of Estonia) and incentives for other targets of cooperative efforts were strengthened.

Even before the 1997 Opinions, the presentation of the Copenhagen accession criteria represented a major shift in the Union's policy of integrating candidate countries into the EU. The definition of membership criteria, however vague and broad, had for the first time indicated that every country would be assessed in terms of its development and ability to meet the criteria. At that time, the concrete strategy for integration, especially in the case of the Baltic countries, was far from clear. In November 1995, the Commission presented its interim report on the effects of EU enlargement on its policies, which stressed that countries 'will accede on an individual basis in the light of their economic and political preparedness and on the basis of the Commission's opinion on each applicant'.[90] This approach was confirmed at the 1995 Madrid Council, where it was decided that each country would be treated separately. The Madrid Council also asked the Commission to 'expedite preparation of its opinions on the applications made so that they can be forwarded to the Council as soon as possible after the conclusion of the intergovernmental conference'.[91] By that time, all three Baltic states had presented their membership applications to the EU.[92] In early 1996, the Commission started collecting necessary information for preparing the Opinions, which were to assess the state of the applicant countries on the basis of the membership criteria. The Opinions recommended opening accession negotiations with Estonia (among other countries), but not with Latvia and Lithuania. After intense debates inside the EU during the second half of 1997, the European Council in Luxembourg confirmed the differentiation of the applicant countries, although in a somewhat 'softer' form of 'ins' and 'pre-ins' and new multilateral arrangements including all candidates.[93] At the same time, the Council declared that 'each of the applicant states will proceed at its own rate, depending on its degree of preparedness'.[94]

The ambiguity of the EU group approach during the period leading to the explicit differentiation of the Baltic states in 1997 was reflected in the attitudes of Baltic policy-makers in assessing to what extent 'preparedness' of their countries for accession could be advanced by intra-Baltic cooperation. This was particularly evident in Estonia's policy. As early as November 1994, the Estonian Foreign Minister Jüri Luik declared that Estonia prefers admission to be decided on the basis of 'individual countries rather than groups,' and 'should any of the Baltic states meet the admission criteria, its admission should proceed immediately'.[95] Likewise, in a statement made during his visit to the Commission in March 1996, Estonian President Lennart Meri declared that 'each of the applicant countries must be dealt with separately, namely, on its own merits'.[96] Such statements elicited criticism from the other Baltic states, and in particular, Lithuania. Thus, several months later the presidents of the three countries declared that their nations would integrate into the EU together, 'making a show of their common front'.[97] Still, the ambiguity of Estonia's policy towards intra-Baltic cooperation was reflected in negotiations regarding its bilateral free trade agreements with the EU. While both the EU and the Baltic Assembly encouraged Estonia to coordinate with the other two Baltic countries, the Estonian attitude was expressed by one official from the Ministry of Foreign Affairs, who said 'had we agreed [to coordinate negotiations] it would have been like having weights tied to our feet, waiting until the others catch up'.[98]

It is important to note that before the EU's differentiation of the Baltic states through its policy of enlargement in stages, intra-Baltic economic cooperation was perceived in all three countries as an important instrument for individual integration into the EU, especially against the backdrop of intensive support for sub-regional cooperation expressed by the EU. The agreement on free trade in agricultural products should be seen in this light. As Estonian Foreign Minister at the time, Siim Kallas, declared after signing the agreement, 'we are going to build our relationship in such a way as to further integrate into the EU'.[99] Although the agreement on abolishing non-tariff barriers in intra-Baltic trade was signed in November 1997, i.e., after the announcement of the Opinions, its conclusion can also be largely attributed to the 'effect of the EU'. The agreement illustrates both the potential scope of intra-Baltic economic cooperation and its future limits taking into account individual integration of these countries into the EU. The preamble of the agreement explicitly stated that the final objective of the parties to the agreement is EU membership. Thus, the agreement was instrumental for their integration into the EU. Moreover, EU rules were taken as a reference for the provisions of the agreement, thereby illustrating most clearly the role of the EU in solving the coordination problem and choosing an appropriate framework for cooperation. In addition, the costs of economic cooperation measures were minimised since each of the Baltic states was in the process of approximating domestic legislation – including norms governing veterinary and technical product standards – as a part of their integration into the EU internal market.

Yet, coordination problems also explain the *failure* of Estonia, Latvia and Lithuania to advance positive intra-Baltic market integration beyond the scope of EU integration, namely the intra-Baltic customs union. The divergent trade regimes of the three countries, the estimated costs of a possible alignment, unclear potential benefits as well as the method of sharing the customs duties among the three, proved to be obstacles that policy-makers in the three countries were unable to overcome in the absence of a leader who could supply the rules and side-payments for the disadvantaged. The role of the EU in promoting areas of positive integration beyond the scope of integrating candidate countries into the EU turned out to be limited. Any proposed economic arrangements among the Baltic states exceeding the scope of their integration into the EU acquired grim prospects, particularly after Estonia began accession negotiations. Differentiation of the Baltic states further reduced the incentives for intra-Baltic economic cooperation, as policy-makers of these states were provided with new opportunities (or constraints) for achieving their main objectives.

The analysis presented above and a discussion of possible future developments regarding intra-Baltic economic cooperation as well as the linkages between EU policy and the intra-Baltic economic agreements are suggested in table 8.2. The scheme is based on the categorisation of integration stages presented in the theoretical section of this chapter.

Several remarks need to be made concerning the linkages between EU policy and intra-Baltic economic cooperation. Although it is possible to attribute changes in EU policy to concrete decisions or agreements, the categorisation of stages masks the fact that policy changes occur gradually, and cause reactions from outsiders, sometimes during the initial stages. Another feature of this scheme is its emphasis on an adaptive policy of the Baltic states based on responses to developments within EU policy. In the area of intra-Baltic economic

Table 8.2 Linkages between EU Policy and intra-Baltic economic cooperation

EU policy towards Baltic states	*Policy characteristics*	*Baltic states' integration into the EU*	*Intra-Baltic economic cooperation*
Establishment of diplomatic and economic relations; search for policy options (1991–95)	Group approach; *ad hoc* support for sub-regional cooperation	Negative market integration (trade and cooperation agreements; free trade agreements) supported by financial assistance (PHARE)	Agreement on free trade in industrial goods
Pre-accession (1995–98)	Group approach with increasing emphasis on individual developments; strengthened support for sub-regional cooperation	Negative market integration supplemented by unilateral aligning of regulatory policies (Europe agreements, White Paper), political dialogue and continued financial assistance	Agreement in free trade in agricultural products; agreement on abolishing non-tariff barriers
Accession negotiations (1998–2001)	Differentiation, individual progress and caching-up principles; some support for sub-regional cooperation	Positive integration complemented by continued financial assistance; opening of the accession negotiations with Estonia in 1998, Latvia and Lithuania in 2000	Failure to implement customs union and agreements on free movement of production factors; unilateral protectionist measures
Membership and transition periods (2004–?)	Initial differentiation; formation of issue sub-groups, possibly extending to the whole Baltic sea region	Positive integration; delegation of authority, participation in decision-making	Possible coalitions inside the EU on certain policy issues (regional, foreign and security, transport policies etc.)

cooperation, Baltic policy-makers cooperate when it is likely to increase their chances of membership, which in turn is facilitated by being a part of the same group in respect to the EU.

The 1997 differentiation of the Baltic states by the EU reduced possibilities and incentives for intra-Baltic economic cooperation. Indeed, the issue was no longer perceived as how the development of intra-Baltic economic cooperation could facilitate EU integration, but, rather, as how differentiation was likely to affect the intra-Baltic economic agreements implemented thus far. This shift was rather clearly illustrated by a declaration made by Estonian Foreign Minister Toomas Hendrik Ilves during the opening of accession negotiations with the EU in April 1998. He stated, 'we shall seek to ensure that the existing political, cultural and economic relations with our neighbouring countries are preserved'.[100] The future status of Estonia's trade regime with the other two Baltic states was to become one of the first negotiation subjects at the beginning of 1999.

Indeed, one could even say that EU differentiation actually *created* incentives for alternative cooperative dynamics among CEE countries, namely those who are at a similar stage of integration. In February 1999, the five prospective 'ins' met in Prague prior to the Luxembourg summit to discuss their integration strategies, and to jointly urge the EU to speed up internal reforms and alter its export policies with regard to CEECs.[101] Another sign of the new dynamics of cooperation was the high number of bilateral meetings between Latvian and Lithuanian officials in 1998 and 1999. That said, however, it was unlikely that cooperation between the new groups of 'ins' and 'pre-ins' would be extended beyond coordination of their policies towards the EU. The combined effects of divergent integration rates among individual candidates, limited benefits to be derived from stronger economic coordination, and the concentration of resources on accession-related measures, all worked to reduce the incentives and opportunities for extending the scope of sub-regional cooperation.

Lastly, these dynamics of trilateral cooperation among the Baltic states were confirmed after the EU Helsinki and Nice summits in 1999 and 2000. Despite the launch of membership negotiations with Latvia and Lithuania in February 2000 the incentives for trilateral cooperation were not strengthened since the policy of the EU was based on the principles of individual progress in negotiations and preparation for the accession. The application of these principles prevented the return of the EU to the same 'group approach' policy towards the Baltic states; on the contrary, it strengthened the incentives to concentrate resources on the integration of each country into the EU. Such unilateral competitive measures were encouraged by statements from EU representatives such as Gunther Verheugen to the effect that 'there are no guarantees that all three Baltic states would be accepted as one group'.[102] Some initiatives advanced by Lithuania, for example, on asking for a transition period to preserve the existing trade regime in case all three countries did not simultaneously accede to the Union or to form a common Baltic position towards the EU on the chapter of free movement of labour, were not supported by Estonia, which until late 2001 was ahead of the other two in the negotiating process. However, by the end of 2001 this situation changed, as both Lithuania and Latvia had succeeded in provisionally closing more chapters than Estonia, and the EU itself had begun clearly indicating that up to ten countries might be accepted into the Union after 2004.

Interest groups and intra-Baltic economic cooperation

Demands for protection

Radical changes in political and economic institutions in the Baltic states have, to various degrees, deprived former economic groups of their influence, while stabilisation gradually has produced favourable conditions for new organised groups to emerge. This section does not seek to analyse the patterns of organised economic groups' development and activities in the Baltic states. Such a task would be beyond the scope of this chapter, and it is highly complicated by the non-transparent nature of lobbying processes. Rather, the section will focus on identifying the demands of divergent economic groups, particularly as they pertain to intra-Baltic market integration. First, the conditions that seem to have influenced the survival or emergence of new groups are discussed. Then the emergence of demands for protection, inasmuch as they impact on intra-Baltic economic cooperation, is addressed, followed by a discussion of demands for market integration, or, rather, the lack thereof.

The degree to which divergent demands of economic groups have been transmitted to governments, and to which governments have been responsive to them, depends on a number factors, including the structures of national economy, institutional policy-making structures, ideological commitments and reform strategies. In Latvia and Lithuania, demands for protection have been stronger due to a large agricultural sector, slower privatisation involving foreign businesses and more gradual economic reforms, whereas in Estonia successive technocratic right-wing governments have largely disregarded such pressures. In Lithuania, the left-wing government formed as a result of the 1992 'protest vote' was particularly more responsive to protectionist demands from groups with whom it had connections from the Soviet era. Moreover, a special prerogative of the Lithuanian government to introduce changes to the trade regime by simple decree further increased the opportunities for the demands of economic groups to be satisfied. Gradually, new sectoral organisations for channelling demands were formed, and groups such as the Association of Sugar Producers in Lithuania were relatively successful at receiving protection from competing imported goods. In some cases, organised economic groups also officially supported certain political parties and had their representatives in government.

In Latvia, trade policy and responsiveness to protectionist demands during the early 1990s were similar to those in Lithuania. Agricultural interests were strongly represented in the government by the coalition partner Farmers'

Union. As a result of this strong lobby in Latvia, the intra-Baltic free trade agreement signed in 1993 did not cover trade in agricultural products. Moreover, soon thereafter the Latvian parliament voted to increase import tariffs on a number of agricultural products including livestock, pork, beef, lamb, butter, cheese and eggs, although not without some disagreements with other cabinet members. As in the Lithuanian case, the Latvian government looked to industrialised countries for prescriptions on how to satisfy protectionist demands. An 'explanation' provided at the time by a representative of the Latvian government was that 'these tariffs exist throughout Europe'.[103]

Yet, in the view of some authors many of the differences evident in the Baltic states' tariff liberalisation schedules (as set by their bilateral agreements with the EU) were also attributable to the demands of domestic groups.[104] In Lithuania, for example, import duties were changed over ten times between 1993 and 1994.[105] In both Latvia and Lithuania, market price support measures and trade barriers to imports of agricultural products increased in 1995–96, although some barriers were reduced following pressure from the IMF and the WTO. In 1997, average import tariffs on agricultural products equalled about 40 per cent in Latvia and about 30 per cent in Lithuania, although conventional import tariffs for industrial goods were much lower.[106] The high dispersion of import tariff rates with tariffs for some agricultural products (particularly sugar and dairy products) as well as income support measures linked closely to specific products and inputs rather than income groups, indicated that organised economic groups were likely to have had an impact on economic policy in these countries.[107] Even in Estonia, an appreciation of the currency, the kroon, caused demands for protection of agriculture to move gradually to the centre of political debate. Nevertheless, the centrist government formed after the 1995 elections remained unresponsive to these demands. The possibility of introducing some trade barriers was considered by the government in 1997 and particularly in 1998, under heavy pressure by local producers and references to future EU accession.[108] However, a law passed by the Estonian parliament giving the government the right to impose agricultural tariffs was subsequently ruled unconstitutional by the Estonian Supreme Court. This move therefore also dampened enthusiasm for protectionism.

A further example of effective lobbying by a domestic economic interest group involves the timing of the free trade agreement, which the Baltic states ultimately did conclude on agricultural products. Although the agreement was foreseen in the three countries' original 1993 free trade agreement and was subsequently encouraged by the EU, it took until May 1996 for the actual agreement to be adopted. Among the contributing factors here was a decision by the new Latvian prime minister Andris Šķele to fire his Minister of Agriculture, who had been advocating higher protection for farmers. Likewise important was the fact that Šķele himself came from the food processing industry, which stood to gain from cheaper imports of raw agricultural products. Thirdly, the agreement was seen as most beneficial for Estonian producers, who could access new markets in the other two states, as well as for Lithuanian producers who could increase their sales in the Latvian market.[109] The agreement thus succeeded in 'locking-in' free trade for about a year and a half before the economic crisis in Russia increased adjustment pressures from agricultural exporters.

The economic crisis in Russia, which began in the summer of 1998, increased adjustment pressures on producers in the Baltic states. After an initial decline following the reorientation of trade flows to Western Europe, the share of Russian (and CIS) trade remained significant in the Baltic states, especially for Lithuania, where exports to Russia comprised about 20 per cent of foreign trade turnover. A majority of exports to Russia from the Baltic states involved raw and processed agricultural products as well as locally processed or re-exported industrial goods. The demand for these products declined after the start of the economic crisis. As a result, some domestic groups responded to these pressures via demands for protection of domestic markets, while those not directly impacted by the crisis tried to take advantage of the situation by advocating protectionist measures vis-à-vis imports of competing products. The latter group was successful in Lithuania, where the government responded to well-organised sugar and fertiliser producers by increasing conventional import tariffs for these products and others in October 1998 despite inter-ministerial disagreements.[110]

Local producers' demands for protection eventually spilled over into the area of intra-Baltic economic relations. The possibility of reintroducing agricultural protection measures was discussed at a joint meeting of the three countries' agriculture ministers in September 1998. The Latvian delegation presented the possibility of introducing protective measures against exports of meat products and eggs from Estonia and dairy products from Lithuania in order to protect Latvian farmers and producers.[111] Indeed, despite protests from its regional partners, at the end of 1998 the Latvian government presented to parliament a proposal to introduce quotas for meat imported from Estonia and Lithuania. Although the Latvian parliament subsequently rejected the proposal, the country's protectionist rhetoric succeeded in prompting Lithuania and Estonia to introduce their own protectionist measures in October and November 1998, by exchanging allegations that various meat products imported from the other country did not conform to domestic veterinary standards – this despite an agreement to respect each other's veterinary decisions.

In the beginning of 1999, intra-Baltic free trade was again distorted by disagreements between Latvia and Lithuania concerning rules of origin, and between Lithuania and the other two countries regarding threshold prices applied by Lithuania.[112] From 1 January 1999, Latvian authorities refused to recognise product certificates issued in Lithuania for re-exported goods. Mutual accusations of rule-breaking were exchanged, and retaliatory measures were threatened. Officials from the Lithuanian Ministry of Foreign Affairs accused Latvia of violating the free trade agreement while the Latvian Ministry of Economy responded by stating that their decisions complied with the new rules of origin initiated by the EU Commission. The disagreement focused on when the new rules were supposed to be enforced. During a meeting in Vilnius in January 1999, the Baltic prime ministers agreed to remove the obstacles to trade. Yet in a new version of protectionist pressure, a number of domestic producers in Latvia and Lithuania raised for the first time demands for anti-dumping policies to be imposed with regard to bilateral exports. For example, in response to certain Latvian producers' demands to restrict the import of eggs from Lithuania based on non-compliance with veterinary standards,[113] Latvian veterinary officials announced on 17 March that they would impose restrictions on certain imports from Lithuania. Although during a trilateral meeting several days later, Latvian representatives denied that such measures had been implemented, the threat had been made. Meanwhile, in March the Estonian government accused Lithuania of trade discrimination by providing subsidies and purchasing support to its pork industry. Finally, in June, under pressure from local farmers, Latvia introduced temporary import tariffs on pork imported from Estonia and Lithuania. The latter threatened to retaliate, but for the first several months the import tariffs remained in place.

On the one hand, these retaliatory protectionist policies might be explained by either a lack of confidence in the partner countries' practices and institutions, a general lack of accurate information, or simply divergent domestic policies.[114] However, taking into account the existence of a set of coordinating institutions and the general market situation in the Baltic states, it seems more likely that these measures represented responses to demands by domestic economic groups. Although the Baltic governments' decision to begin mutual recognition of standards was valid from the standpoint of market integration, it also provided new opportunities for manipulation of these standards depending on domestic demands. The standards could be manipulated even when they were based on EU norms. Regulatory institutions became a new target of demands for protection, and in some cases non-cooperative measures were prevented only after taking the issue to the highest political levels. At the same time, budgetary limits for side-payments to groups facing adjustment pressures made the reintroduction of import protection measures a more feasible instrument for responding to domestic demands. Ultimately, it was likely that as even more new standards and norms were implemented as part of the EU *acquis*, the increasing regulatory role of the state and the complexity of regulation would provide more targets for domestic groups' demands and more opportunities for demands to be met. It was also likely that references to the EU Common Agricultural Policy would increasingly be used as a bargaining tool by domestic interest groups and by governments vis-à-vis other governments.

Demands for market integration

During the 1990s, business-sector demands in favour of intra-Baltic market integration remained relatively silent. One important reason for this can be found in the non-existence of functioning market institutions at the outset of economic reforms. While demands for protection were often channelled through old connections or open protests and the power of numbers, there was little organised resistance to protectionist measures or lobbying for the further removal of barriers to exchange. Food processing firms in the three countries supported the conclusion of an intra-Baltic agreement on free trade in agricultural products. It seems likely that market pressures also contributed to the abolition of non-tariff barriers to intra-Baltic trade, although their impact on the scope and timing of the agreement was difficult to estimate. Still, in the absence of a strong external motivating force, the Baltic governments, Latvia and Lithuania in particular, were more receptive to demands for protection, which proved to be stronger and better organised.

The absence of market demands for integration was also related to an initially low level of business internationalisation and the small size of the intra-Baltic market. It should be noted, however, that the level of internationalisation of the Baltic economies did increase rapidly during the 1990s. International market transactions were liberalised around 1993, and as a result the share of foreign trade in the GDP of each country reached considerable levels. In parallel, domestic laws governing foreign direct investment (FDI) were adopted, although the latter's share was until recently relatively low compared to other CEECs. Moreover, FDI regimes differed in each of the three states. In Estonia, a relatively liberal regime along with extensive privatisation opportunities allowed larger inflows of foreign capital. In Latvia and Lithuania, FDI caught up only during the late 1990s, mainly as a result of large-scale infrastructure privatisation. In 1998, net FDI was expected to reach 200 million USD in Estonia, 344 million USD in Latvia and 800 million USD in Lithuania.[115] These facts, however, reveal little without considering the size and nature of economic relations between the Baltic states.

The combined size of the Baltic states market is around 7.5 million people. Although GDP per capita increased significantly during the 1990s, it was still significantly below the EU average. The share of the intra-Baltic market was well illustrated by a comment made by one Western businessman, who noted that the combined incomes of Estonians, Latvians and Lithuanians did not reach the combined incomes of all the workers in the Empire State Building in New York.[116] The limited potential for intra-Baltic trade growth was also indicated by gravity models, according to which intra-Baltic trade flows exceeded their potential.[117] The potential for trade growth with EU countries was estimated to be significantly higher than for intra-Baltic trade. Furthermore, a low level of intra-industry trade tended to limit opportunities for economies of scale. For example, observers have noted that labour-, skill- and resource-intensive industries, such as clothing, footwear or textiles, favour small and flexible units of production.[118] Gains from economies of scale were restricted further by the relatively large share of trade in agricultural goods. Similarities in production structures were likely to constrain potential for complementarities in trade.[119] Nevertheless, increasing imports of updated technology and growing FDI could create new opportunities for gains and alter specialisation patterns in the long run.

Thus, the gains from active lobbying for intra-Baltic market integration have thus far seemed low, especially taking into account the transition-related problems, which businesses have had to address in each of the countries. The issue of customs administration was perhaps the only one to provoke strong criticism from business circles in the three countries. The Baltic governments acknowledged such problems; however, the necessary improvements in these areas were undertaken only with the technical and financial assistance of the EU. The EU also played a role in encouraging the creation of intra-Baltic business organisations, which could press for the removal of obstacles to market exchanges. Proposals for setting up intra-Baltic business organisations such as a Baltic Chamber of Commerce were voiced during meetings organised by the EU, the OECD and the CBSS, which also provided opportunities for an exchange of information between business and government within the sub-region.[120] However, for a number of reasons, including the absence of a single institutional target for demands and relatively small gains from organised lobbying efforts, joint business actions did not really materialise.

Indeed, it was often only the market strategies employed by foreign investors and domestic companies, which contributed to an informal integration of the three economies. For example, among some multinational corporations there was an increasing tendency to establish operations in one of the three Baltic states as a base from which they serve the entire Baltic market.[121] For instance, Coca-Cola established its bottling factory in Estonia, Kellogg based its headquarters in Latvia, and McDonald's set up shop in Lithuania. Examples in the service sector included the French bank Société Générale in Riga, and the opening of an office of the German Norddeutsche Landesbank in Vilnius. These examples illustrated how international companies perceived the intra-Baltic sub-region, and the degree to which investment in the region might be tied to intra-regional trade. Still, it should be noted that the dominant motivation of foreign investors to locate in the Baltic states remained related to opportunities offered by eastern markets, which could be served from the Baltic countries.

Another phenomenon illustrating the emergence of a regional approach towards the Baltic states in business was the growth of intra-regional investment. For example, in October 1998, Estonian investments in Lithuania equalled about 40 million USD, while Latvian investments in Lithuania made up about 9 million USD.[122] One of the first examples was the Estonian Hansapank, which expanded its financial services activity in the other two Baltic states. As some observers have noted, Estonian enterprises started turning into 'Baltic transnationals' at a faster rate by relying on either subcontracting or the establishment and/or purchase of a company in one of the other Baltic states.[123] A similar trend was demonstrated by other business activities. For example, after buying the Latvian financial firm Latvijas KIF Grupa, Vilnius Bank of Lithuania started business on the Latvian securities market. Meanwhile, a strategic cooperation agreement signed in March 1998 by three major Baltic banks – Estonian Ühispank, Latvian Unibanka and Lithuanian Vilnius Bank – opened the prospects for the creation of a joint banking unit providing cross-border customer service, investment projects, and inter-bank services. Indeed, it should be noted that inflows of FDI into the Baltic states – and in particular from the Nordic countries – contributed especially to this emergence of Baltic alliances, since foreign money was frequently behind the new ownership ties. Moreover, such cooperation and participation later expanded to include insurance, leasing and brokerage services. For example, in 1998 the representatives of the three Baltic stock exchanges discussed the idea of a joint stock exchange, although Lithuanian representatives were reluctant to advance the project, suggesting that gains from an intra-Baltic stock exchange would not significantly exceed the costs of its establishment.[124] Later the idea was modified into creating a joint Baltic–Nordic stock exchange. The recent developments illustrate an increasing level of informal economic integration with both Baltic and foreign, in particular Nordic, investors increasingly operating in all three countries. This has been further facilitated by privatisation of large infrastructure and financial companies in the Baltic states purchased by the same investor. This was paralleled by increasing trade flows among the three countries, in particular Latvia and Lithuania.

Conclusions

This chapter has argued that the scope and timing of intra-Baltic economic cooperation can be explained by 'the EU effect' and by the demands of economic interest groups. First, the EU has acted as a supplier of rules when a number of EU–Baltic and intra-Baltic cooperative measures have been forged. Second, and more broadly, the EU has acted as a supporter of sub-regional cooperation by making the latter an informal precondition for EU integration. Thus, although Baltic policy-makers have generally given a higher priority to EU integration than to intra-Baltic cooperation, it has been the latter's instrumental utility in advancing EU integration that has nevertheless spurred an overall willingness to pursue sub-regional economic cooperation. Third, this instrumental value was higher when the three countries were at the same stage of integration into the EU; after Estonia was granted entry into the group of first wave applicant countries, and with the extension of principles of individual progress, differentiation and catching-up into membership negotiations this value decreased.

By the end of 2001, when all three Baltic countries had closed over 20 chapters of the *acquis* with Brussels and the EU seemed determined to complete accession negotiations by the end of 2002 and accept up to ten countries by 2004, the incentives to compete were somewhat diminished. However, it was unlikely that new trilateral measures would be agreed before accession into the EU. Lastly, there remained the issue of whether the sub-regional approach could be maintained after all three Baltic states became EU members. It seemed unlikely that the Baltic states would follow the example of the Benelux in coordinating their positions in the internal EU negotiations, mainly due to differences in the structure of their economies and lobbying patterns. It was more likely that a regional Baltic Sea group would form within the EU on certain cross-border issues, which would have a blocking minority in the EU under the rules agreed in the Nice Summit.

Regarding domestic economic interest groups we have seen that these, too, have exerted considerable influence on the dynamics of intra-Baltic economic cooperation. Their demands for protection, in particular by agricultural groups, accounted for a number of stops in intra-Baltic market integration and for specific retaliatory policies. During the 1990s the governments in Lithuania and Latvia were generally more receptive to demands for protection than they were to demands for trade liberalisation. This imbalance appeared due to institutional differences, transition-related domestic problems, and limited potential gains from intra-Baltic market integration. Although during the turn of the decade some pressure began to appear in favour of extending the scope of economic cooperation, its impact on policy-making was not significant. Rather, the actual alignment of Baltic trade regulations tended to take place on the basis of individual Baltic adoption of the EU *acquis.*

Finally, the 1998–99 instances of Baltic protectionism and non-cooperative polices provided some interesting grounds for making future projections. Faced with adjustment pressures, disadvantaged economic groups seemed likely to strengthen their demands for protection, while governments, constrained by budgetary limits, were likely to be more responsive to such demands. The extension of market regulation and its increasing complexity also provided more opportunities for protectionist measures to be introduced. Meanwhile, EU rules themselves were often set to be used as a bargaining tool by economic groups, especially as actual EU accession drew closer. In sum, the interplay between domestic interests, EU norms and sub-regional cooperation seemed destined to continue.

Notes

I am grateful to Jan Zielonka, Walter Mattli, Susan S. Nello, Pekka Sutela, Judy Batt, Heather Grabbe, Jean Trestour and two anonymous reviewers for their comments and suggestions regarding this paper. Additional thanks go to Niina Pautola, Vitalis Nakrošis, Erika Wilkens, Nida Gelazis and Effi Tomaras. Finally, I benefited from the comments and information provided by the officials at the Lithuanian Ministry of Foreign Affairs. I am responsible for all expressed views and errors.

1 See, for example, P. Van Ham (ed.), *The Baltic States: Security and Defence after Independence* (Paris, Institute for Security Studies, 1995) Chaillot Papers 19; see also the chapters by D. Bleiere ('Integration of the Baltic states in the European Union: The Latvian Perspective'), A. Lejiņš ('The Quest for Baltic Unity: Chimera or Reality?') and A. Stranga ('The Baltic States in the European Security Architecture'), all in A. Lejiņš and Ž. Ozoliņa (eds), *Small States in a Turbulent Environment: The Baltic Perspective* (Riga,

Latvian Institute of International Affairs, 1997); additionally, H. Rebas, 'Baltic Cooperation: Problem or Opportunity?', in *Perspectives (Review of Central European Affairs)*, 9 (winter 1997/98), 67–76; P. Van Ham, 'The Baltic States and Europe', in B. Hansen, B. Heurlin (eds), *The Baltic States in World Politics* (Richmond, Curzon Press, 1998), pp. 24–45; K. Kreslins, 'A Baltic Military Alliance: An Opinion on the Military Integration of the Baltic states', in T. Jundzis (ed.) *The Baltic states at Historical Crossroads* (Riga, Academy of Sciences of Latvia, 1998), pp. 377–390; and the papers by C. Laurinavičius and E. Motieka, 'Geopolitical peculiarities of the Baltic States', V. Made, 'Estonian Geostrategic Perspectives', and Ž. Ozoliņa, 'The Geopolitical Peculiarities of the Baltic States: Latvian Perspective', all presented at the conference 'Baltic States: Cooperation and Search for the New Approaches', Vilnius, 24 April 1998.

2 One particularity common to a majority of the literature on inter-Baltic relations is an explicit or implicit emphasis on 'regional identity' or 'regional awareness' of the Baltic countries resulting from cultural, historical or linguistic characteristics. While this constructivist tendency is displayed by many scholars, it is often mixed with rationalist arguments and recommendations. Another frequent feature is a normative tone implying desirability of cooperation.

3 See, for example, the papers by M. Jurkynas, 'Baltic System of Cooperation: Internal Resources' and J. Kapustans, 'Inter-Baltic Cooperation and Common Institutions: The Latvian Perspective', both presented at the conference 'Baltic States: Cooperation and Search for the New Approaches', Vilnius, 24 April 1998.

4 See B. Lesser, T. Muravskaya and E. Shumilo, 'Baltic Regional Economic Integration: Past Trends and Future Prospects', paper for the workshop 'Cross-border Trade and Its Finance in the Baltics', Riga, 5–6 June 1997; OECD *Regional Integration and Transition Economies: The Case of Baltic Rim* (Paris, OECD, 1996); N. Pautola, 'Intra-Baltic Trade and Baltic integration', *Review of Economies in Transition*, 3, 12–13 P. Sorsa, *Regional Integration and Baltic Trade and Investment Performance* (Washington, DC, International Monetary Fund, 1997) IMF working paper WP/97/167; R. Vilpišauskas, 'Baltic States' Economic Relations in the Context of European Integration', paper presented at the conference 'Baltic States: Cooperation and Search for the New Approaches', Vilnius, 24 April 1998.

5 W. Mattli, *The Logic of Regional Integration. Europe and Beyond* (Cambridge, Cambridge University Press, 1999), p. 19.

6 See P. B. Evans and H. K. Jacobson, R. D. Putnam (eds) *Double-Edged Diplomacy: International Bargaining and Domestic Politics* (Berkeley, University of California Press, 1993).

7 R. O. Keohane, *After Hegemony: Cooperation and Discord in the World Political Economy* (Princeton, Princeton University Press, 1984), pp. 51–52.

8 H. Milner, *Interests, Institutions, and Information* (Princeton, Princeton University Press, 1997), p. 7.

9 Milner, *Interests*, p. 7.

10 M. Feldstein (ed.), *International Economic Cooperation* (Chicago, University of Chicago Press, NBER, 1988), p. 9.

11 Sorsa, *Regional Integration*, p. 16.

12 Milner, *Interests*, p. 8. In the case of the Baltic states, the issue has often been framed in terms of cooperation versus competition, leading some to conclude that 'we are economic competitors' (Made, 'Estonian', p. 38). In many cases, Baltic policy-makers as well as analysts tend to extend the model of competing firms to the level of the three countries, mix the notions of firms' competition with states' competition for status and prestige, and locational competition for foreign direct investment. All of these issues would be an interesting matter for separate analysis.

13 For example, Lainela and Sutela have suggested that 'the Baltic free trade agreement of

September 1993 is largely due to outside European pressures'. S. Lainela and P. Sutela, *The Baltic Economies in Transition* (Helsinki, Bank of Finland, 1994), p. 11.

14 Mattli, *The Logic*, p. 59.

15 Although in his reformulation of a 'pretheory' of regional integration Haas discussed the possible impact of the 'external world' on the dynamics of regional groupings, this factor was not completely conceptualised. See E. B. Haas, 'The Study of Regional Integration: Reflections on the Joy and Anguish of Pretheorising', in L. Lindberg and S. A. Scheingold (eds) *Regional Integration: Theory and Research* (Cambridge, Harvard University Press, 1971), pp. 3–42

16 Among the exceptions are Friis and Murphy, who address the external role of the EU by using a multi-level governance approach. A second example, involving the application of 'classical' political integration perspectives to EU enlargement, is provided by Balazs. See L. Friis and A. Murphy, 'EU Governance and Central and Eastern Europe: Where Are the Boundaries?', *The European Policy Process Occasional Paper* 35 (1997); P. Balazs, 'Strategies for the Eastern Enlargement of the EU: An Integration Theory Approach', in P. H. Laurent and M. Maresceau (eds), *The State of the European Union. Vol. 4. Deepening and Widening* (Boulder, Lynne Rienner Publishers, 1998), pp. 67–86.

17 J. Gower, 'EU Policy to Central and Eastern Europe', in K. Henderson (ed.) *Back to Europe: Central and Eastern Europe and the European Union* (London, UCL Press, 1999), p. 8.

18 See J. Viner, *The Customs Union Issue* (New York, Carnegie Endowment for International Peace, 1950). The concepts of trade diversion and trade creation have remained popular and are used to estimate the possible welfare effects of economic integration. For a general theory of economic integration see B. Balassa, *The Theory of Economic Integration* (London, George Allen & Unwin Ltd, 1961).

19 On the new regionalism see, for example, R. Fernandez and J. Portes, 'Returns to Regionalism: An Analysis of Nontraditional Gains from Regional Trade Agreements', *The World Bank Economic Review*, 12:2, (1998) 197–220 and W. J. Ethier, 'The New Regionalism', *The Economic Journal*, 108 (1998), 1149–1161. For an analysis of recent regional trade agreements centred around the EU and 'me-too' effects, see J. Pelkmans and P. Brenton, 'Free Trade with the EU: Driving forces and the Effects of "Me-Too"', *CEPS Working Paper*, 110 (1997). Baldwin has addressed the external impact of regional economic integration in the framework of the 'domino effect' applied to the study of the EFTA countries' response to the deepening of integration in the EU. Later he extended his 'domino' explanation of regionalism to other regional schemes. See R. Baldwin, 'The Causes of Regionalism', *The World Economy* 20:7 (1997), 865–888.

20 See Mattli, *The Logic*. For other recent political economy approaches to studies of regional integration and regionalism see E. D. Mansfield and H. V. Milner (eds), *The Political Economy of Regionalism* (New York, Columbia University Press, 1997).

21 This assumption of rational actors can be criticised in general, and specifically as applied to the transition countries. For a reflectivist ('sociological institutionalist') critique of rationalist premises applied to the EU enlargement see F. Schimmelfenning, 'The Eastern Enlargement of the European Union: A Case for Sociological Institutionalism', paper presented at a joint conference of the Austrian, German and Swiss political science associations, Vienna, 1998. More specific disagreements as applied to the analysis of transition economies can be distinguished. For example, policy-makers characterised as 'technopols' might be motivated by concerns for 'general good' and think that 'there are more important things in life than remaining in office' thereby disregarding the re-election consequences of their policy that are assumed to be the main concern of policy-makers in times of 'normal' politics. See J. Williamson (ed.) *The Political Economy of Policy Reform* (Washington, DC, Institute for International Economics, 1994), p. 22. Certain constraints on actors' behaviour are discussed in the text. Still, 'by starting with the assumption of . . . rational motivation we may obtain predictions that serve as a

useful benchmark by which to assess the extent and impact of other actions' (Hardin cited in Mattli, *The Logic*, pp. 16–17).

22 Mattli, *The Logic*, p. 42.

23 As one transition expert has maintained, '[T]he essence of both political and economic transition is a change in a country's institutional system', L. Balcerowicz, 'The Interplay between Economic and Political Transition', in S. Zecchini (ed.) *Lessons from the Economic Transition: Central and Eastern Europe in the 1990s* (Dordrecht, Kluwer Academic Publishers, 1997), p. 153.

24 K. Nicolaidis, 'East European Trade in the Aftermath of 1989: Did International Institutions Matter?', in R. O. Keohane, J. S. Nye and S. Hoffman (eds) *After the Cold War: International Institutions and State Strategies in Europe, 1989–1991* (Cambridge, Harvard University Press, 1993).

25 Nordic regional cooperation institutions or the Benelux model have been often referred to as the ones to be followed by the Baltic states.

26 And has often resulted in a mixture of 'positive reference models' both from the external environment and from the past. See C. Offe, 'Designing Institutions in East European Transitions', in R. E. Goodin (ed.) *The Theory of Institutional Design* (Cambridge, Cambridge University Press, 1996), pp. 212–213. For example, interwar cooperative experiences have often been referred to in the discussion on the models of intra-Baltic cooperation.

27 K. Jurgaitiene and O. Waever, 'Lithuania', in H. Mouritzen, O. Waever and H. Wiberg (eds), *European Integration and National Adaptations* (New York, Nova Science Publishers, 1996), p. 215.

28 The same argument could equally, or even more strongly, be applied to the case of security motivations. EU membership is perceived by the Baltic states to give better chances for providing the public good of security than intra-Baltic cooperation.

29 In this respect, strong parallels can be found in the case of Visegrad countries and creation of the CEFTA in particular. However, there seem to be important differences among the Baltic states and CEFTA countries in both the level of institutionalisation of sub-regional cooperation and the scope of sub-regional market integration. The comparative analysis of these two sub-regions and their dynamics could be an interesting issue in itself.

30 For critical analysis of the EU's policy towards Central and Eastern Europe see H. Kramer, 'The EC's Response to the 'New Eastern Europe', *Journal of Common Market Studies*, 31–2 (1993), 213–244; U. Sedelmeier and H. Wallace, 'Policies towards Central and Eastern Europe', in H. Wallace and W. Wallace (eds), *Policy-Making in the European Union* (Oxford, Oxford University Press, 1996) pp. 353–385; J. Zielonka, 'Policies without Strategy: The EU's Record in Eastern Europe', in J. Zielonka (ed.) *Paradoxes of European Foreign Policy* (Hague, Kluwer Law International, 1998) pp. 131–145; for insiders' views see G. Avery and F. Cameron, *The Enlargement of the European Union* (Sheffield, Sheffield Academic Press, 1998), A. Mayhew, *Recreating Europe: The European Union's Policy towards Central and Eastern Europe* (Cambridge, Cambridge University Press, 1998).

31 Motives for the EU to promote sub-regional cooperation among applicant countries have been summarised by Inotai, and include expectations that sub-regional cooperation would serve as a training ground and learning process for EU membership, geopolitical and security interests and interests in easier market access for its goods and capital. A. Inotai, 'Correlations between European Integration and Sub-Regional Cooperation: Theoretical Background, Experience and Policy Impacts', *Hungarian Academy of Sciences Working Paper*, 84 (1997), 14–15.

32 S. Arnswald, 'The Politics of Integrating the Baltic States into the EU: Phases and Instruments', in M. Jopp and S. Arnswald (eds), *The European Union and the Baltic States* (Helsinki, Ulkopoliittinen instituutti 1998), p. 22.

33 The pro-integrationist role of economic interest groups have been given central role in the neo-functionalist account of the early EC integration. For recent explanations of EC/EU integration dynamics emphasising the role of economic interest groups see W. Sandholtz and A. Stone Sweet (eds) *European Integration and Supranational Governance* (Oxford, Oxford University Press, 1998). Of course, the main difference in the Baltic case is the absence of a supra-national institution towards which transnational groups direct their demands.
34 J. S. Nye, 'Comparing Common Markets: A Revised Neo-Functionalist Model', in L. Lindberg and S. A. Scheingold (eds) *Regional Integration: Theory and Research* (Cambridge, Harvard University Press, 1971), p. 197.
35 H. Milner, *Resisting Protectionism: Global Industries and the Politics of International Trade* (Princeton, Princeton University Press, 1988). It should be noted, however, that foreign investors in certain cases are likely to demand protection, as has been observed in some CEECs. See A. L. Winters, 'Trade Policy Institutions in Central and Eastern Europe: Objectives and Outcomes', in A. L. Winters (ed.), *Foundations of an Open Economy: Trade Laws and Institutions for Eastern Europe* (London, CEPR, 1995), pp. 1–18.
36 Mansfield and Milner, *The Political Economy*, p. 12.
37 P. Bofinger, *The Political Economy of the Eastern Enlargement of the EU* (London, CEPR, 1995), p. 21. This observation seems to be in line with Olson's argument that radical changes in societies destroy rent-seeking organisations for collective action. Interestingly, applying his theory to the transition countries Olson himself has used his argument in a different manner stating that 'since the enterprises and industries are not destroyed by the transition to democracy, but are, on the contrary, given a new freedom to lobby for their sectional interest, this problem is magnified during the transition.' The issue seems to be whether the conjuncture was critical enough to completely destroy channels of influence established during the previous regimes. See M. Olson, 'The Varieties of Eurosclerosis: The Rise and Decline of Nations since 1982', in N. Crafts and G. Toniolo (eds), *Economic Growth in Europe since 1945* (New York, Cambridge University Press, 1996), p. 77.
38 O. Norgaard, *The Baltic States after Independence* (Cheltenham: Edward Elgar, 1996).
39 Norgaard, *The Baltic States*, p. 162.
40 *Ibid.*, p. 3.
41 Mattli, *The Logic*, p. 42. This argument also works for the supply side – governments might be less willing to advance market integration if it does not promise to improve significantly economic welfare. Intra-Baltic market integration developments illustrate, however, that it is not a necessary condition and other factors might be at work.
42 Pautola, 'Intra-Baltic Trade', p. 15.
43 In game theory terms, tit-for-tat is the policy of cooperating first and then doing whatever the other player did on the previous move. See R. Axelrod, *The Evolution of Cooperation* (New York, Basic Books, 1984).
44 S. S. Nello, 'Applying the New Political Economy Approach to Agricultural Policy Formation in the European Union' *Robert Schuman Centre Working Paper*, 21 (1997), p. 17.
45 On discussion of these concepts see N. Petersen, 'National Strategies in the Integration Dilemma: An Adaptation Approach', *Journal of Common Market Studies*, 36:1 (1998), 33–54.
46 Winters, 'Trade Policy', p. 2.
47 Lejiņš, 'The Quest', pp. 162–163.
48 Environmental protection, transportation, and defence are examples of the areas where a number of common policy measures have been agreed upon. They all are characterised by negative or positive externalities which cooperative measures are targeted to reduce or increase. The most conflictual area has proved to be border issues: it took several years of protracted negotiations between Estonia and Latvia to settle a border dispute with the

help of an external mediator, and the border between Latvia and Lithuania is still to be settled. In both cases, the issue at stake is natural resources – fishing in the first, and oil in the second.

49 Quotation from the speech of the Latvian Prime Minister Valdis Birkavs, cited in A Gricius, 'The Baltic Countries: Partners, Competitors or Going Their Own Way?', in P. Joenniemi, J. Prikulis (eds), *The Foreign Policies of the Baltic Countries: Basic Issues* (Riga, Centre of Baltic-Nordic History and Political Studies, 1994), p. 39.

50 For example, there were four meetings of Baltic states' customs officials (Gricius, 'The Baltic Counries', p. 35).

51 J. Prikulis, 'The European Policies of the Baltic Countries', in P. Joenniemi and J. Prikulis (eds), *The Foreign Policies of the Baltic Countries: Basic Issues* (Riga, Centre of Baltic-Nordic History and Political Studies, 1994), p. 93.

52 *The Baltic Independent*, 'Baltics Sign Trade Deals with EC' (15–21 May 1992), 4.

53 *The Baltic Independent*, 'Balts Want Triangular Trade' (29 May–4 June 1992), 1.

54 *Bulletin of the EC* (1992), 5, p. 80.

55 Although some observers have concluded that the emphasis on sub-regional cooperation reflected a lack of a clear strategy on the part of the EU with which to respond to the urgent needs of the region (see Inotai, *Correlations*, p. 15).

56 *Bulletin of the EC* (1992), 7/8, p. 142.

57 Already during the founding meeting of the CBSS German Foreign minister H. D. Genscher declared that the Baltic states 'must be offered association accords with the EU similar to those signed with Poland, Czechoslovakia and Hungary'. *The Baltic Independent*, 'Baltic Region Forms Council to Build Democracy and Speed Growth' (13–19 March 1992), 5.

58 *The Baltic Independent*, 'New Strains on Baltic Unity' (5–11 June 1992), 1.

59 *The Baltic Independent*, 'Lithuania Seeks to Join Baltic Trade Deal' (20–26 August 1993), 1.

60 Estonia has even been voicing doubts about the necessity of the Baltic Assembly. *The Baltic Independent*, 'Trade Row Highlights North–South gap' (2–8 April 1992), 1; Jurgaitiene and Waever, 'Lithuania', p. 213.

61 R. Martikonis, 'Penkeri Lietuvos ir Europos Sajungos santykiu metai' (draft paper, 1997), p. 8.

62 *Bulletin of the EC* (1993), 4, p. 54.

63 Cited in Arnswald, 'The Politics', p. 50.

64 *The Baltic Review*, 'Politics or Economics', 2–2 (March – June 1993), 9.

65 Prikulis, 'The European Policies', p. 106.

66 *Bulletin of the EC* (1993), 6, p. 13.

67 Prikulis, 'The European Policies', p. 106.

68 *The Baltic Independent*, 'Baltic Leaders Give a New Lease of Life to Cooperation' (3–9 September 1993), 1.

69 *The Baltic Independent*, 'Foreign Ministers Rebuke Russia on "Peacekeeping Forays"' (10–16 December 1993), 1.

70 Prikulis, 'The European Policies', p. 107.

71 *Bulletin of the EU* (1994), 1/2, p. 73.

72 For example, Estonia committed itself to free trade without a transitional period, Latvia negotiated a four-year and Lithuania a six-year transitional period, to gradually remove trade restrictions. For a legal analysis of these agreements see S. Peers, 'The Queue for Accession Lengthens', *European Law Review*, 20:3 (1995), 323–329, for an economic analysis, see Sorsa, *Regional Integration*.

73 Preamble of the free trade agreement between the EU and Lithuania.

74 Lithuania's prime minister Adolfas Slezevicius was even quoted as saying that the 'Europe Agreement, no doubt, is the most significant Lithuanian international agreement this century.' *The Baltic Independent*, 'Baltic States Re-enter Europe' (June 16–22, 1995), 1.

75 See the 'Conclusions of the Essen Summit', *Bulletin of the EU* (1994), 12.
76 *The Baltic Independent*, 'Way Cleared for Baltic Negotiations with EU' (5–11 August 1994), 2.
77 Preamble to the Europe agreement between the EU and Lithuania.
78 *The Baltic Independent*, 'Euro-MPs Call for Baltic Integration' (13–19 January 1995), 4.
79 This referred in particular to the border disputes among the Baltic states. *The Baltic Independent*, 'Haench: Settle Quarrels, Then Think about EU' (9–15 May 1996), 4.
80 *Bulletin of the EU* (1994), 12, p. 13.
81 M. Maresceau (ed.), *Enlarging the European Union. Relations between the EU and Central and Eastern Europe* (London, Longman, 1997), pp. 9. Although the importance attached by the EU to the intra-regional coopeation was largely motivated by security reasons, economic cooperation was seen as an important part of it.
82 *Bulletin of the EU* (1994), 10, pp. 53–54. The communication was adopted the same day as the Commission recommended that the Council authorise negotiation of Europe agreements with the Baltic states.
83 *Bulletin of the EU* (1995), 5, p. 66.
84 See Commission of the EC, *Report on the Current State and Perspectives for Cooperation in the Baltic Sea Region* (Brussels, COM (95) 609 final, 29.11.1995).
85 Commission of the EC, *Report*, pp. 3–4. Statistics of financial support provided to each of the Baltic states bilaterally by EU members and Nordic countries illustrated quite clearly the priorities of different countries.
86 Commission of the EC, *Report*, p. 1.
87 *Bulletin of the EU* (1995), 12, p. 96.
88 *Bulletin of the EU* (1996), 4, p. 69.
89 *The Baltic Review*, 'The Visby Summit: Baltic Europe and EU' (summer 1996), 3.
90 *Bulletin of the EU* (1995), 11, p. 69.
91 *Bulletin of the EU* (1995), 12, p. 18.
92 Latvia applied on 10 October 1995; Estonia, on 24 November 1995; Lithuania, on 8 December 1995. In general the timing was related to the forthcoming EU summit in Madrid, although in the case of Latvia the domestic situation also played a role.
93 For reactions of the member states and applicant countries to the Commission's Opinions see Avery and Cameron, *The Enlargement*, pp. 121–139. For reaction of the Baltic states, in particular, see contributions to Jopp and Arnswald, *The European Union*.
94 Cited in Avery and Cameron, *The Enlargement*, p. 135.
95 *The Baltic Review*, 'The Baltic States and EU Integration' (Winter 1995), 12.
96 *Agence Europe* (Brussels, 27.03.1996).
97 *The Baltic Times*, 'Baltic Presidents: We Go West Together' (30 May–5 June 1996), 1.
98 *The Baltic Independent*, 'Estonia Skips EU Transition Period' (3–9 March 1995), 1.
99 *The Baltic Times*, 'Estonia, Latvia Talk Security' (18–24 July 1996), 2.
100 *Agence Europe* (Brussels, 01.04.1998).
101 *Lietuvos Rytas* (12 February 1999).
102 The statement by EU Commissioner G. Verheugen, *Estonian Review*, 'Verheugen sees Estonia in first round of EU enlargement' (27 March–2 April 2000).
103 *The Baltic Independent*, 'Farmers Push for Higher Import Tariffs' (17–23 June 1994), B1.
104 Jurgaitiene and Waever, 'Lithuania', p. 221. The authors explained the transition period of six years given to Lithuania not only by the reasoning provided by Lithuanian negotiators that a transition period was needed to protect Lithuanian agriculture, but also by 'the powerful lobby of the formerly privileged industries'.
105 OECD, *Regional Integration*, p. 34.
106 OECD, *Agricultural Policies*, p. 19.
107 See OECD, *Agricultural Policies*.
108 *Verslo zinios*, 'Estija keicia kursa' (4 November 1998), 8.

109 *The Baltic Review*, 'Long Awaited Baltic Free Trade Agreement Signed' (summer 1996), 8.
110 *Lietuvos Rytas* (15 October 1998).
111 *Verslo zinios*, 'Del latviu ketinimu diskutuos' (25 September 1998), 5.
112 *Lietuvos Rytas* (28 January 1998).
113 *Lietuvos Rytas* (25 February 1999).
114 *The Baltic Times*, 'Crisis Highlights Faults in Free Trade Agreement' (3–9 December 1998), 11.
115 EBRD, *Transition*, pp. 214–221.
116 *The Baltic Times*, 'Foreign Investment Key to Baltic Success' (3–9 December 1998), 13. Although the relevance of such a comparison is doubtful, it illustrates well the attitude of large foreign investors toward the opportunities provided by the intra-Baltic market.
117 Hernesniemi, H. 'Barriers to Economic Cooperation of Baltic Rim Countries' *The Research Institute of the Finnish Economy*, Discussion Paper, 555 (1996), pp. 6–8. It should be noted that intra-Baltic trade potential might have been underestimated due to a large shadow economy and a rapid growth of incomes.
118 Pautola, 'Intra-Baltic Trade', p. 15.
119 Sorsa, *Regional Integration*, p. 16.
120 The first round table was organised by the EU in May 1994 in Riga and brought together EU industrial representatives, members of the Commission, Baltic states governmental officials and business. Its purpose was 'to unite industrialists and public authorities of all three Baltic republics', as EU Commissioner Bangemann said.
121 Lesser, Muravskaya, Shumilo, 'Baltic Regional', p. 20.
122 Interview with official from the Lithuanian Ministry of Foreign Affairs, March 1999.
123 *The Baltic Review*, 'Moving towards a Common Economic Space' (Spring–Summer 1997), 10.
124 *Verslo zinios*, 'Baltijos saliu birzos nori jungtis' (28 October 1998), 3.

Ville Kaitila and Mika Widgrén

9

Revealed comparative advantage in trade between the European Union and the Baltic countries

Ever since Estonia, Latvia and Lithuania regained their independence in 1991, they have had to reorient their previously Moscow-led trade toward new markets in Western Europe, North America and beyond.[1] Due to its geographic proximity and economic size, the European Union is the most obvious trading partner for the Baltic countries. Indeed, by 1997 48 per cent of Estonia's exports went into the European Union.[2] The corresponding figure for Latvia was 49 and for Lithuania 33 per cent. Of Estonia's imports 55 per cent came from the EU, while for Latvia this figure was 53 and for Lithuania 46 per cent. Judging by these trade figures, Lithuania seemed to be economically less integrated into Western Europe than either Estonia or Latvia as the aggregate share of Russia, Belarus, Ukraine and Latvia in its exports was 52 per cent. That said, this chapter will not deal with the Baltic countries' trade with other transition countries; rather, the emphasis will be on trade between the Baltic countries and the European Union.

A concise history of the Baltic countries' reintegration into the Western European economy starts at the official level in 1992 and 1993 with the signing of free trade agreements with the then non-EU members Finland and Sweden. After this, free trade agreements between the EU and the Baltic countries came into force in 1995. These agreements decreased the trade barriers and helped to increase trade. Further trade liberalisation has taken place since then. In early 1998, the bilateral Europe Agreements between the European Union and each Baltic country came into force. After these agreements, however, there still remained quotas and other regulations for trade in processed agricultural goods and fish. Also, the EU's rules of origin regulations restricted trade in textiles and clothing as the Baltic countries had to import the fibres used in the production of these goods.

The so-called 'hub-and-spoke' nature of the Europe Agreements generally has the effect of diverting trade. As bilateral agreements, they encourage trade between the hub (the EU) and each spoke (Estonia, Latvia and Lithuania) separately. They therefore discourage trade between the Baltic countries and non-EU countries such as Russia. As a counterweight to this, the Baltic countries have signed free trade agreements with each other covering not only industrial products, but also agricultural goods. All the Baltic countries have also signed bilateral free trade agreements with other countries in Central and Eastern Europe.

It is important to note the effects of the remaining obstacles to trade, especially those for processed agricultural products. Only 4 per cent of all Baltic exports to the EU in 1997 were live animals, plants, food products, beverages, tobacco etc., while the food processing industry alone accounted for 30 per cent of industrial production in Estonia, 43 per cent in Latvia and 27 per cent in Lithuania. Even though these goods are partly produced for the domestic market, exports to other transition countries are significant. Currently, the Baltic countries do not show a revealed comparative advantage (RCA) in these goods in the EU market and, before trade is liberalised, it is difficult to say whether such advantage potentially exists or not. Meanwhile, the Russian economic crisis that began in mid-1998 is driving parts of the Baltic food industry into bankruptcy. Consequently, the Baltic countries' potential comparative advantage in the EU market is likely to suffer.

Estonia was included as the only Baltic country in the group of six candidate countries to begin actual negotiations for EU membership in early 1998. Latvia and Lithuania were at the time left to the second wave of eastern enlargement. This division was not carved in stone, however, since other factors such as the success of the political, economic and social restructuring of the candidate countries on the basis of, among other things, the *acquis communautaire*, meant that the accession process would advance at different speeds. That Estonia was included in the original group of 'first wave' countries reflected its advance at the time the division was made. Since then both Latvia and Lithuania, but especially the former, have made progress, and thus the order and timing of the Baltic countries' accession into the European Union is by no means certain.

The following analysis is done using Eurostat trade data at the four-digit level of the Combined Nomenclature (CN) for 1993 and 1996. Between these two years Finland, Sweden and Austria became members of the EU. For these three countries data at the four-digit level were not available for 1993. Even so, we are able to construct a systematic analysis of the trade between the European Union and the Baltic countries for these two years, and these countries' revealed comparative advantage in the EU markets and vice versa for 1996.

The study consists of three sections. First, a description of trade between the EU and the Baltic countries is made. This includes calculations for intra-industry trade (IIT) also making a distinction between horizontal and vertical IIT. Second, an analysis of the comparative advantage in trade is constructed. This section is based on Balassa indices and similarity indices. And third, we will take a look at what clues the evolution of the trade gives as to the future of trade and the countries' comparative advantage, taking into consideration the possibility of a two-phase-accession of the Baltic countries into the European Union.

Trade between the European Union and the Baltic countries

Development and structure of trade

Total EU-15 exports to the three Baltic countries accounted for 1,472 million ECUs in 1993. This had risen to 4,213 million by 1996 (see table 9.1). Total EU-15 imports were 1,799 million ECUs in 1993 and 3,440 in 1996. The EU trade deficit of some 327 million in 1993 had thus become a surplus of 774 million by 1996. There remained a small deficit in EU trade with Latvia, but that too had decreased significantly by 1996, and by the next year it had turned into a surplus.[3]

Table 9.1 Total EU exports to the Baltic countries in 1996, %

	Estonia	*Latvia*	*Lithuania*	*All Baltic countries*
Total EU, mill. ECUs	*1,660*	*1,103*	*1,451*	*4,213*
France	2.1	3.5	5.3	3.6
Belgium-Luxembourg	2.0	4.3	4.1	3.3
Netherlands	3.8	7.7	6.3	5.7
Germany	14.1	29.1	38.6	26.5
Italy	3.7	5.7	8.4	5.9
United Kingdom	3.8	8.3	6.6	5.9
Ireland	0.6	1.0	0.9	0.8
Denmark	3.7	6.3	8.6	6.1
Greece	0.1	0.4	0.3	0.2
Portugal	0.1	0.1	0.3	0.2
Spain	0.6	1.0	2.5	1.3
Sweden	12.0	14.8	7.9	11.3
Finland	52.7	16.8	8.5	28.1
Austria	0.6	1.2	1.7	1.1
Total EU	100.0	100.0	100.0	100.0

In 1996 the largest EU exporter to the Baltic countries was Finland, which accounted for 28 per cent of total EU exports, followed closely by Germany with a share of 27 per cent. The two thus accounted for some 55 per cent of all EU exports to the Baltic countries. This shows how concentrated trade between the EU and the Baltic countries is. The share of Finland, Germany, Sweden and Denmark in all EU exports to Estonia, Latvia and Lithuania was 83, 67 and 64 per cent, respectively.

EU imports from the Baltic countries look somewhat different, however. The largest importer was Germany with a 23 per cent share of all EU imports, but it was followed by the UK and the Netherlands, both accounting for just under 17 per cent of all imports (see table 9.2). Finland's share becomes almost negligible for both Latvia and Lithuania as does Sweden's for the latter.

Table 9.2 Total EU imports from the Baltic countries in 1996, %

	Estonia	*Latvia*	*Lithuania*	*All Baltic countries*
Total EU, mill. ECUs	*1,125*	*1,181*	*1,133*	*3,440*
France	3.2	4.5	5.6	4.5
Belgium-Luxembourg	3.2	3.5	7.3	4.7
Netherlands	12.1	27.9	8.2	16.2
Germany	14.2	21.1	33.5	22.9
Italy	1.7	1.2	5.4	2.8
United Kingdom	12.1	20.1	18.0	16.8
Ireland	0.2	1.3	0.5	0.7
Denmark	5.2	4.9	7.3	5.8
Greece	0.1	0.1	0.2	0.1
Portugal	0.3	0.6	1.6	0.8
Spain	0.3	0.8	3.8	1.6
Sweden	20.5	11.5	4.9	12.3
Finland	26.5	2.4	2.3	10.3
Austria	0.3	0.2	1.4	0.6
Total EU	100.0	100.0	100.0	100.0

The main products in aggregate EU exports to the Baltic countries are fairly similar regardless of the importing nation. The most important product groups are machinery, equipment and vehicles, and mineral fuels. Other important goods are plastics and paper products (see table 9.3).

Table 9.3 Main EU export and import products in trade with Estonia (CN2) in 1996, millions of ECUs and % share of total trade

CN	*EU exports*	*Value*	*(%)*	*CN*	*EU imports*	*Value*	*(%)*
85	Electrical machinery and equipment etc.	225	13.5	27	Mineral fuels and oils	208	18.5
84	Nuclear reactors, boilers, machinery etc.	201	12.1	44	Wood and articles of wood	195	17.3
87	Vehicles, other than railway or tramway	134	8.1	62	Clothing accessories, not knitted or crocheted	99	8.8
27	Mineral fuels and oils	115	6.9	85	Electrical machinery and equipment etc.	79	7.0
39	Plastics and articles thereof	69	4.2	84	Nuclear reactors, boilers, machinery etc.	77	6.8
48	Paper and paperboard	54	3.2	94	Furniture, bedding etc.	64	5.7
73	Articles of iron and steel	52	3.1	72	Iron and steel, mainly scrap	48	4.3

The EU countries' imports from the Baltic countries are slightly less homogenous. The main import products from Estonia were mineral fuels and oils, largely transit trade from Russia, and wood and wood products. Furthermore, non-knitted clothing is fairly important. What differs especially from Latvia but also from Lithuania is the importance of machinery in EU imports from Estonia. These products also contribute to the relatively larger share of intra-industry trade between Estonia and the EU.

EU imports from Latvia are dominated by mineral fuels and oils, again transit trade from Russia (see table 9.4). The variety of Latvia's own exports is fairly limited and dominated by wood and articles of wood. In 1997 the share of oil in Latvia's exports had decreased to less than 30 per cent, and wood and articles of wood had risen correspondingly. This was due to the decrease in world market prices of oil. The trend may have continued during 1998 for the same reason. Clothing is the next most important export product in Latvia's exports to the EU.

Table 9.4 Main EU export and import products in trade with Latvia (CN2) in 1996, millions of ECUs and % share of total trade

CN	*EU exports*	*Value*	*(%)*	*CN*	*EU Imports*	*Value*	*(%)*
84	Nuclear reactors, boilers, machinery etc.	120	11.4	27	Mineral fuels and oils	502	42.5
27	Mineral fuels and oils	90	8.5	44	Wood and articles of wood	308	26.1
87	Vehicles, other than railway or tramway	84	8.0	62	Clothing accessories, not knitted or crocheted	71	6.0
85	Electrical machinery and equipment etc.	82	7.7	72	Iron and steel, mainly scrap	35	2.9
22	Beverages, spirits and vinegar	53	5.0	61	Clothing accessories, knitted or crocheted	32	2.7
48	Paper and paperboard	48	4.5	74	Copper, mainly scrap	31	2.6
39	Plastics and articles thereof	32	3.0	52	Cotton	29	2.4

Lithuania's main export product is clothing, constituting a fifth of all its exports to the EU. But again wood and mineral fuels are also important (see table 9.5). Table 9.6 shows estimates for the maximum significance of transit exports for the Baltic countries. Possible arbitrage goods cover 34 per cent of Estonia's exports, 51 per cent of Latvia's exports and 37 per cent of Lithuania's exports. Out of these the share of oil was 55, 82 and 25 per cent, respectively. The overall significance of transit exports decreased substantially between 1992 and 1994, but the decline seems to have stabilised thereafter. In 1996, transit exports still covered 40 per cent of the Baltic countries' exports to the EU. These figures are strongly affected by the fairly volatile world market price of oil. The transit trade in oil may also under some unlikely circumstances be affected by the political conditions in and around the Baltic countries.

Table 9.5 Main EU export and import products in trade with Lithuania (CN2) in 1996, millions of ECUs and % share of total trade

CN	EU Exports	Value	(%)	CN	EU Imports	Value	(%)
84	Nuclear reactors, boilers, machinery etc.	199	14.0	62	Clothing accessories, not knitted or crocheted	163	14.4
85	Electrical machinery and equipment etc.	130	9.2	44	Wood and articles of wood	150	13.2
87	Vehicles, other than railway or tramway	130	9.1	27	Mineral fuels and oils	140	12.4
39	Plastics and articles thereof	79	5.5	31	Fertilisers	129	11.4
99	Other	53	3.7	85	Electrical machinery and equipment etc.	74	6.6
90	Optical etc. instruments and apparatus	43	3.0	61	Clothing accessories, knitted or crocheted	54	4.8
43	Fur skins and artificial fur and articles thereof	41	2.9	72	Iron and steel, mainly scrap	40	3.5

The absolute value of transit exports from the Baltic countries to EFTA countries was 951 million US dollars in 1992, 1,422 million in 1994 and 1,767 million in 1996. Hence the high relative shares in 1992 can be explained by the low level of the Baltic countries' exports right after regaining their independence. Comparison of 1994 and 1996 figures show that arbitrage goods have maintained their importance in the Baltic countries' exports to the EU, although export growth has been somewhat faster in products other than arbitrage goods (see table 9.6).[4]

Figure 9.1 shows the share of transit exports from each Baltic country to each EU country. There are substantial differences between the latter. In the Baltic countries' exports to the EU the share of transit trade exceeds 50 per cent in exports to France, Belgium, the Netherlands, the UK, Greece and Spain. These countries account for 44 per cent of EU imports from the Baltic countries. If we take the Baltic countries' five most important EU export markets, Germany, the Netherlands, the UK, Finland and Sweden, there are substantial differences as exports to the Netherlands and the UK are almost solely based on transit trade, whereas arbitrage goods have only a negligible importance in exports to Finland and Sweden. Figure 2 gives a more detailed picture of the Baltic countries' transit exports to the EU. It shows the estimated shares of potential arbitrage goods for each Baltic country in their exports to each EU country in 1996.

Intra-industry trade

The share of intra-industry trade (IIT) is usually high between developed industrialised countries and fairly low between countries that are at different stages of

Table 9.6 Estimates for transit exports from Baltic countries to the EU and EFTA in 1992 and 1994 and to EU-15 in 1996

	1992		*1994*		*1996*	
Country	*Share of possible arbitrage goods in exports, (%)*	*Share of possible arbitrage goods in exports excluding oil, (%)*	*Share of possible arbitrage goods in exports, (%)*	*Share of possible arbitrage goods in exports excluding oil, (%)*	*Share of possible arbitrage goods in exports, (%)*	*Share of possible arbitrage goods in exports excluding oil, (%)*
Estonia	44.9	39.2	21.7	16.6	33.7	15.3
Latvia	70.5	14.8	57.8	7.2	51.2	9.1
Lithuania	68.5	28.7	47.3	15.1	37.3	27.9
Baltic countries total	63.6	26.4	45.3	12.2	40.9	16.3

Source: 1992 and 1994 Hoekman & Djankov (B. Hoekman and S. Djankov, 'Intra-Industry Trade, Foreign Direct Investment and the Reorientation of East European Exports', *CEPR Discussion Paper* No. 1377 (1996) and 1996 own calculations.

Note: In 1992 and 1994 transit exports consist of the following 2–digit SITC items: non-metallic minerals and metals, crude fertilisers and metalliferrous ores and scrap (27–28), petroleum and products (33), non-metallic mineral products (66), non-ferrous metals (68), transport equipment (78–79), and gold (97). Estimates for 1996 consist of the following 2–digit CN items: earths and stone etc. (CN25), ores etc. (CN26), mineral fuels, oils, etc. (CN27), inorganic chemicals and compounds etc. (CN28), organic chemicals (CN29), pharmaceutical products (CN30), fertilisers (CN31), natural pearls, precious sones and metals (CN71), iron and steel (CN72), articles of iron and steel (CN73), copper and articles thereof (CN74), nickel and articles thereof (CN75), aluminium and articles thereof (CN76), lead and articles thereof (CN78), zinc and articles thereof (CN79), tin and articles thereof (CN80), other base metals and articles thereof (CN81), railway rolling stock (CN86), automobiles and bicycles (CN87), aircraft and parts thereof (CN88), and ships and boats (CN89).

economic development. IIT has indeed been lower in trade between European countries in transition and the EU than in intra-EU trade. But as the countries of Central and Eastern Europe have been narrowing down the difference in economic structures and income levels, their level of IIT in total trade has also been rising. Previous research shows that most of this IIT is, however, vertical and not horizontal in character.[5] This means that even though the countries are engaged in the export and import of goods that are classified in the same product group, the goods are of dissimilar quality. We shall first look at overall IIT levels and then proceed to the question of the quality of the goods.

The extent of intra-industry trade is calculated using the Grubel-Lloyd index. It measures the sum of the absolute differences between the exports (x) and the imports (m) of commodities k in trade between countries i and j, where k runs through all the products in which the countries are engaged in trade with

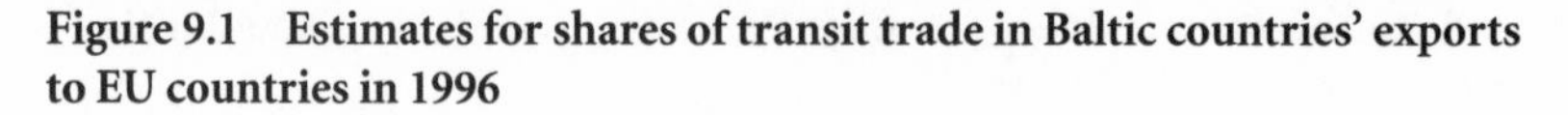

Figure 9.1 Estimates for shares of transit trade in Baltic countries' exports to EU countries in 1996

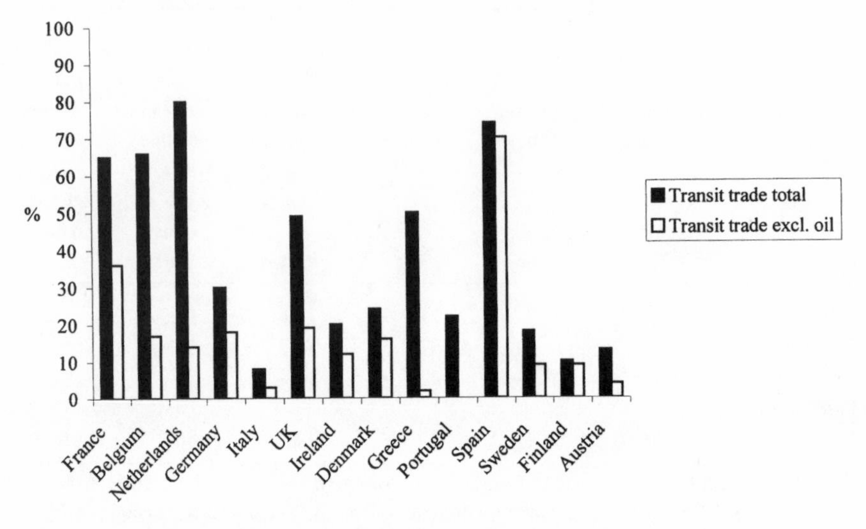

Figure 9.2 Estimates for Baltic countries' transit exports to EU countries, share of total exports in 1996

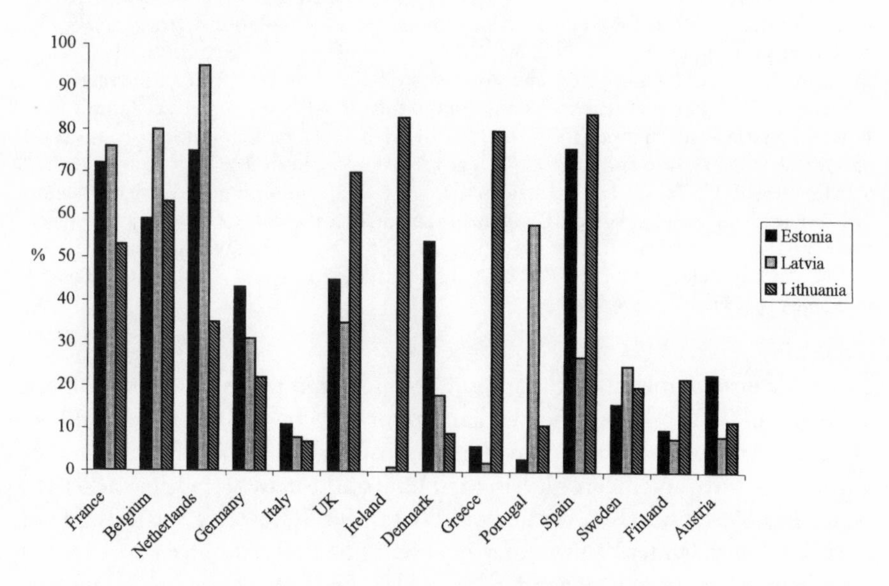

each other. In the denominator we have the total sum of exports and imports between these two countries. If the index takes a value of zero, there is no intra-industry trade between the countries. Moreover, as the index approaches 100, the share of IIT in total trade approaches 100 per cent. More formally the index is given by

$$GL_{ij} = \left[1 - \frac{\sum_k |x_{ij}^k - m_{ij}^k|}{X_{ij} + M_{ij}} \right] * 100.$$

Table 9.7 summarises the results for IIT in EU–Baltic trade with intra-EU trade as a comparison. We may note a few points. First, the overall level of intra-industry trade between the EU and the Baltic countries is fairly low. Second, it has been increasing fairly rapidly. To some extent this may be credited to the Finnish and Swedish EU membership in 1995, even though the other EU countries have also increased their IIT levels. In trade with the Baltic countries in aggregate, all the EU countries, save Greece, have seen their IIT levels rise at the CN4 level. For the individual Baltic countries there are some further exceptions to this general rule, but typically only between countries that do not trade a lot with each other. Third, the EU countries geographically close to the Baltic countries, i.e. Finland, Sweden and Denmark, exhibit by far the highest levels of IIT. The countries farther away from the Baltic Sea have both lower levels of aggregate trade and lower levels of IIT. This also corresponds with the usual observation that country-specific factors explain IIT. The Baltic countries' income levels are so different from those in the EU that geographic proximity remains the only explanatory country-specific factor behind the levels of IIT. Compared to intra-EU levels, the EU-Baltic levels of IIT are, in general, very low.

Table 9.7 Grubel–Lloyd indices of intra-industry trade between the EU and the Baltic countries, and in intra-EU trade (CN4)

Country	*Baltic countries*		*Estonia*		*Latvia*		*Lithuania*		*Intra-EU*
	1993	*1996*	*1993*	*1996*	*1993*	*1996*	*1993*	*1996*	*1996*
France	1.4	5.6	2.2	6.9	0.6	4.3	1.0	6.5	74.3
Belgium-Luxembourg	6.6	10.4	1.1	3.1	1.7	18.1	3.9	5.9	67.9
Netherlands	3.2	5.0	6.7	4.3	1.1	3.4	2.8	10.0	61.5
Germany	10.2	13.1	6.9	12.1	7.0	16.0	8.1	14.9	70.0
Italy	7.0	8.0	2.7	7.2	8.4	9.9	4.8	4.0	52.9
United Kingdom	4.3	5.9	2.5	3.5	2.1	6.4	2.9	4.0	66.9
Ireland	0.0	0.7	0.0	0.7	0.0	0.5	0.0	0.3	39.4
Denmark	14.7	23.0	13.7	20.3	8.0	15.7	15.9	22.7	52.2
Greece	3.2	1.0	0.0	0.0	4.7	0.0	3.0	0.2	19.3
Portugal	0.1	4.7	0.4	1.9	0.0	0.0	0.0	5.1	41.4
Spain	0.2	2.1	0.0	1.7	1.3	3.5	0.1	1.5	59.5
Sweden	–	22.0	–	25.6	–	11.4	–	8.6	55.2
Finland	–	25.1	–	28.7	–	7.4	–	9.7	38.9
Austria	–	5.2	–	5.0	–	3.4	–	6.0	58.3
Total EU	11.1	25.6	11.9	34.8	8.3	19.3	8.4	16.9	–

At the individual country level the picture is, of course, mostly similar to that in the aggregate. Estonia leads in the extent of IIT, which is mostly due to its trade with Finland and Sweden. Indeed, as much as over a third of Estonia's trade with the EU is based on IIT at the four-digit level. Latvia's highest shares of IIT are in its trade with Germany, Denmark and Sweden. For Lithuania, the highest levels of intra-industry trade are with Denmark and Germany. In all trade with the EU, however, Lithuania comes in last, as IIT covers only some 17 per cent of its trade. For each Baltic country IIT is highly concentrated on their trade with their most important trading partners.

Tables 9.8 – 9.10 list those CN4 products where an EU country and one of the Baltic countries have more than 3 million ECUs worth of exports and

Table 9.8 The CN4 product groups with more than 3 million ECUs of total trade between an EU country and Estonia and more than 80% of IIT in 1996

Country	*CN*	*Products*	*Total trade (ECUs)*	*IIT(%)*
Sweden	2710	Oil (not crude) from petrol and bituminous minerals etc.	10,741	83.5
Finland	8544	Insulated wire, cable, electric conductors; optic fibre cable	24,851	97.9
	8522	Parts and accessories of sound/video recording equipment	11,575	93.5
	6403	Footwear, uppers of leather	8,700	80.9
	4407	Wood sawn or chipped length	4,321	93.2
	6110	Sweaters, pullovers etc, knitted or crocheted	4,091	86.4
	9506	Articles and equipment for sports	3,942	82.4
	8431	Parts for machinery for lifting and handling machinery	3,513	89.6
	7307	Tube or pipe fittings, of iron or steel couplings	3,171	84.3
	5209	N/A (52: Cotton)	3,159	92.4

Table 9.9 The CN4 product groups with more than 3 million ECUs of total trade between an EU country and Latvia, and more than 80% of IIT in 1996

Country	*CN*	*Products*	*Total trade (ECUs)*	*IIT(%)*
Germany	8504	Electric transformers, static converters and inductors	14,145	91.0
	6108	Women's or girls' undergarments	3,671	98.1
Italy	4104	Leather of bovine or equine	3,505	99.7
Sweden	6212	Brassieres, girdles, corsets, braces, suspenders etc.	5,998	88.1

Table 9.10 The CN4 product groups with more than 3 million ECUs of total trade between an EU country and Lithuania, and more than 80% of IIT in 1996

Country	*CN*	*Products*	*Total trade (ECUs)*	*IIT(%)*
Germany	1604	Prepared or preserved fish; caviar	4,888	88.1
	6403	Footwear, uppers of leather	4,781	95.9
	2309	Preparations used in animal feeding	3,443	93.9
UK	5208	Woven cotton fabrics	3,346	92.3

imports and the share of intra-industry trade exceeds 80 per cent. This will reveal the products that are both important for a Baltic country and where IIT is prevailing. It is worthwhile noting the most extensive IIT in ECU terms especially where it takes place in mechanical equipment. At the CN4 level there is extensive IIT between Estonia and Finland in wires, cables and electric conductors, but also in sound and video recording equipment. Finnish companies have a lot of subcontracting in Estonia, which is reflected in these figures. Such IIT also exists between Germany and Latvia in electric transformers, static converters and inductors. Between Lithuania and the EU such trade did not exist in 1996. There the large IIT products were in alimentation and textiles.

As already argued, intra-industry trade is usually high between highly industrialised countries. In some cases, however, we may get a misleading picture of the trade as a country may be exporting, for example, high quality electronics, while at the same time importing electronics of lower quality. This results in a high level of IIT even though, due to the difference in quality, the goods are not necessarily substitutes for each other. By making the reasonable assumption that price reflects quality positively, we may analyse whether the countries are engaged in trading goods that are not only of the same type but also of (approximately) the same quality.

The unit export and import prices are calculated as the ratio of trade figures in ECUs to those in tons. There are some problems with this approach as a heavier product is not, *ceteris paribus*, necessarily of poorer quality. Also with the available trade data, an additional problem is presented by the lack of weight data for many products, thus rendering it impossible to calculate the unit prices even when there exists data for trade measured in ECUs.

As shown in table 9.11, the EU's aggregate unit export prices are five to six times higher than its unit import prices in trade with the Baltic countries. There are also very large differences between the countries partly due to the small trade flows. The largest figures, those above ten, are for country-pairs not engaged in extensive trade. But to what extent are the countries trading in goods of similar quality? To analyse this, intra-industry trade is next divided into its horizontal (HIIT) and vertical (VIIT) components. The former refers to trade in goods of similar quality and the latter to goods of dissimilar quality. We adopt here the

Table 9.11 The ratio of the EU's unit export and unit import prices in trade with the Baltic countries, and in intra-EU trade (CN4) in 1996

	Estonia	*Latvia*	*Lithuania*	*Intra-EU*
France	6.78	14.00	11.47	1.00
Belgium–Luxembourg	7.20	3.47	14.89	1.50
Netherlands	5.61	4.66	5.74	0.87
Germany	7.86	8.26	5.28	1.54
Italy	3.41	2.23	3.85	1.68
United Kingdom	5.96	4.36	6.04	0.50
Ireland	21.67	1.60	9.62	4.24
Denmark	4.28	2.04	3.07	0.82
Greece	0.01	16.60	3.96	0.52
Portugal	1.07	15.71	7.44	1.10
Spain	15.13	2.44	7.40	0.87
Sweden	6.56	7.95	5.76	0.56
Finland	2.02	4.71	10.68	0.94
Austria	3.10	3.26	8.45	0.83
Total EU	4.64	5.34	6.66	1.04

approach taken by Greenaway[6] and determine HIIT as those goods where the ratio of unit export prices to unit import prices is at a par, 15 per cent. The 15 per cent should allow for the difference between f.o.b. and c.i.f. prices in trade. Due to the lack of much of the unit price data, it does not make sense to calculate HIIT for many of the EU-Baltic country pairs.

The results are given in table 9.12. There we may first note the last column that shows the extent of horizontal intra-industry trade in intra-EU IIT. It varies from Ireland's 12 per cent[7] to 52 per cent for Belgium–Luxembourg. The share of HIIT between the EU countries and the Baltic countries is, as was to be expected, lower than in intra-EU trade. At the aggregate level, Estonia fares better than either Latvia or Lithuania. Not only is there more IIT in trade between Estonia and the EU, also the share of horizontal IIT is clearly higher than for Latvia or Lithuania. The shares of both IIT and HIIT may be expected to rise in the future as the Baltic countries catch up with the current EU countries.

Due to the lack of simultaneous exports and imports in many product groups and the lack of price data in some others, the extent of vertical and horizontal IIT is only calculated for Estonia's, Latvia's and Lithuania's main EU trading partners and the EU as a whole. But even for the countries that we can calculate any degree of HIIT, one rule seems to exist: the smaller the trade coverage is, the less reliable the results above are. For the EU as a whole the coverage is, however, fairly good, and also the results sufficiently reliable to draw conclusions.

The pattern of IIT may reflect the foreign direct investment (FDI) made between the countries, in this case flowing typically from the EU to the Baltic

Table 9.12 Horizontal intra-industry trade in EU–Baltic trade and intra-EU trade (CN4) in 1996 (% of all IIT)

Country	*Estonia*	*Latvia*	*Lithuania*	*Intra-EU*
France	–	–	–	42.7
Belgium–Luxembourg	–	–	–	52.4
Netherlands	–	1.4	2.5	49.8
Germany	3.1	3.4	3.9	43.2
Italy	–	–	–	25.9
United Kingdom	–	–	–	52.3
Ireland	–	–	–	12.3
Denmark	–	–	3.6	31.3
Greece	–	–	–	20.7
Portugal	–	–	–	23.2
Spain	–	–	–	28.9
Sweden	11.3	6.6	17.5	33.3
Finland	12.1	–	–	15.1
Austria	–	–	–	18.4
Total EU	16.4	5.8	5.7	–

countries. The EU country in question may be using the Baltic country as a base for production partly substituting for, partly complementing domestic production. Indeed, the high level of IIT in Estonia's trade with Finland and Sweden is met by the dominance of these countries in the stock of FDI in Estonia. In particular, many Finnish but also Swedish companies are engaging Estonian companies in subcontracting. Another motivation for FDI is the possibility for firms to expand, as the domestic EU market may already be quite mature and does not offer real growth prospects.

The largest source of FDI in Latvia has been Denmark, which also has the second-largest IIT level. Germany is the second largest EU source of FDI into Lithuania and has the second largest share of IIT. Even though there is thus a positive correlation between FDI flows and the extent of IIT, one should not make too strong judgements on the basis of this evidence. The data should be disaggregated at the level of industries (see table 9.13). Some caution should be exercised with the FDI data also because the country that the data indicates as having made the investment is not always the real country of origin. This may be the case with a joint project by companies from two different countries. One such example is joint-Nordic investment in Baltic beverage companies.

Table 9.14 shows the stocks of foreign direct investment in each Baltic country. Manufacturing industry has been a major receiver of FDI in Estonia and Lithuania with wholesale and retail trade a close second. Latvia displays a somewhat different pattern as the Russian investments into transport and Nordic investment into communications were together the number one receiver of FDI into the country. Also financing has received a lot of FDI.

Table 9.13 The stocks of foreign direct investment in the Baltic countries from the EU, the United States and Russia by country of origin (% of all FDI)

Country of origin	*Estonia, Q2 1998*	*Latvia Q4 1996*	*Lithuania Q4 1997*
France	0	0	2
Luxembourg	0	0	4
Netherlands	3	2	1
Germany	4	5	11
Italy	1	0	1
United Kingdom	4	7	8
Ireland	0	2	5
Denmark	5	27	6
Sweden	18	5	12
Finland	31	3	5
Austria	2	2	2
United States	6	11	26
Russia	4	14	2
Other	22	22	15

Table 9.14 The stock of foreign direct investment in Estonia 6/98, Latvia 9/97 and Lithuania 7/97

Sector	*Estonia*	*Latvia*	*Lithuania*
Manufacturing industry	38	30	40
Wholesale, retail trade	28	8	31
Transport, storage, communication	13	36	11
Real estate, renting and business activities	8	2	1
Financing	3	17	5
Agriculture, hunting, forestry	2	0	1
Hotels, restaurants	2	2	3
Construction	2	1	4
Other	4	4	4

Sources: Bank of Estonia, and Latvian and Lithuanian statistical authorities.

Revealed comparative advantage

Next, we approach the main issue of this study, i.e. revealed comparative advantage in trade between the EU and the Baltic countries. This issue is first analysed with the help of a similarity index of trade and then using the Balassa index of revealed comparative advantage.[8] The products, where a Baltic country has a comparative advantage in its exports to the EU, are usually those in which it is specialising in its exports to the EU. Consequently, these are also the products in which the Baltic countries compete with EU countries in the EU market.

Similarity of Baltic exports to the EU

The similarity index measures the extent to which the exports of two countries are similar. It is calculated here following Drábek and Smith:[9]

$$S(ab,c) = 100^* \Sigma_k \min(X_k(ac),X_k(bc)),$$

where X_k is the share of product k in exports from either country a or country b to country c. In table 9.15, countries a and b are the two Baltic countries in the first row and country c is the EU country in the first column. The index takes values from 0 to 100 as the similarity between the two Baltic countries' exports to an EU country becomes more pronounced.

Table 9.15 Similarity index for the Baltic countries' exports (CN4) to the EU in 1996

EU country	*Estonia v. Latvia*	*Estonia v. Lithuania*	*Latvia v. Lithuania*
France	22.7	22.4	8.6
Belgium–Luxembourg	31.8	40.9	51.7
Netherlands	55.2	44.6	30.1
Germany	44.7	26.9	44.5
Italy	16.4	15.5	31.1
United Kingdom	49.2	53.5	20.2
Ireland	20.8	8.0	8.0
Denmark	34.7	23.8	48.2
Greece	1.0	0.5	0.4
Portugal	13.9	0.9	11.3
Spain	8.0	6.1	27.7
Sweden	38.9	42.3	31.0
Finland	32.5	30.1	26.7
Austria	17.1	14.5	9.3
Total EU	52.0	52.1	43.7

On the basis of these results, Estonia's exports to the EU are more similar to those of Latvia or Lithuania than the exports of the two latter countries are to each other. Consequently, an accession of Estonia to the EU without Latvia and Lithuania would be equally harmful for the two southernmost Baltic countries as Estonia's trade barriers with the EU would then be lower than those of either Latvia or Lithuania.

When comparing the similarity of EU countries' intra-EU exports with the exports of Estonia, Latvia and Lithuania to the EU in aggregate we find in table 9.16 that Estonia's exports are more similar to intra-EU exports than those of Latvia or Lithuania.

On the basis of the similarity indices, no single EU country seems to stand out as being particularly affected by competition from Estonia. The Netherlands, Italy, Denmark, Portugal, Sweden, Finland and Austria score slightly

Table 9.16 Similarity index between the Baltic countries' exports to the EU compared to intra-EU exports (CN4) in 1996

	Estonia	*Latvia*	*Lithuania*
France	19.0	10.7	13.6
Belgium–Luxembourg	21.1	13.9	16.6
Netherlands	24.8	17.2	18.5
Germany	18.7	11.2	13.9
Italy	24.3	13.8	19.2
United Kingdom	20.2	17.0	13.1
Ireland	15.8	8.0	10.6
Denmark	26.5	16.5	18.3
Greece	18.1	15.7	21.4
Portugal	25.3	16.7	25.9
Spain	17.8	10.3	15.1
Sweden	25.7	15.7	17.4
Finland	25.1	16.4	16.2
Austria	25.2	13.8	17.3
Total EU	24.1	15.0	18.1

above-average levels of similarity. In the case of Latvia, the same takes place with the Netherlands, the UK, Denmark, Greece, Portugal, Sweden and Finland. For Lithuania the respective countries are the Netherlands, Italy, Denmark, Greece and Portugal. The Baltic countries are, however, competing more with each other in the EU market than with any of the present EU countries. These results are further given proof in the more statistical analyses using the Balassa indices.

Balassa index of revealed comparative advantage

Balassa indices are calculated here as the ratio of the share of a given product in a country's exports to another country as compared to the share of that product in aggregate intra-EU exports, i.e.

$$BI = \frac{x^k_{ij} \mid X_{ij}}{x^k \mid X},$$

where x is the exports of country i to country j of product k, X_{ij} is total exports of country i to country j, x^k is the intra-EU exports of product k, X is total intra-EU exports.

Using this index, we see that the structure of Latvia's comparative advantage seems to be less diversified than that of either Estonia or Lithuania. Out of the 1,242 product groups at the CN4 level, Estonia has a comparative advantage in 194 groups in the aggregate EU market, Lithuania in 165 groups, while Latvia in only 107 groups. All the EU countries had a more diversified RCA structure in their intra-EU exports (i.e. more product groups with $BI > 1$) than in their exports to the Baltic countries, save Sweden in its exports to Estonia and Finland in its exports to all three Baltic countries.

In tables 9.17–9.19 we find those products where the Baltic countries have not only a relatively high Balassa index but also significant exports to the EU. Even though a higher value of the index does not necessarily denote a higher comparative advantage, this approach may be thought to secure that the year in question was not exceptional. Oil is a product where all the Baltic countries have both a high Balassa index and a significant amount of exports. Oil is, however, mainly transit trade from Russia, and therefore the advantage that the Baltic countries have is mainly geographic and infrastructural. In addition to oil, all the Baltic countries have a comparative advantage in the export of wood and wood products, which is also one of their major export products. Important

Table 9.17 Estonia's exports to the EU: high Balassa indices and high trade intensity (CN4) in 1996

CN	*Description*	*Balassa in exports to EU > 2*	*% of all exports to EU*
2710	Oil (not crude) from petrol and bituminous minerals	9.5	15.5
4407	Wood sawn or chipped	19.0	7.3
4403	Wood in the rough; roughly squared poles, piles, posts	82.8	5.2
8473	Parts and accessories for typewriters and word processing machines	3.5	4.2
9403	Office and household furniture	3.3	2.7
7204	Ferrous waste and scrap	14.4	2.4
5208	Woven cotton fabrics	17.6	2.4
8529	Parts for television, radio and radar apparatus	6.9	2.2
6204	Women's or girls' outer clothing	4.9	2.1

Table 9.18 Latvia's exports to the EU: high Balassa indices and high trade intensity (CN4) in 1996

CN	*Description*	*Balassa in exports to EU > 2*	*% of all exports to EU*
2710	Oil (not crude) from petrol and bituminous minerals	20.5	33.5
4407	Wood sawn or chipped	36.2	13.9
2709	Crude oil from petroleum and bituminous minerals	9.5	8.4
4403	Wood in the rough; roughly squared poles, piles, posts	102.5	6.4
7404	Copper waste and scrap	29.6	2.6
4412	Plywood, veneered panels and similar laminated wood	27.4	2.5
6204	Women's or girls' outer clothing	5.4	2.3

Table 9.19 Lithuania's exports to the EU: high Balassa indices and high trade intensity (CN4) in 1996

CN	*Description*	*Balassa in exports to EU > 2*	*% of all exports to EU*
2710	Oil (not crude) from petrol and bituminous minerals	6.5	10.7
4407	Wood sawn or chipped	25.5	9.8
3102	Mineral or chemical fertilisers, nitrogenous	69.5	7.5
6204	Women's or girls' outer clothing	11.0	4.6
6203	Men's or boys' outer clothing	11.8	4.4
3105	Mineral or chemical fertilisers	46.6	3.8
7112	Waste and scrap of precious metal	186.3	3.5
8540	Thermionic, cold cathode or photo-cathode tubes	22.2	3.5
7204	Ferrous waste and scrap	18.6	3.1
8544	Insulated wire, cable, electric conductors; optic fibre cable	5.1	2.5

RCA product groups are, furthermore, some parts of office and household machinery, some clothing and ferrous waste and scrap for Estonia, some clothing and copper waste and scrap for Latvia, and fertilisers, clothing, and tubes and cables for Lithuania.

To analyse whether the EU countries' RCA in exports to the Baltic countries depends on their revealed comparative advantage in the EU, we calculate a X^2 test for the values of the Balassa indices smaller than or greater than unity. In this case, the null hypothesis is that comparative advantages are independent. The test statistic can be written as follows

$$X^2 = \frac{N\left(|AD - BC| - \frac{N}{2}\right)^2}{(A+B)(C+D)(A+C)(B+D)},$$

where N denotes the number of 4–digit CN classes (1,242 in all), A denotes the number of classes where an EU country has a revealed comparative advantage in both a Baltic market and EU markets, B the number of classes where an EU country has revealed comparative advantage in EU markets but not in the Baltic market in question, C the number of classes where there is comparative advantage in the Baltic but not in EU markets and, finally, D gives the number of classes where an EU country does not have revealed comparative advantage in either market. The results are given in columns 2, 3 and 4 in table 9.20. The values in italic are significant at the 1 per cent level with one degree of freedom. If the value is larger than 6.64, we can reject the null hypothesis, meaning that comparative advantage in Baltic trade is not independent of the comparative advantage in intra-EU trade.

Table 9.20 Chi square tests for the independence of Balassa indices in Baltic–EU trade v. intra-EU trade (CN4)

	EU to Estonia	*EU to Latvia*	*EU to Lithuania*	*Estonia to EU*	*Latvia to EU*	*Lthuania to EU*
France	*19.41*	*8.69*	*20.20*	2.33	0.94	1.02
Belgium–Luxembourg	*29.81*	*19.85*	*18.18*	0.48	0.37	1.81
Netherlands	*45.91*	*59.75*	*20.46*	0.03	0.01	0.37
Germany	*27.80*	*10.02*	*19.73*	*11.79*	3.19	*14.79*
Italy	*135.69*	*168.69*	*86.71*	2.62	0.28	1.40
United Kingdom	*34.84*	*31.55*	*33.94*	0.43	5.42	0.01
Ireland	*66.52*	*30.35*	*72.83*	0.08	0.03	0.39
Denmark	*108.34*	*69.48*	*48.18*	*38.15*	*20.13*	*19.68*
Greece	*25.01*	*14.59*	*34.15*	*18.20*	*7.82*	*22.29*
Portugal	*80.01*	*29.20*	0.28	*50.48*	*25.35*	*48.17*
Spain	*17.90*	*13.82*	*15.45*	0.35	1.39	2.62
Sweden	*37.41*	*13.43*	*47.47*	*6.89*	0.14	0.04
Finland	*7.24*	*29.15*	*12.13*	*11.45*	1.61	1.26
Austria	*9.10*	*15.45*	*7.76*	*15.82*	*9.95*	*15.11*

Note: Values exceeding 6.64 (in italic) are significant at the 1% level.

Table 9.20 shows that in their exports to the Baltic countries the EU countries' RCA clearly depends on their revealed comparative advantage in the EU markets. The only exception to this is Portugal whose RCA in its exports to Lithuania seems to be independent of its revealed comparative advantage in the EU markets. Otherwise the test variables are highly significant. This contradicts earlier studies[10] where no significant correlation between revealed comparative advantage in EU and Baltic markets was found for countries that are the most important exporters in Baltic markets.[11] In terms of the χ^2 statistics the largest exporters obtain the lowest but, still, highly significant values.

In their exports to the EU, the Baltic countries' RCA is mostly independent of EU countries' revealed comparative advantage in the EU markets. There are some exceptions though. In the last three columns of table 9.20, we have country pairs between each EU country and each Baltic country. The EU countries which have a figure in bold in, say, Latvia's column, compete with Latvian exports in the EU market. Such countries are Denmark, Greece, Portugal and Austria. These four EU countries have similar RCA structures with all three Baltic countries. In addition to these, Estonia's revealed comparative advantage in the EU also corresponds to that of Germany, Finland and Sweden, while Lithuania's corresponds to that of Germany. The correspondence between the Baltic countries' RCA and the EU countries' RCA is clearly the widest in Estonia's exports to the EU.

Next, we analyse the dependence of the Baltic countries' RCA in the EU markets. We may thus study whether or not the Baltic countries compete with one another in EU markets and whether the first-wave accession to the EU of one or two, but not all the Baltic countries, matters. If we take the Baltic countries' aggregate revealed comparative advantage in EU markets we find that they are highly dependent. We obtain χ^2 values of 241.5 for a comparison of Estonia's and Latvia's revealed comparative advantage, 236.1 for Estonia v. Lithuania and 207.0 for Latvia v. Lithuania. These numbers are all highly significant, hence indicating that, on average, the Baltic countries specialise similarly in the EU markets. This result is analogous to that given by the similarity indices above.

Next, let us briefly examine which EU countries or fellow Baltic countries a Baltic country might have a most similar revealed comparative advantage with in its most important EU markets. For this we compare, say, Estonia's Balassa indices in its exports to Sweden with the Balassa indices of the EU countries and of Latvia and Lithuania in that market. This analysis gives an idea as to which countries compete the most with Estonia in the Swedish market.

The picture that emerges is fairly similar to the one we get from an aggregate EU analysis. Some interesting details arise, however. First of all, the other Baltic countries remain the fiercest competitors of each Baltic country also at the individual export market level. In Estonia's most important EU markets – Finland and Sweden – the EU countries with the most similar structure of revealed comparative advantage are Portugal, Denmark, Greece and Italy, and also Sweden and Finland, respectively. Consequently, the picture looks similar to that in Estonia's aggregate EU export market.

In Lithuania's most important market, Germany, it faces the most similar structure of comparative advantage with that of Denmark, Greece, Portugal and Austria. Here what is most interesting is that the revealed comparative advantage of aggregate EU-15 exports to Germany is fairly similar to Lithuania's exports there. In Lithuania's exports to the United Kingdom, it mainly competes with Portugal. That the other EU countries do not really compete with Lithuania in the UK market, is, among other things, due to the importance of mineral fuels and oils in Lithuanian exports to the UK. Oil excluded, the RCA structure is then most similar to that of Portugal. Among EU countries, Latvia competes the most with Finland in its largest EU markets, the Netherlands and the UK. In the German market the most similar revealed comparative advantage can be found with Denmark, Portugal and Greece. In sum, it seems that in terms of their revealed comparative advantage, the Baltic countries are very similar to one another in the EU markets. To a large extent this property also holds in their most important export markets. Among EU countries the Baltic countries' specialisation corresponds most with the specialisation of Denmark, Portugal, Greece and Austria.

The results in tables 9.20 and 9.21 confirm that the Baltic countries specialise similarly in their exports to the EU. In their most important export markets they also seem to compete with the same EU countries. There seems to be, however, geographical differences in the Baltic countries' specialisation, as their most important markets are different. Latvia and Lithuania have the Netherlands and the UK among their most important trading partners, but Estonia's trade is more concentrated towards its closest EU neighbours Finland

and Sweden. Note also that the revealed comparative advantage figures show a high degree of dependence between, say, Latvia's and Estonia's specialisation in the German market. As Latvia, however, exports more to Germany than Estonia, we may have a situation where the former also has a wider revealed comparative advantage in its major market area.

Table 9.21 Chi square tests of the correspondence of comparative advantage in the Baltic countries' most important EU markets with the EU countries and the other Baltic countries' comparable comparative advantages

	Latvian exports to:			*Estonian exports to:*		*Lithuanian exports to:*	
	Netherlands	*Germany*	*United Kingdom*	*Finland*	*Sweden*	*Germany*	*United Kingdom*
France	0.06	2.56	0.00	0.01	0.07	0.26	0.34
Belgium–Luxembourg	3.83	0.01	0.00	0.05	0.68	1.48	4.89
Netherlands	..	5.86	3.62	0.92	1.68	5.73	0.00
Germany	0.01	..	0.78	2.45	0.04	..	0.11
Italy	4.10	2.26	2.98	*16.84*	*21.82*	6.45	0.62
United Kingdom	3.01	0.83	..	0.60	2.13	4.59	..
Ireland	4.05	0.02	1.92	0.01	0.23	1.41	3.01
Denmark	0.11	*39.61*	0.06	*40.45*	*60.88*	*33.28*	0.06
Greece	0.02	*8.96*	0.28	*24.04*	*23.97*	*21.65*	0.89
Portugal	0.11	*16.33*	5.67	*85.32*	*78.31*	*16.50*	*33.88*
Spain	0.02	0.07	0.68	2.09	0.05	1.86	0.36
Sweden	0.32	0.94	*9.68*	*19.27*	..	1.46	0.76
Finland	*17.04*	4.44	*18.65*	..	*22.69*	0.10	3.15
Austria	0.09	*7.99*	0.01	*7.76*	4.62	*16.88*	0.01
Total EU-15	0.30	3.55	0.54	1.50	*9.22*	*18.01*	0.18
Estonia	*136.51*	*262.43*	*171.56*	..	..	*213.53*	*177.81*
Latvia	..	..	..	*134.03*	*180.63*	*221.71*	*105.79*
Lithuania	*66.45*	*221.71*	*105.79*	*153.95*	*112.18*	..	..

Note: Values exceeding 6.64 (in *italic*) are significant at the 1% level.

To test whether this is so, we compute Cochran's Q-test statistic for all three Baltic countries. This test takes into account the importance or size of the exports. Our null hypothesis is that the probability of revealed comparative advantage is the same for all the Baltic countries in the EU. Cochran's Q-statistic can be written as follows,

$$Q = \frac{k(k-1)\sum_{j=1}^{k}(G_j - \bar{G})^2}{k\sum_{i=1}^{N} L_i - \sum_{i=1}^{N} L_i^2}$$

where G_j is the total number of 'successes' in the *j*th column, $\bar{G}$ is the mean of the G_j, L_i is the total number of 'successes' in the *i*th row. The test values are distributed approximately as χ^2 with $k - 1$ degrees of freedom, where k is the number of Baltic countries and N is the number of CN classes at the 4-digit level. Here, by successes we mean those product groups where Baltic countries have a revealed comparative advantage. The critical value with 2 degrees of freedom is 9.21 at the 1 per cent level of significance. Test statistics exceeding this level lead to a rejection of the null hypothesis. Consequently, revealed comparative advantage has country-specific differences in the EU country under consideration.

Table 9.22 shows the Cochran's Q-test statistics for the Baltic countries' revealed comparative advantage in different EU countries. Values higher than 9.21 indicate that there are country-specific differences between the Baltic countries' revealed comparative advantage in the EU market in question. Table 9.22 shows that differences do exist. In particular, one finds differences in the Baltic countries' trade with their largest trading partners. Of the Baltic countries' six largest trading partners within the EU, only in their trade with Germany are their comparative advantage patterns similar.

Table 9.22 Cochran's Q-test

EU country	*Value*	*EU country*	*Value*
France	*12.50*	Denmark	3.55
Belgium–Luxembourg	4.19	Greece	1.18
Netherlands	*12.77*	Portugal	1.51
Germany	3.50	Spain	1.27
Italy	1.37	Sweden	*36.38*
United Kingdom	*12.04*	Finland	*305.04*
Ireland	2.67	Austria	1.27

Note: Values in italic show differences between Baltic countries' comparative advantage in separate EU markets.

The main conclusion that can be drawn on the basis of the Q-test is that, although the patterns of the Baltic countries' revealed comparative advantage in the EU market are highly dependent on average, there remain significant country-specific differences in their most important export markets, save Germany. Cochran's test investigates whether the probability of RCA is the same for all the Baltic countries and the results indicate that it is not. Combined with our earlier analysis, it seems that the differences can be explained, on the one hand, by Estonia's wider RCA in Sweden and especially in Finland, and on the other hand Latvia's and Lithuania's wider RCA in the Netherlands and the UK.

Table 9.23 ranks the EU countries according to their importance for the Baltic countries. As a measure of importance we have used the exports and imports per GDP ratios. Similar rankings would tell which of the Baltic countries is more closed toward EU markets than the Baltic average. In exports, Friedman's χ^2 statistic is 0.571 and in imports 0.000. This indicates that in terms of their openness towards the EU there are no differences between the Baltic countries on average. Thus, none of the Baltic countries systematically dominates in EU markets. This also confirms the above conclusion that the patterns of geographical concentration in the Baltic countries' exports and imports differ. The standard conclusion concerning the Baltic countries' trade is that Estonia is more open than Latvia and Lithuania. The results in Table 9.23 indicate that this openness is partially illusory, as it is highly concentrated on trade with Finland and Sweden.

Table 9.23 EU countries' importance to the Baltic countries in their exports and imports relative to their GDP

	Estonia to EU	*Latvia to EU*	*Lithuania to EU*	*EU to Estonia*	*EU to Latvia*	*EU to Lithuania*
France	2	1	3	2	3	1
Belgium–Luxembourg	3	2	1	2	1	3
Netherlands	2	1	3	2	1	3
Germany	3	1	2	3	2	1
Italy	2	3	1	2	3	1
United Kingdom	2	1	3	2	1	3
Ireland	3	1	2	2	1	3
Denmark	1	2	3	2	3	1
Greece	2	3	1	3	1	2
Portugal	3	2	1	1	3	2
Spain	3	2	1	2	3	1
Sweden	1	2	3	1	2	3
Finland	1	2	3	1	2	3
Austria	2	3	1	3	2	1
Sum of scores	30	26	28	28	28	28

Note: Numbers indicate the rank of each Baltic country's export per GDP ratio or import per GDP ratio vis-à-vis the other two states.

Comparative advantage and EU enlargement: an assessment

In this chapter, we have analysed the Baltic countries' trade with the European Union. During the 1990s, the EU has risen from an insignificant trading partner to an important one for all three Baltic countries. In 1997, 48 per cent of Estonia's exports went to the EU, while the corresponding figure for Latvia was 49 and for Lithuania 33 per cent. Respectively, 55, 53 and 46 per cent of these countries' imports originated from the EU. As this major shift in the geographical orientation in trade was intersected by a change in internal economic regime, it is important to study the fundamentals of this trade and the direction it is taking.

The trade of the Baltic countries with the EU is mostly inter-industry, hence based on comparative advantage. This is due to huge differences between the EU countries and the Baltic countries in terms of their resource endowments and economic development. The other side of this is that intra-industry trade, which usually occurs between similarly developed countries, only accounts for 35 per cent of Estonia's trade with the EU, 17 per cent of Latvia's trade with the EU and 19 per cent of Lithuania's trade with the EU. The Estonian figure has begun to approach the lowest levels of IIT reached by EU countries in their intra-EU trade, but Latvia and Lithuania are still lagging behind.

In all cases, IIT is mostly vertical in nature, hence based on quality differences. The Baltic countries' IIT with the EU can be explained by industry-specific factors, not by country-specific factors as mentioned above. Among the Central and Eastern European countries, rapidly increasing vertical IIT has characterised trade development of the more integrated transition countries like the Czech Republic and Hungary, who have also gained the largest flows of foreign direct investments among the CEECs. Among the Baltic countries, Estonia seems to correspond best to this picture.

In the case of Estonia vertical intra-industry trade accounts for nearly 30 per cent of its trade with the EU. Also this figure is very close to the levels reached by countries like Finland or Portugal. In the case of Estonia intra-industry trade is very concentrated in its trade with Finland and Sweden, which, as these countries are also the largest foreign investors in Estonia, confirms similar development as in the Czech Republic and Hungary, where foreign direct investment has boosted vertical intra-industry trade in general and especially with the investing countries. Latvia and Lithuania have lower levels of both general IIT and of horizontal IIT than Estonia.

We find that all of the EU countries' revealed comparative advantage in the Baltic markets depends highly on their revealed comparative advantage in EU markets. The only exception to this is Portugal and its exports to Lithuania. Furthermore, all the EU countries' revealed comparative advantage in the intra-EU market is based on a wider range of product groups at the CN4 level than in their exports to the Baltic countries, save Finland's in its exports to all the Baltic countries and Sweden's in its exports to Estonia.

The Baltic countries' revealed comparative advantage is two-fold in their most important export products. First they have a comparative advantage in oil, which is mainly transit trade from Russia, and thus based on the countries' favourable geographic position by the Baltic Sea and existing infrastructure. The weight of transit oil in the trade figures is strongly affected by the development of the world market price for oil. Another factor that (under some unlikely circumstances) may have an effect on the extent of transit trade are the political conditions in and around the Baltic countries. Second, the Baltic countries have a revealed comparative advantage in wood and wood products, clothing, and some scrap metals. In addition to these, we should note the potential comparative advantage that may lie in processed agricultural goods, but whose trade is still restricted by the Europe Agreements.

In general, the Baltic countries' revealed comparative advantage in the EU markets seems to correspond most with the specialisation patterns of Denmark, Austria, Portugal and Greece. This holds for all three Baltic countries. Furthermore, Estonia's revealed comparative advantage corresponds with those of Finland and Sweden, which is at least partly due to the fairly high intensity of vertical intra-industry trade between these countries. This tendency has also supported Estonia's exports to Finnish and Swedish markets and, at the same time, it seems to somewhat divert Finland's and Sweden's imports of textiles and clothing from Southern European countries to Estonia.

The comparative advantage of the Baltic countries and the competitive pressures that arise from there need to be put into perspective, however. The aggregate population of the Baltic countries is some 7.5 million, i.e. about 50 per cent more than in Finland, while their aggregate gross domestic product measured with purchasing power parity is only a little over a third of Finland's. Productive capacity in the Baltic countries when compared to the EU is negligible, and also the competitive pressures arising from the former are mainly in fairly small product groups.

Furthermore, the Baltic countries' revealed comparative advantage patterns are most similar to each other in the *aggregate* EU market. This means that they compete first and foremost with each other (and perhaps with the other transition countries). Consequently, the one-time proposal to admit the Baltic countries into the EU in several phases would have been harmful for the one(s) left to wait for their turn, since these countries would be deprived of full access to the single market.

However, in their major market areas, except for Germany, we find that the Baltic countries' revealed comparative advantage patterns differ. This is mainly due to Estonia being more focused in trading with Finland and Sweden and the vertical intra-industry nature of its trade with these countries, while Latvia and Lithuania trade more with Germany, the Netherlands and the UK. As to the export and import openness of the Baltic countries vis-à-vis the EU, our analysis shows that there are no systematic differences between them.

Notes

1 This analysis was written in the autumn of 1998 and reflects the trading relations between the Baltic countries and the European Union around the time the former applied for EU membership. The structure of the Baltic contries' foreign trade has changed since then. For example, the share of machinery and equipment in Estonia's total exports has risen from 14 per cent in 1996 to 36 per cent in 2000. This includes exports to third countries as well, however, and partly reflects the collapse of exports to Russia in 1998. Given that our analysis includes 1,242 product groups, the effect of the change in the structure of exports on our calculations is unlikely to be as significant as the above figures would seem to suggest. The financial support of the RSC and the Academy of Finland is gratefully acknowledged. The authors are also thankful for the helpful comments by two anonymous referees and participants at the BOFIT Summer

Workshop on Transition Economics in June 1999 in Helsinki. The usual disclaimer applies.

2 In reality, some of Estonian exports to the EU are exports to Russia. As the tariffs between Estonia and Russia are higher than between the EU and Russia, this is a way to cut costs.

3 Trade potential between the EU countries and the Baltic countries has been analysed in M. Erkkilä and M. Widgrén *Finnish-Baltic Trading Potential and Comparative Advantage* (The Research Institute of the Finnish Economy, ETLA Series B 101, 1995), V. Kaitila and M. Widgrén, *Baltic EU membership and Finland* (The Research Institute of the Finnish Economy, ETLA Series B 139, 1998), and R. Baldwin, *Towards an Integrated Europe* (London, Centre for Economic Policy Research, 1994). In this chapter, we do not analyse trade potential but merely the structure of trade.

4 Note that Switzerland, Liechtenstein, Norway and Iceland are included in the 1994 but not in the 1996 figures.

5 See C. Aturupane, S. Djankov, and B. Hoekman, 'Determinants of Intra-Industry Trade between East and West Europe', *World Bank Occasional Papers* (1997).

6 D. Greenaway, R. Hine and C. Milner, 'Country-specific Factors and the Pattern of Horizontal and Vertical Intra-Industry Trade in the UK', *Weltwirtschaftliches Archiv*, 130 (1994), pp. 77–100.

7 It should be noted, however, that Ireland's unit export prices in its aggregate intra-EU exports are over four-fold its unit import prices, so the small share of HIIT is more to Ireland's favour than vice versa.

8 Originally in B. Balassa, 'Trade Liberalization and "Revealed" Comparative Advantage', *The Manchester School of Economic and Social Studies*, 33 (1965), pp. 99–123 where he states that 'Comparative advantages appear to be the outcome of a number of factors, some measurable, others not, some easily pinned down, others less so. One wonders, therefore, whether more could not be gained if, instead of enunciating general principles and trying to apply these to explain actual trade flows, one took the observed pattern of trade as a point of departure'.

9 Z. Drábek and A. Smith, 'Trade Performance and Trade Policy in Central and Eastern Europe', *CEPR Discussion Paper*, 1182 (1997).

10 See Kaitila and Widgrén, *Baltic EU membership and Finland.*

11 Kaitila and Widgrén used CN data at the two-digit level, which may have contributed to the difference in results. Kaitila and Widgrén, *Baltic EU membership and Finland.*

Niina Pautola-Mol

10

Preferential trade agreements

Specific aspects of EU–Baltic trade integration

The number of preferential trade agreements (PTAs), establishing free trade areas (FTA) and customs unions (CU) has increased rapidly since the early 1980s. These agreements are preferential in the sense that they offer free trade to members but protection against non-members. The first attempt to theorise about the subject was made by the great economist Jacob Viner in 1950. Ever since, the two-sided nature of preferential trade agreements has provoked interest among economists around the world.[1] In the 1950s and 1960s, the theoretical analysis focused, in particular, on static questions concerning welfare effects. During recent years, interest has shifted to more dynamic questions: whether preferential trade arrangements hinder or promote further liberalisation initiatives and the process towards worldwide liberalisation of trade.

Compared to international trading powers such as the United States or the European Union, the three Baltic states, Estonia, Latvia and Lithuania are small. Altogether they form a market size of about 7.5 million people with a GNP per capita of less than 20 per cent of that in the United States. Small economies like those of the Baltic states are price takers in the world market rather than being in the position to significantly influence world prices. Traditional trade theory suggests that trade restrictions such as tariffs and quotas are costly to this type of economy. They divert resource allocation away from more productive uses and distort prices. In the absence of other distortions, a small competitive economy would maximise its welfare by having no tariffs at all. Indeed, the Baltic countries are relatively open economies. For example, the Baltic Free Trade Area for industrial products entered into force in January 1996 and for agricultural products in 1997. An agreement on the abolition of non-tariff barriers to trade among the Baltic states was enacted in July 1998. In addition, negotiations on a liberalisation of the services market is proceeding, and trade with other countries, especially with the EU, other Central and Eastern European countries (CEECs) as well as with the EFTA states, has also greatly been liberalised.

The aim of this study is to analyse preferential trade arrangements between the Baltic states and other countries, and the EU in particular. The theory on regionalism constitutes the overall basis of the study and is used to explain some of the static and dynamic effects related to preferential trade arrangements. The main hypotheses to be tested are the six theses of new regionalism, presented by Wilfred Ethier:

1 the new regionalism typically involves one or more small countries linking up with a large country;
2 regional arrangements are regional geographically;
3 the small countries have recently made, or are making, significant unilateral reforms;
4 regional arrangements often involve deep integration;
5 dramatic moves to free trade between members are not featured; and
6 the liberalisation achieved is primarily by the small countries.[2]

The study is organised into seven sections. Section two presents a theoretical overview of regionalism including some of the static and dynamic effects related to preferential trade arrangements. Section three focuses on the first two hypothesis of new regionalism: the tendency of small countries to link up with a large country, and the role of geographical proximity in regional trade arrangements. In this context, the regional trade arrangements of the Baltic states during the 1990s are reviewed. In addition, the top trading partners, the volume and the composition of Baltic foreign trade are discussed. In section four, the next two hypotheses of new regionalism (concerning the likelihood of small countries making unilateral reforms and regional arrangements involving deep integration) are analysed in the context of the European Union's eastern enlargement process. Section five, meanwhile, takes a closer look at the preferential trade agreements, or Association Agreements, between the Baltic states and the European Union. In particular, the study focuses on the claims that new regionalism involves modest trade concessions and that the stated liberalisation achieved is primarily by small countries. The association agreements themselves are analysed in terms of coverage, the degree of liberalisation in industrial and agricultural trade, rules of origin and other commercial policy measures. Lastly, a sixth section extends the analysis from the EU to the multilateral level. In particular, the discussion returns to the more general, but fundamental question of new regionalism as a phenomenon: do preferential trade agreements hinder or promote further trade liberalisation initiatives? Here, the main principles of the World Trade Organisation (WTO), including its policy towards preferential trade agreements, will be discussed. In addition, the Association Agreements between the EU and the Baltic countries will be assessed from the perspective of WTO principles. Section seven concludes the study.

International trade theory: regionalism and preferential trade agreements

Old regionalism: static and systemic effects of PTAs

Regionalism can generally be defined as a tendency towards some form of preferential trading arrangement between a number of countries belonging to a particular region.[3] Furthermore, the word 'preferential' refers to a club; countries that do not belong to a particular regional arrangement are discriminated against. Thirdly, in recent years the academic literature has begun to make a distinction between old and new regionalism. In the 1950s and 1960s, many attempts were made around the world to form regional trading clubs, including customs unions (CUs) and free trade areas. However, most of these attempts (excluding the European Common Market) did not really succeed. As a result, these efforts came to be known as the 'old' or 'first' regionalism.[4] With the establishment of the European Economic Community, however, a 'new' or 'second' form of regionalism through regional trade agreements (RTAs) emerged. Whereas in the 1960s there were only three essential RTAs among European countries, today the number of RTAs exceeds 90.[5] About 15 of these RTAs are inside Western Europe, 20 inside Eastern Europe, and around 55 between Eastern and Western European countries.[6] Worldwide, the GATT and WTO have tallied the existence of 184 regional trade agreements, of which 109 are still in force.[7]

The discriminatory feature of regional trade agreements (both during the first and second waves of regionalism) has been subject to extensive research among economists. During the first regionalism, the theoretical analysis focused, in particular, on static questions concerning welfare effects. The early development of the theory of preferential trade agreements has been associated with academics such as Jacob Viner, James Meade and Richard Lipsey.[8] Viner, in particular, made a distinction between trade creation and trade diversion. He argued that a trade-creating union increases trade among its members at the expense of inefficient industries inside the member countries themselves, while a trade-diverting union creates trade at the expense of more efficient industries in non-member countries. To put it slightly differently, Viner maintained that a preferential trade arrangement, such as a customs union, is trade-creating when at least one of the members benefits, both members benefit or the two together have a net benefit. In this respect, the outside world loses in the short run; however, it can gain in the longer run due to the general diffusion of the increased prosperity of the customs area. Where trade diversion takes place, at least one of the member countries may be injured, both may be injured or the two together may suffer a net loss. In this case, there will be only losses to the outside world.

Ever since Viner's attempts at theorising about PTAs, trade theorists and policy-makers have been challenged by the question of whether the issue of trade diversion should be taken seriously, or whether any move towards free trade, even if preferential, might unequivocally be considered welfare-improving. In general, economic theory is not fully against PTAs. The rest of this chapter will focus on some of the modern extensions of Viner's analysis.

Wonnacott and Lutz argue that if PTAs are formed among 'natural trading partners', i.e. countries among whom the initial volume of trade is high and the distance between them is low, then one should expect such agreements to be welfare-improving for the members.[9] The argument implies that the high initial volume of trade among members and the short geographical distance between them reduces the potential for trade diversion. This argument has some similarities with traditional gravity theory on bilateral trade patterns, according to which trade between two countries depends positively on the income of the trading countries and negatively on the distance between them.[10]

In contrast to this argument, however, Meade and Lipsey have maintained that actual trade diversion will reflect not the average initial trade volumes (the so-called volume-of-trade criterion), but other underlying fundamentals such as substitution among products.[11] Under these circumstances, with each member country specialised in a different product when all products are imperfect substitutes, the steady preferential reduction of tariffs by one country toward another will first improve its welfare and then progressively reduce it at some stage. Consequently, once an FTA has reached a 100 per cent reduction in tariffs, it may reduce welfare even below the starting level.[12] This argument that PTAs with less than 100 per cent preferences are superior to FTAs was first introduced by Meade.[13] The key to this result is the declining marginal utility for the consumption of each variety. The welfare effects of trade creation become negligible at a certain point, while trade diversion effects become larger. This is because varieties of products with larger marginal utility, meaning those products from other foreign non-member countries, are replaced by product varieties from member countries, which have smaller marginal utility.[14] Another approach along the lines of Viner is that of Kemp and Wan.[15] They showed that if countries were to form a CU, and could choose their external tariff, they could always form a CU, which left the welfare of the non-members unchanged while improving member countries' welfare.

An interesting extension to the static welfare effects of PTAs deals with their systemic effects. These are caused by the fact that one tries to restrict or liberalise trade on the basis of which product comes from which country. In order to do so, a country must establish a 'rule of origin', which often leads to problems of arbitrary definitions of origin. This difficulty is present both in FTAs and CUs. Indeed, the problem becomes even more acute in an FTA because in this case there are different external tariffs among members which, in turn, creates a fear of non-member products coming into one's territory at a lower tariff than one's own by entering through another lower-tariff member country. Finally, FTAs are often negotiated at different points in time and with different time schedules for reaching zero tariffs. As a result, we can find a complicated set of applicable tariffs on the same product. These rules generate a world of preferences increasing transaction costs and facilitating protectionism. This phenomenon is known as the 'spaghetti bowl' phenomenon.[16]

New regionalism and the dynamic approach

Since the era of old regionalism, the whole international trading environment has changed dramatically. First of all, the multilateral liberalisation of trade in manufactured goods among industrial countries is much more complete thanks to the GATT and WTO rounds of multilateral tariff reductions. In addition, less developed and former communist countries are nowadays more actively trying to integrate into the multilateral trading system. The old age of inward-oriented, communist and/or import-substitution policies has given way to more market-oriented and open-trade dispositions.

Although a state's motives behind the formation of a regional trade arrangement may often be country- or region-specific, Ethier maintains that some general characteristics behind the new regionalism do exist, 'Regional integration now usually involves reform-minded small countries that link with a large country or countries located geographically close to them. In addition, regional integration involves deep integration, but confers relatively minor trade advantages.'[17] While a majority of the so-called deep integration schemes are currently taking place in Europe, other regional trade arrangements (e.g. in North and Latin America) have involved relatively shallow integration with long transition periods and a focus primarily on statutory border measures.[18]

In addition to the international trading environment, the focus of theoretical research has also changed amidst the new regionalism. While the first regionalism concentrated on static welfare effects of PTAs, the new regionalism has put more emphasis on dynamic issues: i.e., whether PTAs hinder or promote the worldwide non-discriminatory reduction process of trade barriers. Furthermore, if PTAs pose a threat to global trade liberalisation, what is the nature of this threat? Among the trade theorists, the question of how preferential trade agreements influence trade liberalisation worldwide remains open. Just as there are various interpretations about the static welfare effects of PTAs, theories about dynamic effects provide mixed results as well.[19]

In terms of trade liberalisation in general, it has been argued that the dynamic output effects of trade liberalisation are substantial, and perhaps significantly larger than the static effects analysed in earlier studies.[20] The reasoning behind this argument is that trade liberalisation may, other things being equal, raise the marginal productivity of human and physical capital. Provided that the steady-state levels of these factors are determined endogenously, trade policy can have an influence over these levels. Consequently, liberalisation of trade can have a dynamic effect on output and welfare as the economy moves towards a new steady state. The overall welfare effects resulting from trade liberalisation and additional economic output depends on the degree of external scale economies.[21]

Referring to studies on regional trade liberalisation in particular, it has been argued that when preferential trade agreements are kept separate from multilateral trade negotiations (meaning that one neither hurts nor helps the other), PTAs may either improve or reduce welfare immediately (in the static sense). In either case, the time-path could then be stagnated, which would imply a fragmentation of the world economy and no further expansion of the initial PTA. This type of time-path would also fall short compared to the time-path representing the worldwide freeing of trade on a non-discriminatory basis at a specified time (the ultimate goal). An alternative path would lead to multilateral free trade for all through a continued increase in PTAs. The other situation is when PTAs and multilateral trade negotiations interact. In this case, the negotiations' time-path becomes a function of whether the PTA time-path travels simultaneously.[22]

Likewise, many authors treat PTA time-paths as endogenous conditions. Under this assumption, one of the conclusions has been that the PTA will eventually create a domino effect with outsiders wanting to become insiders and incentives increasing to add members to the preferential trade area.[23] The main idea behind this argument is that the cost for non-membership (tariffs that member countries' firms do not need to pay) drives firms to lobby for pro-integration. If the non-member country's government was previously indifferent to membership, such a change in trends may enlarge the market and add countries one after another (the domino). In the end, this could lead to a point where trade barriers have been freed worldwide, a situation where every country belongs to the same preferential trading area.

While some economists argue that any liberalisation makes further liberalisation easier, provided it increases both imports and exports,[24] others instead suggest that bilateral FTAs can undermine political support for multilateral free trade. In addition, PTAs may reduce the incentive of two member countries to liberalise tariffs reciprocally with the non-member world, and this incentive could be so reduced that it would make multilateral trade liberalisation impossible.

Some of the most recent studies about static welfare effects of regional integration arrangements indicate that effects are more positive than negative. For example, it has been shown that regional trade arrangements are welfare improving if countries, which are predominantly least-cost producers of export goods, form them or if they give rise to increased imports from all trading partners.[25] However, the same study concludes that currently, there are hardly any, if any, such customs unions or free trade areas that would fully meet these criteria. Recent empirical studies, which have focused on regional trade arrangements in Europe and North America, suggest that presently operating regional trade arrangements have caused a modest positive impact on member countries and a minor impact on non-member economies.[26] In addition, there seems to be less evidence indicating that a well-functioning regional trade arrangement has actually had negative welfare effects on member or non-member countries.[27]

Foreign trade and regional trade arrangements in the Baltic states

Table 10.1 illustrates the variety of preferential trade arrangements which existed during the late 1990s between the Baltic countries and other countries.

In addition to the EU, Estonia had free trade agreements with the EFTA countries, the Czech Republic, Slovakia, Slovenia, Turkey and Ukraine. Furthermore, in 1998 negotiations to establish free trade agreements were concluded with Poland and Hungary.[28] For its part, Latvia had concluded free trade agreements with the EU and the EFTA, the Czech Republic, Slovakia, Slovenia and Turkey. Moreover, Latvia had a free trade agreement with Ukraine, while the provisional application of an agreement with Poland was proceeding.[29] Latvia was also negotiating free trade agreements with Hungary and Romania, and was planning to start negotiations with Bulgaria.[30] In the case of Lithuania, free Trade Agreements had been concluded (in addition to the EU and the EFTA members) with the Czech Republic, Poland, Slovakia, Slovenia, Turkey and Ukraine. Moreover, a free trade agreement had been initiated with Hungary, and negotiations with Romania were proceeding.[31] Finally, the three Baltic countries were part of their own Baltic Free Trade Area.

Table 10.1 Regional trade agreements of the Baltic states

Country	*Multilateral*	*Bilateral*
Estonia	Baltic Free Trade Area EU: Europe Agreement EFTA	Czech Republic Slovakia Slovenia Turkey Poland Hungary Ukraine
Latvia	Baltic Free Trade Area EU: Europe Agreement EFTA	Czech Republic Slovakia Slovenia Turkey Ukraine
Lithuania	Baltic Free Trade Area EU: Europe Agreement EFTA	Czech Republic Slovakia Slovenia Turkey Poland Ukraine

All in all, two conclusions can be made. First, the smaller Baltic countries generally had regional trade arrangements with larger countries. Second, all of these countries were in Europe and were geographically relatively close to the Baltic states. Hence, the first two hypotheses of new regionalism – small countries usually link up with a large country and regional arrangements are also regional geographically – seem to apply to the PTAs between the Baltic states and other countries.

However, to what extent were these preferential trade arrangements welfare improving for the Baltic economies? To what extent did they create trade instead of diverting it? Tables 10.2 to 10.4 illustrate the Baltic states' volume of trade with their top trading partners in 1993 and 1998. Tables 10.5 to 10.7 illustrate the product composition of trade during the same years. While these statistics should be treated with a certain degree of caution (given the sometimes differing collection techniques used in the three states), several interesting observations can be made. First, the statistics show that Baltic foreign trade was clearly focused on the European continent, as the collapse of the Soviet Union had broken old trade relations and precipitated a shift towards new, western, markets. Second, Baltic foreign trade was focused not only in terms of the continent, but also as regards the concentration of trade inside Europe. The EU appeared to be the most important trading partner for all three Baltic economies. Trade volume with the EU also increased considerably during the 1990s. This indicates that the preferential trade agreements between the Baltic countries and the EU had a trade-creating influence. Third, inside the EU, some of the members have stronger trade relations with the Baltic states than others. This finding can most likely be

Table 10.2 Estonia's trading partners, % of total exports or imports (million kroons)

1993				*1998*			
Exports		*Imports*		*Exports*		*Imports*	
Total	100 (10,636.2)		100 (11,831.6)		100 (45,236.7)		100 (66,975.5)
Russia	23 (2,408.5)	Finland	28 (3,303.5)	Finland	19 (8,473.3)	Finland	23 (15,163.8)
Finland	21 (2,202.6)	Russia	17 (2,033.3)	Sweden	17 (7,463.2)	Russia	11 (7,437.2)
Sweden	10 (1,007.5)	Germany	11 (1,272.8)	Russia	13 (6,082.3)	Germany	11 (7,258.4)
Latvia	9 (913.5)	Sweden	9 (1,055.0)	Latvia	10 (4,294.7)	Sweden	9 (6,054.5)
Germany	8 (851.3)	Holland	4 (429.1)	Germany	6 (2,492.2)	Japan	5 (3,284.8)
Holland	4 (430.9)	Lithuania	3 (391.0)	Ukraine	5 (2,266.6)	U.S.	5 (3,095.7)
Other	26	Other	27	Other	30	Other	36
EU	48 (1,894.9)	EU	61 (2,760.7)	EU	55 (24,769.4)	EU	60 (40,278.4)
CIS	30 (3,228.7)	CIS	22 (2,551.1)	CIS	21 (9,453.1)	CIS	14 (9,489.3)
Other Baltic states	12 (1,307.4)	Other Baltic states	6 (658.4)	Other Baltic states	14 (6,421.2)	Other Baltic states	4 (2,448.9)

Source: Statistical Office of Estonia.

Table 10.3 Latvia's trading partners, % of total exports or imports (lats)

1994				*1998*			
Exports		*Imports*		*Exports*		*Imports*	
Total	100 (553,437)		100 (694,588)		100 (1,068,852)		100 (1,881,285)
Russia	28 (155,719)	Russia	24 (164,178)	Germany	16 (166,822)	Germany	17 (315,547)
Germany	11 (58,271)	Germany	14 (94,011)	UK	14 (144,343)	Russia	12 (221,290)
UK	10 (53,894)	Finland	9 (59,102)	Russia	12 (129,007)	Finland	10 (179,189)
Sweden	7 (38,114)	Sweden	6 (44,494)	Sweden	10 (110,017)	Sweden	7 (135,096)
Ukraine	6 (32,727)	Lithuania	6 (41,243)	Lithuania	7 (79,325)	Estonia	7 (124,827)
Lithuania	6 (30,694)	Estonia	4 (24,412)	Estonia	5 (48,526)	Lithuania	6 (118,518)
Other	32	Other	37	Other	36	Other	41
EU	39 (217,044)	EU	41 (281,685)	EU	57 (604,459)	EU	55 (1,039,492)
CIS	43 (236,375)	CIS	30 (211,600)	CIS	19 (202,611)	CIS	16 (301,063)
Other Baltic states	8 (45,054)	Other Baltic states	10 (65,657)	Other Baltic states	12 (127,851)	Other Baltic states	13 (243,345)

Source: Statistical Office of Latvia.

explained both by geographical as well as historical reasons. Especially for Estonia and Latvia, the most dominant EU trading partners were Finland, Sweden and Germany. For Lithuania, Germany, together with Italy, Denmark and the UK, were the most active EU trade partners. Another interesting observation that can be made from the trade data is that, contrary to earlier expectations, the preferential trade agreements in industrial and agricultural products among the Baltic states did not substantially increase intra-Baltic trade flows. One of the main reasons for the low level of intra-Baltic trade appeared to be that the trade structure of the three states was largely competitive rather than complementary. Another explanation for low levels of intra-Baltic trade could be the fact that the Baltic market was a relatively small market, and therefore not as attractive as, for example, the EU market. Furthermore, cooperation initiatives may have been dampened to the extent they were seen as competing with efforts aimed at EU accession. In addition, resistance to new bureaucracy and consequently the lack of an official and effective structure that could enforce regional rules were both obstacles to further regional integration efforts.[32] Finally, economic factors also hampered intra-Baltic trade, including a shortage of trade finance as well as the fact the Baltic countries generally had lower price levels than the EU.[33]

Table 10.4 Lithuania's trading partners, % of total exports or imports (million litas)

1993				*1998*			
Exports		*Imports*		*Exports*		*Imports*	
Total	100		100		100		100
	(8,707.0)		(9,798.2)		(14,849.2)		(23,186.2)
Russia	33	Russia	54	Russia	17	Russia	21
	(2,884.7)		(5,256.6)		(2,484.6)		(4,891.2)
Ukraine	11	Germany	10	Germany	13	Germany	18
	(977.5)		(945.3)		(1,919.0)		(4,187.3)
Belarus	7	Ukraine	6	Latvia	11	Poland	6
	(641.2)		(609.3)		(1,659.5)		(1,299.0)
Latvia	7	Belarus	3	Belarus	9	Italy	5
	(635.7)		(325.8)		(1,307.4)		(1,032.0)
Poland	7	Denmark	2	Ukraine	8	Denmark	4
	(608.0)		(239.3)		(1,192.3)		(879.9)
Germany	7	Netherlands	2	Italy	4	UK	4
	(592.0)		(223.9)		(595.9)		(857.1)
Other	28	Other	23	Other	38	Other	42
Europe[a]	93	Europe	94	EU	37	EU	47
	(8,117.5)		(9,244.0)		(5,551.1)		(10,960.0)
CIS	5	CIS	26	CIS	36	CIS	26
					(5,371.0)		(6,022.2)
Other Baltic states	10	Other Baltic states	2	Other Baltic states	14	Other Baltic states	3
	(854.5)		(221.2)		(2,061.2)		(775.3)

Source: Statistical Office of Lithuania.

Note: [a] In 1993, the share of the EU as one trading partner was not registered in Lithuanian national statistics.

Another interesting observation indicated by the trade data concerns Central and Eastern Europe. With the exception of Poland, none of the Central and Eastern European countries, with which the Baltic countries had free trade agreements, appears on the list of top trading partners. To be sure, many of these agreements had only begun to take effect. However, the data show how far this trade still had to go. Finally, although the Baltic countries did not have preferential trade agreements with Russia, the argument linking geographical proximity with trade partners remained particularly true in the case of Russia. Through the 1990s, Russia remained an important trade partner for the Baltic economies.

With regard to the general composition of foreign trade, the main changes are illustrated in Tables 10.5 to 10.7. In Estonia, the share of machinery increased significantly and by 1998 formed the largest part of foreign trade, both in exports and imports. Although the overall share of foodstuffs in foreign trade declined, it still remained significant. In addition to machinery, trade in wood, wood articles, paper and textiles constituted another important share of Estonia's exports.

Table 10.5 Estonia's trade by groups of goods (% of exports or imports)

1993			*1998*		
	Exports	*Imports*		*Exports*	*Imports*
Foodstuffs	23.4	14.7	Foodstuffs	15.9	16.9
Mineral products	7.6	15.5	Mineral products	3.8	5.9
Products of chemical industry	4.7	6.4	Products of chemical industry	7.2	8.1
Textiles and footwear	13.5	11.5	Textiles and footwear	11.6	7.5
Wood, paper etc.	8.1	2.8	Wood, paper etc.	14.5	4.3
Base metals and articles of base metal	10.4	5.0	Non-precious metals and metal products	8.5	9.3
Machinery and equipment	7.6	17.7	Machinery and equipment	19.6	25.4
Transport vehicles	10.6	14.2	Transport vehicles	4.8	9.4
Other	14.1	12.2	Furniture etc.	4.8	1.6
			Other goods	7.0	7.4
Total	100.0	100.0	Total	100.0	100.0

Source: Bank of Estonia, Statistical Office of Estonia.

Table 10.6 Latvia's trade by groups of goods (% of exports or imports)

1995			*1998*		
	Exports	*Imports*		*Exports*	*Imports*
Foodstuffs and animal products	15.7	10.2	Foodstuffs and animal products	5.5	4.7
Mineral products	2.2	21.7	Mineral products	0.4	8.6
Products of chemical industry	6.4	11.3	Products of chemical industry	5.2	8.2
Wood and wood articles	26.4	4.5	Wood and wood articles	32.0	3.6
Textiles and footwear	14.7	8.5	Textiles and footwear	15.1	5.8
Metals	7.9	6.4	Metals	10.0	4.1
Machinery	8.7	17.3	Machinery, transport vehicles	8.5	31.2
Other	18.0	20.1	Other	23.3	33.8
Total	100.0	100.0		100.0	100.0

Source: Statistical Office of Latvia.

Only minor changes took place regarding the shares of chemical products and textiles in Estonian foreign trade. In Latvia, exports were dominated by trade in wood and related articles. Second on the most-traded-product list were textiles. Their share in foreign trade, both in exports and imports, did not change significantly over the years. Likewise, chemical products remained largely unchanged,

Table 10.7 Lithuania's trade by groups of goods (% of exports or imports)

1994			*1998*		
	Exports	*Imports*		*Exports*	*Imports*
Live livestock and animal production	8.8	1.5	Live livestock and animal production	6.6	3.2
Foodstuffs	15.2	8.4	Foodstuffs	4.4	5.0
Mineral products	16.6	32.7	Mineral products	18.9	15.4
Production of chemical and related industries	10.6	8.7	Production of chemical and related industries	9.5	9.2
Wood and wood products	4.0	2.8	Wood and wood products	4.7	-
Textiles and footwear	13.3	7.8	Textiles	18.3	8.9
Metals	6.1	6.4	Metals	3.8	6.2
Machinery and transport vehicles	15.7	22.5	Machinery and transport vehicles	19.8	18.9
Other	9.7	9.2	Other	13.0	20.2
Total	100.0	100.0	Total	100.0	100.0

Source: Department of Statistics to the Government of the Republic of Lithuania.

while foodstuffs declined and machinery increased significantly becoming the biggest share of imports by the end of the decade. Machinery also topped the trade roster in Lithuania. Mineral products and textiles constituted the second and third most important parts of foreign trade. While the share of exported minerals remained relatively steady, the share of imported minerals declined considerably. The export share of textiles slightly increased. Finally, the share of chemical products in the overall trade remained relatively steady, whereas food exports declined considerably.

Referring to the composition of trade with individual PTA partners, the analysis is partly constrained by the limited data available from Baltic statistical sources.[34] Given the importance of the EU as a trading partner for the Baltic states, some comments can be made concerning the composition of EU–Baltic trade.[35] During the 1990s Estonia imported mainly machinery and electrical equipment, textiles and agricultural products from the EU. The main products exported to the EU were machinery, textiles and wood. Latvia's imports from the EU consisted primarily of machinery, foodstuffs and textiles. The most common products exported to the EU were wood products, textiles and base metals. Finally, Lithuania exported mainly textiles, machinery, mineral products and chemicals to the EU. Imports from the EU consisted primarily of machinery, vehicles and textiles.

The Baltic countries' strong reorientation towards the West after the collapse of the Soviet Union and nearly ten years of political and economic cooperation with the EU reflected the importance of the EU to the Baltic countries.

The EU was not only a significant trade partner, but also an international policy-maker, which had influence over political and economic decision-making in the Baltic states. For this reason, the rest of this study will focus on the preferential trade relations of Estonia, Latvia and Lithuania with the EU. In particular, we will analyse the following questions. What role did preferential trade arrangements play in the EU enlargement process and the Baltic states' accession preparations? How did the EU's Association Agreements with the Baltic states contribute to trade liberalisation over the years? Did these preferential trading arrangements pose a threat to WTO principles and the idea of multilateral trade liberalisation?

PTAs as a part of the European Union's enlargement process

The previous section concluded that the Baltic states' regional trade arrangements supported two hypothesis of new regionalism, namely that the smaller Baltic states had preferential trade arrangements with larger countries, and these regional arrangements were also geographically regional. In this section, it will be argued that two other characteristics of new regionalism apply in the Baltic–EU relationship, i.e. that smaller countries tend to be the ones to make significant unilateral reforms, and regional arrangements often involve deep integration.

In June 1997 the Amsterdam European Council called for accession negotiations to begin in 1998. One month later, the Commission published its Agenda 2000 document and opinions on each applicant's ability to accept the *acquis communautaire.* The December 1997 Luxembourg Council decided that negotiations should be started with five Central and Eastern European countries and Cyprus, and with another five countries when they had made the necessary progress required for accession. Negotiations finally began on 30 March 1998 with the first wave of six countries: Cyprus, the Czech Republic, Estonia, Hungary, Poland and Slovenia. These were followed by a second wave of five countries: Bulgaria, Latvia, Lithuania, Romania and Slovakia.

Enlargement was a complex and challenging issue. Much of the work to make enlargement possible was done within the candidate countries themselves. Their economies had to succeed in closing the development gap with respect to the EU, carrying out transition to a market economy and revising national legislation. From the Union's side, the accession strategy was based mainly on five elements:

1. Association Agreements (or Europe Agreements) on economic cooperation;
2. the Commission's White Paper on the approximation of laws;
3. the PHARE programme of economic aid to the associated countries;
4. a system of 'structured dialogue' consisting of meetings of heads-of-state and government as well as ministerial meetings; and
5. accession partnerships or running action plans through which the EU and each accession country would coordinate (a) priority areas in which EU

legislation would be adopted (b) programming for EU financial assistance, and (c) terms to be applied to this aid, including obligations taken under the previous Association Agreements as well as the general Copenhagen criteria.

As a stepping-stone to membership, and in order to boost trade between the Community and the CEECs, the EU began by signing Association Agreements – or Europe Agreements – with each individual Central and Eastern European country. These acknowledged the interest of each partner country in becoming a full member of the EU. In addition, however, the accords were *preferential agreements* designed to establish a close, long-term association between the EU and the individual CEECs. The overriding goal for the Association Agreements was to create a climate of mutual confidence, which would foster stability for the path of political and economic reform in the CEECs. More narrowly, however, the Association Agreements also established a free trade area by the year 2002, liberalising trade in industrial products and providing a basis for economic cooperation in a large number of sectors. In addition, the parties pledged to encourage a climate for trade and investment, improve the transparency of Community financial support and promote a two-way flow of information and cooperation. Thirdly, at the individual policy level, the above-mentioned objectives were manifested via intensified political dialogue, the removal of trade barriers (customs duties, quantitative restrictions and measures having equivalent effect) and the gradual harmonisation of principles covering the movement of workers, establishment of firms and supply of services. Concrete actions also included the liberalisation of payments and capital as well as the harmonisation of competition policies. Finally, the agreements called for improvement of protection of intellectual, industrial and commercial property rights.

The multidimensional feature of the Association Agreements supports our working hypothesis that the regional arrangements between the Baltic states and the EU (as well as between the other CEECs and the EU) involved deep integration and significant reform efforts from the candidate countries. In the next part of this study we will focus more specifically on EU–Baltic progress in trade liberalisation regarding industrial and agricultural goods as laid down in the Association Agreements.

Association agreements between the EU and the Baltic states: how liberal?

When we analyse the preferential trade arrangements between the EU and other countries, the first important point to be made is that there is no standard form of preferential trade agreement with the EU. While such agreements usually cover most or all industrial goods, some products – such as textiles and clothing, coal and steel – have been or are still subject to special quotas. In addition, liberalisation is asymmetric and transition periods vary. With regard to trade in agriculture, access to the EU markets is even more selective, product-based and well protected.[36] These fundamental characteristics apply also to the preferential trade agreements between the EU and the Baltic states.

At the beginning of 1995, Free Trade Agreements between the EU and the Baltic states entered into force. In February 1998, these accords were replaced by the Association Agreements, which the Baltic countries had signed already in June 1995. However, as far as trade in goods was concerned, the Association Agreements neither altered nor added to the provisions of the FTAs already concluded. According to the Association Agreements, a free trade area would be established with each of the Baltic states following transitional periods lasting from four (Estonia and Latvia) to six (Lithuania) years.[37] In the meantime, each agreement had a 'standstill' clause, which proscribed any increase in protection starting from the day before the entry of the agreement (1 January 1995). In other words, the duties in force hitherto constituted the basis of the agreement.[38] As regards industrial goods, the Agreements divided them into three groups: (1) textiles and clothing (2) coal and steel products, and (3) other industrial products. As far as textiles and clothing products were concerned, the Agreements originally covered only customs duties. Quantitative restrictions were dealt with a separate Textiles Protocol. However, after the beginning of 1998 all quantitative restrictions as well as the other restrictive measures were abolished on imports of textiles and clothes into the EU.[39] As for trade in steel products, quantitative restrictions were abolished from the entry into force of the Agreements (February 1998). Customs duties on steel products were eliminated for all associated countries already on 1 January 1996. Lastly, regarding coal and related products, both customs duties and quantitative restrictions were fully eliminated by the beginning of 1996.

Throughout the 1990s, Estonia maintained one of the most liberal trade regimes in the world.[40] Tariffs, quantitative restrictions and other protectionist measures were practically non-existent and trade-related subsidies were limited mainly to the agricultural sector. As a result, Estonia's liberal foreign trade regime also contributed to very liberal trade between Estonia and the EU. Customs duties and quantitative restrictions for industrial products were abolished from the beginning of 1995, upon the entry into force of the FTA.[41] Likewise in Latvia, no customs duties or quantitative restrictions were applied for industrial products traded with the EU.[42] In EU-Lithuanian trade, quantitative restrictions for industrial products were abolished at the beginning of 1995. However, Lithuania still applied customs duties on certain industrial goods, although these were progressively eliminated by 1 January 2001.[43]

In the domain of agricultural or processed agricultural goods, the Agreements did not provide for very liberal trade. Some concessions were enacted, but none of them significantly liberalised trade. Moreover, if the concessions seemed to result in a serious disturbance in the markets of the partner country, the 'suffering' party could adopt measures to restrict imports. At the same time, taking the Baltic states separately, Estonia represented a clear exception in that it fully liberalised market access to EU products, whereas the EU offered only so-called 'selective liberalisation' for products of Estonian origin. Still, no quantitative restrictions were applied to agricultural imports into the Community or to imports into Estonia.[44] In Latvia's and Lithuania's Association Agreements, no quantitative restrictions on trade with the EU were applied. Concessions on a reciprocal basis were mandated.[45] Higher tariffs applied essentially to processed products like sugar and butter.[46]

In addition to the restrictions still applied to trade in agricultural products, the Association Agreements contained various contingent commercial policy instruments, namely a general safeguard clause, an anti-dumping clause, export safeguards, a special safeguard clause, and anti-subsidy measures. The main idea behind these instruments was that they would provide the possibility for deviating from the trade liberalisation agreement when a party's interests were affected. This included, for example, situations where an increase in imports caused or threatened to cause significant losses to either domestic producers or an entire sector of economic activity or region. The same applied to exports in cases of serious shortages. The Agreements' anti-dumping clause furthermore gave the right to penalise products, which are sold in the receiver's market at a lower price than they are sold on the trade partner's own market. The anti-subsidy measure functioned similarly, but it applied when a foreign competitor received state subsidies. Finally, the specific safeguard clause was addressed to the association countries: in the case of infant industries, sectors under restructuring or sectors facing other serious difficulties had the right to adopt protectionist measures against imports coming from the Union. Exceptional duties were usually in the form of increased customs duties.

Rules of origin of any given product are important in implementing trade policy instruments such as anti-dumping and safeguard measures. The EU has general origin rules, which are applied to preferential trade. These rules also conform to WTO rules following from the 1994 GATT agreement.[47] However, these WTO rules do not apply to preferential trade agreements, such as the Association Agreements. In the EU's preferential trade arrangements, therefore, the concepts of 'substantial transformation' and 'sufficient working or processing' serve as a general foundation for the determination of the rules of origin.[48] According to the most common rule applied in the Association Agreements, 60 per cent of the value of the product must be derived from the value added in the associated country. However, interestingly enough, the rules of origin applied in the EU's preferential trade were less stringent than the rules enacted under preferential trade agreements.[49] Nevertheless, after the beginning of 1997, the Baltic countries, as well as the other CEECs and EFTA states, were all covered by the so-called 'pan-European cumulation of origin' rule, in which the origin of products could be moved around while still qualifying for preferential tariff treatment.

PTAs: a threat to the WTO and the multilateral trade system?

During the post-World War II era, the multilateral trading system of the General Agreement on Tariffs and Trade (GATT) no doubt played a crucial role in liberalising worldwide trade to unprecedented levels. Its eight different rounds of negotiations culminated in 1995 with the creation of the World Trade Organisation (WTO). As is well known, the main principle followed by the GATT/WTO in international trade relations has been that of 'most favoured nation' (MFN) treatment (Art. I). According to this rule, any advantage in terms of trade policy applied to one country must be immediately and unconditionally applied in the same way to all other GATT/WTO contracting parties. Discrimination against imports from one country or countries is prohibited. To be sure, this MFN principle is applied only to GATT/WTO members and therefore falls short of being worldwide. However, membership in the organisation is open to all countries that meet the criteria for admission. Secondly, an additional core principle of GATT/WTO is that of reciprocity, according to which any mutual changes in trade policy should result in equal changes in import volumes across trading partners. Finally, the principle of national treatment (Art. III) calls for the equal treatment of nationals and foreigners as regards regulations and/or commercial policy measures.

From a regional point of view, an important nuance is that the GATT makes provision for certain exceptions to the MFN rule. The best known is Article XXIV, which allows countries to establish preferential trading areas: free trade areas and customs unions. For example, regional blocs, such as the European Union, are considered consistent with the GATT/WTO, even though their regional nature can pose a threat to the GATT/WTO's basic conception of a world trading system. In addition, PTAs including partial preferences are allowed for developing countries. Also PTAs are allowed within the Generalised System of Preferences (GSP), according to which developed countries can grant trade preferences to developing countries. All in all, the principal requirement is that the purpose of a regional trade agreement should be to facilitate trade between the constituent territories, not to raise barriers to the trade of other WTO members, which are not parties to the agreement.[50]

In relation to trade theory, the argument in favour of Article XXIV has been presented by Bhagwati and Panagariya.[51] They find justification for PTAs on two occasions: first, when a group of countries aims at deeper economic and political integration including capital and labour mobility and uniform policies in various fields and, second, when the PTA is created using the same multilateral approach to trade negotiations as under the GATT/WTO and according to Article XXIV. Nevertheless, while making these two justifications for PTAs, the authors do express their concern about whether policy-makers can really differentiate between free trade and free trade areas. In addition, they asked whether an increasing number of PTAs will actually be formed in harmony with WTO principles, and finally, whether Article XXIV could be so strengthened as to ensure that its discipline is respected by member states.

The EU's Association Agreements: in line with or against WTO principles?

In principle, the EU's Association Agreements with the countries of Central and Eastern Europe were not bound by the WTO principles. Rather, they aimed at providing preferential treatment over other third countries in trade with the EU. Yet, to the extent that they still affected international trade, to what extent can it be said that these PTAs were in line with the spirit of the WTO and with the idea of multilateral liberalisation of trade? Several concerns are worth discussing, some of them have been raised on a general level, including on the part of individual WTO members. In particular, the special treatment that has been applied to agriculture and earlier also to textiles has been under extensive discussion during trade policy examination sessions in the WTO. For example, during the late 1990s the EU defended the protectionist measures it maintained in different sectors, in which the Baltic countries (and other Central and Eastern European countries) could be expected to have some comparative advantage – despite the possible effect these might have had on economic growth in these countries. In addition, some analysts questioned whether the preferential agreements would raise trade barriers to third countries and whether the consequent economic effects would be positive. Finally, one can ask how different commercial policy instruments have influenced the ultimate motive of preventing new protection and abolishing existing trade barriers.

First, it should be noted that no sectors were excluded from coverage in the Association Agreements. In other words, the aim of 'substantially all trade' was achieved. Nevertheless, changes in the composition of EU–Baltic trade during the 1990s did partly reflect the progress in liberalisation within different sectors. For example, the increase noted above in EU–Estonian and EU–Lithuanian trade in manufactured products could partly be explained by the liberalisation of trade in industrial products. Similarly, the share of textiles in foreign trade between the EU and the Baltic countries did not change dramatically during the 1993–98 period, which again mirrors the EU's protectionist trade policy in this sector. As regards the agricultural sector, the EU indicated that at the end of the transition period, the only sectors where there would still remain some protective measures would be agriculture and fisheries.[52] Nevertheless, if one of the Baltics' future comparative advantages lies in processed agricultural goods, the EU's protectionist policy, if continued, could hamper the exploitation of this advantage in EU markets. In addition, given the fact that the Baltic states constitute only a marginal share of the EU's foreign trade, it is difficult to see any justification for the remaining protection. However, this trade is largely surplus trade for the EU and therefore, in itself, adds to the Community's protectionist attitude. Moreover, it should be remembered that if the EU were to open its agricultural trade with the Baltic states, it would be under political pressure to do so with the other Central and Eastern European associated countries as well. Consequently, the whole issue would no longer be marginal in nature. Furthermore, a part of the access problem related to agriculture had to do with the Baltic states' own difficulties in complying with EU import requirements.[53] Overall, it seems that liberalisation has been lower and the protection is likely to remain for some of the products that constitute immediately and potentially exportable goods for the Baltic economies. This naturally has some implications for the Baltic countries' possibilities for increasing exports.[54]

Regarding rules of origin, the Association Agreements aimed in principle to provide for full cumulation across the agreements in order to reach a simple and transparent system in the overall pre-accession context. As a result, any changes in rules of origin made by either side were related to the harmonisation of these rules and the establishment of a single territory for the determination of origin between the EU, EFTA and the Central and Eastern European countries. Despite this progress, however, further efforts to promote the cumulation of rules of origin remained desirable given that such rules play a crucial role in developing regional trade and creating new business possibilities. This was also the case notwithstanding the fact that some of the CEECs' market access problems relating to origin rules were likely to become less significant as non-agricultural tariffs in the EU approached very low levels or zero.

From the point of view of the Baltic countries (as well as the other associated countries), another interesting observation to be made is that the EU's rules of origin were stricter under the preferential trade agreements than the rules of origin generally applied to the Union's MFN trade.[55] Consequently, although customs duties were lower under the preferential trade agreements, it was still more difficult to obtain origin under the Associated Agreements than under MFN trade. While an estimate of how much the Baltic states were influenced by these 'unequal' origin rules was difficult to come by, as a policy recommendation it would seem natural to support the idea of harmonisation (and simplification) of rules of origin between the EU's preferential and non-preferential agreements.[56] All in all, while rules of origin are often considered to be purely technical arrangements, their power as an important part of commercial policy deserves continuous attention. Rules of origin should not themselves create restrictive or distorting effects on trade.

Whether various safeguards, anti-dumping or anti-subsidy measures in the EU's Association Agreements worked against the ultimate goal of trade liberalisation greatly depended on how easily these measures could be adopted and for how long they could be maintained. As regards the duration of these protectionist measures, the Agreements stated that these cannot be applied for a period longer than two to three years (unless otherwise agreed with the Association Council).[57] However, all measures had to be terminated when conditions no longer justified their maintenance, and at the latest by the end of the transition period. Furthermore, none of the measures could be used in sectors where duties or quantitative restrictions were removed more than three years ago. One of the weak points related to the commercial policy instruments was that both parties could implement measures giving only relatively short notice, i.e. within 30 days or in some extreme cases even immediately. Moreover, these could be imposed without too much procedure. A good example here was a special safeguard concerning protectionist rights for the associated countries. If during trade consultations between the Community and the Association Council no consensus was reached on a particular issue, the associated country could adopt defensive measures without the Community's approval. The only requirement was that the associated country had to submit a plan for phasing these measures out. Moreover, the schedule had to provide for a phasing out of these duties no later that two years after their introduction.

Within the sphere of anti-dumping measures, few cases were raised by the EU against the Baltic states. Although during the late 1990s three definitive anti-dumping measures were in force (one against each Baltic country),[58] the scope of dumping penalties imposed on the CEE associated countries as a whole was low.[59] Still, the EU's anti-dumping regulations and procedures did give rise to criticism, for example with regard to Brussels's degree of secrecy, its method of calculation, and its tendency to underestimate the importance of market structure when measuring injury. In addition, although the actual number of anti-dumping penalties was relatively low, there were other less obvious but nevertheless significant effects, which could cause problems to the associated countries in the long run. For instance, it was maintained that anti-dumping charges could harm the credibility of market reforms and thereby also harm the confidence of investors. In turn, this would cause losses in sectors, which were crucial for economic growth in the affected country. In sum, therefore, the different kinds of safeguarding, anti-dumping or other defensive measures provided for in the Association Agreements could not be viewed as the most effective tools for encouraging further trade liberalisation. This, to some extent, also justified concerns about the possibility of reverse trade liberalisation.

A second interesting aspect relating not only to the EU–Baltic preferential trade arrangements, but also to the Association Agreements in general, was the so-called hub-and-spoke criticism presented by Richard Baldwin.[60] The main idea behind the argument is that where there is a hub, such as the EU, which dominates the economic activity of a certain region and has bilateral trade arrangements with peripheral associate countries which themselves have no free trade, the location of economic activity is likely to concentrate on the hub. This is because firms located in the EU can export freely (at the end of the transition period) within the Union or into the associated countries. However, if these firms were located in an associated country, they could trade freely with the EU, but not necessarily with the other associated countries. With regard to the Baltic region alone, Estonia, Latvia and Lithuania already have industrial and agricultural free trade agreements with each other. However, as was mentioned earlier, their competitive (rather than complementary) trade structures with each other contribute to the hub-and-spoke phenomenon. The hub-and-spoke issue becomes even more relevant when one looks at the whole club of associated countries, among which there was no full free trade with the exception of the Central European Free Trade Association.

Conclusions

The purpose of this study was to analyse the preferential trade arrangements between the Baltic states and the European Union. Regionalism theory constituted the basis of the study and was used to explain some of the static and dynamic effects related to preferential trade arrangements between the EU and the Baltics. In addition, six specific hypotheses of new regionalism were applied to the EU's Association Agreements with the Baltic countries, and in each case these were found to be true. The preferential trade arrangements between the Community and each individual Baltic state embodied, for example, the principle of reform-minded small countries linking up with a large neighbour. The Agreements also involved significant unilateral reforms in the Baltic countries in order to be accepted into the EU. Thirdly, regional integration presupposed deeper integration, from free trade to a common market and harmonised rules and policies. At the same time, this conferred relatively minor trade advantages as most of the bilateral trade had either already been liberalised or remained protected on sensitivity grounds.

During the 1990s as a whole, the European Union's Single Market Program and liberalisation according to WTO principles improved access conditions for the EU's trading partners. There seemed to be a general understanding on the EU side that strengthening European integration both in the Single Market and through regional and bilateral agreements were likely to have increasing effects on the outside world, and on the multilateral system as a whole. This applied not only to the extension of duty-free access on an FTA basis, but also through the adoption of the EU's trading regime by its partners.

Yet, while the EU remained bound by WTO principles and these rules had an influence over the EU's policy-making, criticism of the EU was also justified in some respects. The present analysis of the EU's Association Agreements with the Baltic states showed that while the EU played a significant role in opening up its market for Baltic industrial products, more could be demanded in terms of liberalisation in agricultural trade. In particular, given the fact that agriculture appeared to represent one of the future comparative advantages for the Baltic states, and that the Baltic countries constituted only a marginal share of the EU's overall foreign trade, it was difficult to see the rationale for any remaining protection. Nevertheless, protectionist pressures did exist within the Community, if only because any possible liberalisation of Baltic trade was inexorably linked to liberalisation across the CEE area. Furthermore, given the Community's need to reform its agricultural policy, the level of agricultural protection vs. any future concessions remained highly fluid. Lastly, as regards commercial trade policy measures – e.g. special safeguard clauses, anti-dumping and anti-subsidy regulations – the Association Agreements provided an opportunity to deviate from liberalisation and could therefore be seen as possible obstacles for further trade liberalisation initiatives. Part of this risk, however, was gradually being reduced as the transition periods came to an end, limiting the possibilities to use these measures.

Notes

1 See R. Baldwin, 'Measurable Dynamic Gains from Trade', *National Bureau of Economic Research Working Paper*, 3147 (1989); J. Bhagwati, *The World Trading System at Risk* (London, Harvester Wheatsheaf, 1991), pp. 3–79; A. L. Winters and W. Chang, 'Regional Integration and the Prices of Imports: An Empirical Investigation', paper presented at the North American Economics and Finance Association session of the Allied Social Science Association, San Francisco (1997); P. Wonnacott and M. Lutz. 'Is There a Case for Free Trade Areas?', in J. Schott (ed.), *Free Trade Areas and U.S. Trade Policy* (Washington, DC: Institute for International Economics, 1989), pp. 59–84.
2 W. J. Ethier, 'The New Regionalism', *The Economic Journal*, 108 (1998), 1162–1182.
3 S. Lahiri, 'Controversy: Regionalism versus Multilateralism', *The Economic Journal*, 108 (1998), 1126–1127.
4 Bhagwati, *The World Trading System*, 3–79.
5 A. Sapir, 'Trade Regionalism in Europe: Towards an Integrated Approach', Centre for Economic Policy Research/Yrjo Jahnsson Foundation/ZEI Conference (1998).
6 Eighty-nine of these RTAs are bilateral agreements, and 82 of these bilateral agreements are free trade agreements (FTAs). In addition, 74 of the FTAs involve Central and Eastern European Countries (CEECs).
7 World Trade Organisation, 'Regionalism and the Multilateral Trading System' (Geneva, World Trade Organisation, 1999).
8 J. Viner, *The Customs Union Issues* (New York, Carnegie Endowment for International Peace, 1950); J. Viner, *Studies in the Theory of International Trade* (London and New York, Harper & Brothers Publishers, 1951), 110–118; J. E. Meade, *Problems of Economic Union* (London, George Allen & Unwin, 1953). J. E. Meade, *The Theory of Customs Unions* (Amsterdam, North-Holland Publishing Company, 1955); R. G. Lipsey, *The Theory of Customs Unions: A General Equilibrium Analysis* (London, London School of Economics and Political Science, 1970).
9 Wonnacott and Lutz, 'Is There a Case for Free Trade Areas?'
10 A. V. Deardorff, 'Determiants of Bilateral Trade: Does Gravity Work in a Neoclassical World?', in J. A. Frankel (ed.), *The Regionalisation of the World Economy* (London, National Bureau of Economic Research, 1998), pp. 7–33.
11 Meade, *Problems of Economic Union*; Lipsey, *The Theory of Customs Unions.*
12 J. Bhagwati and A. Panagaryia, *The Economics of Preferential Trade Agreements* (Washington, DC, Centre for International Economics, 1996), pp. 1–78.
13 Meade, *The Theory of Customs Unions.*
14 Frankel, *The Regionalization*, pp. 34–152.
15 M. C. Kemp and H. Wan, 'An Elementary Proposition Concerning the Formation of Customs Unions', *Journal of International Economics*, 6 (1976), 95–98.
16 Bhagwati and Panagaryia, *The Economics of Preferential Trade Agreements.*
17 Ethier, 'The New Regionalism'.
18 R. Baldwin, 'The Causes of Regionalism', *Centre for Economic Policy Research Working Paper*, 1599 (1997) 5–8, 26–33.
19 At the end of 1998, the Committee on Regional Trade Agreements of the WTO started to examine 62 regional trade agreements, including the European Community's free trade agreements with various Central and Eastern European Countries, the North American Free Trade Agreement, the Central European Free Trade Agreement, etc. The Committee was set to address especially the systemic implications of these agreements and the repercussions such agreements could have on the functioning of the WTO system of rights and obligations.
20 Baldwin, 'Measurable Dynamic Gains'.
21 The degree of external scale economies equals the divergence between the social and

private marginal productivity of capital. K. Bagwell and R. W. Staiger, 'Reciprocity, Non-Discrimination and Preferential Agreements in the Multilateral Trading System', *National Bureau of Economic Research Working Paper*, 5932 (1997) 10–19.

22 See Bhagwati, *World Trading System*; also J. Bhagwati, D. Greenway and A. Panagariya, 'Trading Preferentially: Theory and Policy', *The Economic Journal*, 108 (1998), 1128–1148.

23 Baldwin, 'Measurable Dynamic Gains'; and Baldwin, 'The Causes of Regionalism'.

24 Baldwin, 'The Causes of Regionalism'.

25 D. A. DeRosa, 'Regional Integration Arrangements: Static Economic Theory, Quantitative Findings, and Policy Guidelines', A background paper prepared by the Trade, Development Research Group for the World Bank Policy Research Report *Regionalism and Development* (1998).

26 Baldwin, 'The Causes of Regionalism'.

27 The study by Winters and Chang measures the welfare effects of regional integration on the terms of trade. They show how Spanish accession to the EU affected the prices of imports from the EU, Japan and the United States. One of the conclusions made is that non-members (Japan and the USA) suffered significant losses in terms of trade relative to European Community competitors in Spanish import markets for differentiated goods. Winters and Chang, 'Regional Integration and the Prices of Imports'.

28 European Commission, 'Regular Report from the Commission on Estonia's Progress Towards Accession' (1998). The agreements have been in force since 1 January 1999. *Estonian Economy 1998–1999* (Tallinn, Ministry of Economic Affairs, 1999), p. 129.

29 E. Elgar, 'Latvia: Trade Growth in Transition Economies. Export Impediments for Central and Eastern Europe', *Working Papers International Institute for Applied Systems Analysis*, 118 (1997).

30 European Commission, 'Regular Report from the Commission on Latvia's Progress Towards Accession' (1998).

31 European Commission, 'Regular Report from the Commission on Lithuania's Progress Towards Accession' (1998).

32 A. Mayhew, *Recreating Europe: The European Union's Policy Towards Central and Eastern Europe* (Cambridge, Cambridge University Press, 1998), p. 89.

33 For more on intra-Baltic integration, see Vilpisaukas in this volume (chapter 8).

34 Country-specific data on the composition of trade flows is not collected for each country. In this study, information concerning the trade structure with the EU is based on the Eurostat statistics, the EU Commission Opinion and trade statistics provided by the Baltic national statistical offices.

35 For a more detailed analysis of trade between the Baltic states and the European Union, see also Kaitila and Widgren in this volume (chapter 9).

36 World Trade Organisation, 'Policy Reviews' (1997); J. Pelkmans and P. Brenton, 'Free Trade with the EU: Driving Forces and the Effects of "Me-Too"', *Centre for European Policy Studies Working Document*, 110 (1997), 1–17.

37 These transitional periods apply starting from the entry into force of the Agreement of Free Trade and Trade Related Matters: on 1 January 1995.

38 For Estonia, the basic duty for each product covered by the Association Agreement was that applied on January 1994 (Art. 8). In case of Latvia, the basic duties, with few exceptions, were mainly those applied on January 1995 (Art. 8). For Lithuania, the basic duty, depending on the product, was that applied either on March 1994, or January 1995 (Art. 8).

39 Mayhew, *Recreating Europe*, p. 63.

40 As an example, in 1998 the foreign trade turnover of goods and services in Estonia amounted to 168 per cent of the country's GDP. There were few other countries in the world where the foreign turnover of goods and services exceeds GDP to such an extent, *Bank of Estonia, Newsletter*, 1 (1999).

41 Europe Agreement between the European Community and Estonia, Document 298A0309(01): Articles 9–16; Mayhew, *Recreating Europe.*
42 Europe Agreement between the European Community and Latvia, Document 298A0202(01): Articles 9–17; Mayhew, *Recreating Europe.*
43 Europe Agreements between the European Community and Lithuania, Document 298A0220(01): Articles 9–17. Industrial products on which customs duties still apply, see Annex II, III, IV and V. Mayhew, *Recreating Europe.*
44 Europe Agreement between the European Community and Estonia, Document 298A0309(01): Articles 17–20. 'Agenda 2000: Commission opinion on Estonia's application for membership of the European Union', in *European Commission Bulletin of the European Union Supplement,* 11 (1997).
45 Europe Agreement between the European Community and Latvia, Document 298A0202(01): Articles 18–21. Europe Agreements between the European Community and Lithuania, Document 298A0220(01): Articles 18–21.
46 It is worth noting that after July 1996 the Association Agreements were modified to take into account the Agreement on Agriculture concluded during the GATT Uruguay Round, and also to reflect further improvements in the concesions on agricultural products granted to the Baltic states. The GATT-related adjustments, together with new concessions decided by the Community, increased the preference level for all agricultural products from 60 to 80 per cent. Furthermore, the general applicable duty decreased from 40 to 20 per cent. The European Commission. Free Trade and Association Agreements with the EU, 1997.
47 Article IX.
48 The European Commission. 1998. Comm(98)0389 final. Rules of origin defined in the context of preferential arrangements.
49 1) Community Legislation Doc. 394D0800 'Relations in the Context of the General Agreement on Tariffs and Trade'. 2) The Europe Agreements between the EU and Estonia, Latvia and Lithuania.
50 World Trade Organisation, 'Regionalism and the Multilateral Trading System' (1999).
51 Bhagwati and Panagaryia, *The Economics of Preferential Trade Agreements.*
52 World Trade Organisation, 'Policy Reviews. Examination of the Free Trade Agreements between the European Communities and Estonia, Latvia, and Lithuania' (1997).
53 For example, in terms of an important concession granted to Latvia in January 1998 six dairy processing establishments were given licenses to export to the EU. However, during that same period no Latvian slaughterhouse received authorisation for export to the EU, which was important given the fact that Latvia's export potential to the EU lay partly in meat and dairy products.
54 Similar conclusions concerning the effects of the Association Agreements have been made regarding the other CEECs. S. Schultz, 'Countries in Transition and GATT/WTO: Issues, Expectations, Prospects', *German Institute for Economic Research Discussion Paper,* 121 (1995), 11–16.
55 Mayhew, *Recreating Europe.*
56 Upon the implementation of the harmonisation, the origin of a particular good is either the country where the good has been wholly obtained, or when more than one country is concerned in the production of the good, the country where the last substantial transformation has been carried out.
57 See The Europe Agreements, Article 27 in the case of Estonia, and Article 28 in the case of Latvia and Lithuania.
58 The European Commission, DG1, Information Office. 12.4.1999.
59 See related discussion: Mayhew, *Recreating Europe,* pp. 93–99.
60 R. Baldwin, *Towards an Integrated Europe* (London, Cambridge University Press, 1994).

Iikka Korhonen

11

Some implications of EU membership on Baltic monetary and exchange rate policies

The entry of up to ten Central and Eastern European countries (CEECs) into the European Union will affect these states in myriad ways. This study will confine itself to the possible effects of EU membership on monetary and exchange rate policies in the case of the Baltic states. As these countries prepare for full participation in the euro area, we will also examine what Stage Three of the Economic and Monetary Union (EMU) might mean for the conduct of monetary policy and exchange rate policies in the Baltics. While there most certainly is a political dimension to all this, I will confine the analysis to economics.

The start of Stage Three of EMU, beginning in 1999 and concluding with the introduction of euro notes and coins in January 2002, changed the global environment for monetary and exchange rate policies. Obviously, those countries with the most extensive trade and investment ties with the euro area felt this change the strongest. Among the most affected were the transition economies of Central and Eastern Europe, including the Baltics. The Estonian kroon, once pegged to the D-Mark, was now pegged to the euro. In Lithuania the litas was likewise anchored to the euro in February 2002, while in Latvia the lats was re-valued according to a currency basket with a heavy euro weighting.

The choice of an appropriate exchange rate arrangement in the pre-accession countries posed a series of hard choices. For example, some of the larger transition economies in Eastern Europe opted for relatively free-floating exchange rates. Such was the case in Poland, where this kind of arrangement was feasible due to the size of the country's economy and the liquidity of its foreign exchange market. By contrast, in the Baltic states a more rigid exchange rate arrangement was chosen, which in turn had the consequence of limiting the type of monetary policy their central banks can pursue. Through 2002, all of the Baltic countries continued to use fixed exchange rate regimes. Estonia and Lithuania employed a currency board – an arrangement whereby the country's foreign currency reserves were maintained at a level sufficient to cover the monetary base at all times. Latvia, meanwhile, pledged to continue pegging its currency to the notional currency of the International Monetary Fund, the Special Drawing Right, at least until EU membership. Because the Baltic economies were small and open to foreign trade, they were excellent candidates for a fixed exchange rate regime. Furthermore, since the euro-area bloc constituted the largest single trading partner for the Baltics, the euro was also the natural anchor currency for the Baltic countries. Lastly, because of the thinness of Baltic capital and foreign exchange markets, free-floating regimes would have exposed these countries to large swings in the external value of their currencies.

Whatever regime was chosen, the Baltics would still need to keep a close watch on the development of the real value of their currencies. Most economists agree that the Baltic currencies were considerably undervalued when they were first introduced in 1992–93. However, real effective exchange rates later appreciated so much that by the end of the decade overvaluation was the main issue. In the cases of Estonia and Latvia, brisk growth in labour productivity appeared to stave off severe overvaluation, even in the face of large external imbalances. In Lithuania, however, labour productivity growth clearly failed to keep pace with real wages.

The chapter is structured as follows. Section two reviews the historical development of both the exchange rate and monetary policy in the three Baltic countries since regaining independence. In addition, we look briefly at the development of the Baltic banking systems, as they are very important to the conduct of monetary policy. Section three explores the possible and probable consequences of the introduction of the euro in the Baltic countries. In addition to monetary and exchange rate policies, we consider integration of the Baltic countries with the euro area in terms of foreign trade, capital flows, and financial systems. Section four examines exchange rate and monetary policy options in the period leading up to EU membership.

A brief history of Baltic monetary and exchange rate arrangements

Within the former Soviet Union, the Baltic states were one of the first areas to undertake serious economic reform. Indeed, the first commercial bank in the Soviet Union was established in Estonia in 1989.[1] Banks soon followed in the other two Baltic states as well. This section provides an overview of economic development in the Baltic countries during this decade.[2]

Currency reforms and exchange rate arrangements

Currency reform was an important component in the economic reforms of the Baltic countries. Although the three states became independent from the Soviet Union in August 1991, monetarily they remained linked to the ex-Soviet, now Russian rouble through mid-1992. This connection became especially problematic when prices in Russia were freed at the start of 1992 and monthly inflation quickly jumped to over 30 per cent as prices rose to eliminate the monetary overhang.[3] After this first initial change in the price level, monthly inflation ran at approximately 10 per cent during the first half of 1992. In June 1992, monthly inflation jumped to almost 30 per cent and stayed there for nearly five months. In turn, the external value of the rouble depreciated strongly and a general malaise set in. In the Baltic countries, this instability prompted monetary authorities to seek alternative monetary arrangements. New currencies were the only answer.

Estonia was the first Baltic country to introduce its own currency, the kroon, in June 1992. Moreover, its authorities decided to adopt perhaps the most rigid and credible form of currency peg, a currency board system, whereby a central bank's outstanding liabilities would always be backed 100 per cent by its foreign currency reserves. Under the strictest possible currency board, variations in currency reserves would translate immediately into changes in the monetary base. In practice, countries that adopt currency boards usually retain some discretion over the monetary base. Nevertheless, the common feature of such arrangements is that the monetary base must be backed *at least* 100 per cent by foreign currency reserves. A currency board also presupposes free movement of capital and precludes central bank lending to the public sector, so in effect adopting a currency board means giving up independence in monetary policy altogether. Money supply is wholly endogenous and dependent on capital flows. In return for this loss of independence, the currency board offers a quick way to gain confidence in a currency. This consideration apparently weighed heavily in the case of Estonia, which successfully launched a new currency in the midst of a complex political situation. Estonia's monetary regime, generally regarded as highly credible, benefited specifically from the fact that its currency board arrangement was so rigid and immutable. In addition, other components of Estonia's economic policy supported the currency board arrangement. For example, Article 116 of the Estonian Constitution does not allow the state to run any budget deficits. This consistent adherence to chosen policies during the transition process conferred credibility on Estonia's monetary arrangements and its economic policies in general.

In May 1992, the Estonian parliament passed three laws regarding monetary and exchange rate policy: a currency law, a law on the backing of the Estonian kroon, and a foreign exchange law.[4] Estonia balked at the strictest possible version of a currency board as the Bank of Estonia retained some discretion as to the amount of capital inflows allowed to boost the monetary base. In addition, the Bank of Estonia retained its right to set minimum reserve requirements for commercial banks, which again is not in accordance with orthodox definitions of a currency board system.[5] Even so the Bank of Estonia never wavered from the guiding rule that the country's foreign currency reserves had at all times to cover the currency in circulation and the deposits of commercial banks at the central bank. In practice, reserve coverage averaged around 110 per cent. The Estonian kroon was pegged to the D-Mark at a rate of eight to one (i.e. DEM

1 = EEK 8). Following the actual changeover the kroon remained totally convertible for current account purposes. While the Bank of Estonia required exporters to surrender their export earnings within two months, it is unclear how strictly this rule was applied in the early years. Foreign currency deposits were allowed, but no new accounts were permitted. This regulation was repealed in March 1994. Thereafter the kroon was fully convertible and the movement of capital virtually free.[6] The exchange rate arrangement was quite successful in initially bringing inflation down, especially when compared to other countries of the former Soviet Union, including the other two Baltic countries. Figure 11.1 shows the monthly inflation rates for the three Baltic countries from June 1992 to December 1994. Note that Latvia and Estonia succeeded in bringing inflation down quickly, while Lithuania struggled considerably longer with high and variable inflation. Eventually, monthly inflation subsided in all cases. By the end of the 1990s, annual inflation was in the low single digits throughout the Baltics.

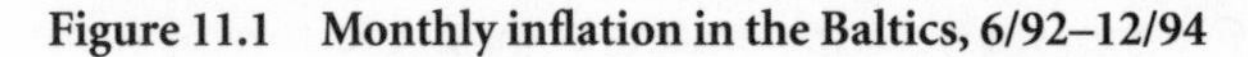

Figure 11.1 Monthly inflation in the Baltics, 6/92–12/94

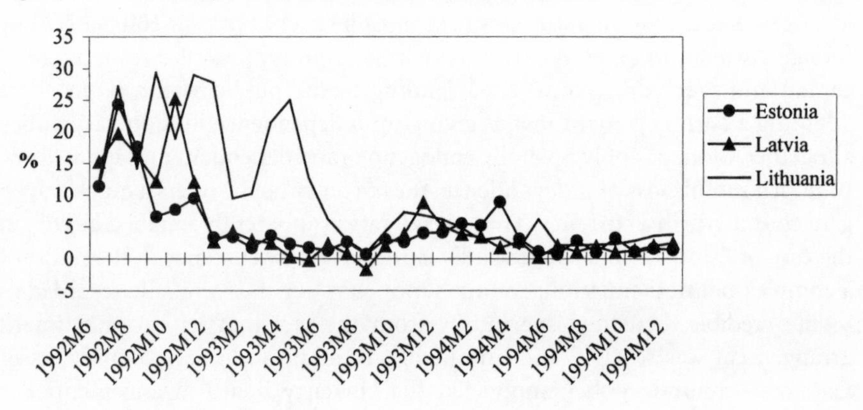

The first years of Estonia's economic transition saw declining economic activity, much as in all the transition countries. Yet, in the countries of the former Soviet Union the output collapse was more precipitous. The severity of the initial drop can be largely explained by the fact that the trade ties between the republics of the Soviet Union were closer than those between the independent nations in the CMEA (Council of Mutual Economic Assistance).[7] In Estonia, economic activity reached its lowest point in 1994–1995, and eventually revived to a rapid pace. Indeed, by the time growth reached 10.6 per cent in 1997, concerns about an overheating of the economy were expressed. At the same time, Estonia's vibrant economic growth ran parallel with a deteriorating external balance. In 1997, the current account deficit reached 12 per cent of GDP. The steadily worsening external balance and rapid growth in domestic credit (bank lending to the private sector increased 77 per cent from December 1996 to December 1997) further contributed to doubts about the sustainability of Estonia's exchange rate regime. In October 1997, the kroon came under speculative pressure. Nevertheless, the currency board arrangement proved resilient. Interbank interest rates went up sharply, but soon capital flows reversed and interest rates started to fall. During the summer of 1998, the Russian crisis sparked some speculation about the monetary arrangement of Estonia, as Estonia was expected to suffer substantially from the drop of exports to Russia. Through 2001, however, Estonia seemed to have weathered the crisis reasonably well, and the credibility of the kroon remained strong.

Like Estonia, Latvia also had ideas for an independent currency already in 1990. However, after independence Latvia chose to ease itself out of the rouble area by first introducing a temporary currency, the Latvian rouble, in May 1992. Moreover, from the start of currency reform, the use of other currencies was allowed. The Latvian currency was also freely convertible for current and capital account transactions. Initially, the Latvian authorities announced that a new permanent currency would be issued as soon as inflation had been brought under control. The introduction of the new currency, the lats, was supposed to take place in 1992. Ultimately, however, it was postponed until March 1993. Moreover, the switch to the lats was gradual. In July 1993, all Latvian rouble bank deposits were converted into lats and all taxes were collected in lats. Latvian roubles were definitively withdrawn from circulation in October 1993.

Initially the Latvian rouble and the lats were floating currencies. There has been some debate as to how freely the currencies floated, but nevertheless the Latvian rouble and the lats appreciated strongly against the US dollar from summer 1992 to spring 1994. In March 1994, the lats was pegged to the International Monetary Fund's SDR at a rate of just under eight to one (SDR 1 = LVL 0.7997).[8] Thereafter Latvia maintained this peg rigorously. Although Latvia did not have a currency board system, the policy of the Bank of Latvia was to ensure that its currency reserves were sufficient to back the monetary base at over 100 per cent. The Bank of Latvia also introduced a number of monetary policy instruments. As for economic output, Latvia's initial contraction was larger than Estonia's. When the economy started to recover in 1994–95, the country was hit by a severe banking crisis. The resulting monetary contraction curtailed growth once again during 1995. Thereafter, growth accelerated to 8.6 per cent in 1997. Yearly inflation, meanwhile, declined steadily to a level below 2 per cent. The Russian crisis hit also Latvia, but it recovered quite rapidly from the recession.

Lithuania also took a gradualist approach to monetary reform. Although the Lithuanian parliament adopted a law on the creation of a national currency in December 1991, political debates about the new currency prevented Lithuania from leaving the rouble zone for quite some time. In May 1992, the Lithuanian authorities introduced an interim currency that lacked even an official name. It was simply called the 'coupon', or *talonas* in Lithuanian, and was issued at a par with the Russian rouble. In September 1992, the Lithuanian authorities began to withdraw roubles from circulation, and from the beginning of October they forbid use of the rouble. In June 1993, the authorities announced the introduction of the new currency, the litas. From August 1993, the talonas ceased to be legal tender and the use of foreign currencies was banned. The litas was convertible for current account purposes, but Lithuania retained restrictions on capital account transactions longer than its Baltic neighbours.

Lithuania also differed from the other Baltic countries at the beginning of economic reforms in its exchange rate arrangement. The country maintained a dual exchange rate system until autumn 1993. Secondly, due to a lax monetary stance, inflation was considerably higher than in Estonia or Latvia, and was reflected in the external value of the Lithuanian currency. The talonas depreciated markedly against the dollar up to summer 1993. Tightened monetary policy eventually stopped the depreciation, and the litas even appreciated slightly. Partly as a result of this observed volatility of the exchange rate and the low credibility of monetary policy, debate about a more appropriate exchange rate regime intensified in autumn 1993. Ultimately, Lithuania decided to adopt a currency board in March 1994. The new arrangement became effective in April 1994. The litas was pegged to the US dollar at a rate of USD 1 = LTL 4. Although the Bank of Lithuania subsequently introduced several monetary policy instruments, the country also maintained a currency board, and the monetary base was still 100 per cent backed by foreign currency reserves. In February 2000, the anchor currency was switched from the US dollar to the euro at a rate of 1 euro = 3.45 litas.

Of all the Baltic countries, Lithuania suffered the largest output collapse at the beginning of transition. Real growth returned only in 1995. Nevertheless, at the end of 1995 and the beginning of 1996, Lithuania also experienced a banking crisis, although this was less severe than in Latvia and had little impact on the real economy. By 1997, real GDP growth had recovered to 7.3 per cent. The exchange rate stability conferred by the currency board helped bring inflation down. At the beginning of 1994, annual inflation was almost 200 per cent. By 1999, it was close to zero. Much like Estonia, however, Lithuania's external balance has continued to deteriorate as a function of economic growth. In 1997, the current account deficit was approximately 10 per cent of GDP; in 1998, it exceeded 12 per cent of GDP. Of all the Baltic countries Lithuania was the hardest hit by the Russian crisis, and in 1999 GDP contracted by 4.2 per cent. Recovery was not as rapid as in Estonia and Latvia.

The development of banking systems

The number of banking institutions started to increase in all the Baltic countries even before the countries regained their political independence. The first commercial bank in the Soviet Union was founded in 1989 in Tartu, Estonia. Thereafter, when Baltic independence was restored, the number of banks ballooned. By the end of 1993, there were 22 banks in Estonia, 61 in Latvia, and 32 in Lithuania. One of the reasons behind this expansion was the fact that many businessmen saw banks as a relatively easy way to earn money in the new economic environment. Banks in the Baltic countries were involved in financing foreign trade and speculating in the currency markets. The volatile economic environment following the break-up of the Soviet Union offered ample opportunities for these activities. More traditional types of banking were not seen as lucrative, especially in the virtual absence of relevant laws and regulations.

Yet, when these easy sources of revenue began to dry up and the authorities in the Baltic countries stepped up their efforts at banking regulation (for instance, by introducing new minimum capital requirements), the number of banks began to diminish dramatically.[9] The consolidation and privatisation of banking sectors continued from 1994 onwards, although at varying speeds in different countries. During 1996 and 1997, Baltic banks expanded their businesses rapidly. Estonian banks especially, grew very fast with some even moving into the Latvian market. After more general uncertainty over emerging markets rocked the international financial sector at the end of 1997, Baltic banks curbed their lending growth. Moreover, 1998 witnessed several takeovers of Baltic (mainly Estonian) banks by large foreign (mainly Swedish) banks.

Throughout the Baltics, banks were able to expand their business as inflation declined and economies stabilised. Estonian banks started by issuing short-term credits to private companies. During 1998–99, bank lending to households increased very rapidly as a mortgage market developed and leasing operations expanded. The average maturity of loans extended also increased. Already at the end of 1998, approximately 85 per cent of the loan stock had a maturity of more than one year. Stabilisation was also associated with the emergence of a positive real interest rate. Real interest rates on short-term loans turned positive in early 1994.

In Latvia, the country's macroeconomic stabilisation was characterised by an increase in both the volume of bank lending and the average maturity of loans. This positive development was, however, interrupted by the collapse of the largest bank (Banka Baltija) in 1995. The closure meant a severe contraction in the broader monetary aggregates. After this, the development of the Latvian banking sector was on a more secure footing. During 1997, bank lending to the private sector increased by 77 per cent. If at the end of 1993 only 16 per cent of all bank lending had a maturity of more than one year, then by the end of 1998 this figure was up to 67 per cent.

The development of Lithuania's banking sector has been somewhat slower than in the other two Baltic countries. This is reflected both in the volume of lending and maturities. During 1997 the volume of loans grew 21 per cent. From 1993 to 1998, the proportion of loans with a maturity of over one year rose from 12 per cent to 46 per cent; however, this was clearly lower than in Estonia or Latvia.

Stage Three of European Monetary Union and the Baltic exchange rate arrangements

The start of Stage Three of European Monetary Union and the launch of the euro as an accounting unit in early 1999 profoundly affected the economic environment of the three Baltic countries. With a common monetary area now encompassing over 300 million people and a nominal gross product of approximately EUR 6.4 trillion in 2000, the euro's impact would be felt first in terms of trade and financial flows, and later with regard to monetary and exchange rate policies in the Baltic countries. This section outlines some of these possible effects, giving special emphasis to issues related to monetary and exchange rate arrangements.

The direct effect of the euro on the exchange rate policy

The change to the euro most directly affected Estonia, which previously pegged its currency to the German mark. After the mark ceased to exist as an independent currency at the beginning of 1999, Estonia needed to change several laws. The law on the security for the Estonian kroon stated that the external value of the kroon is expressed in terms of the mark. For the sake of practicality, however, Estonian authorities took the view that the mark would exist until the beginning of 2002 when euro notes began to circulate and national currencies were withdrawn from circulation. This gave them until the end of 2001 to amend all necessary legislation, and in December 2001 the D-mark was officially replaced by the euro in Estonian legislation.

In Latvia, the composition of the SDR currency basket (to which the lats was pegged) changed with the introduction of the euro. In 1999, the euro represented approximately 28 per cent of the SDR. Thus, Latvia's monetary integration into the euro area was not as tight as that of Estonia's, provided Latvia continued to peg to the SDR. In 2002, the share of the euro in the SDR basket was slightly higher, 30 per cent.

In 1997, Lithuania announced a decision to give up its currency board arrangement. According to the Bank of Lithuania's original program, the currency board was to have been abandoned during the first half of 1999. However, general instability in the emerging markets prompted the Lithuanian authorities to reconsider their decision. In the end they decided to maintain the currency board, but its anchor currency was changed to the euro in February 2002. This reflected a clearly better foreign trade orientation for Lithuania, and was also understandable given Lithuania's bid for EU membership.

Trade flows between the euro area and the Baltic countries

The twelve countries comprising the euro area are the single most important trading partner for all Baltic countries. This section looks at the trade between the Baltic countries and the euro area. Tables 11.1 to11.3 depict the evolution of the geographical distribution of the Baltic countries' foreign trade from 1996 to 2000. Note that while the euro area's importance as a trading partner grew fairly steadily for Latvia and Lithuania during 1994–98, in 1999 the Russian crisis redirected even more foreign trade towards the EU and the euro area. Estonia's shift to Western markets happened earlier, so there was no significant upward trend in the share of the euro area until 1999. Generally speaking, the Baltic countries were able to shift their trade quickly from the other former countries of the Soviet Union to Western European markets.[10]

Table 11.1 Geographical distribution of Estonian foreign trade (%)

	1996		1997		1998		1999		2000	
	Exp.	*Imp.*	*Exp.*	*Imp.*	*Exp.*	*Imp.*	*Exp.*	*Imp.*	*Exp.*	*Imp.*
Euro area	36.0	53.8	35.3	51.8	36.7	51.0	39.7	48.4	45.8	47.4
Sweden	13.2	8.8	18.2	10.6	20.8	10.7	22.7	10.7	20.5	9.8
Denmark	4.0	2.8	4.1	2.7	4.3	3.0	4.7	2.8	3.4	2.5
UK	3.6	2.9	4.7	3.2	4.8	3.1	5.6	2.6	4.4	2.3
Russia	14.2	11.2	9.8	8.8	5.9	7.8	3.4	8.0	2.4	8.5
Latvia	8.2	2.0	9.0	2.0	9.4	2.1	8.3	2.4	7.0	2.6
Lithuania	5.2	1.5	4.9	1.4	4.4	1.6	3.4	1.8	2.8	1.6
Total value (USD bn)	1.8	2.9	2.1	3.5	2.5	3.9	2.4	3.4	3.2	4.3

Source: Statistical Office of Estonia and author's own calculations

Table 11.2 Geographical distribution of Latvian foreign trade (%)

	1996		1997		1998		1999		2000	
	Exp.	*Imp.*	*Exp.*	*Imp.*	*Exp.*	*Imp.*	*Exp.*	*Imp.*	*Exp.*	*Imp.*
Euro area	23.3	34.5	22.3	38.6	27.6	41.0	29.3	40.2	30.6	39.4
Sweden	6.6	7.9	8.3	7.7	10.3	7.2	10.7	7.2	10.8	6.7
Denmark	3.7	2.3	3.9	3.5	5.1	3.8	6.1	3.9	5.8	3.6
UK	11.1	2.8	14.3	3.3	13.5	3.1	16.4	3.3	17.4	2.7
Russia	22.8	14.2	21.0	15.6	12.1	11.8	6.6	10.5	4.2	11.6
Estonia	3.7	5.7	4.2	6.0	4.5	6.6	4.7	6.4	5.3	6.2
Lithuania	7.4	6.3	7.5	6.4	7.4	6.3	7.5	7.3	7.6	7.6
Total value (USD bn)	1.4	2.3	1.7	2.7	1.9	3.2	1.7	2.9	1.9	3.2

Source: Central Statistical Office of Latvia and author's own calculations.

Table 11.3 Geographical distribution of Lithuanian foreign trade (%)

	1996		1997		1998		1999		2000	
	Exp.	*Imp.*	*Exp.*	*Imp.*	*Exp.*	*Imp.*	*Exp.*	*Imp.*	*Exp.*	*Imp.*
Euro area	25.7	31.5	24.0	35.4	26.8	36.0	34.6	35.0	30.8	32.3
Sweden	1.7	3.1	1.9	3.2	2.5	3.7	4.2	3.4	4.4	3.4
Denmark	2.6	3.8	3.4	4.2	4.0	3.8	6.2	3.9	4.9	3.1
UK	2.8	3.9	3.2	3.3	3.4	3.7	5.1	4.2	7.8	4.5
Russia	24.0	25.9	24.5	24.3	16.7	21.1	7.0	20.1	7.1	27.4
Ukraine	7.7	2.6	8.8	2.0	8.0	1.9	3.7	1.5	4.4	1.5
Belarus	10.2	2.4	10.3	2.4	8.8	2.2	5.9	2.2	2.9	1.8
Latvia	9.2	3.3	8.6	3.4	11.1	1.8	12.8	2.0	15.0	1.6
Estonia	2.5	2.2	2.5	2.4	2.6	1.5	2.4	1.5	2.3	1.2
Total value (USD bn)	3.4	4.6	3.9	5.6	3.7	5.8	3.0	4.8	3.8	5.5

Source: Lithuanian Department of Statistics and author's own calculations.

Naturally there were differences among the countries.[11] In Estonia, the share of the euro area was significantly larger in imports than in exports. This was largely due to the predominance of Finland in exports and imports. For example, the 2000 share of Finland in total Estonian exports was 32.3 per cent, whereas imports from Finland were 27.4 per cent of total imports. In Latvia the relative importance of Russia and other CIS countries (most notably Ukraine) declined during the 1990s. Both Latvian producers and consumers turned to the more stable markets of Western Europe. Toward the end of the decade, the economic problems in Russia (which spread to Ukraine and Belarus) also hastened this trend. Euro-area countries thus formed the single largest trading partner; already in pre-euro 1998 the share of the euro-area countries in Latvian foreign trade was 36 per cent. Sweden and the UK are also very important to Latvia. Lithuania was clearly the most dependent on CIS markets, although the importance of Russia did decrease during the 1990s. In 1997, the CIS was still as important an export market as the eleven countries of the euro area. By 1998, the relative importance of the euro area was much larger. The euro-area countries were also by far the largest exporters to Lithuania. In 1999 and 2000 also Latvia gained importance in Lithuania's foreign trade.

There are numerous arguments for and against fixed exchange rates, but the consensus, *ceteris paribus*, is that the advantages of fixing a currency become pronounced as the country's dependence on foreign trade increases.[12] The Baltic countries surely qualify as countries highly dependent on foreign trade. In 1999, the ratio of foreign trade (exports and imports) to GDP was 112 per cent for Estonia, 70 per cent for Latvia and 74 per cent for Lithuania. Moreover, the geographical distribution of the Baltic countries' foreign trade would suggest that the three states would benefit from some sort of exchange peg to the euro area. Despite the fact that Russia and several other CIS countries remained important trading partners for the Baltics, it was too much of a stretch to argue for a rouble peg. Indeed, including any currency as volatile as the rouble in a currency basket stood to degrade the credibility itself of a currency (although it might help to stabilise the nominal effective exchange rate).

The desirability of a fixed exchange rate naturally depends on a host of other factors (including possible political reasons). Nevertheless, it would be a non-trivial task to analyse, for example, the correlation of business cycles in the Baltics with those of the EU or the euro area. During the 1990s, all of the transition countries underwent profound structural adjustments, and thus the economic data covering recent years was of relatively little use in predicting future correlations with economic growth in other countries. For this reason, it is worth considering instead the intensity of trade as the most significant indicator of economic integration.

The costs and benefits of fixing the currency to the euro did not depend solely on the amount of trade the Baltic countries conducted with the euro area. Fixing to the euro was more desirable if other significant trading partners had also fixed their currencies to the euro. Thus, the decision of a single Baltic country about its foreign exchange rate regime depended to some extent on what the other two decided. For example, Lithuania had the lowest share of trade with the countries of the euro area. However, if Estonia and especially Latvia decided to peg their currencies to the euro (or at least to a basket where the euro played a major role), the argument for a similar peg for Lithuania would be stronger. It should also be remembered that Denmark, which was a reasonably large trading partner for all the Baltic countries, decided not to participate in the adoption of the euro. Thus, this would be a deterrent factor. Still, table 11.4 shows how much the foreign trade of the Baltic countries might be with the entire euro bloc (i.e. the euro area plus the countries that have pegged to the euro). The first two columns use the assumption that the euro bloc consists only of the euro area and the sole country still a member of ERM2, i.e Denmark.[13] The next two columns assume that the three Baltic countries are also all pegged to the euro. The last two columns assume that Sweden and the UK also join the euro area or at least peg their currencies to the euro.

Table 11.4 Baltic foreign trade with the euro bloc under three assumptions (%)

	Euro area + ERM2		*Euro area + ERM2 + Baltic countries*		*Euro area +ERM 2 + Baltic countries + Sweden and UK*	
	Exp.	*Imp.*	*Exp.*	*Imp.*	*Exp.*	*Imp*
Estonia	49.2	49.9	59.0	54.1	83.9	66.2
Latvia	36.4	43.0	49.3	56.8	77.0	66.2
Lithuania	35.7	35.4	53.0	38.2	65.2	46.1

Source: Author's own calculations with national data from 2000.

We can see that the exchange rate regime chosen by one or two countries may have strong externalities on others. For Latvia and Lithuania, the exchange rate arrangements of the other two Baltic countries are quite important, as a large share of their foreign trade is conducted with the other Baltic economies. For Estonia, the additional incentive from Latvia and Lithuania choosing a euro peg would be quite small. It appears that the Baltic countries have fairly similar comparative advantage in their exports to the European Union.[14] If all the Baltic countries fix their currencies, this would decrease the risk of gaining competitive advantage in EU markets through devaluations.

The costs and benefits of monetary integration with the euro area depend not only on trade flows, but also on the currencies used in foreign trade. While data on invoicing currencies is generally scarcer than data on trade flows, Baltic central banks did publish estimates about the share of different invoicing currencies. In Estonia's case, the US dollar's share in June 1998 was approximately a third, which was not as much as in the other Baltic countries. Estonia's particularity, however, was its great use of the Finnish markka in invoicing foreign trade, approximately a quarter. The D-Mark was used in slightly less than a fifth of foreign trade transactions, and all other foreign currencies accounted for 5 per cent of invoicing or less. In Latvia, the share of the US dollar in foreign trade remained around 50 per cent. The D-Mark was used in about a fifth of foreign trade transactions, and no other currency significantly exceeded the 5 per cent level. For Lithuania, the share of the US dollar was approximately 60 per cent of all foreign trade for several years. The second most important invoicing currency was the D-Mark; its share was around 20 per cent of trade. All other foreign currencies played a very minor role in the invoicing of foreign trade.

The future development of invoicing currencies in Baltic foreign trade will naturally depend on the acceptance of the euro as an international means of payment. If the euro takes a significant share in global trade from currencies joining EMU, and if the CIS countries also switch some of their foreign trade to the euro from the dollar, the Baltics can be expected to conduct a significant share of their foreign trade in euros. However, this might take years.

The formal introduction of the euro in 2002 was expected to additionally lower barriers to trade among the countries participating. This in turn had the potential to shift some of the trade previously conducted with countries outside EMU to inside the new currency union. However, Temprano-Arroyo and Feldman argue that for the CEECs generally the effects from such trade diversion would be small and counterbalanced by the positive effect EMU would have on growth within the euro area.[15] Likewise, De Grauwe and Skudelny estimate that eliminating exchange rate uncertainty inside the original EMU-11 could generate an extra 6 per cent of trade inside this bloc in the long run. Such a trend would equally be attractive to the Baltic states.

Lastly, if the Baltics pegged their currencies to the euro or a basket in which the euro was a major component, then movements in the value of the euro against other currencies would naturally affect the extra-euro foreign trade of the Baltic countries. However, the larger the Baltics' foreign trade within the euro area, the smaller this effect would be. Further, the relative importance of EUR/USD and EUR/JPY cross-rates would not be considerable for the Baltic countries, because a relatively small share of their trade was with these countries or with countries that had pegged their currencies to the dollar or yen.

Capital flows between the euro area and the Baltics

In addition to trade flows, capital movements can also have a profound effect on exchange rate regimes. For example, large fluctuations in investment can serve to destabilise any arrangement. Moreover, in systems with fixed exchange rates authorities must take particular care that rapid inflows do not lead to overtly inflated asset prices and/or encourage excessive domestic lending. A reversal of capital flows might then lead to economic contraction and endanger the stability of the domestic financial system.

The Baltic countries received substantial capital inflows after regaining their independence. Indeed, Estonia was among the highest receivers of per capita foreign direct investment (FDI) among all transition economies in Europe.

Likewise, Estonia received large (relative to its size, of course) bank loans and portfolio investment during these years, although the later crises in emerging markets also affected these flows. Meanwhile, Latvia and Lithuania also began to catch up during the late 1990s, as their privatisation processes accelerated. Table 11.5 shows the geographical distribution of FDI stock in the Baltics at the end of 1998. All in all, the stock of FDI to Estonia was approximately USD 1.8 billion. This represented approximately one-third of nominal GDP. In 1997, the flow of FDI was 2.7 per cent of GDP, but in 1998 the value of investments jumped to almost 11 per cent of GDP. This increase in FDI was largely associated with the acquisition of the two largest Estonian banks by Swedish companies, so in reality it did not represent a permanent shift in the level of FDI. Meanwhile in Latvia, the total of FDI stock was USD 1.1 billion (slightly more than 15 per cent of nominal GDP); for Lithuania, USD 1.6 billion (approximately 15 per cent of GDP). In 1998, FDI flows corresponded to 4.3 per cent of GDP in Latvia and 8.6 per cent of GDP in Lithuania. In Lithuania's case, the high FDI figure was mostly due to the privatisation sale of Lithuanian Telecom.

Table 11.5 Geographical distribution of FDI stocks in the Baltics, end-1998 (%)

	Estonia	*Latvia*	*Lithuania*
Euro area	35.4	22.5	31.0
Sweden	32.4	6.9	16.9
Denmark	4.7	15.5	6.6
Russia	1.8	8.7	1.7
United States	5.2	10.7	18.7
Norway	4.8	3.8	4.2
Estonia	–	3.4	4.3

Sources: Bank of Estonia, Central Statistical Bureau of Latvia, Lithuanian Department of Statistics, and author's own calculations.

Yet, note also the substantial differences between the three states. In Estonia's case, euro-area countries contributed the highest share of FDI, approximately 35 per cent, albeit here the contribution of Finland was 27 per cent. Euro-area countries also contributed a large amount of FDI to Lithuania, almost one-third of the whole stock. In Latvia's case, however, the euro-area share was smaller. Here, Russia and Denmark made up a significant portion of the entire investment stock.

Other capital flows into the Baltics were minor before 1997. However, their absolute size and relative importance did grow. In 1997, Estonia received substantial inflows of capital both as portfolio investments and bank lending. For example, portfolio investments totalled USD 260 million (5.6 per cent of GDP). In addition, Estonian banks borrowed USD 300 million from abroad (6.4 per cent of GDP). In 1998, the net portfolio investments were practically zero, reflecting the difficult situation in emerging markets everywhere. Net borrowing by banks was less than USD 40 million, less than 1 per cent of GDP. In Latvia's case, the net flow of portfolio investments was actually negative in 1997, i.e. Latvians made more portfolio investments abroad than were invested into Latvia. The net outflow of portfolio investments was USD 600 million, or 10 per cent of GDP. One would be tempted to conclude that Latvian banks invested quite heavily in neighbouring markets, namely to Russia. This conclusion was supported by a report by the Bank of Latvia that approximately 8 per cent of Latvian bank assets were invested in Russia before the crisis in August 1998. At the same time, the Russian government's subsequent de facto default on state debt meant considerable losses for many Latvian banks. Other net investments into Latvia (mainly borrowing by Latvian banks) amounted to USD 350 million (6.1 per cent of GDP) in 1997. In 1998, the net outflow of portfolio investments was clearly smaller, less than USD 10 million. Other investments also declined. Lastly, Lithuanian net portfolio investments were approximately USD 190 million (2 per cent of GDP) in 1997, and other investments USD 250 million (2.6 per cent of GDP). In 1998 the net portfolio investments into Lithuania were USD –50 million (–0.5 per cent of GDP), but other investments USD 550 (5.1 per cent of GDP).

Integration of Baltic financial systems into the euro area

A decade after restored independence, the Baltic financial systems had progressively become more integrated into global financial markets. Nevertheless, their equity and debt markets were still at a very early stage of development, the only exception being Estonia where the equity market was somewhat more active than in Latvia or Lithuania.[16] This section concentrates mainly on the integration of the Baltic banking systems into the euro area and the possible effects of the euro on Baltic banking.

As noted above, the Baltics witnessed a boom in the number of banks during the early years of transition. However, the number of banks soon started to decrease through closures and mergers. By 1999, Estonia was down to six banks, Latvia 28, and Lithuania 12.[17] At the same time, foreign ownership in the larger Baltic banks also increased. In October 1998, the Swedish Swedbank announced that it had acquired 48 per cent of Estonia's largest financial institution, Hansapank. Later it increased its share to over 60 per cent. Meanwhile, Sweden's SEB owns almost completely the second largest bank in Estonia (Eesti Ühispank), the largest bank in Latvia (Unibanka) and the second largest bank in Lithuania (Vilniaus Bankas). Among foreign banks, who set up shop in their own name, Finland's Nordea operated in Estonia; Latvia had Estonian, French and German banks; and in Lithuania, French and Polish banks maintained offices. Thus, at the level of ownership and operations the Baltic banking systems are already quite integrated into the EU and the euro area. Yet, from the standpoint of exchange rate and monetary policy it was probably more significant that a notable share of these banks' balance sheets were also denominated in foreign currencies. Thus, unless bank liabilities and assets in foreign currencies were equal, any changes in exchange rates would add to volatility in the net value of banks.

As table 11.6 indicates, the Estonian banking system had at the end of 1998 both significant assets and liabilities in foreign currencies, i.e. 50 per cent of consolidated assets and 43.7 per cent of liabilities were denominated in foreign currencies. In particular, Estonia's fixed exchange rate regime gave banks strong incentives to conduct much of their business in D-Marks. The overwhelming majority of the foreign-currency-denominated assets and liabilities were denominated in D-Marks, which is to say, euros. In addition to this, many loan contracts, which were denominated in kroons also included a clause tying the principal of the loan to the external value of the kroon. This meant that banks had even more assets denominated in foreign currency than the above figures would suggest[18], and likewise that the difference between the banking sector's foreign currency assets and its liabilities was more than ten percentage points of its consolidated balance sheet. In sum, if the Estonian kroon were to depreciate, Estonian banks would benefit, provided that their customers would be able to service their loans.

Table 11.6 Share of foreign-currency-denominated assets and liabilities in the consolidated balance sheets of the Baltic banking systems, end-1998 (%)

	Assets	*Liabilities*
Estonia	50.0	43.7
Latvia	47.3	65.4
Lithuania	38.0	30.3

Sources: National central banks, end-March 1999.

In Latvia, the banks had an even larger share of their balance sheets in foreign currencies than in Estonia. On the liabilities side, simple demand deposits denominated in foreign currencies made up almost 45 per cent of all foreign currency liabilities. On the assets side, it is noteworthy that foreign-currency-denominated assets constituted fully 65 per cent. Foreign-currency-denominated debt instruments and especially claims on foreign banks make up the bulk of these foreign currency assets. In this sense, the Latvian banking system was very much integrated into the international financial system. The large share of foreign currency assets and liabilities on bank balance sheets implied that Latvian banks would be vulnerable to changes in the external value of the lats.

In Lithuania, the banking sector conducted more of its business in the domestic currency than in the other two Baltic countries. Foreign currency assets represented slightly less than 40 per cent of all assets. Foreign-currency-denominated liabilities were less than one-third of all liabilities. One reason for these differences may have been that Lithuanian banks had more difficulties in attracting foreign financing because of Lithuania's lower credit rating. Lithuanian banks also had less business with Russian companies and individuals than Latvian banks.

The effects of EU membership on exchange rate and monetary policies

In this section we will examine what effects preparation for EU membership will have on the monetary and exchange rate policies of the Baltic countries. First, I will look at criteria on the desirability of a fixed exchange rate regime and how well the Baltic countries fulfil these. The choice of exchange rate regime largely determines monetary policy, but there are also some technical issues related to monetary policy that the Baltics must address before joining the EU. I will try to highlight at least some of these. A second, related, question (and admittedly, more distant) is how the Baltic countries might best prepare for participation in the euro area once they become EU members.

Monetary and exchange rate policies before EU membership

As noted above, the introduction of the euro as a unit of accounting in 1999 already meant some changes for exchange rate policies in the Baltics. The anchor currency in Estonia changed, the composition of the currency basket to which the Latvian lats was pegged also changed. Later Lithuania would peg the litas to the euro. The Baltic currencies, therefore, are already extensively integrated with the euro area.

Even so, EU membership was still years away for all three countries. Therefore, Baltic monetary authorities needed to decide on the type of exchange rate and monetary policy to pursue before membership. What would be the best policy for attaining sustainable long-term growth? How could monetary and exchange rate policies best help in pursuing EU membership? As mentioned in the introduction, we concentrate here on the economic issues related to the choice of an exchange rate system. Countries may, obviously, also peg their currencies to the euro for such political reasons as demonstrating a desire for quick integration with the EU.

Fixed or flexible exchange rates?

The analytical literature on the desirability of fixed exchange rates begins with Mundell.[19] As mentioned above, most economists agree that when countries are more open to foreign trade, they have more to gain from a regime of fixed exchange rates.[20] It is usually argued that the more open an economy is, the faster changes in the exchange rate will translate into changes in nominal wages and prices, thus rendering exchange rate policy less effective in maintaining external balance. At the same time, movements in the exchange rate threaten domestic price stability. One could therefore argue that smaller countries are natural candidates for fixed exchange rates as they are more likely to be more open to international trade. The currency of a very small country may also not be very effective in the traditional functions of money, i.e. as a unit of account and medium of exchange. For the currency of a tiny country, fixing to a more widely known currency could enhance its usefulness in the aforementioned functions.

If a country has a high level of factor mobility, then the costs of maintaining a fixed exchange rate (either in terms of inflation or unemployment) will be smaller than in the case of low-factor mobility. If a group of countries generally faces dissimilar real shocks, then fixing their currencies will entail larger economic costs than letting the currencies float. A flexible exchange rate can shield a country from nominal shock originating from abroad, but a fixed regime can stabilise the effects of a domestic nominal shock. Given the brief period the Baltics have been independent and the immense structural change they have experienced, it is impossible to say even with the customary low degree of confidence how the shocks to Baltic countries will correlate with shocks to the EU and euro-area economies in the future. Further, separating nominal from real shocks is clearly impossible at this stage. Thus, we have to rely on cruder measures of integration. One could argue that as the Baltic countries are highly integrated with the EU via trade links, their economic development will be closely integrated as well.

By fixing the external value of its currency, a country surrenders one tool with which to correct possible over-appreciation. For example, if wage growth exceeds the growth in productivity for an extended period, domestic producers will lose their competitiveness in export markets. If nominal wages are inflexible downwards, then the fastest way to change real wages and restore international competitiveness is to devalue the currency.

Wages could rise exceptionally fast because of, for example, large capital inflows, which cause a boom in domestic lending, inflate the value of assets in the economy and create a large increase in domestic demand. When capital flows stop or perhaps even reverse, and if domestic prices and wages do not adjust downwards, the country might either adjust its exchange rate or face an economic downturn.

A rigid currency peg may also hamper a central bank's ability to act as a lender of last resort if the banking system experiences widespread difficulties. Consider a situation where the central bank would otherwise extend credit to banks it deems solvent, but illiquid in the short term. A rigid peg may prevent the central bank from intervening if it fears that the additional liquidity would endanger the currency peg. In such a situation, it is even likely that the currency is already under speculative attack, making the situation more difficult. This danger is even more pronounced in a currency board system. Under the strictest currency board rules, the monetary authority would be forbidden from issuing liquidity credits to the banking system. However, the two Baltic countries with currency boards have opted for a system whereby the central bank can credit the domestic banking system to the extent it has currency reserves over the required 100 per cent backing. The Bank of Lithuania used this option during the 1995–96 banking crisis; the Bank of Estonia did so in 1994. This option would naturally not be available to the countries if they faced large capital outflows draining their excess reserves. Here, the stability of the financial system would have to be ensured by the fiscal authorities. (We assume that such authorities would be concerned about stability and perhaps willing to protect depositors.) However, if a deposit insurance system is in place and it can cover the ensured deposits in full, then bank runs might not take place. Of course, this would not wholly negate the danger of systemic risk to the banking sector as a whole. It might even induce excessive risk-taking in banks because of the moral hazard deposit insurance systems are often thought to cause.

Stability of the banking system might actually be enhanced if a significant share of the domestic banking system consists of subsidiaries or branches of larger and well-capitalised foreign banks. Interestingly, Baltic countries seemed to be moving in this direction in the 1990s with Estonia leading the way. The largest bank in Estonia, Hansapank, was already half-owned by a Swedish bank, and a Finnish bank, Nordea, was rapidly expanding its business in Estonia in retail banking. A large foreign presence in the banking sector also was likely to be beneficial in the sense that it would promote a more arm's length relationship between the authorities and the banks. It has been observed that in many transition and developing economies, close connections between banks and the political system can lead to problems, especially if these connections hinder the work of banking supervisors. Close ties between the banks and the political system might also lead to sub-optimal lending decisions under political pressure, even if a full-blown banking crisis does not materialise.[21]

What should the Baltics do?

As the Baltic states consolidated their economies during the 1990s, they already fulfilled many of the conditions outlined above for the desirability of a fixed exchange rate. They were certainly small and very open to international trade. In 1998, the nominal value (at the average annual market exchange rate) of Estonia's GDP was USD 5.2 billion, Latvia's USD 6.4 billion, and Lithuania's USD 10.7 billion. In total, the Baltic countries had slightly less than 8 million inhabitants and a combined GDP of slightly over USD 20 billion.

Moreover, the Baltics' openness to foreign trade was also easy to quantify. In 1999, for example, the ratio of combined exports and imports of goods to GDP was over 110 per cent in Estonia, and over 70 per cent both in Latvia and in Lithuania. To this one could add that international trade in services was also important. Transportation and, especially in Estonia, tourism, had become important sources of revenue. The three countries served as transportation links for trade between Russia and Western Europe. Lastly, Baltic labour markets were relatively unregulated, which provided a certain degree of flexibility in dealing with, for example, the aftershocks of the Russian financial crash of 1997 or the events of 11 September 2001. In particular, one could expect flexibility in wage-setting, which was almost completely decentralised. As a result, and in sum, the Baltic countries had quite a bit of the flexibility, which was needed in a regime of fixed exchange rates.

However, there were also certain complicating factors in this situation. For example, it was not known how much labour mobility existed inside the countries or between sectors. It was also largely unknown how fast education systems could respond in teaching new skills to people in outmoded occupations. Here, a certain degree of pessimism seemed advisable. For example, Kuddo argued in 1998 that a large portion of the labour force in the Baltic countries (as well as in other transition economies) was 'functionally illiterate,' i.e. lacking the skills needed in a market economy.[22] He maintained there was very little training and retraining for people in the labour force. Furthermore, Kuddo argued that vocational training did not offer skills that would be in demand in the labour market. This quite pessimistic view of the present situation in the Baltic labour markets was reinforced by Hazley and Hirvensalo.[23] They conducted a survey among Finnish companies that had made investments in the Baltic countries and/or Russia. According to their results, most companies listed lack of qualified labour as a hindrance to their business. Thus, the flexibility of Baltic labour markets might have been illusory. If the example of the existing EU countries was anything to go by, labour mobility to other countries would clearly be lower still, even at the future moment when the Baltic countries would join the EU. From the viewpoint of exchange rate policy, therefore, it would be advisable to increase various retraining programs and redesign at least parts of the education system to enable people to change occupations more easily, that is, create more factor mobility. On the other hand, flexibility in wage-setting might offset other rigidities in the labour market to a large degree.

A second complicating factor for the Baltic economies during the 1990s was their large external imbalances, which many commentators took as evidence of an overvalued exchange rate. They predicted that the Baltics would face exchange rate realignments in the near future.[24] However, trade and current account deficits alone do not dictate whether a currency is overvalued. Countries starting from a low level of economic development will probably offer investment opportunities with reasonably high expected returns. These investment opportunities would entice a capital inflow to the country and, if domestic investments exceed domestic savings, then the country will have a current account deficit as a matter of definition. It is hard to dispute that all post-socialist countries offered a great number of investment projects with a high expected return, although the associated risks, both economic and political, were also large. Thus during the decade after the collapse of communism, as risks decreased, the investment flow into the transition economies increased. In particular, much of the foreign direct investment was associated with privatisation of former state-owned companies.

Another oft-cited piece of evidence for the eroding competitiveness of Baltic economies was the fast increase in dollar wages. Figure 11.2 shows the evolution of monthly US dollar wages in the three Baltic countries during the mid-1990s. The upward trend is apparent. However, mere wage costs do not tell us anything about competitiveness of the companies. One must also take into account changes in labour productivity. Table 11.7 therefore shows the changes

Figure 11.2 Monthly gross wages (USD) 1/95–12/98

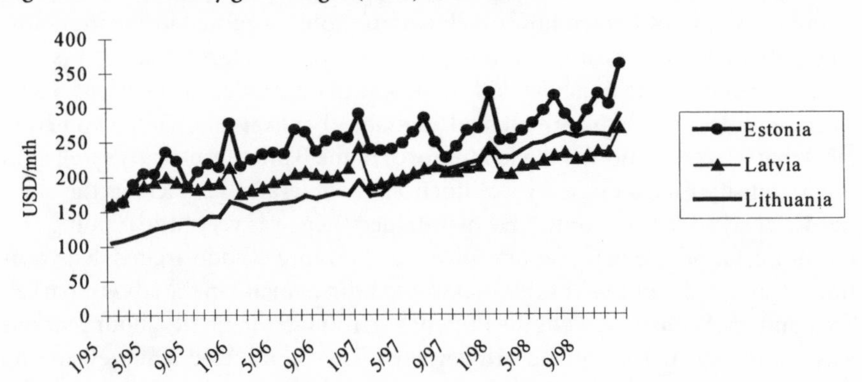

Note: Latvia wages before 1997 based only on public sector.

in productivity in manufacturing during roughly this same period. Since it is the manufacturing industry which is most exposed to foreign competition, it is appropriate to focus on its productivity. One can see that productivity increased during the latter half of 1990s in all the Baltic countries, but at diverse rates. After 1993, productivity in manufacturing increased almost 45 per cent in Estonia, 53 per cent in Latvia, and 27 per cent in Lithuania. However, these changes in productivity exhibited considerable volatility, so one should consider this evidence with caution.

Table 11.8 shows the change in the annual unit labour costs in the manufacturing industries of the three Baltic countries. The general trend in Estonia and Latvia seemed to be towards lower increases in unit labour costs, although in Estonia their growth accelerated somewhat in 1998. In Lithuania, increases in

Table 11.7 Changes in productivity in manufacturing (%)

	1994	*1995*	*1996*	*1997*	*1998*
Estonia	6.7	0.4	3.7	26.3	2.3
Latvia	9.5	–1.0	8.6	28.0	1.9
Lithuania	–12.1	12.0	8.5	7.6	11.0

Source: European Bank for Reconstruction and Development, *Transition Report Update* (London, EBRD, 1999).

Table 11.8 Changes in D-Mark unit labour costs (%)

	1994	*1995*	*1996*	*1997*	*1998*
Estonia	61.7	35.2	19.2	–5.3	13.6
Latvia	73.0	17.9	5.2	4.2	3.3
Lithuania	85.1	23.3	30.5	32.9	7.5

Source: European Bank for Reconstruction and Development, *Transition Report Update* (London, EBRD, 1999).

unit labour costs were quite large up until 1997. It is hard to explain this large difference between Lithuania and the other two Baltic countries. One might claim that the restructuring of manufacturing progressed more slowly in Lithuania than in the other countries. Lithuania received less FDI, and foreign owners were generally thought to be better at restructuring.

Another approach to assessing the real value of exchange rates is offered by Halpern and Wyplosz, who try to determine equilibrium exchange rates in transition economies.[25] They use the monthly dollar wage as a proxy for the real exchange rate. In general terms, dollar wages rose in almost all of the European transition countries during the 1990s. However, the estimated equilibrium dollar wages did not always trend upwards.[26] For the Baltic countries there was an upward trend in the equilibrium dollar wages that was consistent with the evidence presented on the evolution of productivity in the Baltic countries. In Estonia and Lithuania, wages had not reached their equilibrium levels by 1997, but in Latvia this happened during 1997, and thus wages might have been too high according to this model.

Continuing with fixed exchange rates had its risks. If a country lost external competitiveness, for example, then rectifying this without exchange rate adjustment would be costly, especially if prices and wages were sticky downwards. Especially in Lithuania, where the development of productivity had lagged behind Estonia and Latvia, this risk was quite real. Naturally, the authorities in Estonia and Latvia also needed to monitor their economies closely, especially given their large external imbalances. Yet, despite all of these caveats, the benefits of fixed exchange rates seemed to outweigh the apparent risks in the case of the Baltics. It also appeared that all of the Baltic countries were continuing with fixed exchange rates.

When to join the monetary union?

When new members join the European Union, they take upon themselves the commitment to fulfil the stipulations of the Maastricht Treaty. That this condition applied also to the CEE applicant countries was clearly stated in the conclusions of the Copenhagen Council meeting in June 1993. Among other things, membership would require 'the ability to take on the obligations of membership, including adherence to the aims of political, economic and monetary union'. Nevertheless – and this cannot be overstated – the Maastricht criteria for joining Economic and Monetary Union *were not* formal criteria for membership in the European Union.[27] Applicant countries therefore needed to concentrate on structural changes in their economies for many years to come, and not on a strict interpretation of the Maastricht criteria.[28]

Yet, despite the fact that the criteria were not of immediate importance for accession, it is of interest to see where the applicant countries stood in this regard during the early accession period. This sort of exercise gives an indication of how far the countries had to go in their nominal convergence before participation in EMU could be considered. For example, experience from Italy and Belgium during the 1990s illustrates how difficult it can be to lower the general government debt once it has been allowed to rise to over 100 per cent of GDP.

Table 11.9 shows how the applicant CEECs fared in 1999 with regard to the Maastricht criteria. (The interest rate criterion is omitted, as there was at this point in time no truly functioning market for domestic long-term debt instruments in any of the applicant countries.) Clearly, no applicant country fulfilled the criteria completely, even if we do not take into account the interest rate criterion. However, there were clear differences between the countries. In 1999 the fiscal criterion presented problems for the Baltic countries because of the Russian crisis, but after 1999 their budget deficits have decreased substantially. For the Baltic countries, the debt criterion in particular portended few problems in the coming years. When the Soviet Union disintegrated, Russia took over the USSR's foreign assets and liabilities, and thus for example the Baltic countries started with no external debt. Latvia and Lithuania incurred quite large deficits during the first half of 1990s (Lithuania for longer than Latvia), but their public debt was still quite modest and was likely to remain so. Concerning inflation, Latvia and Lithuania have managed to push inflation lower than any other CEEC applicant country. Lastly, if one believes that past inflation performance is useful in predicting future inflation (insofar as it reflects authorities' preference for and/or commitment to low inflation), then low inflation would also mean low long-term interest rates. That said, the rates would not be as low as in the current euro-area countries, because the applicant countries' debt instruments would still carry a significant risk premium for many years to come.

The changes that preparation for EMU participation will mean for the conduct of monetary policy in the new members will be quite large. First, when

Table 11.9 Maastricht criteria for ten CEEC applicant countries in 1999

	Inflation (%)	*General government balance (% of GDP)*	*General government debt (% of GDP)*
Bulgaria	0.3	–1.0	93.6
Czech Republic	2.1	–4.2	29.0
Estonia	3.3	–4.7	11.0
Hungary	10.0	–3.9	72.7
Latvia	2.4	–3.8	10.6
Lithuania	0.8	–8.6	28.6
Poland	7.3	–3.7	43.0
Romania	44.8	–4.0	32.3
Slovak Republic	10.6	–4.1	26.5
Slovenia	6.1	–0.7	24.3
Criteria	2.0	–3.0	60.0

Source: Deutsche Bank, *EU Enlargement Monitor* 1 (2000).

the new members join European Union, the Maastricht Treaty stipulates that the economic and exchange rate policies of member countries are a matter of common concern. In a sense, discussions concerning economic policies have already started with the Commission's Joint Assessments of medium-term economic policy concerns.[29] The intensity of dialogue will naturally increase as accession talks progress.

When the applicant countries have joined the European Union, they must then decide on whether to join the EU's Exchange Rate Mechanism (ERM2) as their first step toward monetary union. Since no new member country was expected to opt out from joining the euro area, it was probable that they would all join the ERM2. Generally, the consensus was that a minimum of two years of exchange rate stability was necessary for membership in the Exchange Rate Mechanism. Of course, a country could in principle stay in ERM2 longer than two years.

When is a country ready to join the Exchange Rate Mechanism? Presumably when it is ready to peg its currency to the euro and eventually join the monetary union. When the present member countries of the monetary union were chosen, the emphasis was very much on nominal convergence between the countries. This was reflected in the criteria on inflation, long-term interest rates, and exchange rate stability. These same criteria would naturally apply also to the CEE applicant countries when they are ready to join the monetary union. But for them the issues related to structural adjustment were also very important. The new member countries, including the Baltics, were not therefore advised to join until their structural adjustment was more or less complete. Of course, one could argue that if a country had been accepted into the EU, its structural adjustment to a functioning market economy must have been, by definition, complete. In this case, however, the criteria for choosing new members for the monetary union would be identical for the present members of the monetary union, i.e. one based on the nominal convergence between the countries and the stability of their fiscal position.

Yet, the countries of Central and Eastern Europe had considerably lower GDP per capita than the countries already in the monetary union, and this disparity was set to persist for years to come, even if the high growth of the mid-1990s were to have continued in the more developed accession countries. To be sure, there was a wide disparity of per capita GDP and income already inside the current euro zone. In 1996, for example, per capita GDP (based on purchasing power parities) was $21,200 in Germany and $13,100 in Portugal. In other words, income disparities as such did not prevent CEECs from joining monetary union. There could also be persistent inflation differentials inside the monetary union, as productivity would probably grow faster in the countries with lower levels of income.[30] In this situation, the process of catching up should naturally be advanced so far that the possible inflation differential is small enough to fall inside the Maastricht criterion on inflation. In a system of truly fixed exchange rates, the appreciation of the real exchange rate accompanying relative improvements in productivity must come in the form of higher inflation.[31]

Therefore one can argue that the new member countries of the European Union could join the monetary union (and before that ERM2) when their productivity levels have risen sufficiently. A sufficient level would be one where changes in productivity no longer threaten the attainment of the inflation criterion in a regime of fixed exchange rates. Countries could naturally participate in ERM2 for several years and use readjustments of their central parities to attain the needed appreciation of their real exchange rate. Here, the authorities must weigh the costs these readjustments might bring in the form of lost credibility.

Given the aforementioned arguments, one must conclude that the lower the current income level of an accession country, the longer it should wait for membership of the monetary union and perhaps ERM. This is especially important for the Baltic countries, because their income levels are lower than in most other applicant countries.

Conclusions

The start of Stage Three of the Economic and Monetary Union – including the formal launch of the euro – changed the economic environment of the Baltic countries to a considerable degree. Firstly, the introduction of the euro meant that the Baltic countries would henceforth conduct a very significant part of their foreign trade with countries who had a common currency. If these countries were counted as a single entity, then the euro area was the single most important trading partner for all the Baltic countries. As a result, questions of exchange rate policy arose, particularly for Lithuania, which previously had pegged its litas to the dollar. Secondly, the Baltic countries were integrated to the euro area via direct foreign investment as well as developments in the global financial system. The capital flows through these channels also represented factors to be taken into account when managing exchange rate regimes and monetary policy.

Thirdly, we saw that the introduction of the euro did not necessarily need to change the exchange rate regimes in the Baltic countries. But since the countries were in the process of joining the European Union, it was of interest to contemplate the choice of an appropriate exchange rate regime (which in turn determines the conduct of monetary policy). The Baltic countries were extremely small and open to international trade. This meant that they were natural candidates for a regime of fixed exchange rates. When one also considers the fact that the present exchange rate arrangements had been quite successful in reducing inflation and maintaining macroeconomic stability, and as a result of this they had gained popular support and credibility, the case for maintaining fixed exchange rates was quite strong. However, this approach was not without its dangers. In a regime of fixed exchange rates the fiscal authorities need to react with sufficient speed to threatening imbalances, which is difficult even under the most benign conditions. Maintenance of a fixed exchange rate also places heavy demands on the flexibility of the markets, especially the labour market. During the Baltic states' early accession period, it appeared that they had sufficient flexibility in their labour markets with regard to wage setting. In this context it should be remembered, however, that the Maastricht criteria on joining the currency union were not immediate criteria for joining the European Union.

The form of the currency peg was also a matter of some importance. When capital movements are completely liberalised (as they were in the Baltic countries), maintaining a currency peg is very difficult if the underlying economic policies are not strictly in line with the peg. Perhaps the only solution for this dilemma is a currency board, which seems to have performed reasonably well in different countries also during the recent volatility in the global financial markets (with the possible exception of Hong Kong). For Estonia this meant continuing with the present arrangement as long as possible. Also Lithuania has decided to maintain its currency board until it joins the monetary union.

Once the Baltic countries become members of the European Union, they must decide when to join the monetary union. As a first step towards this, they must join the Exchange Rate Mechanism II. In this chapter it is argued that the countries should have developed enough economically so that the inevitable[32] appreciation of the real exchange rate does not threaten the attainment of the criterion on inflation. This would mean that membership of the monetary union was still quite far off, especially for the Baltic countries, which had quite low per capita GDP. One could naturally join ERM2 and then use readjustment of the central parity to achieve the needed appreciation of the real exchange rate, but this could damage the credibility of the exchange rate policy and would essentially be counterproductive.

Notes

I would like to thank Ville Kaitila, Péter Mihályi, Jan Zielonka, and two anonymous referees for extremely useful comments and suggestions regarding this chapter. All errors and omissions are naturally mine.

1 I. Korhonen, 'Banking Sectors in Baltic Countries' *Review of Economies in Transition*, 3 (1996), 33–54.
2 The discussion of currency reforms and exchange rate arrangements draws heavily on S. Lainela and P. Sutela, *The Baltic Economies in Transition* (Helsinki, Bank of Finland, 1994); as well as I. Korhonen, 'Baltian vuosikatsaus', *Review of Economies in Transition*, 2 (1996), 45–54, I. Korhonen and N. Pautola, 'Baltian vuosikatsaus 1996', *Review of Economies in Transition*, 5 (1997), 15–26 and N. Pautola, 'Baltian talouskatsaus 1997', *Review of Economies in Transition*, 3 (1998), 27–38. The main reference for the section on banking sectors is Korhonen, 'Banking Sectors'.
3 Monetary overhang was the result of forced saving during the Soviet era. Households and companies could not increase their consumption at the same rate as their money holdings increased. Prices were fixed, so excess demand could not be eliminated by raising prices, i.e. open inflation.
4 Eesti Pank, *The Monetary Reform in Estonia* (Tallinn, 1992).
5 See, e.g. S. H. Hanke, L. Jonung and K. Schuler, 'Estonia: It's Not a Currency Board', *Transition*, 1 (1993) 5.

6 Restrictions on foreigners buying real estate, however, remained in force for some years.

7 Much has been written on the reasons for economic downturn at the beginning of transition. While some authors blame overtly strict monetary and fiscal policies for declines in output, it is perhaps more realistic to treat transition as a structural shock that severs old trading patterns and reveals the inefficiency of many existing enterprises. In such situations, conventional demand management policies have little relevance. For an analysis along these lines, see e.g. O. Blanchard, *The Economics of Post-Communist Transition* (Oxford, Clarendon Press, 1997).

8 The current composition of the SDR is as follows: USD 43 per cent, EUR 28 per cent, JPY 17 per cent, and GBP 12 per cent.

9 It is interesting to note that most of these bank failures and closures had little impact on ordinary households or companies despite the lack of an official deposit insurance scheme.

10 For an assessment of the early years of Baltic foreign trade, see I. Korhonen, 'The Baltic Countries' Changing Foreign Trade Patterns and the Nordic Connection', *Review of Economies in Transition*, 3 (1996) 17–32.

11 In addition to the usual problems relating to the quality of data in transition economies used in assessing trade flows, one should bear in mind that at least some Estonian exports to Finland, the remaining Baltic countries and Ukraine were also actually destined to Russia. The reason for this rerouting was to circumvent the high tariffs Russia applied to imports from Estonia.

12 See, for example, B. T. McCallum, *International Monetary Economics* (Oxford, Oxford University Press, 1996). On the other hand, openness to trade might very well be influenced by the foreign exchange rate regime, see J. A. Frankel and A. K. Rose, 'The Endogeneity of the Optimum Currency Area Criteria', *The Economic Journal*, 108 (1998), 1009–1025.

13 African countries with currencies pegged to the French franc are omitted as their share in Baltic foreign trade is minuscule.

14 See also Kaitila and Widgren in this volume (chapter 9).

15 H. Temprano-Arroyo and R. A. Feldman, 'Selected Transition and Mediterranean Countries: An Institutional Primer on EMU and EU relations', *International Monetary Fund Working Paper*, 82 (1998).

16 In mid-1998, the market capitalisation of Tallinn Stock Exchange was less than $600 million; at the Riga Stock Exchange it was $360 million; and at the National Stock Exchange of Lithuania it was $1.8 billion. Trading was by far most active in Tallinn.

17 I have included the branches of foreign banks in all Baltic countries with the exception of the Lithuanian Development Bank and Turto Bankas, which was set up to sort out bad loans the Lithuanian banking system had incurred before the banking crisis in late 1995/early 1996.

18 Another matter was whether the clients who had in effect taken foreign currency loans would be able to service these loans in full if the external value of kroon were to change.

19 R. A. Mundell, 'A Theory of Optimum Currency Areas' *American Economic Review*, 51 (1961), 657–665.

20 See, e.g. P. Isard *Exchange Rate Economics* (Cambridge, Cambridge University Press, 1995) and references therein.

21 On this point, see for example P. Honohan, 'Banking System Failures in Developing and Transition Countries: Diagnosis and Prediction', *BIS Working Paper*, 39 (1997).

22 A. Kuddo, 'Social Developments in Transition Economies: The Case of Baltic States', paper presented at conference 'Economic Development in the Baltic Region: The Path Ahead', 20 October 1998.

23 C. Hazley and I. Hirvensalo, 'Barriers to Foreign Direct Investment in the Baltic Sea Region', *ETLA Discussion Paper*, 628 (1998).

24 The inertia of monetary regimes is hard to foresee. For example, Lainela and Sutela describe the Estonian currency board as 'transient'. Lainela and Sutela, *The Baltic Economies.*

25 L. Halpern and C. Wyplosz, 'Equilibrium Exchange Rates in Transition Economies: Further Results', paper presented at CEPR/EastWest Institute Economic Policy Initiative Forum, Brussels, 20–22 November 1998.

26 The determinants of equilibrium dollar wages were obtained from panel data consisting of 85 countries and spanning the period 1970–95. In the final specification the determinants of monthly dollar wages were GDP per capita, age dependency ratio, government consumption (per cent of GDP), openness of the economy, net foreign asset position and credit to private sector (per cent of GDP).

27 J. Dixon, 'Implications of the Euro for the Eastern Enlargement', paper presented at Seminar on the Implications of the Euro on Enlargement, Brussels, 22–23 October 1998.

28 At the same time, it was still desirable to aim for low and stable inflation in the medium-term regardless of the Maastricht criterion per se, since experience over decades has shown that high inflation hinders economic growth. See, for example, R. J. Barro, 'Inflation and Economic Growth', *NBER Working Paper*, 5326 (1995). That said, it has been difficult to find any significant difference between the growth experience of, say, countries with average inflation rates of 3 per cent and 5 per cent.

29 Dixon, 'Implications of the Euro'.

30 For evidence on the scope for inflation differentials in the current monetary union, see E. Alberola and T. Tyrväinen, 'Is There Scope for Inflation Differentials in EMU? An Empirical Evaluation of the Balassa-Samuelson Model in EMU Countries', *Bank of Finland Discussion Paper*, 15 (1998).

31 This argument relies on the Balassa–Samuelson model of real exchange rates, whereby traded and non-traded goods sectors have different productivity. The relative price of traded goods is proportional to the ratio of average labour products in the two sectors. Furthermore, it is assumed that the price of traded goods is the same in different countries, i.e. purchasing power parity holds in the traded goods sector. If the ratio of traded goods productivity to the productivity in the non-traded goods sector grows faster, for example, in Estonia than in the EU, then the relative price of non-traded goods will also rise faster in Estonia than in the EU. Because the price of traded goods is similar in Estonia and the EU, the Estonian currency will experience real appreciation as the price of Estonian output rises relative to the price of output in the EU.

32 Inevitable in the sense that all accession countries are expected to grow faster than the current EU members, because they start from a lower level. Of course, bad economic policies could derail growth, but one tends to be optimistic in this regard, at least in the case of the Baltic countries.

Chronologies

Chronology of Estonia's accession to the EU

27 August 1991	The EU recognizes Estonian independence.
1 January 1992	The Baltic states are included in the EU's PHARE programme.
11 May 1992	EU and Estonia conclude an Agreement on Trade and Commercial Economic Cooperation.
18 July 1994	Free trade agreement signed between EU and Estonia.
9–10 December 1994	EU adopts a pre-accession strategy for future candidate countries, including Estonia.
1 January 1995	EU–Estonian free trade agreement enters force.
12 June 1995	Estonia and EU sign Europe (Association) Agreement, beginning the general integration process toward membership.
28 November 1995	Estonia formally applies for membership in the EU.
6 June 1996	Estonian Government adopts Activity Plan for joining the EU.
15 July 1997	EU Agenda 2000 report recommends starting negotiations with Estonia, noting that the country has fulfilled the Copenhagen criteria, including the ability to cope with the EU's internal market. More work on administrative capacity will be needed, however.
12–13 December 1997	EU Luxembourg summit confirms Estonia's place among first round of applicant countries.
1 February 1998	Europe (Association) Agreement between the EU and Estonia enters force.
31 March 1998	Estonia formally begins accession talks with EU along with other first-wave countries.
4 November 1998	The EU's first Regular Report on Estonia recaps the country's progress, but notes that naturalization for stateless children must be eased and the judiciary must be strengthened.
11–12 June 1999	Tallinn hosts one of the regular meetings of chief accession negotiators among the six first-wave countries.
13 October 1999	EU Commission criticizes Estonia's adoption of a new language law in second Regular Report. It also calls for progress in pension reform, customs administration and energy sector restructuring.
8 November 2000	The EU's third Regular Report praises Estonia for its adoption of a minority integration strategy as well as amendments to the controversial language law. It warns, however, about the country's growing current account deficit as well as mounting public sector debt.

4 December 2000	Estonia completes 16 out of 31 negotiation chapters in advance of Nice summit.
13 November 2001	The Commission's fourth Regular Report notes progress in the areas of pension reform and administrative modernisation. It reiterates calls for reform in the energy sector and for measures to combat piracy and counterfeit goods.
30 July 2002	Estonia concludes 28th negotiation chapter on energy sector, preparing the way for final talks during upcoming Copenhagen summit.
9 October 2002	EU's final Regular Report on Estonia declares the country has 'achieved a high degree of alignment with the *acquis* in the large majority of areas'. Still, it recommends greater efforts to tackle unemployment, minority integration, and a restructuring of Estonia's oil shale industry.
13 December 2002	Estonia officially concludes accession negotiations with the EU at the Copenhagen summit.

Chronology of Latvia's accession to the EU

27 August 1991	The EU recognizes Latvian independence.
1 January 1992	The Baltic states are included in the EU's PHARE programme.
11 May 1992	EU and Latvia conclude an Agreement on Trade and Commercial Economic Cooperation.
18 July 1994	Free trade agreement signed between EU and Latvia.
9–10 December 1994	EU adopts a pre-accession strategy for future candidate countries, including Latvia.
1 January 1995	EU–Latvian free trade agreement enters force.
12 June 1995	Latvia and EU sign Europe (Association) Agreement, beginning the general integration process toward membership.
27 October 1995	Latvia formally applies for membership in the EU.
26 July 1996	Latvia submits its answers to the EU's questionnaire on candidate countries' readiness for accession.
18 December 1996	Latvia adopts first National Programme for Integration with EU.
15 July 1997	EU Agenda 2000 report does not recommend the start of accession negations with Latvia, stating that Latvia would face serious difficulties in coping with EU market conditions and needs to do more work on non-citizen naturalization.
12–13 December 1997	The Luxembourg summit confirms Commission's recommendation to begin direct negotiations with only 6 candidate countries, not including Latvia.
1 February 1998	Europe (Association) Agreement between the EU and Latvia enters force.
23 February 1998	First meeting of EU–Latvian Association Council.
4 November 1998	The Commission's first Regular Report on Latvia highlights the country's progress since the publication of the Agenda 2000 report, but does not recommend beginning direct negotiations.

11–12 December 1998	EU Vienna summit does not agree to begin enlargement talks with second-wave counties.
13 October 1999	The EU Commission publishes its second Regular Report on Latvia, recommending that accession negotiations be opened in 2000. The Report cites, however, corruption and weak administrative capacity as the main challenges to integration.
10–11 December 1999	EU Helsinki summit agrees to open accession talks with second-wave countries, including Latvia.
9 February 2000	Latvian parliament adopts 'Strategy of the Republic of Latvia for Integration into the European Union' as framework document for accession talks with EU.
15 February 2000	Latvia and EU begin official accession negotiations.
8 November 2000	In its 2000 Regular Report, the European Commission notes that corruption remains a 'serious obstacle', despite the adoption of an anti-corruption program. Following controversy surrounding the adoption of a new Language Law in 1999–2000, the EU declares itself satisfied with the final result.
27 June 2001	Latvia provisionally closes 16th chapter in negotiations, representing nominal half-way point in 31-chapter accession process.
13 November 2001	European Commission releases 2001 Regular Report on Latvia, praising the adoption of a civil service law and of new measures against corruption. The Report also commends new minority integration policy, but notes that non-citizens' rights continue to be a concern.
11 June 2002	Latvia closes its last negotiation chapters, leaving just agriculture, financial matters and EU institutions to be worked out at the final enlargement summit in December.
9 October 2002	EU Commission issues final Regular Report confirming that Latvia is ready to join the EU. It notes, however, that judicial reform, anti-corruption measures and minority integration must continue.
13 December 2002	Latvia officially concludes accession negotiations with the EU at the Copenhagen summit.

Chronology of Lithuania's accession to the EU

27 August 1991	The EU recognizes Lithuanian independence.
1 January 1992	The Baltic states are included in the EU's PHARE programme.
11 May 1992	EU and Lithuania conclude an Agreement on Trade and Commercial Economic Cooperation.
18 July 1994	Free trade agreement signed between EU and Lithuania.
9–10 December 1994	EU adopts a pre-accession strategy for future candidate countries, including Lithuania.
1 January 1995	EU–Lithuanian free trade agreement enters force.

12 June 1995	Lithuania and EU sign Europe (Association) Agreement, beginning the general integration process toward membership.
8 December 1995	Lithuania formally applies for membership in the EU.
6 September 1996	Lithuanian government adopts national legislation harmonisation programme for EU integration.
15 July 1997	EU Agenda 2000 report does not recommend the start of accession negations with Lithuania, citing the need for more enterprise restructuring, agricultural modernisation and banking sector development.
12–13 December 1997	The Luxembourg summit confirms Commission's recommendation to begin direct negotiations with only 6 candidate countries, not including Lithuania.
1 February 1998	Europe (Association) Agreement between the EU and Lithuania enters force.
23 February 1998	First meeting of EU–Lithuanian Association Council.
4 November 1998	First EU Regular Report on Lithuania again defers the start of negotiations, saying among other things a long-term energy plan is needed to close down Ignalina nuclear power plant. Corruption is also cited.
11–12 December 1998	EU Vienna summit does not agree to begin enlargement talks with second-wave countries.
13 October 1999	Commission accedes to the start of negotiations with Lithuania in its second Regular Report. While welcoming the country's decision to phase out the Ignalina nuclear power plant, it calls on Vilnius to lower its budget deficit and improve administrative capacity.
10–11 December 1999	EU Helsinki summit agrees to open accession talks with second-wave countries, including Lithuania.
15 February 2000	Lithuania and EU begin official accession negotiations.
8 November 2000	Third Regular Report praises Lithuania for legal reforms and creation of an anti-corruption strategy.
11 June 2001	Lithuania's total of closed negotiation chapters tops 17.
13 November 2001	Fourth Regular Report calls on Lithuania to maintain enforcement of civil service reform, enterprise restructuring measures, and fiscal discipline.
11 June 2002	Lithuania closes its last two negotiation chapters on energy and regional policy, preparing the way for the final Copenhagen summit.
9 October 2002	Final EU Regular Report stresses implementation of adopted reforms, saying Lithuania has achieved 'good degree of alignment with the *acquis*.'
13 December 2002	Lithuania officially concludes accession negotiations with the EU at the Copenhagen summit.

Bibliography

Äimä, K. 'Central Bank Independence in the Baltic Countries', *Review of Economies in Transition*, Vol. 4, No. 4 (1998).

Alston, P., Bustelo, M. R. and Heenan, J. (eds), *The EU and Human Rights* (Oxford: Oxford University Press, 1999).

Arnswald, S. *EU Enlargement and the Baltic States* (Helsinki: The Finnish Institute of International Affairs and Institut für Europäische Politik, 2000).

Artéus, G. and Lejiņš, A. (eds), *Baltic Security: Looking towards the 21st Century* (Stockholm: Latvian Institute of Foreign Affairs and Försvarshögskolan, 1998).

Avery, G. and Cameron, F. *The Enlargement of the European Union* (Sheffield: Sheffield Academic Press, 1998).

Balazs, P. 'Strategies for the Eastern Enlargement of the EU: an Integration Theory Approach', in P. H. Laurent, M. Maresceau (eds), *The State of the European Union. Vol. 4. Deepening and Widening* (Boulder: Lynne Rienner Publishers, 1998), 67–86.

Baldwin, R.E. 'The Causes of Regionalism', *Centre for Economic Policy Research Working Paper*, No. 1599 (1997).

Baldwin, R. E. *Towards an Integrated Europe* (London: Centre for Economic Policy Research, 1994).

Barr, N. (ed.), *Labor Markets and Social Policy in Central and Eastern Europe: The Transition and Beyond* (Oxford: Oxford University Press, 1994).

Blanchard, O. *The Economics of Post-Communist Transition* (Oxford: Clarendon Press, 1997).

Bofinger, P. *The Political Economy of the Eastern Enlargement of the EU* (London: Centre for Economic Policy Research, 1995).

Breslauer, G. W. and Dale, C. 'Boris Yeltsin and the Invention of a Russian Nation-State', *Post-Soviet Affairs*, Vol. 13, No. 4 (1997), 303–332.

Burnell, P. 'Good Government and Democratization: A Sideways Look at Aid and Political Conditionality', *Democratization*, Vol. 1, No. 3 (1994), 485–503.

Caddy, J. 'Harmonization and asymmetry: environmental policy coordination between the European Union and Central Europe', *Journal of European Public Policy*, Vol. 4, No. 3 (1997), 318–336.

Commission of the European Communities, 'Report on the current state and perspectives for cooperation in the Baltic Sea Region' (Brussels, COM (95) 609 final, 29.11.1995).

Commission of the European Communities, 'Agenda 2000: Commission opinion on Estonia's application for membership of the European Union' (Brussels: DOC/97/12, 1997).

Commission of the European Communities, 'Agenda 2000: Commission opinion on Latvia's application for membership of the European Union' (Brussels: DOC/97/14, 1997).

Commission of the European Communities, 'Agenda 2000: Commission opinion on Lithuania's application for membership of the European Union' (Brussels: DOC/97/15, 1997).

Cremona, M. 'Movement of persons, establishment and services' in M. Maresceau (ed.), *Enlarging the European Union: Relations Between the EU and Central and Eastern Europe* (London and New York: Longman, 1997).

Drábek, Z. and Smith, A. 'Trade Performance and Trade Policy in Central and Eastern Europe', *Centre Economic Policy Research Discussion Paper*, No. 1182 (1997).

Erkkilä, M. and Widgrén, M. *Finnish-Baltic Trading Potential and Comparative Advantage* (Helsinki: The Research Institute of the Finnish Economy, ETLA Series B 101, 1995).
Ethier, W. J. 'The New Regionalism', *The Economic Journal*, No. 108 (1998), 1149–1161.
Fournier, J. 'Administrative Reform in the Commission: Opinions Concerning the Accession of the Central and Eastern European Countries to the European Union', in OECD, *Preparing Public Administrations for the European Administrative Space*, Sigma Papers, 23 (Paris: OECD, 1998).
Friis, L. and Murphy, A. 'EU Governance and Central and Eastern Europe – Where are the Boundaries?' *The European Policy Process Occasional Paper*, No. 35 (1997).
Gelazis, N. 'Institutional Engineering in Lithuania: Stability through Compromise' in A. Pravda and J. Zielonka (eds), *Democratic Consolidation in Eastern Europe: Institutional Engineering* (Oxford: Oxford University Press, 2001).
Gold, M. (ed.), *The Social Dimension: Employment Policy in the European Community* (London: Macmillan, 1993).
Grabbe, H. 'A Partnership for Accession? The Nature, Scope and Implications of Emerging EU Conditionality for CEE Applicants', *Robert Schuman Centre Working Paper*, No. 12 (1999).
Hanf, K. and Soetendorp, B. (eds), *Adapting to European Integration: Small States and the European Union* (London: Longman, 1998).
Hansen, B. and Heurlin, B. (eds), *The Baltic States in World Politics* (Richmond: Curzon Press, 1998).
Haslam, J. 'Russia's seat at the table: a place denied or a place delayed?' *International Affairs*, Vol. 74, No.1 (1998), 119–130.
Henderson, K. (ed.), *Back to Europe: Central and Eastern Europe and the European Union* (Philadelphia: UCL Press, 1999).
Hernesniemi, H. 'Barriers to Economic Cooperation of Baltic Rim Countries' *The Research Institute of the Finnish Economy Discussion Paper*, No. 555 (1996).
Hesse, J. J. 'Rebuilding the State: Public Sector Reform in Central and Eastern Europe', in J.-E. Lane (ed.), *Public Sector Reform: Rationale, Trends and Problems* (London: Sage, 1997).
Holmes, P. *et al.* 'The European Union and Central and Eastern Europe: pre-accession strategies', in *Sussex European Institute Working Paper*, No. 15 (1996).
Howard, A. E. D. (ed.), *Constitution Making in Eastern Europe* (Washington, D.C.: The Woodrow Wilson Center Press, 1993).
Hubel, H. (ed.), *EU Enlargement and Beyond: The Baltic States and Russia* (Berlin: Arno Spitz GmbH, 2002).
Joenniemi, P. and Prikulis, J. (eds), *The Foreign Policies of the Baltic Countries: Basic Issues* (Riga: Centre of Baltic–Nordic History and Political Studies, 1994).
Jopp, M. and Arnswald, S. (eds), *The European Union and the Baltic States* (Helsinki: The Finnish Institute of International Affairs and Institut für Europäische Politik, 1998).
Jundzis, T. (ed.), *The Baltic States at Historical Crossroads* (Riga: Academy of Sciences, 1998).
Jurgaitiene, K. and Waever, O. 'Lithuania', in H. Mouritzen, O. Waever, and H. Wiberg (eds), *European Integration and National Adaptations* (New York: Nova Science Publishers, 1996).
Kaitila, V. and Widgrén, M. *Baltic EU membership and Finland* (Helsinki: The Research Institute of the Finnish Economy, ETLA Series B 139, 1998).
Karklins, R. *Ethnopolitics and Transition to Democracy: The Collapse of the USSR and Latvia* (Baltimore: The Johns Hopkins University Press, 1994).
Knill, C. 'European Policies: the Impact of National Administrative Traditions', *Journal of Public Policy*, Vol. 18, No. 1 (1998), 1–28.
Korhonen, I. 'Baltian vuosikatsaus' *Review of Economies in Transition*, No. 2 (1996), 45–54.
Korhonen, I. 'Banking Sectors in Baltic Countries' *Review of Economies in Transition*, No. 3 (1996), 33–54.
Korhonen, I. and Pautola, N. 'Baltian vuosikatsaus 1996', *Review of Economies in Transition*, No. 5 (1997), 15–26.

Kramer, H. 'The EC's Response to the 'New Eastern Europe', *Journal of Common Market Studies*, Vol. 31, No. 2 (1993), 213–244.

Krenzler, H. G. 'The EU and Central-East Europe: The Implications of Enlargement in Stages', *Robert Schuman Centre Policy Paper*, No. 2 (1997).

Lainela, S. and Sutela, P. *The Baltic Economies in Transition* (Helsinki: Bank of Finland, 1994).

Laitin, D. 'The Russian-Speaking Nationality in Estonia: Two Quasi-Constitutional Elections', *East European Constitutional Review*, Vol. 2, No. 4/Vol 3, No. 1 (1993–1994).

Larson, D. and Kairys, J. (eds), *Lithuanian Economic Reforms: Practice and Perspectives* (Vilnius: Margi Raštai, 1997).

Lauristin, M. and Vihalemm, P. (eds), *Return to the Western World: Cultural and Political Perspectives on the Estonian Post-Communist Transition* (Tartu: Tartu University Press, 1997).

Lejiņš, A. and Ozoliņa, Ž. *Small States in a Turbulent Environment: The Baltic Perspective* (Riga: Latvian Institute of International Affairs, 1997).

Lejiņš, A. and Apinis, P. *The Baltic States on Their Way to the European Union: Security Aspects* (Riga: Latvian Institute of International Affairs and Konrad Adenauer Stiftung, 1995).

Lieven, A. *The Baltic Revolution: Estonia, Latvia, Lithuania and the Path to Independence* (New Haven: Yale University Press, 1993).

Linz, J. and Stepan, A. *Problems of Democratic Transition and Consolidation: Southern Europe, South America, and Post-Communist Europe* (London: The Johns Hopkins University Press, 1996).

MacFarlane, S. N. 'Russian Conceptions of Europe', *Post-Soviet Affairs*, Vol. 10, No. 3 (1994), 234–269.

Malcolm, N., Pravda, A., Allison, R. and Light, M. *Internal Factors in Russian Foreign Policy* (Oxford: Oxford University Press, 1996).

Maniokas, K. and Vitkus, G. *Lithuania's Integration into the European Union: Summary of the Study on the Status, Perspectives and Impact* (Vilnius: European Integration Studies Centre, 1997).

Mansfield, E. D. and Milner, H. V. (eds), *The Political Economy of Regionalism* (New York: Columbia University Press, 1997).

Maresceau, M. (ed.), *Enlarging the European Union: Relations Between the EU and Central and Eastern Europe* (London and New York: Longman, 1997).

Mayhew, A. *Recreating Europe: The European Union's Policy towards Central and Eastern Europe* (Cambridge: Cambridge University Press, 1998).

Meny, Y., Muller, P. and Quermonne, J-L. (eds), *Adjusting to Europe: the Impact of the European Union on National Institutions and Policies* (London: Routledge, 1996).

Müllerson, R. *et al.* (eds), *Constitutional Reform and International Law in Central and Eastern Europe* (The Hague: Kluwer Law International, 1998).

Nello, S. S. and Smith, K. E. 'The Consequences of Eastern Enlargement of the European Union in Stages' *Robert Schuman Centre Working Paper*, No. 51 (1997).

Norgaard, O. *et al. The Baltic States after Independence* (Cheltenam: Edward Elgar, 1999).

Ozoliņa, Ž. 'The Impact of the European Union on Baltic Co-operation' *Copenhagen Peace Research Institute Working Paper*, No. 3 (1999).

Pautola, N. 'Baltian talouskatsaus 1997', *Review of Economies in Transition*, No. 3 (1998), 27–38.

Pautola, N. 'Intra-Baltic Trade and Baltic integration', *Review of Economies in Transition*, No. 3 (1998).

Pelkmans, J. and Brenton, P. 'Free Trade with the EU: Driving forces and the Effects of "Me-Too"', *Centre for European Policy Studies Working Document* 110 (1997).

Pettai, V. 'Estonia: Positive and Negative Engineering,' in A. Pravda and J. Zielonka (eds), *Institutional Engineering in Eastern Europe* (Oxford: Oxford University Press, 2001), 111–138.

Pettai, V. "Estonia and Latvia: International Influences on Citizenship and Minority Integration", in A. Pravda and J. Zielonka (eds), *International Influences on Democratic Transition in Central and Eastern Europe* (Oxford: Oxford University Press, 2001), 257–280.

Pettai, V. and Kreuzer, M. 'Party Politics in the Baltic States: Social Bases and Institutional Context', *East European Politics and Societies*, Vol. 13, No. 1 (1999), 150–191.

Preston, C. *Enlargement and Integration in the European Union* (London and New York: Routledge, 1997).

Rebas, H. 'Baltic cooperation – problem or opportunity?', *Perspectives, Review of Central European Affairs*, No. 9 (1997/98), 67–76.

Rollo, J. 'Economic aspects of EU enlargement to the East', in M. Maresceau (ed.), *Enlarging the European Union: Relations Between the EU and Central and Eastern Europe* (London and New York: Routledge, 1997).

Roosma, P. 'Constitutional Review under 1992 Constitution', *Juridica International*, III (1998), 35–42.

Roosma, P. 'Protection of Fundamental Rights and Freedoms in Estonian Constitutional Jurisprudence', *Juridica International*, IV (1999), 35–44.

Schneider, H. 'Relations Between State Bodies in Implementing Constitution', *Juridica International*, III (1998), 10–24.

Sedelmeier, U. and Wallace, H. 'Policies towards Central and Eastern Europe', in H. Wallace and W. Wallace (eds), *Policy-Making in the European Union* (Oxford: Oxford University Press, 1996), 353–385.

Shlapentokh, V. 'Early Feudalism – The Best Parallel for Contemporary Russia', *Europe-Asia Studies*, Vol. 48, No. 3 (1996), 393–412.

Shlapentokh, V. 'How Russians Will See the Status of Their Country by the End of the Century', *Journal of Communist Studies and Transition Politics*, Vol. 13, No. 3 (1997), 1–23.

Smith, D. J. *et al. The Baltic States: Estonia, Latvia and Lithuania* (London: Routledge, 2002).

Sorsa, P. 'Regional Integration and Baltic Trade and Investment Performance', *International Monetary Fund Working Paper*, No. 167 (1997).

Spanou, C. 'European Integration in Administrative Terms: A Framework for Analysis and the Greek Case', *Journal of European Public Policy*, Vol. 5, No. 3 (1998), 467–84.

Taagepera, R. 'Estonia's Constitutional Assembly, 1991–1992', *Journal of Baltic Studies*, Vol. 25, No. 3 (1994), 211–232.

Taagepera, R. *Estonia: Return to Independence* (Boulder: Westview Press, 1993).

Timmerman, H. 'Relations Between the EU and Russia: The Agreement on Partnership and Co-operation', *Journal of Communist Studies and Transition Politics*, Vol. 12, No. 2 (1996).

Van Ham, P. (ed.), 'The Baltic states: security and defence after independence', *Chaillot Papers*, No. 19 (1995).

Varblane, U. (ed.), *Foreign Direct Investments in the Estonian Economy* (Tartu: University of Tartu Press, 2001).

Verheijen, T. 'The Management of EU Affairs in Candidate member states: Inventory of the Current State of Affairs', in *Preparing Public Administrations for the European Administrative Space*, Sigma Papers, 23 (Paris: OECD, 1998).

Von Rauch, G. *The Baltic States: The Years of Independence, Estonia, Latvia, Lithuania, 1917–1940* (New York: St. Martin's Press, 1974).

Winters, A. L. (ed.), *Foundations of an Open Economy: Trade Laws and Institutions for Eastern Europe* (London: Centre for Economic Policy Research, 1995).

Zecchini, S. (ed.), *Lessons from the Economic Transition. Central and Eastern Europe in the 1990s* (Dordrecht: Kluwer Academic Publishers, 1997).

Zielonka, J. 'Policies without Strategy: the EU's Record in Eastern Europe', in J. Zielonka (ed.), *Paradoxes of European Foreign Policy* (Hague: Kluwer Law International, 1998) 131–145.

Ziemele, I. 'Incorporation and Implementation of Human Rights in Latvia' in M. Scheinin (ed.), *International Human Rights Norms in the Nordic and Baltic Countries* (Dordrecht: Martinus Nijhoff Publishers, 1996) p. 78.

Ziemele, I. 'The Citizenship Issue in the Republic of Latvia' in S. O'Leary and T. Tiilikainen (eds), *Citizenship and Nationality in the New Europe* (London: Sweet and Maxwell, 1998), 187–204.

Ziemele, I. 'The role of state continuity and human rights in matters of nationality of the Baltic States' in T. Jundzis (ed.), *The Baltic States at Historical Crossroads* (Riga: Academy of Sciences, 1998).

Index

administrative capacity 9, 104–134
Afghanistan 31
Alston, Philip 61
Andrikiene, Laima Lucija 113
Austria 22, 120, 144, 223, 224

Balassa, Bela 218
Baltic Assembly 167, 175
Baltic Council 167, 176
Baltic Council of Ministers 167, 175
Baltic states
  citizenship disputes 5, 18, 28, 29, 35, 46–69
  citizenship policy 49–54, 67–69
  customs union plans 178
  economic cooperation among 163–197
  economic interest groups 190–196
  economic protectionism 190–193, 197
  foreign direct investment 194, 216–217
  human rights 63–69
  interwar history 3
  intra-Baltic investment 195
  intra-Baltic trade 10–11, 174–175
  minorities 4–5, 6, 17–18, 46–69
  nationalist movements 4, 47–48
  regional trade agreements of 236
  relations with Russia 5–6, 17–18, 25–42
    minority issues within 30–31, 35
  Stalinism 3
  state continuity in 47–48
  trade with Russia 192
  trade with the EU
    intra-industry trade 210–220
    revealed comparative advantage in 218–229
    structure and development 207–210
  transit trade 210, 221
  trilateral trade agreements 176–177
  see also Estonia; Latvia; Lithuania
Belarus 20, 33, 36, 205
Belgium 144, 216
Birkavs, Valdis 4
border issues 5, 18, 20
Brazauskas, Algirdas 4
Brewer-Carías, Allan 77
Bulgaria 127
Burnell, Peter 58

Chechnya 31, 41
Commonwealth of Independent States (CIS) 38, 40, 41, 181
constitutionalism 76–78
Council of Baltic Sea States 180, 184–185, 195
Council of Europe 35, 54, 57, 58, 69
Czech Republic 33, 36, 59, 131, 228

democratic transition 12–13
Denmark 19, 119, 124, 143, 207–229 *passim*
Drábek, Zdenek 219

Estonia
  accession negotiations with the EU 6–7
  Accession Partnership with EU 148, 150
  citizenship policy 53–54, 68
  Constitutional Assembly 78–79
  Constitutional Review Chamber 75–100, 191
  constitutional system 4, 78–81
  Europe Agreement with EU 146–147
  foreign trade 238
  gender equality 153–154
  Legal Chancellor 75–100 *passim*
  minorities 88–89, 97–99, 152–153
  party politics 4
  social policy 9, 141–144, 150–153, 155–158
  trade with EU 207–208
  see also Baltic states
Ethier, Wilfred 11
euro 12
European Convention on Human Rights (ECHR) 62, 67, 96
European Court of Justice 18, 46, 61, 62
European Free Trade Association 181, 210
European Social Charter 148, 154
European Union
  Accession Partnerships 8, 59, 60, 63

acquis communautaire 8, 9, 59, 60, 62, 75, 104–134 *passim*
Agenda 2000 59, 60, 62, 63, 64, 68, 75, 148, 150, 185
Common Agricultural Policy (CAP) 110, 111
Common Foreign and Security Policy (CFSP) 21–22
conditionality 58–60, 64–69, 132
Copenhagen criteria 8, 59, 62, 75, 128, 185
Council 20, 22, 121, 181–186 *passim*
demands for Baltic cooperation 180–185
diplomatic recognition of the Baltic states 7, 179
Economic and Monetary Union 12, 23
economic cooperation with Baltic states 8, 188
enlargement, first wave 6, 16, 121, 104, 185, 189–190
Europe Agreements with the Baltic states 8, 60, 183, 205
European Security and Defense Policy (ESDP) 21–22
Northern Dimension 19, 42
Parliament 1, 18, 62, 183
PHARE programme 6–8, 60, 105, 132, 179, 180, 184
Regular Reports 60, 63, 66
relations with Russia 5, 19
social policy in 144–145, 148–150, 154–158
Treaty of Amsterdam 20, 22
Treaty of European Union 46, 60, 62
Treaty of Nice 1, 20–21, 197
twinning programmes 8, 129
White Paper 145, 149, 150

Feldstein, Martin 166
Finland 11, 19, 22, 36, 42, 143, 182, 205–229 *passim*
Framework Convention for the Protection of National Minorities (FCPNM) 63–64
France 118, 144

Germany 117, 144, 207–229 *passim*
Gorbachev, Mikhail 3, 26–27, 47
Gower, Jackie 168
Greece 117, 144, 220, 223, 224, 229
Greenaway, David 216

Hungary 33, 36, 59, 118, 121, 127, 131, 228

International Monetary Fund 12, 191
Ireland 22, 119, 144, 156, 216
Italy 144, 224

Kaliningrad 6, 22, 29, 32, 33, 41
Kallas, Siim 187
Kazakhstan 32, 38
Kemp, Murray 234
Keohane, Robert 166
Klaar, Toivo 15
Kozyrev, Andrei 28
Krushchev, Nikita 31
Kyrgystan 38

Laar, Mart 4
Landsbergis, Vytautas 4
Latvia
accession negotiations with the EU 6–7
citizenship policy 50–53, 67
constitutional system 4
foreign trade 239
party politics 4
trade with EU 208–209
see also Baltic states
Lebed, Aleksandr 30
Lebow, Richard 31
Light, Margot 27
Lipsey, Richard 233, 234
Lithuania
accession negotiations with the EU 6–7
Accession Partnership with EU 121–123, 128
citizenship policy 49–50
constitutional system 4
foreign trade 240
National Programme for the Adoption of the Acquis (NPAA) 121–125
party politics 4, 113
PHARE programme in 126–130
trade with EU 208
see also Baltic states
Luik, Jüri 186
Lukashenko, Aleksandr 33
Lutz, Mark 234
Luxemburg 144, 216

Maastricht Treaty *see* European Union: Treaty of European Union
March, J. G. 108

Maruste, Rait 97
Mattli, Walter 168–169
Meade, James 233
Meri, Lennart 83, 84, 85, 86, 90, 96, 182, 186
migration, Slavic 5, 50
Milner, Helen 166
minority integration 5, 18, 67

Narva 88–89
national identity 15–16, 22–23, 165
Netherlands 219, 144, 208, 210, 220, 229
North Atlantic Treaty Organization (NATO) 10, 16–17, 21–22, 28–31, 33–37

Offe, Claus 12
Olsen, Johan 104
Organization for Economic Cooperation and Development (OECD) 195
Organization for Security and Cooperation in Europe (OSCE) 18, 35, 46, 55, 58, 69, 88

Parekh, Bhikhu 15
Päts, Konstantin 78
Poland 33, 36, 59, 112, 116, 117, 118, 121, 127, 128, 131
Portugal 117, 144, 220, 223, 224, 228, 229
preferential trade agreements (PTAs) 233–236
Primakov, Yevgeny 28, 34
Putin, Vladimir 31, 37, 41, 42

regionalism 232–236
Russia 5–6, 10, 25–42, 56, 205, 206, 217
  foreign policy orientations of 25–28

September 11 2001 34, 42
Shlapentokh, Vladimir 26–27
Sillamäe 88–89
Šķēle, Andris 191
Slezevičius, Adolfas 4
Slovenia 59, 112
Smith, Alasdair 219
social dumping 158–159
Sokov, Nikolai 34
Spain 117, 118, 123, 144
Special Drawing Rights 12
Sweden 11, 19, 22, 36, 143, 182, 205–229 *passim*
Switzerland 156

trade creation/diversion 11, 233
Truuväli, Eerik-Juhan 80, 89

Ukraine 11, 32, 36, 38, 147, 205
Union of Soviet Socialist Republics (USSR) 3–4, 15, 26–27
United Kingdom 118, 119, 144, 156, 207–229 *passim*
United States 39

Vagnorius, Gediminas 104
Vähi, Tiit 93
Viner, Jacob 233, 234

Wan, Henry 234
Weiler, J. H. H. 61
Western European Union 21, 35
Wonnacott, Paul 234
World Trade Organization 191, 237

Yeltsin, Boris 5, 25, 26, 28–30, 31, 34
Yugoslavia 28, 33, 36